Damp d[illegible] but good!

GARDENING ON WALLS

GARDENING ON WALLS

Christopher Grey-Wilson
and Victoria Matthews

illustrated with paintings by
Victoria Goaman
and drawings by the authors

COLLINS

St James's Place, London, S.W.1.

William Collins Sons & Co Ltd
London · Glasgow · Sydney · Auckland
Toronto · Johannesburg

First published 1983

ISBN 0 00 219220 9

Filmset by Electronic Village Ltd, Chiswick
Colour reproduction by Adroit Photo Litho Ltd, Birmingham
Made and printed by William Collins Sons & Co Ltd, Glasgow

Contents

List of Colour Plates

Abbreviations in the text

subsp.	subspecies
var.	variety
Pl.	Plate
p.(pp.)	page (pages)
R	repeat flowerer (roses)
NR	non-repeat flowerer (roses)
=	indicates that the following scientific names are synonyms also used by some sources for the species named
N	North
S	South
E	East
W	West
C	Central
×	crossed with (hybrid forms) (placed *before* a single name indicates a cross-genetic hybrid)

Other codes and symbols used in species descriptions are explained on pages 9-10.

Preface

This book is intended primarily for the gardener and botanist or indeed anyone interested in a wide selection of interesting and colourful plants. Although the title is *Gardening on Walls* the book covers all structures that plants can be grown up or trained against, and so includes walls, fences, posts, pillars, pergolas, tree stumps and even live trees.

Walls provide a wonderful environment against which to grow an exciting range of rare and everyday garden plants. Every house has at least one or two walls of different aspect on which plants can be grown. This provides a dimension to gardening which, although old in practice, is nevertheless often overlooked or underestimated.

One of the difficulties faced in compiling this book is that almost any plant can be grown against a wall or fence, provided that it will survive our winters. However, some plants need them for support or for the shelter which they provide. As a result the plants included are to some extent a personal selection, though we have tried to include all popular wall plants. In addition there is a wide selection of lesser-known plants, some very rare in cultivation, which deserve to be more widely known and grown. Unless otherwise indicated all the plants mentioned in the book are commercially available in Britain and Europe.

A very wide selection of plants are good 'wall' subjects. The most obvious are the shrubby climbers as exemplified by the Clematis and the Honeysuckle. However, in addition, there are quite a number of annual climbers as well as herbaceous climbers which die down to ground level each autumn. The largest group of plants is the tender evergreen and deciduous shrubs which thrive best in a wall-sheltered environment, but which rarely succeed in the open garden except in the very mildest parts of the country. Besides these there are many fruits, such as the apples, pears, peaches and grapes, that are suitable for wall culture, which both provide fruit and greatly enhance the look of a wall or fence. Lastly, there is a bewildering array of small plants such as the wallflower and the houseleeks that can be grown in the cracks and crevices of walls. Many of these appear spontaneously, providing one of the most delightful features of wall gardening.

We are very grateful to Vicki Goaman for her careful and painstaking work on the colour plates, which are an integral part of this book. We would like to thank the former Director of the Royal Botanic Gardens Kew, Professor J.P.M. Brenan and the Regius Keeper of the Royal Botanic Garden, Edinburgh, Mr. D.M. Henderson, for allowing us to use the facilities, especially the living collections, of these two establishments, whilst preparing this work.

Introduction

'Walls' provide a protected environment, a favourable microclimate in which more tender subjects can be grown, and they help to extend the range of plants that can be grown in the average garden. Walls not only provide a milder zone in the garden, especially in temperate latitudes, but, more importantly perhaps, they protect plants from cold and buffeting winds which can often create havoc. Thus in many parts of Britain plants from the Mediterranean or California, or even as far away as New Zealand or Tasmania, can be grown in wall-sheltered environments. In the open garden they would soon perish.

Plants are grown against walls simply for their charm and beauty or to enhance a building in some way. Alternatively, suitable subjects may be chosen to cover an unsightly fence or wall or to smother an old tree or tree stump. They may be grown for their flowers or fruit, or simply for their attractive foliage.

There are a number of general considerations that need to be borne in mind besides purely cultural techniques. The size of the wall or space to be filled is critical: it is no good trying to confine a vigorous subject into too small a space, for it will simply spend all its time trying to escape. Self-adhering climbers can cause some damage to walls, especially old walls, in which the mortar may perhaps be a little rotten. Vigorous climbers may, if not checked, grow to block

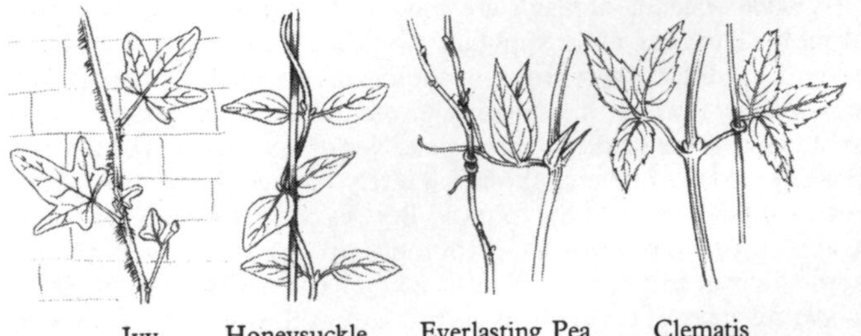

Ivy Honeysuckle Everlasting Pea Clematis

Plants climb by a variety of means: Ivy has short clinging, adventitious roots; Honeysuckle twines its stems around suitable supports; Everlasting Peas *(Lathyrus)* climb with coiling tendrils; many Clematis have twisting leaf stalks.

gutters or, worse still, creep under the roof and pull the tiles off. Plants with a strong root system may invade drains and foundations and cause all manner of unexpected problems. There are of course more aesthetic considerations. Some wall plants can obscure the architectural beauty of buildings, especially fine old buildings. On the other hand they can greatly enhance a building or boundary wall or fence; indeed many modern buildings could well do with more judicious wall plantings. It may be undesirable to fix a plant-supporting framework to walls of certain buildings, especially historic ones.

Often a combination of plants can be chosen for a particular position so that each enhances the other in its colour of flowers, or leaf shape, or general habit. Climbers and shrubs can be happily intermingled if carefully selected, as car evergreen and deciduous subjects.

This book is arranged in two parts.

Part One deals with culture; preparation of soils, planting, types of support, pruning and training, propagation, pests, diseases and disorders.

Part Two deals with the plants themselves, giving a wide range of common and uncommon species and cultivars for wall culture. These are split up into manageable categories such as 'evergreen shrubs' or 'deciduous climbers'. Clematis, Honeysuckles and Roses are treated separately as they are all very popular and are large groups in themselves. Shrubs or climbers that are normally evergreen, but which in a severe winter may lose all their leaves, are treated as evergreens.

In each section genera are treated in alphabetical order. Species on the other hand, are arranged so that similar-looking species come next to each other.

Each species has its latin name in full (**Campsis radicans** for instance). Synonyms are placed immediately following *(= Bignonia radicans, Tecoma radicans)*; they are important because the plant in question may sometimes appear under these other names in nurserymen's catalogues and lists. If the plant is illustrated in colour a reference to the Plate on which it appears is given in brackets (Pl.12). If a particular plant has a common name then it follows the latin name (**Berberidopsis corallina**, the Coral Plant).

An asterisk * immediately preceding the latin name indicates that the species is particularly recommended by the authors. This applies also to cultivar names.

Descriptions of plants are relatively brief, though enough to give the reader a general impression of the subject. Particular attention is paid to habit and flower shape and colour, and indeed to any other feature that is important from a gardening point of view. Use of measurements is kept to the minimum, although plant height is generally given as well as leaf length and flower size. A glossary of terms such as lanceolate, ovate or bipinnate is included at the end of the book. p.305.

In the margin beside each species text will be found one or more symbols which indicate the aspect and the amount of sun which the plant prefers and, when appropriate, if acid or neutral soil is needed:

Aspect and sunshine requirements.

- ☼ needs full sun; south- and south-west-facing walls ideal, south-east often also suffice.
- ◐ needs semi-shade: west- and east-facing walls generally suitable, south-facing walls shaded for part of day may also suffice.
- ● needs full shade: provided by many north-, north-east- or north-west-facing walls.
- ☼◐ needs full sun or semi-shade.
- ●◐ needs full shade or semi-shade.
- ✹ tolerates full sun, semi-shade and full shade.

Aspect for cultivars is the same as for the species unless otherwise indicated.

Soil type Plants requiring an acid or neutral soil are marked △

Immediately following each species description further information is presented within square brackets in abbreviated form, set out in a strict order. The meaning of these symbols and abbreviations is as follows:

Flowering period (e.g. May–June). On the whole this covers the main flowering period in an average season. It does not include the occasional out of season blooms which some species produce.

Hardiness. Three categories are recognised.

H the plant is hardy throughout the British Isles and the Irish Republic.

HH the plant is only half-hardy. In the milder parts of Britain and Ireland such plants will be hardy in all but the severest winters. In other districts some form of winter protection is advisable. In the coldest districts plants will not survive out-of-doors except in exceptionally mild winters. However, bear in mind that quite a number of plants are hardier than is generally supposed so it is worth experimenting sometimes with half-hardy species in a sheltered nook, especially in the angle between two high walls.

T tender species. These will only succeed in the very mildest parts of the country where frosts and biting winds are rare, and even there it is advisable to give the plants some form of winter protection. Remember that the wall environment can often be a frost-free niche in which tender species can survive quite happily through many a winter. It is generally wise to propagate tender species regularly to ensure a stock of young plants which can be housed in a frost-free place over winter in case the parent plant is killed.

Both half-hardy and tender species can be grown in frost-free conservatories or greenhouses in many parts of the country.

Pruning. This is discussed in greater detail on p.17.

PN plants need no regular annual pruning except to remove old, diseased, dead or weak unwanted growths.

PA plants should be pruned immediately after flowering. This includes most of the species that flower on the previous year's wood and these generally flower during the first half of the year. Pruning is carried out as soon as flowering ceases in order to promote a good amount of growth to carry the following season's blooms. *Forsythia* is typical of this group.

PS plants should be pruned in early spring once the worst frosts have passed. Many of the species in this group flower in the second half of the year on the current season's growths. Pruning too late will reduce the amount of flowers produced. *Campsis* belongs to this group.

PW really a subdivision of the preceding category. Plants should be pruned during the winter. Hardy subjects such as Blackberries and Loganberries belong here.

Origin. The country of origin of individual species is given e.g. China.

The coded information for a particular species may thus look as follows [Aug – Sept H, PS, SE USA]. This indicates that the plant in question normally flowers in August and September, is hardy throughout the United Kingdom and the Republic of Ireland, should be pruned in the spring and its country of origin is the South-Eastern United States of America. The symbols in the margin beside this paragraph indicate that the plant prefers a sunny south- or south-west-facing wall or fence and that it prefers an acid or neutral soil.

Information may follow on particular aspects of cultivation of that species together with interesting points about the plant's history.

Cultivars of a particular species are given after the species descriptions (e.g. 'Phylis Moore', which is a cultivar of *Chaenomeles speciosa*). Cultivars are generally selected forms which usually are propagated vegetatively to maintain uniformity. They may have particularly fine-coloured flowers, or large flowers, or a different habit which distinguishes them from the wild plant, or indeed from the ordinary form of the species in cultivation. There are often innumerable cultivars, especially of roses, large-flowered clematis or fruit trees, so that we have had to make a careful selection of those we consider are most worth mentioning. In nurserymen's catalogues and lists cultivars may either be found under the appropriate species — *Chaenomeles speciosa* 'Phylis Moore', or simply as *Chaenomeles* 'Phylis Moore'.

The illustrations have mostly been prepared from living specimens. Colour illustrations are of the typical form of the species or cultivar, especially as regards flower colour, a feature particularly prone to variation. They present the specimens at two-thirds their natural size.

PART ONE

Culture

Soils and Planting

Careful preparation of the soil is essential if plants are to have a good start and to continue to grow well. Remember that some shrubs and climbers may remain in the same position for many years, so a little extra trouble at the start is well worth while.

The soil underneath walls is generally drier than the surrounding soil. The stone or brickwork tends to absorb water from the soil immediately adjacent to it. Besides this, walls will often prevent much of the rain reaching the soil beneath. This is especially true of the outside walls of buildings which may have deeply overhanging eaves. Fences and pergolas may have a similar, though often less marked, effect. By the same token, walls may protect the adjacent soil from frosts and freezing and thus they enable less hardy plants to survive.

Soil by walls which has not been previously worked may be full of bricks and mortar rubble and need careful 'cleaning', digging down to at least 45cm if this is possible. Diligent gardeners will, in all probability, have previously dug their soil to a good depth, in which case a careful forking over is all that is required.

As all gardeners will know a good rich, deep moisture-retentive loam is an ideal soil, though it is a lucky person who can claim to have such a luxury. Most have to be content with the soil they have and to try to improve it as much as they can.

Sandy soils by their very nature, dry out quickly and are unsuitable for most wall plants. They can be greatly improved by adding humus in the form of peat, well-rotted farmyard manure, compost, finely chopped straw or spent hops, or even sawdust or wood chippings. Once improved, the soil must not be abandoned but topped up from year to year by adding mulches or forking in further compost around the plants.

Heavy clays can be greatly improved by judicious additions of 'humus' and coarse composts. In many instances it is probably better to dig out an area, say 45cm square and as deep, entirely filling it with a good friable mixture of loam and compost with added peat.

Acid soils can be improved, unless wanted for acid-loving species, by adding lime. However, limy soils cannot in the average garden be made suitable for 'acid' plants. Clever gardeners often devise methods for enclosing small areas of acid peaty soils in limy gardens. However, on the whole, the best advice is to concentrate effort on improving existing soils — there is always a wide range of plants that can be grown on most soil types.

Soils, however good, may dry out at almost any time of year, especially during the summer, and watering should be anticipated. Do not assume that because the rest of the garden is moist that soils beneath walls and fences are equally well blessed. It is especially important to ensure that young plants and newly planted ones are kept well watered. Mulches of moist compost or peat around the base of plants are always beneficial and can greatly help to establish new plants.

Once the soil has been prepared it should be firmed down and levelled, although you should be careful not to firm clayey soils too much or they will become compacted and airless. Before planting it is a good idea to add about 60g (2oz) of fine bone meal to each planting site, forking it lightly into the surface.

Now you will be ready to start planting having selected your subjects with care. Today matters are made much simpler by the fact that many plants are container-grown and in this way a wide range of suitable wall plants can be obtained, often by just going down to the local garden centre or nursery. If you are seeking rarer or more unusual subjects then they will have to be ordered by post and probably will arrive without containers. The advent of the container has meant that plants can be purchased and planted at almost any time of the year except during frosty weather. Those planted during the height of summer must be well watered-in, and regularly watered thereafter until they are established. There is nothing more disheartening than to lose plants for no other reason than a lack of water.

Plants arriving without containers will do so in the autumn or spring. If it is frosty then plants should be kept in a cool frost-free place for a few days until the weather is milder. On the whole deciduous subjects can be planted at any time from late October until early April, whilst most gardeners will tell you that early spring, March and early April, is the best time to plant evergreens. However, in milder districts and by walls early autumn planting is just as good and allows plants a little time to settle in before winter arrives.

Plants should be planted at the same depth as they were previously, taking care not to disturb the roots too much. Any damaged roots should be removed with secateurs or that sharp knife which most gardeners seem to carry in their pockets. If the roots are tangled in a tight ball in the container then they should be teased out a little, otherwise plants may find it difficult to put out new roots. If transplanting from another place in the garden then it is wise to ensure that plants have a good ball of soil around the roots. Whatever the source, all plants should be firmed in well, though don't be too heavy-footed on clayey soils.

One question that is always asked is how far from the base of a wall or fence, or indeed pergola, should plants be placed. If too close to the wall then not enough room is allowed for the stems to develop, besides which it may also be very dry. Walls can also get very hot in strong sunshine and this may damage the base of the plant. On the other hand, if you plant too far away from the wall, you lose some of the protection provided by it. Plants which need the wall for support should be planted not closer than 15cm from the base of the wall and not further away than 30cm. Free-standing subjects can be planted a metre away from the base, or more, depending on the width of the border and the tenderness of the subject.

It is time for another word of advice. Never plant too near a drain or too near an exposed corner of a building. Roots may break and block drains, which can be a most annoying if not maddening experience. Deciduous species in particular can often be trained successfully around a corner, though the young foliage may be scorched by persistent winds. Sites near corners are often rather exposed and evergreen subjects may suffer badly, so plant well back, one or two metres if possible. At the same time this will allow plenty of room for expansion.

Shrubs will not usually require any means of support. Climbers, however, will need tying carefully to wires, hooks or nails fixed to the wall, fence or pergola; various forms of support are outlined below. Alternatively, temporary canes or sticks can be used to secure the plant until it is able to reach more permanent supports. It is wise to push these into the ground immediately before planting for if done afterwards it is all too easy to damage the new plant. At the same time any damage or bruised stems can be pruned back to a bud or leaf in order to promote healthy new shoots when growth commences.

Do not be too disappointed if some plants take a long while to settle in. Some are very fickle at first, while others will romp away as though they had never been disturbed. It is in the second and third seasons that you should expect to see a good deal more growth and the framework of your plants building up.

A word needs to be said about conditions around other forms of support. Pergolas and pillars have a less localising effect on the adjacent soil, the tendency to drying out being less pronounced. However, unless they are in a well-sheltered position the plants trained up them will be very much more exposed. In general they are suitable only for the hardy species and you should choose climbers for them with a good deal of care. Lists of plants suitable for differing aspects are presented on p.24. Tree stumps provide the same sort of problems but you will need to be more wary of living trees. Trees may create a dense shade, whilst also drawing much of the moisture from the surrounding soil. At the same time they may prevent some, or indeed a good deal, of rain from reaching the soil. Suitable subjects therefore need to be vigorous and deep rooted. New plants should be placed away from the base of the tree, preparing the soil with extra care and watering them judiciously through the first season. Liberal moist mulches are very beneficial to such plants.

Don't give up on plants once they are established. They will welcome a careful light forking around the base and a sprinkling of bone meal in the spring. Additional mulches are always a good idea and plants will repay you with their strong healthy growth from year to year.

Supports

Careful consideration needs to be given to the type and amount of support required by the various kinds of wall plants. It is all too easy to ruin the natural beauty of the plant, or indeed the wall or fence itself, by providing an unsightly or untidy support.

Some plants such as the ivies and the Climbing Hydrangea need no support for they will cling by natural means. It is, however,sometimes necessary to fasten one or two strong shoots of young plants to the 'wall' to start them off. Lead-headed wall nails of the type used for securing electric wires are very suitable for such a purpose. Once they have attached themselves, plants will be quite happy finding their own way about.

Quite a few wall shrubs are tough and rigid and require little or no support except for an occasional tie to help to train the direction of growth of the main shoots or to keep the plant close to the wall. Simple strong galvanised screw-eyes (vine-eyes as they are commonly called), or hooks fixed to the walls will prove most effective. Place them wherever they happen to be needed.

However, many 'wall' plants will require more extensive forms of artificial support. These include many climbers that will not cling naturally and shrubs with weak, flexuous or straggling growths that require more careful training. The main considerations to take into account are the size and bulk of the plant in question, its permanence and the cost of the various types of supports available. Annual or herbaceous climbers will require only temporary, lightweight supports, which can be removed at the end of the growing season, if necessary. Shrubby climbers, on the other hand, may remain in position for many years and much stronger and more permanent supports will be required. Often such plants may become not only bulky, but very heavy. There is nothing more irritating or disappointing than to find a beautiful climber in full bloom collapsed on the ground because it lacks adequate support.

Supports need to be as neat and efficient as possible. Reflect a moment on what sort of growth and habit the plant will have, remembering that, in general, climbers need more support than shrubs. To what is the support being fixed? — wall (brick or stone), fence, pillar and so on. Will the support look nice? This is a vital question. Ideally it is best if the support is as inconspicuous as possible so that the form and beauty of the plant is obstructed as little as possible, taking into consideration at the same time that it may take a plant several years to fill a space completely. Whatever happens, a conspicuous support, such as lattice work or wire mesh should be completely shrouded by the plant at maturity, unless, of course, you particularly like the look of wire or wooden lattice work.

Annual and herbaceous climbers can be trained up ordinary pea sticks stuck in the soil close to the wall or fence. They can, of course, be grown up more permanent supports, and such climbers are often used as 'fillers' to hide gaps until such time as the permanent shrubs or shrubby climbers cover the wall space adequately. The advantage of pea sticks is that they can be removed in the autumn, an important consideration if walls are painted or fences creosoted.

There are many types of permanent support that can be used, indeed inventive gardeners often devise their own means from available materials. Lattice work of narrow lathes, painted or creosoted, is frequently used and can be bought as collapsible pieces in various sizes. It is relatively cheap to buy and quick to put up, though wooden lattice work can look rather unsightly on many walls. It is best suited to quick-growing climbers, particularly clematis and honeysuckles and various other evergreens. It is unsuitable for shrubs. Lattice work needs to be 3–5cm away from the wall to allow room for the plant which will push up stems on either side. This can be accomplished by first fixing small wooden blocks or long, 5cm square, battens to the wall and nailing the lattice to them. The lattice should start 20–30cm above the soil surface. Alternatively, a wooden framework can be built up from narrow battens to form a trellis. Lattice or wooden trellis can be fixed to the wall with the aid of masonry nails, or, better still, by wall-plugs and screws. Masonry nails are banged into the mortar between bricks whilst wall-plugs are best placed in holes drilled in the brickwork. The latter are generally better on old walls where the mortar may have begun to crumble and could be damaged by nails.

Today there are many types of wire or plastic netting available, some of which are good for supporting wall plants. These range from plastic or nylon mesh to plastic-coated steel or galvanised wire netting. Various mesh sizes are available although 5cm square and 10cm square are perhaps the best. Ordinary galvanised mesh is probably the cheapest and certainly is longer-lasting than plastic or nylon mesh and less conspicuous. It can be protected from eventual rusting by painting it with bituminous paint before it is put up. Nylon and plastic meshes come in various colours, white, green and brown being the most favoured. Mesh, of whatever it is made, can be fixed to horizontal wood battens. The battens should be about 3–5cm square, the length determined by the width of the space to be filled. The mesh can be nailed to the battens using galvanised U-staples — make sure that it is pulled tight between the battens which should be spaced about 90cm apart. Metal mesh is better for the stronger growing and heavier climbers, plastic and nylon for the lighter-weight ones, both shrubby and herbaceous.

Simple galvanised wires are undoubtedly the best way of securing wall plants. They do not disfigure walls and they are easily disguised, a prime factor on old or historic buildings or walls. Furthermore they are relatively cheap to put up, will last a long time and are strong. If the correct gauge of wire is purchased it will support the weight of most wall plants with ease. However, they do take time to put up, though the effort is well worth while. Horizontal wires starting about 30cm from the soil surface and spaced at 50cm intervals will suit most wall plants. However, some climbers, especially the twining forms, need vertical wires spaced at a distance of 20–30cm. Some gardeners prefer a system of horizontal and vertical wires, especially for some of the larger climbers, *Clematis* species, *Campsis* and so on. Galvanised wire of 12-gauge is ideal, though 10- to 14-gauge may also be used; it needs to be drawn as tightly as possible. The wires are fixed

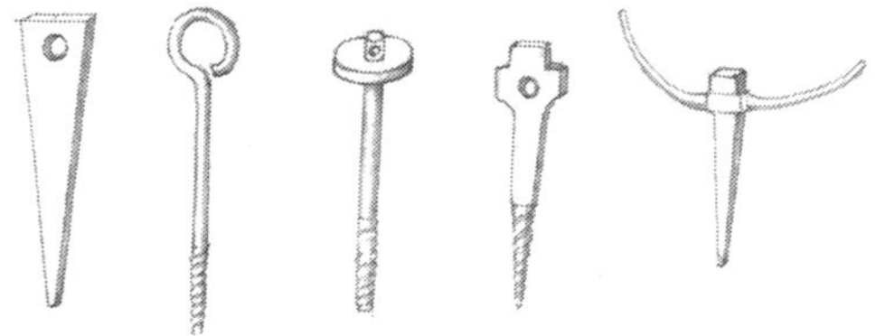

A number of fixings are available for securing wires to walls and fences. Some are knocked directly into mortar or wood, others being screwed into wall plugs or wood. The fixing on the extreme right is driven home and then the two soft metal 'arms' are wrapped around the plant stem to hold it in position.

to galvanised vine-eyes drilled into the wall about 1.5–2m apart. The vine-eyes should be 8–10 cm long to allow them to stand away from the wall sufficiently. Lead wall nails with eyes can also be used and these can be knocked into the mortar. Some types have a screw-thread and for these the wall first needs to be drilled and plugged. For short widths of wall the wires can be strained sufficiently by securing one end then pulling the other as tight as possible by hand or using a pair of pincers. For long lengths of wire it is usually impossible to strain the wires sufficiently. In such cases galvanised straining bolts are most useful, placing one of these at one end of each wire. Many gardeners use eyelet-holed metal pins for holding the wires between the end vine-eyes. These are simply strong pointed narrow wedges of metal with a hole in the broad end, which are knocked into the mortar for 2cm or so until secured. A system of horizontal wires is ideal for supporting and training wall fruits, p.256.

Some types of fencing, especially old ones, may not take wires or supports or indeed the weight of the plants. This problem can be overcome by securing

Adjustable straining bolts are employed to tighten long lengths of galvanised wire. On walls the bolts are fastened to wooden battens. Horizontal wires are suitable for most wall plants but vertical ones are best for twining climbers.

horizontal wires between stout wooden, concrete or iron posts set just in front of the fence. Posts need to be sunk a sufficient depth into the ground and, if necessary, embedded in a plug of concrete. Ideally the posts should be 3–4m

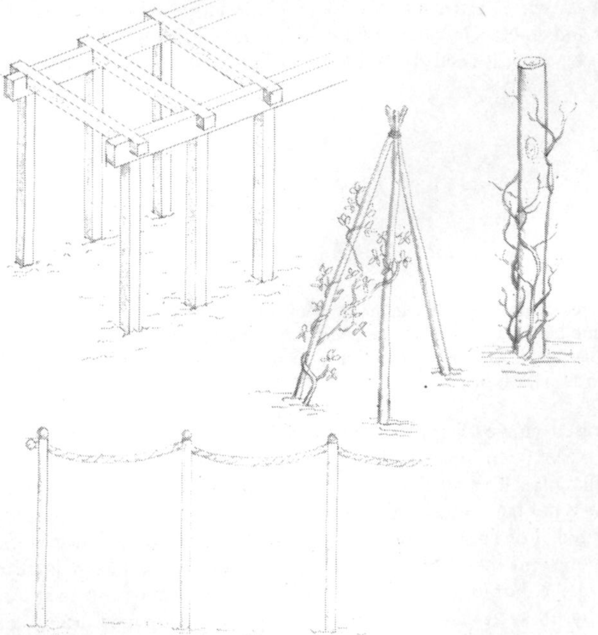

Climbers can be trained up various types of support other than walls and fences. Pergolas are ideal for roses and some clematis. They vary considerably in design, but a simple wooden structure (top left) can be very effective. A tripod or quadropod of poles or stakes is useful for vigorous climbers, such as *Actinidia* and *Celastrus* species. A stout wooden pole or tree trunk (top right) can make an ideal support for many climbers. A colonnade (lower left) composed of vertical poles or pillars linked together by stout rope is an effective support for rambler roses.

apart with 1.5–2m above the ground. Wooden posts should be treated carefully with preservative before being sunk in the soil, otherwise the basal part will rot rapidly. Wires can be strained, as already described, using galvanised straining bolts. End posts may often need to be braced to keep them absolutely upright.

Other methods of securing plants to walls include loops of rubber, especially pieces of old tyre cut into 2.5cm widths, looped around the stem and fixed to the wall with masonry nails. Shreds of strong cloth can be used in a similar manner. However, in very exposed situations such nails can be easily pulled out during a strong wind. This system is useful when just a few branches of a particular shrub need securing to the wall.

Branches and stems can be tied to wires and other supports with string, especially tarred string, or lengths of cloth, or plastic coated wire. Various proprietary ties can be purchased but these can work out very expensive if you have a lot of shrubs and climbers to secure, although some of them are long-lasting. Whatever ties are used they should be checked annually to see that they are not constricting stems or about to wear out.

Pruning and Training

To prune or not to prune is a question that vexes many gardeners. Pruning is a mystery to many, a complicated operation that only the skilled can understand. However, once understood, pruning is a fairly simple procedure, one that, with a little patience and practice, anyone can quickly learn. To see a well-pruned shrub or tree is to admire the skill of the pruner, yet we so often see bad pruning — tortured, misshapen plants all too drastically cut back. Bad pruning is certainly far worse than no pruning at all.

Nowhere in the garden is the need for pruning of some sort more apparent than with those plants grown on or against walls and fences. Many books have been written on the art of pruning and it is certainly not possible here to give more than an outline of the subject.

At the outset it must be pointed out that many wall plants, particularly shrubs, do not require any regular pruning other than to remove old, diseased, weak or unwanted growth.

Pruning is carried out for a number of reasons. Excessive growth may have to be cut out to keep a particular plant in check, especially when it has outgrown its allotted space, or one or two branches may need removing to keep a good shape. When some shrubs become old they may need rejuvenating by cutting back some or all of the older branches in order to promote strong young growths from the base of the plant. This has to be done with caution as some species do not take kindly to overpruning and may repay the gardener by dying. It is wise to find out how the subject will react before setting about it with saw and secateurs. The most important reason for pruning is to promote good healthy growth and to ensure good regular crops of flowers and fruits.

Pruning and training can be regarded as one and the same operation, or at least ones that closely complement each other. The type of growth and the flowering

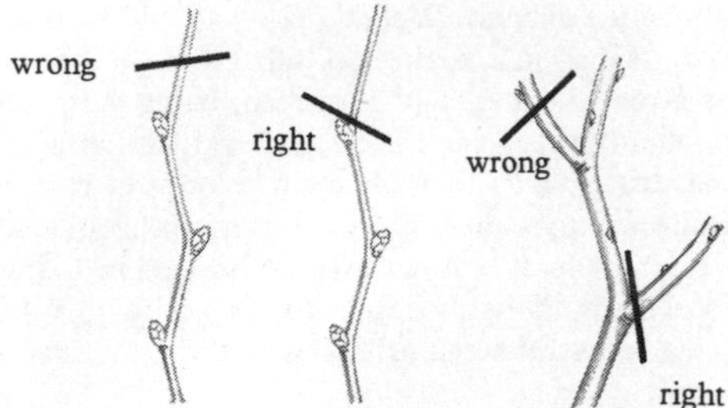

When pruning always produce a clean cut, using a sharp pair of secateurs or a pruning knife. Make cuts immediately above a suitable bud (centre). Take care not to leave a snag of wood above a bud (left) as this will prevent healing of the wound and cause die-back to the nearest bud, the dead 'wood' being a potential source of infection for various diseases. This applies equally to the removal of a branch (right). The correct cut should be made close to the main stem, as in the lower cut shown.

time of a particular species or cultivar are critical factors that must be ascertained before any pruning is carried out. If you are not sure, don't prune.

Plants that flower on the current season's shoots. Such plants generally flower in midsummer and autumn and should be pruned in the late winter or the very early spring. This gives the plant the longest possible time to produce plenty of new shoots before flowering. If pruning is carried out too late in the spring flowering may be delayed or even prevented during the same year. The idea is to cut back into old growth, if possible to a dormant bud near the base of shoots. This should be consistent with leaving a sufficient amount of wood as a framework for the new growth.

Plants that flower early in the year on shoots formed during the previous season. Many of these flower between March and June. To prune them early in the year, let us say in the late winter, would be to remove the potential flowering shoots. Pruning should therefore be carried out immediately flowering has ceased, cutting back strong growths that have just flowered to encourage new shoots which will bear the flowers during the following year. Examples are *Forsythia* spp. *Jasminum nudiflorum*, *Prunus triloba*, and *Clematis montana*. The very early flowering subjects in this category, such as the Forsythias, are pruned in much the same way as those shrubs which are winter pruned, for they have not made any new growth by the time the flowers fade: they are pruned immediately after flowering as the new shoots begin to emerge, shortening back many of the older shoots to strong new buds, leaving one or two shoots to grow at the base of each. The majority, however, flower later at a time when a good deal of new young growth has already been made. These require more careful pruning, the general aim being to thin the shoots, removing all the weak ones or overcrowded ones to produce a well-balanced specimen. This is again undertaken immediately after flowering, a process of thinning rather than shortening back.

The point to remember is that pruning should be carried out at the time of year that allows the plant the maximum period in which to produce new growth before the next flowering season. Pruning should not allow the natural grace and beauty of the shrub or climber to be spoilt.

Of course many shrubs do not need pruning, or at least do not require regular pruning. This applies to many evergreen shrubs. If pruning becomes necessary, because the shrub may have become too lanky or too large, then it is best carried out in the spring, allowing the plant the maximum possible time to grow and recover before the winter comes round again. Obviously if such shrubs are summer-flowering then the flowers will be sacrificed for a season.

As pruning is carried out any weak, diseased, dead or unwanted growths can be cut out, removing them close to a main stem if possible; avoid leaving unsightly 'snags'. Any large cuts are best dressed at the same time with a proprietary bituminised paint which will seal the wound, to make it watertight and prevent disease from entering the plant.

Pruning time is also a good time to check the ties of those shrubs and climbers which are tied to wall supports.

Having said all this it must be stressed that there are no hard and fast rules to pruning. There is no universal system that covers all plants, although the general principles will be found quite satisfactory for the majority of species. Not everyone will agree on the best way to prune a particular subject or when to prune it. Pruning was always and will long remain one of the most controversial of gardening practices. Those shrubs that flower during mid-summer on the current season's growth and are followed by attractive fruits in the autumn should not, of course, be pruned immediately after flowering otherwise the autumn display of fruit will be lost. Such subjects need to be pruned with caution and generally speaking need little pruning. However, a few shoots can be cut back from time to time to encourage some strong new growths, even if this means sacrificing some of the fruiting wood.

Plants grown primarily for their foliage are less exacting — *Actinidia* spp., various vines such as *Ampelopsis*, and *Parthenocissus* and the Loquat, *Eriobotrya japonica* for example. On the whole the best procedure to adopt is winter pruning for the deciduous plants and early spring for the evergreen ones.

Young plants in the early stages of wall-training generally need only very light pruning. This should aim at encouraging branching in the right direction or at stimulating more vigorous growth to help to build up a good framework on which the future flowers or foliage will be borne. Once the plant has filled its allotted space then, if it is a species or cultivar that requires it, a programme of regular pruning can be initiated.

The pruning of Clematis, Roses and wall fruits is covered in more detail in the appropriate chapters. Through the other chapters the type of pruning is indicated by the system of coding described at the end of the introduction.

A few shrubs such as *Buddleia fallowiana* and *Fuchsia magellanica* can be pruned hard back close to the ground every spring — to within 30cm of ground level during April.

Shrubs or climbers that have suffered frost damage during the winter will require some pruning in the spring, preferably in May when danger of further frosts has receded. The aim should be to cut back damaged shoots to clean healthy tissue. After severe winters a hard prune of such subjects may well be necessary.

The suckers produced by some shrubs and climber should be removed soon after they appear, unless they form an integral part of the framework of the particular subject.

One last point needs to be stressed. Hard pruning may not necessarily produce the desired results. It is often a fine procedure for promoting strong new growth from some old 'tired' shrubs. However, others may not respond to a hard pruning and may die back, or even die completely. Hard pruning is not a satisfactory way of keeping many shrubs 'within bounds'. It may often result in over vigorous leafy growth and reduction in the amount of flowers produced. Many mature shrubs settle down into a routine of flowering and/or fruiting, producing a small amount of extension growth each year. These often require very little pruning save for thinning or the removal of old, weak or diseased growth.

Propagation

Propagation is one of the most exciting and rewarding of gardening techniques. It is most satisfying to be able to grow plants from seeds or cuttings and to be able to give spare plants to one's friends. Anyone who has a plant of which they are particularly fond will want to propagate it, not only to have more than one plant but also to ensure that it won't be lost from the garden.

You do not need an expensive propagating frame with warming cables and careful temperature control to be able to propagate plants, although some of the rarer and more difficult species and cultivars do need the special conditions afforded by such propagators. Many plants can be rooted or germinated using cheap homemade equipment.

The simplest form of propagator is a flowerpot covered by a polythene bag or jam jar. Placed indoors on a warm windowsill, out of the direct sunlight, it is surprising what will root. A deep box with a generous layer of a mixture of equal parts of peat and sand will provide space for a greater number of cuttings. A sheet of glass placed over the box will keep the cuttings or pans of seeds warm and the atmosphere moist. Such propagators are good in greenhouses or cold frames, although strong sunlight should be avoided.

Cuttings Cuttings vary greatly in their rooting abilities. Some will root in a jar of water or simply stuck into a corner of the garden and left to their own devices. However, these are the minority; the remainder vary from moderately difficult, to difficult to root or downright impossible, and some form of propagator will be needed. Having said this though, it has to be admitted that some gardeners can manage to root almost anything — perhaps the green-fingered amongst us might even root a pencil, put to the test. Joking apart, cuttings can be temperamental. Even within a batch of the same cultivar, some may root whilst others simply wither or linger on for some time without rooting. Knowing when to take cuttings and the type of cutting to make will lead to a far greater degree of success.

There are three main types of cutting — softwood, half-ripe or semi-hardwood and hardwood.

Softwood cuttings are generally taken in late spring and early summer. Healthy young shoots are cut immediately below a leaf-joint or node. The ideal cutting should be 5–8cm long and the lowermost leaves should be removed with a sharp knife close to the stem leaving only the upper third with leaves.

Semi-hardwood cuttings are taken during mid or late summer, selecting firmer

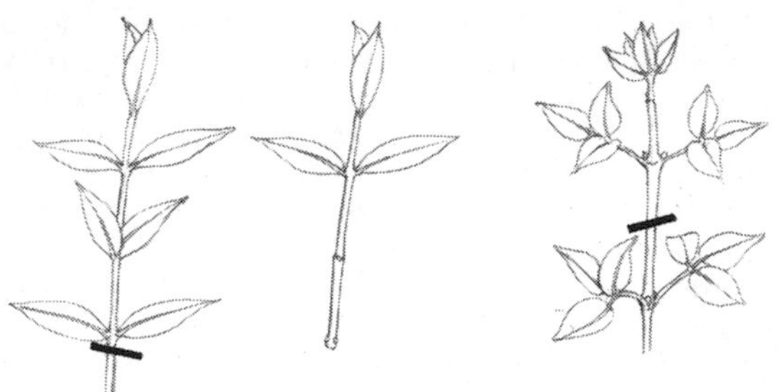

Most softwood cuttings are made immediately below a leaf-joint (node) of a suitable young shoot (left & centre). The lower leaves are trimmed from the cutting. Internodal softwood cuttings (right) are employed for some plants, especially clematis.

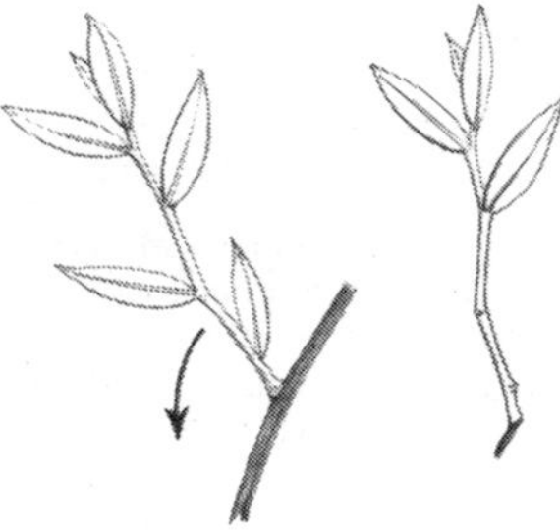

Semi-hardwood cuttings consist of semi-mature growth with a 'heel' of old wood.

shoots which have half-ripened. These can be longer, 8–12cm long. Semi-hardwood cuttings are generally removed with a 'heel' of hardwood at the base. This is obtained by pulling lateral shoots downwards removing a small portion of the previous year's growth. This base is trimmed neatly to leave a small 'heel'. Clematis are generally rooted from semi-hardwood cuttings, however, internodal cuttings are more satisfactory — the cut being made mid-way between two leaf-nodes or joints. Leaves are removed in the same way as for softwood cuttings.

Hardwood cuttings, as the name implies, are taken of mature wood which has ripened well through the season. Such cuttings are taken during the autumn or early winter. At this time they may have lost some or all of their leaves if deciduous. Hardwood cuttings can be made with a 'heel' or cut immediately beneath a node. Hardwood cuttings are generally between 15 and 25cm long.

Hormone rooting powders greatly help the rooting of various cuttings. Several types are available and are intended for the different kinds of cuttings listed above. The cut ends of the shoots are dipped in water and then into the rooting compound. Excess powder is tapped off and the cuttings are then inserted in a suitable rooting compost.

The best compost is one of equal parts peat and coarse sand and this will suit the majority of plants referred to in this book. Cuttings can be placed around the inner edge of 10cm-diameter pots or in rows in a propagating frame. They should be firmed-in and well watered-in immediately. Once rooted (the time taken to do so varying greatly from one plant to another) they can be potted on singly into 8cm pots, using a standard potting compost. Rooting of softwood or semi-hardwood cuttings is often indicated by a sudden increase in growth. Hardwood cuttings can be placed in a propagating frame or, alternatively, hardy cultivars can be placed directly out-of-doors in a suitable corner of the garden. Slender slip trenches lined with coarse sand are most suitable, placing cuttings in rows and firming them in carefully. Those rooted out-of-doors are best left for a full season and removed to their permanent positions the following autumn.

Cuttings of tender or half-hardy species and cultivars are best over-wintered indoors or in a protected frame and not planted out until the late spring. Young plants are generally less hardy than mature plants.

Layering Layering is a way of rooting many difficult plants, especially those that often fail as cuttings. Layering can take two forms, but the essential feature is that

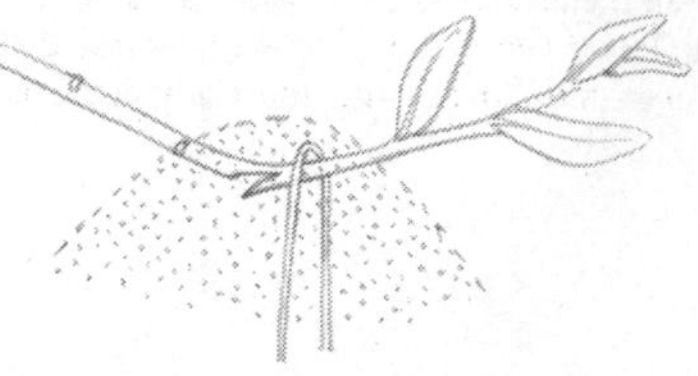

Layering is a method of rooting new plants of difficult species. An upwardly directed cut is made in the stem which is pinned to the ground or weighed down with a stone. Soil is piled up over the layered portion. Stems well above the ground can be air-layered, wrapping the cut portion of the stem in moss and surrounding this with polythene. Layers are detached from the parent plant only when rooting has taken place.

the chosen shoot remains firmly attached to the parent plant until it has rooted. Ordinary layering involves pegging down a strong, conveniently placed, mature shoot to the ground. A short upward-slanting cut should be made in the lower surface of the shoot, 30–50cm from the tip, producing a short 'tongue' of tissue. This cut area is dusted with hormone rooting powder and then pegged down to the ground with a loop of wire, a bent bamboo slither or a convenient rock and soil is built up over the pegged area to form a small mound. Some plants layer themselves readily — Brambles, *Rubus* spp., do this frequently without any assistance.

Often, however, there is not a convenient shoot near ground level so that layering is done in the air — air layering. The process is the same as ordinary layering except that the cut zone is enclosed in a tight wall of moist sphagnum moss kept in place by ties of raffia or soft string. The whole is then wrapped in polythene to form a sausage.

When the layers have become well-rooted they can be severed from the parent plant and either potted up or planted out in their permanent site. Layers may take a full year or more to root properly.

Suckers and division Suckering shrubs can be increased by simply removing suitable suckers with a few attached roots from the parent plant, using a sharp knife or spade. Care should be taken not to damage the main plant.

Herbaceous climbers can often be increased by careful division of the whole clump into suitably-sized portions. The whole plant should be lifted in the autumn or early spring and teased apart by hand. Tough clumps can be split using two forks back to back and forcing the clump into two. Some gardeners simply cut plants into sections with a spade though one certainly would not recommend this for rare or delicate species. Divisions should be replanted immediately, certainly before they have had a chance to dry out or get frosted.

Propagation by seeds Seeds provide a ready means of increasing many plants. For those annual and herbaceous climbers mentioned in this book it is perhaps the only, or at least the easiest, way to produce new plants. Many gardeners find a great deal of satisfaction in raising a plant from a seed to a mature plant in full flower. However, others find that for many shrubs and trees the time lag between seedling stage and flowering is too tedious. It is easier to buy a container-grown plant from a nursery centre with a good chance that it will flower within a couple of years.

Many species come true from seed, that is the offspring closely resemble their parents. Others, especially selected cultivars and hybrids, may not come true and even the offspring of some species may prove a mixed bunch. If you want to keep a particular cultivar true then propagate it from cuttings or layers. This applies particularly to many rose and clematis cultivars, and of course all hybrids.

Seeds of annual climbers can be sown in plant pots or boxes in the early spring, using a suitable seed compost. Unless large numbers are being sown, 10cm pots are a very suitable size for most seeds. Pots should be well-crocked to allow free drainage, for bad drainage can inflict all sorts of trouble on to the seedlings when they appear. The compost should be firmed down and flattened before sowing, and watered. Large seeds can be spaced evenly and can be pushed into the compost using the end of a pencil. Fine seeds should be scattered thinly, a process which can be made easier by mixing them with fine sand and sprinkling the mixture thinly over the surface of the compost. Thin sowing is the key to success with nearly all seeds. Once sown, seeds should be covered with a thin layer of finely-sifted compost — equal in depth to the size of the seed. Pots can be labelled so that one is not left puzzled as to what the seedlings are when they appear. The sowings should be covered with glass and paper or just paper if placed in a frame, and placed in a warm place in a greenhouse or on a windowsill, though direct sunlight should be avoided at first. The moment the first seedlings appear the paper should be removed and this requires a daily inspection otherwise seedlings may become leggy.

As soon as they are large enough to handle, generally having produced one or two leaves beyond the seed leaves (cotyledons), the seedlings are best pricked off individually into pots using a standard potting compost — most gardeners have their own preferred type of compost, though the heavier, loam-based red ones have been in decline in recent years. Pricked-out seedlings should be firmed in and watered well. A cold greenhouse is adequate for most except the more tender species. As the weather warms young plants can be gradually hardened off and finally planted out — say by the end of May. More tender subjects such as Morning Glory *(Ipomoea)* and the Glory Vine *(Eccremocarpus)* are best left until June, especially if the weather is cool and damp. It is always a temptation to plant out at the first sign of a warm spell and this may often be regretted later.

Now what about those seeds of precious trees and shrubs? Many of these are hard-coated and have a long dormancy. Sown normally, germination may be very slow or erratic or perhaps no seeds will germinate at all. To assist germination a pre-sowing treatment, stratification, can be recommended. Seeds are mixed with moist sand or a sandy soil and placed in layers, one above another, sandwiched between further layers of moist sand. Pots, boxes or tins perforated at the bottom are suitable containers. Once full the containers are placed out of doors, preferably in the autumn. The ideal place is one which receives a lot of frost or cold such as the north side of a fence or wall — the more severe the better. Containers can be partly buried or left on the surface. By late winter the seeds should have received enough cold treatment and the seed coats will have been softened or partly broken down. The seeds can then be removed and sown in the normal way. Hardy species can be placed in cold frames whilst the less hardy ones are best started off in a propagator. Care should be taken to protect stratified and sown seeds from the ravages of mice and other rodents.

Seedling shrubs and trees may take several years before they are large enough to plant out in their permanent sites. Nursery beds can be prepared for hardy species, where they can be placed in rows until large enough to plant out. Some will of course be large enough in their second season.

Patience is required in growing shrubs and trees from seed, however, the eventual rewards more than repay the early frustrations.

Shrubs and Climbers for Different Aspects

Choosing the right plant for the right place can prove a nightmare. Plants are relatively expensive to buy and there is nothing more infuriating than to find that the chosen plant dies or simply fails to flower.

The first thing to decide is whether you want an evergreen or deciduous subject, a shrub or a climber. Other factors will obviously play an important part — flowering time, colour and so on. In any event a suitable subject can always be found, even for those nasty cold north-facing walls.

The following lists are intended as a guide only and include a selection of the plants to be found in this book. The selections should be used in conjunction with the text so that as much information as possible can be gained about a particular plant. Latin names are given, despite their tongue-twisting names, for they act as a direct cross-reference with the text.

Experimenting with plants is one of the great joys of gardening. It can be exciting to succeed with plants that the neighbours haven't got or can't grow, so it is often worth hunting out some of the rarer or lesser- known plants.

Evergreen shrubs for south- or west-facing aspects

Abelia ×grandiflora
Abutilon megapotamicum
A. ×suntense 'Jermyns'
A.vitifolium 'Veronica Tennant'
Acacia baileyana
A. dealbata
Callistemon salignus
Carpentaria californica
Ceanothus impressus
C. ×lobbianus
C. rigidus
C. ×veitchianus
Cestrum elegans
Choisya ternata
Coronilla glauca
Crinodendron hookerianum
Cytisus battandieri †
Fremontodendron californicum
Hoheria angustifolia
H. populnea
Itea ilicifolia
Leptospermum scoparium
Magnolia grandiflora 'Exmouth'
Myrtus communis & cultivars
Olearia — many species & cultivars
Phygelius capensis
Piptanthus laburnifolius
Pittosporum eugenioides 'Variegatum'
P. tenuifolium & cultivars
P. tobira
Romneya coulteri

† sometimes only partially evergreen.

Deciduous shrubs for south- or west-facing aspects

Abeliophyllum distichum
Buddleia colvillei 'Kewensis'
B. crispa
B. fallowiana
Chaenomeles species & varieties
Chimonanthus praecox
Clianthus puniceus
Forsythia suspensa
Hoheria glabrata
H. lyallii
Lippia citriodora
Punica granatum
Ribes speciosum
Robinia hispida

Evergreen shrubs for north- or east-facing aspects

Azara microphylla
Berberis × stenophylla
Camellia — many species & varieties
Choisya ternata
Cotoneaster franchetii
C. microphyllus
Crinodendron hookerianum
Daphne odora 'Aureomarginata'
Drimys winteri
Escallonia macrantha
Euonymus fortunei & varieties
Garrya elliptica
Illicium anisatum
Lomatia myricoides
Mitraria coccinea
Piptanthus laburnifolius†
Pyracantha — most species & varieties
Viburnum × burkwoodii

†sometimes only partially evergreen.

Deciduous shrubs for north- or east-facing aspect

Chaenomeles species & varieties
Cotoneaster horizontalis
Forsythia suspensa
Jasminum nudiflorum
Kerria japonica 'Pleniflora'

Evergreen climbers for south- or west-facing aspects

Clematis armandii
C. cirrhosa
C. finetiana
Lonicera henryi
L. japonica 'Halliana'
Passiflora caerulea
Rosa — various species & varieties
Solanum crispum 'Glasnevin'
S. jasminoides

Deciduous climbers for south- or west-facing aspects

Actinidia chinensis
A. kolomikta
Campsis radicans
C. × tagliabuana
Clematis alpina
C. chrysocoma var. *sericea*
C. florida 'Sieboldii'
C. macropetala
C. montana & varieties
C. tangutica
C. vernayi 'Orange Peel'
Jasminum officinale
Lonicera etrusa
L. periclymenum & varieties
Rosa — many species & varieties
Schizophragma hydrangeoides
Vitis vinifera & varieties
Wisteria species & varieties

Evergreen climbers for north- or east-facing aspects

Akebia quinata
Berberidopsis corallina
Hedera — species & many varieties
Pileostegia viburnoides

Deciduous climbers for north- or east-facing aspects

Berchemia racemosa
Celastrus orbiculatus
Clematis alpina
C. macropetala
C. montana & varieties
C. — many large-flowered varieties
Hydrangea petiolaris
Lonicera ×*americana*
L. caprifolium
L. periclymenum & varieties
L. ×*tellmaniana*
L. tragophylla
Parthenocissus — most species & varieties
Rosa — various varieties, particularly 'Aloha', 'Mme Caroline Testout', 'Gloire de Dijon', 'Mme Alfred Carrière', & 'Danse du Feu'
Schizophragma hydrangeoides
Vitis coignetiae

Annual or herbaceous climbers

Aconitum volubile
Bowiea volubilis
Cobaea scandens
Dicentra chrysantha
Eccremocarpus scaber
Lathyrus latifolius
Ipomoea species & varieties
Maurandia barclaiana
Mina lobata
Phygelius capensis
Tropaeolum speciosum
T. tuberosum

Scented shrubs & climbers for walls or fences

Abelia chinensis
Azara microphylla
Buddleia auriculata
B. crispa
B. fallowiana
B. farreri
Chimonanthus praecox
Choisya ternata
Clematis armandii
C. flammula
C. paniculata
C. finetiana
Daphne odora
Drimys winteri
Holboellia latifolia
Lonicera caprifolium
L. fragrantissima
L. japonica
L. periclymenum
L. ×*purpusii*
L. standishii
Pittosporum eugenioides
P. tobira
Trachelospermum species
Viburnum ×*bodnantense*
V. ×*burkwoodii*
V. farreri
Wisteria species

Winter or early spring flowering shrubs or climbers

Acacia baileyana
A. dealbata
Buddleia auriculata
Camellia sasanqua
Chimonanthus praecox
Clematis cirrhosa subsp. *balearica*
Daphne bholua
Garrya elliptica
Jasminum nudiflorum
Lindera praecox
Lonicera fragrantissima
L. ×*purpusii*
L. standishii
Viburnum ×*bodnantense*
V. farreri

Pests, Diseases and Disorders

Good cultivation is the best way to prevent ill-health and attack by pests and diseases. Strong, well-grown plants are more resistant. Garden hygiene is also important; the incidence of pests and diseases can be reduced by sweeping up and burning all dead fallen leaves and fruits as they can harbour fungal spores, insect eggs and slugs.

However, once a pest or disease has got a hold it will be necessary to use chemicals as a control. It is extremely important to follow the manufacturer's instructions exactly, noting not only the amount to be used but how often, and whether the chemical is safe to use on the intended plants, e.g. HCH is harmful to members of the cucumber family, Cucurbitaceae. The chemicals must be stored in a cool dry dark place where children and pets cannot reach them. Spraying is best carried out in the evening once the sun is off the plants as most beneficial insects, especially bees, will have retired by then. Windy weather should be avoided because the wind can carry the spray away from the infected plant on to plants which do not need it and they may even be damaged as a result.

The pests and troubles which affect clematis, honeysuckles, roses and wall fruits are dealt with in the relevant chapters in the second part of the book. Those mentioned below are the ones most likely to occur on other climbers and wall plants.

PESTS

Aphids affect a wide range of plants and the commonest are species of greenfly and blackfly. They suck sap from the stem and leaf tissues and often tend to congregate towards the tips of shoots and around flower buds. Heavy infestations can result in stunted growth, curly leaves and a reduction in flowering. Another disadvantage of aphids is that they exude a sticky substance, known as honeydew, which soils the leaves, encouraging the growth of sooty mould. Aphids are known to spread various virus diseases of plants, so aphid control goes hand-in-hand with virus control. Aphids reproduce very rapidly in warm weather, and so can become a great problem during a hot dry summer.

Control is by spraying with Derris, Malathion, Pirimicarb, Dimethoate or Formothion. Exposed colonies are easily dealt with in this way, but protected aphids, e.g. those inside curled leaves, must be killed by means of a systemic insecticide. Tar oil washes kill the over-wintering eggs of aphids on fruit trees.

Bryobia Mites are tiny red mites which feed on leaves, producing a silvery or light-coloured speckling on the upper surface. Eventually the leaves become chlorotic, or turn brown and shrivel. Bryobia mites are an especial nuisance on ivies, *Hedera*, and apples, and should be sprayed with Derris or Malathion as soon as they are noticed.

Capsid Bugs are brownish long-legged insects about 0.5cm long in the adult stage, whilst the larvae are smaller and greenish. They suck the sap from buds and young leaves and inject a poisonous saliva into the plant which kills the plant tissue where they feed. When the affected young leaves expand, the dead areas tear into many small holes giving the leaves a characteristic appearance. In addition, the shoots usually become distorted. The worst damage usually occurs in dry weather when the numbers of capsids increase. There are several species which attack different plants; the most susceptible are roses, apples, hydrangeas and forsythia.

Control is by spraying with HCH or Fenitrothion. Some capsids overwinter in plant débris, so cleaning away dead leaves helps to keep the population down.

Caterpillars are the larval stage of butterflies and moths and are common garden pests. There are about fifty species which eat the leaves and young stems of many garden plants. Caterpillar damage usually shows itself as irregular holes in the leaves, but generally the culprits are visible, except in those species which feed at night, when inspection by torchlight is necessary!

Control is by spraying with HCH, Derris or Malathion, as soon as the damage is noticed. Caterpillars have enormous appetites and the older bigger ones eat more than the younger ones.

Cutworms are caterpillars of various species, which live in the soil, feeding on the roots and the stems of plants at soil level. Their feeding usually results in slow growth and a tendency for the plant to wilt in the sun, even when the soil moisture is adequate. In extreme cases, the cutworm damage completely encircles the stem and the plant dies.

To control them the soil should be teated with HCH dust, preferably while the cutworms are still small, since the fully grown ones are difficult to kill. It is worth looking for and destroying the larger grubs which are usually found close to the plant, near the soil surface.

Earwigs feed at night, eating young stems, petals and the soft parts of leaves and often leaving only a network of veins. They do most damage in warm still evenings and affect a wide range of plants. They can be trapped using the traditional method of a flower pot filled with straw and inverted on top of a cane — the flower pot must be emptied each morning and the earwigs destroyed. If the infestation is bad, control the pests by spraying at dusk with HCH, Fenitrothion or Trichlorphon.

Leaf Miners live inside the leaves, eating a tunnel between the upper and lower surfaces. This can be seen as a white or brown rambling line, marking the progress of the leaf miner. There are a number of different species which attack different plants; of the climbers, the honeysuckles, *Lonicera* can be badly affected.

Control is by spraying with HCH or Trichlorphon as soon as the tunnels are noticed.

Red Spider Mites are minute reddish-brown mites which suck the sap from the undersides of leaves which then turn yellowish. They produce a fine silky web which often covers the withering leaves. They attack various plants but roses, vines and figs are especially susceptible, and warm dry conditions encourage them to breed, so that plants grown on a warm sheltered wall are likely to be attacked. Merely spraying with water may help to check their numbers as they dislike wet conditions, but for proper control it is necessary to spray with Malathion, Derris, Dimethoate or Formothion, taking care to wet the undersides of the leaves. The plant should be sprayed at least three times at weekly intervals.

Scale Insects are usually brownish or yellowish, oval, flat insects about 3-4mm long, which suck the sap from leaves and stems. There are several different kinds, e.g.soft scales, which tend to attack ivies, *Hedera*, and *Camellia*, or brown scales, which affect wall fruits, roses and *Ceanothus*. Control is by spraying with Malathion as soon as the scales are seen, making sure that the undersides of the leaves are sprayed.

Slugs attack a wide range of plants and eat young shoots and stems as well as leaves and flowers. They betray their presence by leaving silvery shiny trails behind them. They are most active in the spring and autumn and thrive in mild moist weather. They are especially troublesome in soils which have a high organic content. Most of their feeding is done at night, and during the day they hide below stones and plant pots and among plant débris.

Control is by slug bait based on Metaldehyde or Methiocarb, or by watering or spraying a Metaldehyde solution on to the soil and plants. These chemicals will poison animals, so that bait should be hidden under a tile or put in a place where animals cannot reach it.

Weevils are small or medium-sized beetles, usually dark brown or grey and with a long snout. They feed mainly at night and eat the leaves of a range of plants, although *Camellia* and vines are particuarly prone to attack.

Control by spraying with HCH when damage is seen.

White flies are small, white, moth-like insects which hatch from flat oval scale-like larvae. They congregate like aphids, excreting honeydew which encourages sooty mould. The larvae are often not noticed, but as soon as adults are seen the plant should be sprayed with Malathion.

Woolly aphids are troublesome on members of the Rose family such as apples, pyracanthas and cotoneasters. They cluster on the twigs and branches and produce tufts of protective white wool. Affected twigs become swollen. Control is by spraying with Malathion, making sure that, later in the year, the spray penetrates into cracks and crevices in the bark where the woolly aphids overwinter.

DISEASES

Fireblight is a bacterial disease affecting members of the Rose family and occurs mainly in the southern half of the British Isles. It usually attacks the flowers which turn blackish, and then spreads down the twigs into the main branches. Leaves and stems wilt and turn brown but, characteristically, the leaves do not fall. In the Autumn, cankers appear at the base of dead twigs.

The only remedy is to dig up and burn affected plants or, if the disease is caught early, to cut back diseased wood at least 5cm below the affected part. Pruning tools should then be disinfected.

Grey Mould can affect many plants, producing a grey-brown furry fungal growth on the affected part which may be flower buds, stems or fruits. It is especially bad in a wet season, causing flowers, or even whole herbaceous plants to rot. Infection may be prevented by spraying with Benomyl or Thiophanate-methyl when the first flowers open, repeating twice more at fortnightly intervals. Herbaceous plants already infected should be sprayed with Captan, Thiram or Zineb. In woody plants the affected tissue should be removed and the wound coated with a protective paint.

Honey Fungus affects a wide range of plants, although woody plants are more susceptible than herbaceous. It produces honey-coloured toadstools in autumn, but these rarely spread the disease. Infection occurs by means of black boot lace-like structures called rhizomorphs which live on both living and dead wood and grow through the soil until they find more roots to penetrate. The symptoms of infection are that the plant suddenly wilts and dies, and when the roots are dug up, the black strands of the fungus can be seen. All dead and dying plants should be removed and destroyed and the soil should be sterilized with a 2% solution of Formalin. Nothing should be planted in the soil for two months.

Powdery Mildew is usually seen as a whitish powdery deposit on leaves, stems, buds and even fruit. Many species of fungus cause this disease and it affects many different plants. Powdery mildew is worse when the soil is dry, so it is a good idea to mulch to help to conserve moisture, and to water in dry weather. Lack of circulating air, e.g. against a very sheltered wall, also encourages the disease. Very severely affected plants should be removed; those less badly affected can be sprayed with Benomyl, Dinocap or Triforine.

Scab occurs on members of the Rose family, apples, pears and pyracanthas being the most susceptible. It appears as greenish-brown blotches on the leaves which usually fall early. The fruits bear brown or black scabs and pyracantha berries may be completely coated in a thick felt. Diseased leaves should be collected and burnt and affected shoots removed. The plants should be sprayed with Captan at fortnightly intervals up to the middle of July.

Silverleaf is a fungus disease which commonly affects plums, cotoneasters and honeysuckles. The fungus usually enters the plant through a pruning wound and the leaves turn silvery and then sometimes brown. Affected branches die back and sometimes the whole plant will die. Purplish fruiting bodies are produced on the dead wood, which become brownish or fawn, and the internal tissues are stained with purplish-brown. The dead wood should be cut back to at least 30cm below any wood which is stained.

Virus Diseases are often carried by aphids, so aphid control helps to control the viruses. There are a number of different virus diseases which usually attack a limited range of species, e.g. Cucumber Mosaic Virus affects cucumber, passion flowers, *Passiflora,* and *Daphne.*

A plant with a virus disease usually lacks vigour and the leaves become distorted and mottled. Any affected plant should be dug up and burnt. It is best not to plant the same species in a virus-affected site. Hands and tools should be washed after contact with infected plants.

NUTRIENT AND TRACE ELEMENT DEFICIENCY

Plants require a number of food materials and lack of any particular nutrient, e.g. potassium, magnesium, phosphorus or nitrogen, produces characteristic symptoms. Substances which the plant needs in minute amounts, e.g. manganese, iron, are known as trace-elements, and deficiency in these results in chlorosis.

Nitrogen deficiency occurs mainly when the plants grow in light soils which lack organic content. The growth of both roots and stems is stunted and the young leaves are pale yellow. Eventually the leaves turn bright yellow, red and occasionally purplish. Fruit production is reduced and fruits are usually small and brightly coloured.

The deficiency can be corrected by the application of a nitrogenous fertilizer such as ammonium sulphate or nitro-chalk.

Phosphorus deficiency is at its worst in areas of high rainfall and therefore is most prevalent in the north and west, and on clay soils. It is difficult to distinguish it from nitrogen deficiency because the symptoms are similar, but the leaf colours are somewhat more subdued, usually being purple or bronze. The remedy is to apply superphosphate every second or third year at 40gm per sq m (1½oz per sq yd). Bone meal, which has a high phosphorus content can be used at 140gm per sq m (4oz per sq yd), before sowing seed or planting.

Potassium deficiency usually occurs on sandy, peat or chalk soils. Growth is stunted and the leaves turn a dull bluish-green, often with browning around the margin or at the tips. In addition, the leaves may curl downwards or even fall. Flowering and fruiting is usually poor. To correct the deficiency, apply sulphate or nitrate of potash at 17–25gm per sq m (½–¾oz per sq yd).

Magnesium deficiency often occurs on light acid soils, and on all soils after heavy rain, as magnesium is easily washed out from the soil. An excess of potassium renders magnesium unavailable to plants, thus deficiency symptoms can occur when the plants have been over-fed with potash fertilizers. The most usual symptom is chlorosis (yellowing) of the leaves, affecting the older leaves first and spreading gradually upwards. Often the leaves turn yellow between the veins and eventually become orange, red or brown and fall off.

Magnesium deficiency can be corrected by spraying with a solution of magnesium sulphate (Epsom salts) made from 275gm (½lb) dissolved in 10l (2½ gallons) of water, plus a spreader such as soft soap or detergent. The spraying should be carried out two or three times at intervals of a fortnight.

Manganese deficiency is found on sandy, peat and alkaline soils and is often accompanied by iron deficiency. The symptoms are very similar to those of magnesium deficiency, i.e. the leaves become chlorotic. The remedy is to spray with a manganese sulphate solution made from 70gm (2oz) dissolved in 10l (2½ gallons) of water plus a soap or detergent spreader.

Iron deficiency occurs on very alkaline soils which have a pH of over 7.5 (pH is the degree of acidity or alkalinity of a soil; if the pH is below 7.0 the soil is acid; above 7.0 it is alkaline). Limy soils are alkaline and another name for iron deficiency is 'lime-induced chlorosis'. In mild cases, it is not easy to distinguish between iron deficiency and lack of magnesium and manganese, so it is necessary to determine the pH of the soil.

Acid-loving plants such as the Camellia, will show symptoms of iron deficiency when the soil pH is between 7.0 and 8.0. When it rises above 8.0, species of *Ceanothus*, *Chaenomeles*, *Hydrangea* and *Prunus* may be affected.

The pH of the soil can be reduced by adding acidic materials such as peat or crushed bracken, or acidifying chemicals. On sandy soils, flowers of sulphur can be added at 140gm per sq m (4oz per sq yd).

Aluminium sulphate or ferrous sulphate at the rate of 140gm per sq m (4oz per sq yd), should only be used on bare ground and plants should not be put in until the required pH has been attained.

PART TWO

The Plants

Deciduous Climbers

This chapter contains some of the finest and greatest favourites of all wall plants, the Climbing Hydrangea, *H. petiolaris*, the ever-popular Wisterias and various vines, *Vitis*, *Ampelopsis* and *Parthenocissus*, plus many more, some very little known. Although deciduous climbers include many species and cultivars of clematis, roses and honeysuckles these are dealt with in separate chapters.

Apart from the tender species and cultivars most deciduous climbers can be planted at almost any time from the late Autumn until the Spring, weather permitting. Container-grown specimens can in fact be planted almost throughout the year, however, those planted during the spring and summer will require careful attention in the way of regular watering and heavy mulches to prevent the roots from drying out.

Tender species are best planted out in the spring, and even then should be protected at first lest the weather turn cold and windy. Wise gardeners will protect such plants through the winter, even when they are well established, insuring against loss by striking cuttings during the summer. These are kept in a frame or greenhouse over winter in case the parent plants succumb to low temperatures.

Deciduous climbers are particularly valuable when a permanent curtain of green foliage is not required. If walls or fences need regular painting or other treatment then it is much easier to get behind deciduous rather than evergreen subjects.

ACTINIDIA (Actinidiaceae)

A genus of usually hardy, twining, mostly deciduous climbers of which the Chinese Gooseberry is the best-known species. The leaves are simple and alternate, often heart-shaped. The flowers are small and often white, plants having either male or female or hermaphrodite flowers. The fruits are fleshy, sometimes edible, berries.

Actinidias are easily grown in most average garden soils, though not in dry soils, and are ideal subjects for walls, fences, pergolas or on stout poles. On the whole they prefer cool, partially shaded positions, especially those that avoid sun during the midday hours — west-, north-west- and north-east-facing aspects are perfect. *Actinidia kolomikta* however, does best on a sunny south- or west-facing wall. Young plants are best placed in their permanent positions in early March. Those species or varieties grown for their fruits should be planted in twos or threes. Propagation is from midsummer cuttings or layerings placed in a propagating frame.

Some species are greatly attractive to cats which will chew the leaves and young shoots. *Actinidia kolomikta* and *A. polygama* are particularly prone to such attacks.

◐ **Actinidia chinensis** (Pl.1), the Chinese Gooseberry or Kiwi Fruit, is a vigorous climber reaching 9–10m tall, with reddish-hairy shoots. The heart-shaped leaves are pointed, 13–20cm long, with a bristly margin, dark rather vivid green above but greyish-downy beneath. The leaves of flowering shoots are smaller and relatively broader than those of vegetative shoots, rounded and notched at the apex. The flowers are white, turning cream and then buff-yellow, 38–40mm across, fragrant, borne in small clusters on short lateral shoots. Fruit a walnut-sized berry covered in reddish-brown hairs, with the flavour of gooseberry. [Aug–Sept, H, PW, China]

A handsome climber for a large old wall which was introduced from Hupeh in 1900 by Ernest H. Wilson. Plants are hardy and will often bear fruit in Britain. They are grown commercially in large numbers in New Zealand where a number of selected clones have been developed and where the name 'Kiwi Berry' is generally used. Most plants are either male or female, though hermaphrodite flowers may also occur.

'Aureovariegata' has leaves marked with yellow and cream.

◐ **Actinidia arguta** is a very vigorous climber reaching 15m or more in height. The oval or oblong leaves, 8–13cm long, have a rounded or heart-shaped base, dark shiny green above, paler beneath and downy along the veins. The leaf-stalk is long and pinkish. The fragrant white flowers are produced in small lateral clusters, each flower being rather globular, 15–20mm across, with purple anthers. Male and female flowers are borne on separate plants. The greenish-yellow berries are oblong, 25mm long, edible but rather tasteless. [June–July, H, PW, Japan, Korea, & Manchuria]

One of the most vigorous and hardy species flowering well in the garden, particularly in the south and west of Britain. The fruits are widely eaten in Japan.

var. **cordifolia** has leaves which are more prounouncedly heart-shaped with purple leaf stalks.

◐ **Actinidia purpurea** is closely related to *A. arguta* but less vigorous, seldom climbing more than 8m in height. The leaves are oval or oblong, 7.5–12.5cm long, dull green above, green and downy beneath. The white flowers are 12–20mm across, the male in clusters of five to seven, the female ones solitary or in threes. The small egg-shaped fruits are about 25mm long, purple when ripe, edible and sweet. [June, H, PW, SW China (W Szechwan & Yunnan)]

A handsome species introduced at the beginning of the century.

☼ ***Actinidia kolomikta** (Pl.1) is a handsome and striking climber reaching about 2–4m in height with slender stems. The heart-shaped leaves are coarsely toothed, 8–16cm long. They are remarkable for their coloration, some or all of the leaves having the terminal half creamy-white flushed with pink, a feature particularly well marked early in the season. The small, slightly fragrant, white flowers are borne in clusters of one to three, each 12–13mm across, male and female on different plants. The yellowish fruits are oval in outline, 2.5cm long, sweet to taste. [June, H, PW, N China, Japan & Manchuria]

Probably the most decorative species, less vigorous than the others and worth a place in any garden where a sunny sheltered wall can be provided. Plants will, in fact, tolerate walls of most aspects though the unusual leaf colorations are best developed on sunny walls. Young plants may take a year or two before the leaf colours are produced. The white ends to the leaves look as though they have been dipped in whitewash; after a few days they take on a pink tinge, later becoming quite deep pink. Unruly shoots can be shortened back during the summer, though the main pruning effort is best undertaken during the winter, cutting side growth to two or three buds, but leaving a good framework to the plant.

A. kolomikta was first introduced to cultivation round about the middle of the nineteenth century. The form usually cultivated is the male plant, and it is possible that all the plants grown have been developed from a single clone.

***Actinidia polygama**, the Silver Vine, is a slender-branched climber 4.5–6m tall. The elliptic or oblong, sometimes heart-shaped, leaves are 7.5–12.5cm long, with a bristly-toothed margin, green but tinged with bronze when young. The fragrant white flowers are usually borne in clusters of three, each 18–24mm across; they may be male or female or bisexual. The translucent canary-yellow fruits are egg-shaped, 25–40mm long, juicy and edible, though poorly flavoured. [June, H, PW, Central Japan] ◐

The end half of the leafblades, or occasionally the whole leaf, is sometimes white or yellowish and for this reason this species is often confused with the more widely grown *A. kolomikta*. However, the leaves of *A. polygama* are tapered or rounded at the base, whereas those of *A. kolomikta* are heart-shaped.

A. polygama is a good species for the smaller garden, especially on a pergola, or for scrambling up a tree. It is not nearly so vigorous a climber as either *A. chinensis* or *A. arguta*.

Actinidia coriacea is another vigorous, often semi-evergreen, climber reaching 8m high, the young shoots hairless, turning dark brown with age and speckled with white lenticels. The leathery leaves are dark green above, paler beneath, lanceolate or oval, tapered at both ends, 7.5–12.5cm long, the margin with distant sharp teeth. The flowers are borne on short lateral shoots, solitary or two together, a deep rather lurid red with yellow anthers, 12–13mm across. Fruit, juicy, brown, dotted with white, rounded to egg-shaped, about 18mm long. [May–June, HH–T, PW, W China (Szechwan)] ◐

An attractive plant in flower, though the flowers are short-lived. It is sometimes found under the name *A. henryi* in nurseries, though this is a distinct but closely allied species described next.

Actinidia henryi = *A. callosa* var. *henryi* can be distinguished by its slightly ribbed young shoots which are clothed in curly reddish bristles. Older shoots are hairless. The ovate or oblong leaves have a heart-shaped or rounded base and a pointed apex, 7.5–12.5cm long, green above contrasting with the bluish-green slightly downy undersurface. Flowers white, 12–13mm across, borne in small lateral clusters. Fruit cylindrical, 18–25mm long. [May–June, HH, PW, China (Yunnan)] ◐

Actinidia melanandra is a very vigorous climber reaching 10m or more high, with hairless stems. Leaves oblong or oval, abruptly pointed, 7.5–10cm long, green above but bluish-green beneath. Flowers white, 18–25mm across, female solitary, the male in small clusters of three to seven, with purple anthers. Fruit egg-shaped, 25–30mm long, reddish-brown with a plum bloom. [June–July, HH, PW, Central China (Hupeh and Szechwan)] ◐

Actinidia callosa is a vigorous climber reaching 10m in height with hairless young shoots covered in oval lenticels. The oval or oblong leaves are 7.5–12.5cm ◐

long with a straight or rounded base, hairless. White or cream-coloured flowers are borne in lateral clusters of two to five or solitary, on hairless stalks. The egg-shaped fruits are 18–25mm long, green tinged with red and spotted [May–June, HH, PW, N India, Himalaya & W China]

Actinidia venosa is similar and closely related to *A. callosa*; however, the leaves have prominent netted veins and the sepals and flower stalks are clothed in rusty down.

AKEBIA (Lardizabalaceae)

This attractive genus of climbing shrubs is quite frequently seen in gardens, grown as much for its elegant foliage as for its small reddish or purplish flowers. There are only two cultivated species which are vigorous growers suitable for covering walls, fences or pergolas, and even old tree stumps. The stems are twining and fasten themselves securely to their supports and need little training other than to remove old or untidy growths. The leaves consist of three or five leaflets radiating from a central point. The flowers are borne in drooping racemes and are interesting to examine closely. Those at the base of the raceme are female and are larger than those towards the end which are male. All flowers have three spreading elliptic petals. The large attractive fleshy fruits are unfortunately only rarely produced in cultivation. Akebias thrive in any good garden soil, but resent disturbance and once planted should not be moved; container-grown plants are the best to purchase. They are excellent plants for north- or east-facing walls or fences.

◐ **Akebia quinata** (Pl.1) is the most commonly grown species and may reach a height of 10m or more if left unchecked. The vivid green leaves usually have five oblong untoothed leaflets and are only evergreen in mild winters or in the warmer localities of the south and west. The spicy fragrance of the flowers is reminiscent of vanilla. The female flowers are a rich chocolate-purple, 20–35mm in diameter. The male flowers are pale purple and much smaller, only 7–8mm in diameter. Fruits, if produced, are sausage-shaped, greyish-violet or purple, 6.5–10cm long. [May, HH, PN, China, Japan & Korea]

◐ **Akebia trifoliata.** A plant superficially like the previous species, but always deciduous and with leaves with three leaflets that have an irregular margin and a notched apex. The flowers are purple, the female ones about 18–20mm in diameter. The fruits are sausage-shaped, pale violet, and 8–13cm long, but are seldom produced. [April, HH, PN, China & Japan]

This species flowers earlier than the preceding and for this reason the blooms are sometimes caught by a late frost unless particularly well protected.

There is an hybrid between the two species, *A.* ×*pentaphylla*, which occurs both in the wild and in cultivation and is more or less intermediate in habit between the parent species.

AMPELOPSIS (Vitaceae)

A handsome genus of deciduous climbers from North America and Asia grown mainly for their attractive foliage, though a few produce clusters of small rather interesting fruits. Their flowers are small, generally greenish and of little consequence horticulturally. Most of the species are too vigorous for small gardens and require ample space in which to mature satisfactorily. *Ampelopsis* are easy to grow though they require a warm sheltered niche in the garden and a loamy soil. Most should be given plenty of root room, although *A. brevipedunculata* should be constricted if a good crop of berries is desired. Plant in the autumn or early spring, tying in young stems to their supports as they extend to start them off. Most species are vigorous and grow rapidly and care must be taken that the growth does not get under roof tiles or clog the guttering. The shoots require a certain amount of support and plants are ideal on a sheltered pergola where the shoots can be tied in and trained. Alternatively, plants can be trained up stout posts allowing the shoots to hang free eventually and this can give a most pleasing effect. Like most vines the species and varieties are easily rooted from short cuttings of firm young growths struck in July and August.

The genus *Ampelopsis* contains in all some 20 species which are much confused with *Vitis*, the true Grapes; indeed most of the species were once included within that genus. Most people can be forgiven for getting the two confused and the characters of separation may seem rather slight; in *Vitis* the petals are united together at the tips whilst in *Ampelopsis* they are free from one another and spread widely apart. Both genera have climbing tendrils which cling to supports by simply coiling around them, however, these are not enough to support the weight of plants on pergolas, pillars or walls and some artificial support will be required. In the allied genus *Parthenocissus*, on the other hand, the tendrils are tipped by sticky pads like small suckers which cling readily to any support and make any tying unnecessary.

***Ampelopsis brevipedunculata** = *Cissus brevipedunculata, Vitis heterophylla* var. *cordata* and var. *amurensis,* is a vigorous climber with rough hairy young stems. The leaves are three- or occasionally five-lobed with a heart-shaped base, 5–15cm long, long-stalked, deep green above but paler and rough-hairy beneath. The inflorescence is hairy, once or twice forked and followed by attractive small bright amethyst-blue berries 6–8mm diameter. [July–Aug, HH, PW, China, Japan, Korea & E USSR]

A fine species with hop-like leaves which is at its best on a south wall, though only reliably hardy in the milder districts. Unlike the other species a restricted root run is preferable if plants are to be grown to their best advantage.

var. **maximowiczii** = *Vitis heterophylla* var. *maximowiczii* exhibits an extraordinary range of leaf shapes and sizes even on the same plant. Plants are less hardy than the type and are often sold in nurseries as plain *Vitis heterophylla*.

'Citrulloides' has deeply five-lobed leaves.

'Elegans'= *Ampelopsis heterophylla* var. *variegata* has pinkish young shoots and leaves freckled and splashed with pink and white. A tender cultivar, only at its best on a warm sheltered wall in the mildest parts of the country. This attractive plant is sometimes sold as a pot plant.

***Ampelopsis aconitifolia** = *Vitis aconitifolia* is a slender deciduous climber with hairless young shoots. The leaves are glossy green above but paler and duller beneath, very variable in shape and size with basically three or five leaflets 2.5–8cm long, which are coarsely toothed as well as each being deeply cut into three to five lobes. The greenish flowers are followed by dull orange berries 6mm long. [Aug–Sept, H, PW, China]

A fine plant seen at its best on a pergola or stout post. The dense deeply cut foliage gives the species a luxuriant appearance. It is sometimes confused with *A. japonica*.

Ampelopsis arborea = *Vitis arborea, Ampelopsis bipinnata*, the Pepper Vine, is a handsome climber with slender purplish, scarcely hairy stems and forked tendrils. The leaves are large, twice or thrice pinnate with numerous oval leaflets each 3.5–4.5cm long, dark green above, paler and downy beneath at first. The small green flowers are followed by dark purple berries 8mm across. [July–Aug, H, PW, SE USA]

A rather splendid hardy vine which has been in cultivation since about 1700. It is perhaps seen at its finest against a sheltered wall where its striking leaves show to the best advantage. In the very mildest districts it may behave as a semi-evergreen.

Ampelopsis orientalis = *Cissus orientalis* is a rather lax climbing shrub to 5m, with hairless, somewhat ridged shoots. The hairless leaves are dark green and somewhat dull above contrasting with the grey-green under surface; they are variable in shape from twice-trifoliate to pinnate or bipinnate, the oval or diamond-shaped leaflets 2.5–7.5cm long and coarsely toothed. The small greenish flowers are followed by red berries, 6mm across, in clusters rather like redcurrants. [Aug–Sept, H, PW, Asia Minor & W Asia]

Closely related to *A. arborea* but a coarser plant of only marginal garden value.

Ampelopsis megalophylla = *Vitis megalophylla* is a vigorous hairless climber with rather bluish-green young shoots. The large leaves are pinnate or bipinnate, 45–60cm long, sometimes more, with seven to nine leaflets which vary in shape from oval to oblong, being deep green above but bluish-green beneath. The green flowers are borne in a sparse loosely branched inflorescence, followed by small black berries, 6mm across. [Aug, H, PW, W China]

A handsome vine with the largest leaves of any in cultivation. It is a strong grower on the richer soils often making as much as 3m growth in a season. A stout post to 5m tall or an old tree are its best supports.

Ampelopsis chaffanjonii = *Vitis chaffanjonii* is allied to the previous species but the leaves are smaller, rarely exceeding 30cm in length and with five to seven oval or oblong, sparsely toothed leaflets that are shiny green above and strikingly reddish-purple beneath [Aug, HH, PW, W China]

An attractive vine brought back from Hupeh by E.H. Wilson at the turn of the present century. *A. chaffanjonii* is a good plant on a south wall in sheltered areas or on a stout pole where its striking foliage can be admired.

Ampelopsis delavayana = *Vitis delavayana* is another vigorous climber with hairy young stems which are noticeably swollen at the nodes. The leaves have three or five narrowly oval rather tapered leaflets which are coarsely toothed, 4–10cm long and rather downy beneath. The small flowers are followed by attractive, dark blue berries 6mm across. [July–Aug, H, PW, W China]

An attractive species which is unfortunately rare in cultivation. The young shoots and leaf-stalks are pinkish in most plants.

Ampelopsis cordata = *Vitis indivisa* is a vigorous climber with rather warted bark and hairless or slightly downy young stems and forked tendrils or no tendrils at all. The leaves are rounded or oval with a rather obscure heart-shaped base, sharply toothed margin, and 5–13cm long, borne on downy stalks. The greenish flowers are borne in branched clusters on slender stalks. The berries are small, blue or greenish-blue. [July–Aug, H, PW, S & SE USA]

A rather dull species with grape-like leaves of no great attraction and certainly not worth a place in most gardens. The shoots die back part-way during the winter and generally break off at the nodes.

ARISTOLOCHIA (Aristolochiaceae)

An extraordinary and quite remarkable group of plants, mostly from the tropics but including several herbaceous species from Mediterranean latitudes. However, it is the hardy or half-hardy climbing species that are most sought-after as wall subjects. The climbing species possess twining stems and deciduous heart-shaped leaves. The flowers of Aristolochias are very curious though no one could call them beautiful — there is no corolla but the calyx is strangely inflated, partly tubular but bent to resemble a siphon. This curious twist gives the plant its common name of Dutchman's Pipe. The flowers (at least in some tropical species) act as insect traps, producing a strong foetid odour which entices flies in particular. Once lured into the bloom the insect is unable to climb out again due to the lining of downward pointing hairs inside the tube. Thus trapped the insects fulfil pollination.

The cultivated species require a good loamy soil and respond to liberal summer mulches. The climbing species need plenty of wall space. Plants can be propagated easily, by dividing existing plants or from cuttings, and are best planted out in March and early April. Sheltered walls of west or south-west aspect are preferable. After flowering, plants can be pruned by removing unwanted, weak or straggling growths.

***Aristolochia macrophylla** = *A. sipho, Isotrema sipho,* the Dutchman's Pipe, is a vigorous climber 6–10m tall with heart- or kidney-shaped leaves, which are downy beneath to begin with and rather a pale green. The flowers are generally borne in pairs on separate stalks, each 7–8cm long with a yellowish-green tube which expands after a constriction into three flat spreading lobes which are yellowish-brown bordered with purplish-brown. Each flower stalk is clasped by a large oval bract below the middle, making this species easy to identify. [June, H, PA, E USA]

This is a fine plant worth growing as much for its handsome foliage as for its curious flowers which, though not beautiful, have a good deal of appeal, *Aristolochia macrophylla* is a quick grower for walls, pillars or pergolas. The bark has a pleasantly aromatic smell. The species has been cultivated in Britain since the end of the eighteenth century.

Aristolochia tomentosa = *Isotrema tomentosum* is a vigorous climber, 7–10m tall when mature, with densely downy leaves, flowers and young shoots, giving the plant a distinctive appearance. The oval or rounded leaves have a heart-shaped base, each leaf being 7–20cm long and rather a dull pale green. The solitary flowers are greenish-yellow with a brown throat and yellowish lobes, 40mm long and half as broad. The angular fruits are about 5cm long when fully grown. [June–July, H, PA, SE USA]

This species has been in cultivation almost as long as *A. macrophylla* but is seldom seen today.

Aristolochia californica = *Isotrema californicum* is another vigorous climber, 4–6m tall, with downy stems and leaves similar to *A. tomentosa*. The solitary flowers are borne on slender stalks, each flower about 50mm long, dull purple in colour, the tube double-bent, constricted at the mouth and with three only slightly expanded lobes. [June–July, HH, PA, SW USA (California)]

This species is closely related to *A. tomentosa* but the flower colour and shape serve to tell them apart.

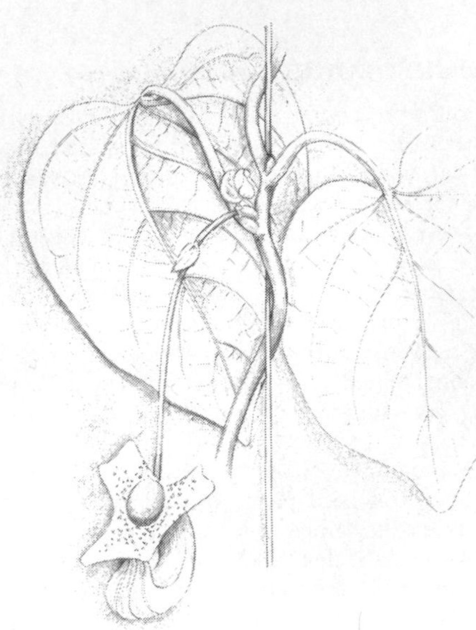

Aristolochia moupinensis.

◐ **Aristolochia moupinensis** = *Isotrema moupinense* is a vigorous climber to 6m tall with downy stems. The heart-shaped leaves are 6 – 12cm long, rather downy beneath but only slightly so above. The solitary pendulous flowers are borne on slender drooping stalks, each flower, about 38mm long, has an inflated pale green tube which is bent back to expose a yellow throat, whilst the spreading lobes are yellow, dotted with reddish-purple, with a green margin. The fruits are about 7cm long when mature with six prominent ridges. [June, H, PA, W China]

Aristolochia moupinensis is not often seen in cultivation, though hardy. The first plants were brought back from China by E.H. Wilson in 1903. However, it was first discovered in the district of Moupin some years earlier by Père David. The plant is not perhaps as showy as the previous species but the flowers are quite pretty and worth a close look.

☼ ***Aristolochia chrysops** is a climbing or rather rambling shrub with finely downy young shoots and leaves. The leaves are narrow or broadly oval with a heart-shaped base, dull green and 4 – 10cm long. The flowers are solitary or borne in pairs on practically hairless stalks, each flower 48 – 52mm long, a typical Dutchman's Pipe shape with a downy yellow tube, a bright yellow throat and spreading lobes of deep reddish-purple, sometimes almost black. The fruit is 5 – 6.5cm long with six ribs. [June, HH, PA, W China]

This species is the most handsome of all the climbing species cultivated often being found in gardens under the incorrect name of *A. heterophylla*. It is another plant brought into cultivation by that intrepid plant hunter E.H. Wilson, being first grown in Britain in 1904.

Plate 1 Deciduous Climbers 1 *Actinidia kolomikta* (p.34), 2 *A. chinensis* (p.34), 3 *Akebia quinata* (p.36), 4 *Schisandra rubriflora* (p.53), 5 *Campsis × tagliabuana* 'Madame Galen' (p.42).

1
2
3
4
5

2
1
2
3
4

BERCHEMIA (Rhamnaceae)

A genus of deciduous twiners with small greenish flowers carried in terminal clusters. The leaves are alternate, untoothed and with conspicuous veins. The fruits are sausage-shaped and contain a single seed.

It is scarcely worth growing Berchemias for their flowers which are not attractive, but the plants can be quite ornamental when in fruit. An added advantage is that they can be grown in partial shade as well as sun. They are best grown on a wall, using wires or trellis for support, but can also clamber over unwanted bushes or small trees.

Berchemia scandens = *B. volubilis*, known as Supple Jack, has hairless twining stems which reach 3–5m. The leaves are oval, 3–7.5cm long, with a fine bristle-like point at the tip, a wavy margin and nine to twelve pairs of veins. The small flowers are greenish-white, in clusters 2.5–5cm long and borne at the ends of the main and the side branches. The fruits are dark blue or nearly black, about 1cm long. [July–Aug, HH, PN, SE USA]

The only American Berchemia in cultivation, the others being Asian. Unfortunately in Britain it fruits only rarely.

Berchemia racemosa produces hairless stems which usually reach about 4–5m, although vigorous plants can attain 12m. The leaves are ovate, heart-shaped at the base, 3–7.5cm long and pale beneath. The small flowers are greenish and produced in terminal clusters 5–15cm long. The fruits are green when young, changing to red and finally black when mature. [July–Aug, H, PN, Japan & Taiwan]

Berchemia racemosa is attractive in fruit but a good crop is produced only in a warm year. It is hardier than *B. scandens* and can be grown further north. The leaves turn yellow before they are shed in the autumn.

'Variegata' has leaves which are more creamy-white than green. The variegation is more pronounced towards the ends of the shoots.

CAMPSIS (Bignoniaceae)

This genus contains two of the most glorious of all deciduous climbing plants which well deserve to be better known and more widely cultivated. Their striking trumpet-shaped flowers in shades of red or orange and their opposite pinnate leaves give them an exotic appearance. They are probably seen at their best in the south of France or in Italy, where they are widely grown. In many parts of Britain they are quite hardy when grown on a wall. *Campsis* require a good loamy soil and a warm sunny wall if they are to flower with any profusion. However, the roots should not be allowed to dry out during the summer months and this can be easily overcome by careful watering or the application of mulches around the base of plants during dry periods.

Both species are easy to cultivate. They are best planted during March and for the first year or two left to fill the wall space allotted to them. Thereafter they can be treated as other climbers, cutting shoots back to within a few buds of the old wood after the leaves have fallen or in the early spring. They are readily propagated from cuttings of both stems or roots, by the careful removal of suckers when they appear or by layerings.

Campsis was at one time included in the genus *Tecoma* and may still be found as such in some nurserymen's catalogues. However, species of the latter genus are

---

Plate 2 Deciduous Climbers 1 *Parthenocissus henryana* (p.51), 2 *Hydrangea petiolaris* (p.47), 3 *Schizophragma integrifolium* (p.54), 4 *Parthenocissus tricuspidata* (p.51).

natives of the warmer parts of Central and South America, whereas *Campsis* is confined to cooler districts in the Northern Hemisphere.

☼ ***Campsis radicans** = *Bignonia radicans, Tecoma radicans*, the Trumpet Vine, is the more commonly grown species. It is a vigorous climber up to 12m tall with stout main stems and branches that climb by means of tiny roots which cling to the wall like ivy. The leaves have seven to eleven ovate dark green leaflets which are coarsely toothed and downy beneath. The flowers occur in small clusters at the tips of the current season's shoots and are rich scarlet and orange, 6–8cm long. The pod-like fruits, which are occasionally produced in this country are spindle-shaped, about 12cm long. [Aug–Sept, H, PS, SE USA]

Although this fine climber is self-clinging it requires some support from nails driven into the wall to aid the heavier stems. This species was cultivated in Britain as long ago as 1640 and today a number of forms and cultivars are available.

'Atropurpurea' has deep scarlet flowers.
'Flava' has yellow flowers.
'Minor' is a less vigorous form with smaller flowers.
'Praecox' is similar to the typical plant but flowers earlier.

☼ **Campsis grandiflora** = *Bignonia grandiflora, Campsis chinensis, Tecoma grandiflora*, is a more splendid plant than the previous in many ways. It grows 7–10m tall with twining stems, each leaf bearing seven to nine ovate leaflets that are coarsely toothed and quite hairless. The flowers occur in rather pendulous, slightly branched clusters at the end of shoots of the current season and are deep orange and red, 5–7.5cm long. Fruits are rarely produced in Britain. [Aug–Oct, HH, PS, China]

This beautiful climber is not as hardy as *C. radicans* in this country and unfortunately seldom flowers as well here as it does on the Continent. The stems need more support as it does not produce self-clinging roots. It has long been cultivated in Japan.

'Thunbergii' = *Tecoma thunbergii* is a hardier form with rather smaller flowers.

Campsis × tagliabuana, *C. radicans* × *C. grandiflora* = *Tecoma tagliabuana, T. grandiflora* var. *princei*, (Pl.1). In Southern Europe both the parents flower and fruit readily and hybrids occur from time to time. This particular hybrid was raised on the nursery of the Tagliabue Brothers in Milan in the last century and a number of forms are in existence, indeed they are more often seen in cultivation than either of the parents. The best cultivar is ***'Madame Galen'** which is more or less intermediate in character between the parents [Aug–Oct, H, PS]

CIONURA (Asclepiadaceae)

There is only one species in *Cionura* which used to be included within the tropical genus *Marsdenia*.

☼ **Cionura erecta** = *Marsdenia erecta* climbs to 3m with numerous slender hairless stems which twine at their tips. The opposite leaves are heart-shaped, 3.5–6cm long. The sweetly scented flowers are borne in many-flowered axillary clusters which are 5–10cm long. Each white flower is about 1cm across, with five spreading corolla lobes. The fruits are narrowly egg-shaped, 7.5–8cm long. [June–Aug, HH, PA, SE Europe]

Cionura erecta should be grown on a sunny wall if it is to flower well and produce its fruits. It is a vigorous plant and the many twining stems will need to be thinned out in the autumn. Great care must be taken when pruning as the cut stems exude a milky sap which is not only poisonous but can blister the skin. For this reason, it is sensible to wear gloves when handling the plant.

CELASTRUS (Celastraceae)

A genus of vigorous hardy deciduous climbers and shrubs which are grown for their magnificent displays of brightly-coloured autumnal fruits. They are related to the spindle trees, *Euonymus*, though less well known and all too seldom planted.

Most of the cultivated species are strong growers highly suitable for covering old walls, trellises, pergolas, trees or stout posts stuck into the earth. They succeed in most average garden soils, but they tend to be gross feeders and relish regular feeds and mulches. They are suitable subjects for an east- or north-east-facing wall. Little pruning is required other than to remove old wood or to shorten back unduly long shoots, this being carried out in the early spring once the fruits have finally fallen.

The leaves are alternate and toothed and the flowers are small, greenish-yellow or whitish, and of little attraction. Some species possess hermaphrodite flowers, although the two most well known, *C. orbiculatus* and *C. scandens* bear male and female flowers on separate plants. With these species it is essential to ensure that a plant of each sex is planted, otherwise no fruits will be produced. The fruits often occur in large numbers and they generally split into three segments to reveal brightly-coloured seeds. Fruits are borne for two months or more during the winter months and fortunately are not attractive to birds in this country.

***Celastrus orbiculatus** = *C. articulatus* is perhaps the best and most widely grown species. Plants are very vigorous and may ultimately reach a height of 14m. The young stems are twining and at first are armed with pairs of spines at each bud. The leaves are obovate or more or less orbicular and shallowly toothed, 5–12cm long. The flowers are green, small, only 4mm across, occurring in clusters of two to four. The green pea-sized fruits eventually turn black as they split to reveal a golden inner surface and shining scarlet seeds of great beauty. [June, H, PN, NE Asia]

Celastrus orbiculatus in fruit.

A magnificent plant seen at its best in the late autumn when the yellowish leaves are mixed with the brightly-coloured fruits. The fruits themselves survive generally until after Christmas, long after the leaves have fallen. Hermaphrodite clones exist in cultivation, but plants grown from seed usually will be either male or female.

◐ ***Celastrus scandens**, the Staff Tree, is a handsome twining climber, ultimately reaching a height of 10m. The leaves are ovate to elliptic, finely and rather irregularly toothed, 5–10cm long. The small yellowish-white flowers occur in terminal racemes or panicles of little attraction, male and female occurring on separate plants. The fruits are borne in heavy masses 5–8cm long; each is pea-sized and splits to reveal an orange inside and brilliant scarlet-coated seeds. [June–July, H, PN, E N America]

A very beautiful plant when seen in fruit in the late autumn, though plants seldom fruit as well in Britain as they do in the United States; it is said to be particularly fine in the area around the Niagara Falls. It was introduced to cultivation as long ago as 1736 and is one of the most splendid species to grow, though it requires quite a lot of room.

◐ **Celastrus glaucophyllus**, a hairless plant reaching 7m tall. The shoots are green at first but become purplish-brown in the second season. The leaves are oval and shallowly toothed, 5–10cm long, green above but bluish-green beneath. The small greenish flowers are inconspicuous and occur in small groups at the leaf axils or in short racemes at the shoot tips. The fruits are about 10mm long, yellow when ripe, and splitting into three to reveal bright scarlet seeds. [June–July, H, PN, W China]

A rather distinctive plant first introduced by E.H. Wilson in 1904 and occasionally seen in cultivation today. Plants are less vigorous than other species and the shoots scarcely twine and need some tying in at first.

◐ **Celastrus hypoleucus** = *Erythrospermum hypoleucum* is rather similar to the previous species, but the young shoots are covered in a purplish waxy bloom and the oblong leaves are larger, 10–15cm long, dark green above and a striking blue-white beneath. The yellowish flowers are produced in racemes up to 20cm long at the shoot tips; each flower is about 6mm across. The green fruits are the size of a large pea and split to reveal a yellow interior and red-coated seeds. [June–July, H, PN, China]

A handsome plant like the previous species and perhaps even less vigorous and therefore more suitable for smaller gardens or more confined spaces.

◐ **Celastrus variotii** var. **laevis** = *C. spiciformis* var. *laevis* is like *C. hypoleucus* but with rather smaller leaves that are dark green above and pale green, not bluish-white, beneath. The small yellowish-white flowers are mostly borne in slender panicles 8–13cm long at the shoot tips. The 6mm fruits are orange-yellow when ripe, splitting into three to expose the shiny brown-coated seeds. [June–July, H, PN, SW China]

The typical form of this plant from the wilds of Szechwan is not in cultivation.

◐ **Celastrus hookeri** is a deciduous climber which grows to 7m tall, its young shoots reddish-downy at first and with whitish lenticels. The oval or ovate leaves are coarsely toothed and pointed, 7.5–15cm long, with reddish down along the midrib and main veins on the under surface. The inconspicuous greenish flowers are borne in short-stalked lateral clusters of no beauty. The orange fruits are about 7mm long, and contain red-coated seeds. [June, H, PN, Himalaya & S China]

An attractive species introduced from Szechwan in 1908 by that prolific plant hunter E.H. Wilson. In cultivation it is vigorous and sets abundant fruit.

Celastrus rosthornianus is a hairless climber to 7m tall with very slender shoots and rather pendulous branches. The shiny green leaves are oval-lanceolate or ovate, finely toothed and 4–8cm long. The greenish flowers are of no great beauty but are followed by small pea-sized orange-yellow fruits in groups of two to three at each node; each fruit splits into three or four valves to reveal startling scarlet-coated seeds. [June–July, H, PN, W China]

The fruits are borne well into the new year. With its slender appearance this plant looks rather more elegant than most of the other species.

Celastrus rugosus is a vigorous climber to 7m tall with hairless stems dotted with tiny lenticels. The oval leaves are coarsely toothed and distinctively wrinkled (rough) above, 6.5–14cm long, the midrib and veins with small warts or downy beneath. The small greenish flowers are solitary or borne in small clusters, laterally or at the shoot tips. The orange-yellow fruits are about 8mm long and contain red-coated seeds. [June–July, H, PN, W China]

A handsome and strong growing species which does not always fruit heavily in this country.

CLEMATOCLETHRA (Actinidiaceae)

A genus of deciduous climbers closely related to *Actinidia* but distinguished by their flowers which possess ten stamens and a solitary style, rather than numerous stamens and several styles. There are other differences which need not concern us here.

There are about 25 species of *Clematoclethra*, all of them Asian in origin. They are easily cultivated on most well-drained loamy soil, but in most districts they require the protection of a sheltered wall or fence; in milder districts they can be trained on stout stakes or over tree trunks. Propagation is from late summer cuttings.

The leaves are alternate and in the cultivated species are margined by fine bristle-like teeth. The flowers are usually five-petalled and the sepals persist at the base of the fruit which is a small rounded berry.

Clematoclethra actinidioides is a vigorous climber reaching 12m tall, sometimes more, with hairless young shoots. The ovate or heart-shaped leaves are 4–7cm long, borne on slender stalks. Flowers are white tinged with rose, about 10mm across, and borne in small lateral clusters of one to three. Berry black or purplish-black, 6mm. [June, HH, PN, SW China]

Clematoclethra integrifolia is closely related to *C. actinidioides* and may indeed be a form of the same species. The plant can reach 7.5m and the ovate-oblong leaves are hairless, green above but bluish-green beneath. The white flowers are fragrant, slightly smaller than the previous species. [June, HH, PN, W China]

A finer plant than *C. actinidioides*, first discovered by the Russian traveller Potanin in 1887, whilst travelling in Kansu.

Clematoclethra lasioclada is a vigorous climber reaching 6m, sometimes more, with downy young shoots. The ovate leaves are 5–10cm long and have tufts of down in the vein angles beneath. Flowers white in small lateral clusters of two to seven. Berry black, 8mm. [July, HH, PN, W China]

This species is uncommon in cultivation.

Clematoclethra scandens is another vigorous climber reaching 8m in height with densely bristly young shoots. Leaves oblong-lanceolate, pointed, rounded or tapered at the base, 5–13cm long, bristly along the midrib, green above but bluish-green and downy beneath. Flowers white, 7–8mm across, borne in small axillary clusters of three to six. Berry red when ripe, 8mm. [June, HH, PN, W China]

A handsome species, hardy in southern and southwestern areas in all but the severest winters. Equally good on a wall or tree in sun or partial shade.

COCCULUS (Menispermaceae)

A genus of some eleven species native to the tropics and subtropics of the Old World and North America, and including both climbers and erect shrubs. They may be deciduous or evergreen and have entire or lobed, alternate leaves. The flowers are small and unisexual and borne in axillary clusters; they have six sepals and petals. The male flowers have six to nine stamens and the female flowers have three to six ovaries. The fruit is spherical, fleshy and one-seeded.

Cocculus trilobus has twining downy stems growing to 3.5–4.5m tall and becoming woody with age. The leaves are heart-shaped or ovate, occasionally with three to five lobes, 3.5–10cm long and downy beneath, particularly when young. The flowers are cream, borne in axillary clusters. The fruits, about 1cm across, are black with a blue bloom. [Aug, H, PN, China, Japan & Korea]

This species can be grown up a wall, or trained on a pergola, pillar or tree. An attractive sight in October when covered in fruits, though to fruit well it needs plenty of sunshine.

Cocculus carolinus, the Carolina Moonseed, has twining woody stems reaching 5m. As in *C. trilobus* the stems are downy. The leaves are ovate or heart-shaped, sometimes three- to five-lobed, 5–12cm long and whitish-downy beneath. The flowers are white, the male ones in axillary clusters and the female in racemes. Occasionally male and female flowers are carried on separate plants. Fruits red, about 6mm across, borne in dense clusters. [July, HH, PN, SE USA]

Cocculus laurifolius is an evergreen shrub and is described on p.189.

DECUMARIA (Hydrangeaceae)

Decumaria barbara is sometimes deciduous but is treated with the evergreen *D. sinensis*.

FALLOPIA (Polygonaceae)

Woody twiners with alternate, stalked, heart-shaped leaves. The small flowers are borne in lax terminal and axillary panicles, and usually have five perianth segments of which the three outer are winged or ridged on the back. The fruit is a three-angled nut, enclosed by the perianth which persists.

There are three species in cultivation, all of which thrive in full sun. They can be grown on a wall, provided there are supporting wires, over pergolas or arches, or alternatively left to scramble up an old tree. They will succeed in most average soils and are readily propagated from soft summer or hard winter cuttings.

Fallopia baldschuanica = *Polygonum baldschuanicum, Bilderdykia baldschuanica,* is a vigorous, indeed rampant twiner reaching 12m, sometimes more. The stems are slender, hairless and greyish. The leaves are broadly heart-shaped, 3–10cm long, hairless and pale green. The small white or pale pink flowers are borne in panicles 20–40cm long. The three outer perianth segments are winged on the back, each wing continuing downward to the flower stalk. [June–Sept, H, PS, Afghanistan, W Pakistan & S USSR]

***Fallopia aubertii** = *Polygonum aubertii, Bilderdykia aubertii* (Pl.4), the Russian Vine, is similar to *F. baldschuanica,* differing mainly in having narrower, erect, scabrid panicles carrying smaller, white or greenish flowers which become pinkish in fruit. [June–Sept, H, PS, W China & Tibet]

It is scarcely necessary to tell gardeners about the Russian Vine, however, *F. aubertii* and *F. baldschuanica,* which are very similar, have been much confused in gardens. Many of the plants sold and grown under the latter name are in fact *F. aubertii,* which is more common in cultivation. No pruning is strictly necessary, but it may be desirable to keep them within bounds. Another common name for *F. aubertii* is 'A Mile a Minute' which sums up its vigorous growth. If you have a large wall or fence space to cover this plant is the ideal answer. It is rather dull out of flower but it does reward the grower with a prolonged flowering season.

Fallopia multiflora = *Polygonum multiflorum* is a woody climber with slender red stems twining up to 4.5m tall. The leaves are heart-shaped, 5–12cm long and dark shiny green. The white or greenish flowers are borne in loose downy panicles. [June–July, HH, PS, China & Taiwan]

Less commonly grown and less hardy than the other two species, it is normally deciduous, but in a mild winter in the south or west, it may retain its leaves.

HYDRANGEA (Hydrangeaceae)

The climbing members of this popular genus attach themselves to walls by aerial roots which are produced from the stems, similar to those of ivy. They have opposite leaves and bear their flowers in flat-topped clusters. These clusters are composed mainly of tiny fertile flowers with very small sepals and four or five petals, although in a few species large showy sterile flowers (composed of three to five sepals) are produced at the edge of the cluster.

A well-drained soil is preferable, especially when enriched by mulches of compost or well-rotted manure. Cuttings of well-ripened shoots placed in a propagating frame in the summer should root fairly readily.

***Hydrangea petiolaris** = *H. anomala* subsp. *petiolaris* (Pl.2), the Climbing Hydrangea, reaches as much as 15m, the stems producing aerial roots. The older stems have a peeling brown bark. The leaves are broadly ovate, toothed, 3–11cm long. The flat flower clusters are 15–25cm in diameter and have white marginal sterile flowers. The fertile flowers are very small, dull white and have 15–22 stamens. [June, H, PS, Japan, Korea & Taiwan]

H. petiolaris is the most commonly grown climbing hydrangea and what a fine plant it is. It can be grown on walls or fences of any aspect though especially valuable on a north wall where it will flower well. Plants can take time to become established and may need support until enough aerial roots have been produced.

The flowers are borne on lateral shoots which develop from the main clinging stems, so very young plants are unlikely to flower. In addition to any spring pruning which may be required, unwanted growth can be removed as it is produced during the summer. *H. petiolaris* can be allowed to climb up trees or indeed it can be very effective when used to cover old tree stumps when it will eventually develop a bush-like habit.

This species has been confused in nurserymen's catalogues and some of the plants offered as *Schizophragma hydrangeoides* turn out to be this plant.

Hydrangea anomala is very similar to *H. petiolaris* but the flower clusters are less flat, the creamy fertile flowers have fewer stamens (9–15) and the leaves coarser teeth. [June, HH, PS, Himalaya to W China]

Hydrangea serratifolia is an evergreen climber described on p.100.

JASMINUM (Oleaceae)

The undermentioned species, although described in the chapter on evergreen climbers, often behave as deciduous subjects in the north of Britain, or elsewhere in a severe winter. *J. beesianum, J. dispermum, J. officinale,* the commonly grown sweetly-scented summer jasmine, *J. ×stephanense* and *J. subhumile.*

MANDEVILLA (Apocynaceae)

Mandevillas come from Central and tropical South America where there are more than 100 species. They are graceful twiners whose cut stems exude a milky sap. The leaves are opposite and the flowers, which have five sepals and petals, are borne in racemes. The stamens are attached to the corolla-tube. The seed pods are usually produced in pairs.

***Mandevilla suaveolens**, the Chilean Jasmine, in a favourable situation reaches 4.5m tall, or more. Its leaves are heart-shaped, long-pointed, untoothed, 5–8cm long, dark green and hairless above, paler beneath with tufts of white hairs in the vein-axils. The flowers are very fragrant; the corolla is white or creamy, funnel-shaped, 5cm long and 5cm wide at its mouth with spreading lobes, the tube hairy inside. The five yellow anthers hide the stigma. The seed pods are narrowly cylindrical, 30–40cm long. [June–Sept, T, PS, Argentina]

A showy species for training on a wall. The flowers open each day and close at night. Spring pruning consists mainly of the removal of weak growth or dead wood. Despite its common name, it is native only to the Argentine.

MENISPERMUM (Menispermaceae)

A small genus of woody or semi-woody twiners with deciduous alternate long-stalked leaves. The flowers are unisexual and male and female are borne on separate plants. Each fruit contains one crescent-shaped seed, often known as 'Moon Seeds'.

Menispermum species are attractive in fruit, but plants of both sexes are needed if fruits are to be produced.

Menispermum canadense, the Canada Moonseed, is a vigorous climber spreading by underground suckers. The slender downy stems will attain a height of 3.5–4.8m, usually producing a dense tangle. The leaves are ovate to heart-shaped and usually have three, five or seven shallow angular lobes; the leaf stalk is not attached to the base of the blade, but a little way up from the base. The leaves are dark green above, paler and strongly veined beneath. The flowers are greenish-yellow, rather inconspicuous, carried many together in axillary long-stalked racemes. The fruits are blackish when ripe, blackcurrant-like, about 7–9mm across, in long loose clusters. [June–July, H, PN, E North America]

Menispermum canadense grows rapidly and will quickly cover a wall or trellis. It should not be planted near slow-growing or more fragile shrubs or climbers, lest they be smothered. Although no pruning is actually necessary, the plant may be tidied by removing weak or dead wood, but this is a difficult task with such a tangled mass of stems. It may be preferable to cut the plant nearly to the ground every two or three years — this should be done in the winter; new shoots will rapidly grow up during the following spring.

Fruits ripen in October and November; both fruits and seeds are poisonous.

Menispermum dauricum is similar to *M. canadense* but less often seen in gardens. The leaf lobes are more pointed and the apex of the leaf is more attenuated. The racemes of flowers are shorter and denser and produced in pairs above each leaf axil. The fruits are slightly larger. [June–July, H, PN, NE Asia from Siberia to China]

Treatment is similar to that of *M. canadense.*

MUEHLENBECKIA (Polygonaceae)

Semi-woody shrubs or climbers from the southern hemisphere. The leaves are alternate and the unisexual flowers are green or whitish, with a deeply five-lobed perianth. The male flowers have eight stamens. The fruit is a three-angled nutlet enclosed in the persistent perianth. Only one species is generally cultivated in Britain.

Muehlenbeckia complexa is a deciduous twiner growing to 6m and producing numerous slender, dark, interlaced stems. The leaves vary enormously in size and shape and may be roundish, oblong, heart-shaped or fiddle-shaped, 3–18mm long, dull green and hairless with a rough warty stalk. The greenish-white flowers are about 4mm long, produced in terminal and axillary spikes about 1.5cm in length. [Sept–Oct, T, PN, New Zealand]

Not a plant to be grown for its beauty, but mainly of botanical interest, a curiosity for those wanting something different. It produces a matted tangle on a wall and is best used to disguise an old tree stump in a sheltered position, or to cover an unimportant shrub. It is hardy only in the south or west, and is normally killed to ground-level in the winter further north.

var. **trilobata** = *M. varians* has deeply three-lobed leaves.

PAEDERIA (Rubiaceae)

A small genus seldom seen in our gardens but well deserving to be tried if plants can be acquired. Only one species, *P. scandens*, is cultivated out of doors, a plant for a sunny sheltered wall or fence, succeeding on most average garden soils, if they are well drained.

Paederia scandens = *P. chinensis, P. wilsonii,* is a vigorous climber reaching 5m high. Leaves ovate, finely-pointed, 5–15cm long, dark green, downy beneath. The tubular flowers are white with a purple throat, 8–12mm long, borne in branched clusters at the shoot tips amongst smaller, narrower, leaves.

The pea-sized fruits are orange when ripe. [July – Sept, T, PS, China, Japan & Korea]

The young growths and leaves have an unpleasant foetid odour when crushed. This species has been cultivated since 1907.

PARTHENOCISSUS (Vitaceae)

A genus of about ten species of ornamental climbers from North America, Eastern Asia and the Himalaya. Most are quick growing with alternate, palmate, rarely simple, leaves, and climb by means of tendrils. The tendrils are branched, each branch often tipped by a sticky sucker-like pad by which they attach themselves firmly to wall, fence, pillar or tree. This is the main means of distinguishing *Parthenocissus* from its two close allies, *Vitis* and *Ampelopsis*. Their culture is the same.

In *Parthenocissus* the greenish, rather insignificant flowers are borne in lateral-branched (cymose) panicles, the flowers being followed by small blue or black berries during hot dry summers.

◐ **Parthenocissus quinquefolia** = *Vitis quinquefolia*, the Virginia Creeper, is a tall deciduous climber to 15m tall, sometimes more, with slender hairless stems that are reddish at first. The leaves are composed of five, more rarely three, oval or rather obovate, coarsely toothed leaflets, 2.5 – 10cm long, that are a rather dull green above but paler and bluish-green beneath. The small greenish flowers are followed by clusters of bluish-black berries. [July – Aug, H, PS, C & E North America]

A handsome creeper grown mainly for its decorative foliage which turns a striking and vivid rich crimson in the autumn. This species has been cultivated for many years, records going back as far as 1629. *P. quinquefolia* is the true Virginia Creeper though this common name is often wrongly applied to *P. tricuspidata* which does not even come from North America but from China and Japan. The fact is that although *P. quinquefolia* was widely grown in former times, particularly in the eighteenth century, it has largely been replaced by its 'oriental cousin' which has, at the same time, taken up the name Virginia Creeper with the public at large, although erroneously so. The correct common name for *P. tricuspidata* should be the Japanese Creeper.

Nevertheless, *P. quinquefolia* is a fine climber, quite hardy and suitable for growing up tall walls, fences, towers and massive tree trunks. The species is a variable one and a number of botanical varieties and forms are recognised.

var. **hirsuta** = *Ampelopsis graebneri* has hairy shoots, leaves and inflorescences. The leaves have very intense autumn coloration.

var. **murorum** = *Ampelopsis hederacea* var. *murorum, Parthenocissus radicantissima*, has tendrils with more and shorter branches enabling the shoots to cling very tightly to their supports. A variety from the southern USA.

var. **saint-paulii** = *Parthenocissus saint-paulii* has young shoots and undersurface of the leaves finely downy and leaflets more deeply and more sharply toothed than the other varieties.

forma **engelmannii** = *Vitis* or *Ampelopsis engelmannii*, has smaller leaves than the type which are pleasantly bluish-green during the summer but turn fiery red during the autumn.

◐ **Parthenocissus inserta** = *Vitis* or *Ampelopsis inserta, Parthenocissus quinquefolia* var. *vitaceai* is a vigorous deciduous climber closely related and often confused with *P. quinquefolia* but lacking the sticky suckers on the tendrils. The tendrils instead coil around suitable supports or insert themselves into crevices. The leaves have five obovate-lanceolate leaflets which are rather larger and a brighter green than those of *P. quinquefolia*. [July–Aug, H, PS, E, C & SW USA]

This species has been often confused with *P. quinquefolia*, and indeed the two are closely related and do hybridise readily. The autumn colouring is just as fine and this species is the one to choose if a non-clinging plant is required.

var. **laciniata** = *P. quinquefolia* var. *laciniata* has very deeply toothed leaflets giving the plant a striking appearance. A variety found growing wild in parts of the SW USA.

***Parthenocissus tricuspidata** = *Ampelopsis tricuspidata, Ampelopsis* or *Cissus veitchii*, (Pl.2), is a vigorous and very handsome deciduous climber growing up to 20m. The shoots bear tendrils with sticky suckers and shiny leaves that vary enormously in size and shape. In young plants leaves are 5–12cm across, heart-shaped and scarcely lobed, or they have three distinct leaflets, whilst in mature plants the leaves are coarser and generally three-lobed, larger, up to 20cm across. The yellowish-green flowers are borne in branched clusters on short lateral shoots and are followed by small dull dark blue berries. [July–Aug, H, PS, China & Japan]

This is one of the largest and most spectacular of all climbing plants and one that is commonly planted on expansive walls thoughout Britain where the vivid and spectacular crimson autumn leaves are a familiar sight. Indeed it is so often planted that it is frequently decried for this very reason, but there are few better plants for large bare old walls. However, care should be taken to keep plants in check keeping shoots away from window and door frames and not allowing plants to obscure the architectural lines of old buildings.

This species is commonly found under the name *Ampelopsis veitchii* in catalogues or as 'Virginia Creeper', a common name that rightly applies to *Parthenocissus quinquefolia*.

'Lowii' is an elegant cultivar with rather small three- to seven-lobed leaves which are crinkled and have fine autumn colours.

'Veitchii' = 'Purpurea' has smaller leaves than the typical plant which are oval or three-lobed, and reddish-purple, even when young.

***Parthenocissus henryana** = *Vitis henryana*, (Pl.2) is a very handsome and rather vigorous deciduous climber to 10m tall, sometimes more. The stems are hairless and noticeably four-angled. The leaves have three to five oval, coarsely toothed leaflets, 4–13cm long. The leaf coloration is very striking, the upper surface being a rich dark velvety-green or bronze with the veins picked out in pink and reddish or purplish. The small greenish flowers are borne in terminal leafy clusters 15–18cm long. The small berries are dark blue. [July–Aug, HH, PS, Central China]

This is without doubt the finest and most handsome species. The leaves are delightful to see throughout the summer and in the autumn the entire leaf turns red. The stems cling readily to supports by sticky padded tendrils. A fine plant for a sheltered wall — it is not reliably hardy in all districts. Walls of north or east aspect are best and in such positions the leaf colorations are most marked.

***Parthenocissus thomsonii** = *Vitis thomsonii* is an attractive vine closely related to the previous species, the young stems slender and ribbed, crimson-purple at first, but becoming greenish-purple with age. The glossy green leaves have five oval or obovate leaflets, 2.5–10cm long, which are sharply toothed in the upper half. The greenish flowers are followed by small black berries. [July–Aug, HH, PS, Assam, China & the Himalaya]

A delightful plant, hardier than *P. henryana* and more slender and graceful in habit. The leaves turn rich crimson and scarlet in the autumn and colour best on a shaded or partially shaded wall.

◐ **Parthenocissus himalayana** = *Ampelopsis himalayana* is a vigorous deciduous climber with hairless stems which bear tendrils with sticky suckers. The leaves have three leaflets, each oval or obovate, toothed, 5–15cm long, dark green above, paler and rather bluish-green beneath. The leaves turn a rich crimson in the autumn. The small berries are deep blue, when produced. [July–Aug, T, PS, Himalaya]

A fine species but rather tender in all but the mildest districts and only suitable for growing on a sheltered wall.

var. **rubrifolia** has smaller leaves which are purple when young. [W China]

PERIPLOCA (Asclepiadaceae)

Deciduous or evergreen climbers or shrubs native to the Old World. The stems exude poisonous milky juice when cut. The leaves are opposite and untoothed. The calyx is five-lobed as is the corolla which also bears a five-lobed corona. The seed pods are produced in pairs and contain winged seeds each bearing a tuft of hairs.

Two deciduous species are described below; a third semi-evergreen species *(P. laevigata)* is described on p.110. They are easily grown climbers, especially good on fences, pergolas and arches.

☼ **Periploca graeca**, the Silk Vine, has brown, hairless, twining stems up to 9m tall. The leaves are oval or ovate, 5–12cm long, dark green and shiny. The flowers are carried in clusters 5–7.5cm across which bear eight to twelve flowers together. The flowers are brownish-purple inside and greenish-yellow outside, with spreading corolla lobes, 2.5cm in diameter. The seed pods are cylindrical and 12–13cm long. [July–Aug, H, PN, SE Europe & Asia Minor]

An interesting plant although not immediately beautiful. It can be grown on a wall, with supporting wires or trellis, but is perhaps most suitable for a pergola or old tree. It is generally considered that the flowers smell unpleasant, although a few people like the scent.

☼ **Periploca sepium**, the Chinese Silk Vine, is a smaller, more delicate climber than *P. graeca*. The stems reach 3m and the leaves are lanceolate to narrowly ovate, 4–10cm long, shiny and dark green. The fragrant flowers are borne in clusters of two to nine. The corolla is dark purple inside and greenish outside, about 2cm wide, the lobes recurved and woolly on the margins. The seed pods are usually twisted, 10–15cm long. [June–July, H, PN, N China]

P. sepium is a more hardy species than *P. graeca*.

SARGENTODOXA (Sargentodoxaceae)

The family Sargentodoxaceae contains but a single species, *Sargentodoxa cuneata*, as generally agreed by botanists. However, it was at one time included in the family Lardizabalaceae as a species of *Holboellia* and it is probably to this genus that it finds the closest affinity, although in the general characteristics of the leaves it more closely resembles *Sinofranchetia chinensis* (p.55).

The reader may well ask how Sargentodoxaceae is separated from Lardizabalaceae and indeed the differences do seem rather slight. In the former the fruit consists of a head of many single-seeded, stalked, berries arranged in a spiral fashion. In the latter there are only a few, borne in whorls and each contains several seeds.

The genus is named in honour of Professor C.S. Sargent of the Arnold Arboretum (Boston, USA).

Sargentodoxa cuneata = *Holboellia cuneata* is a twining deciduous shrub of great vigour, reaching a height of 8m or more. Its leaves are trifoliate, rather dark glossy green in appearance and borne on long stalks, the leaflets oval, 6–12cm long, untoothed. The male and female flowers are greenish-yellow, borne on separate plants in loose drooping racemes, 10–15cm long. Each flower is small and rather starry, 18–22mm across, with six narrow, petal-like sepals, there being no true petals. The clusters of berries carried by the female plants are each produced from a single flower, each berry is about 6mm across and purplish-blue when ripe. [May–June, HH, PA, Central China] ◐

A rare plant in cultivation and scarcely attractive in flower, although the male flowers are said to have a pleasing fragrance. The hardiness of this species is unknown but a warm sheltered wall would seem an obvious choice of site. The species was first discovered in 1887 by Augustine Henry, the Irish botanist.

SCHISANDRA (Schisandraceae)

There are some 25 species of *Schisandra* which grow in tropical and warm temperate Asia and eastern North America, but only five are commercially available in Britain at present. They are deciduous or evergreen woody climbers with alternate leaves. The flowers are unisexual and usually carried on different plants. The 5–20 sepals and petals are similar to one another and there are 5–15 stamens in the male flowers. The female flowers have numerous crowded carpels, which separate as the fruits ripen, eventually forming a spike of berries.

The name is often erroneously given as ‘Schizandra’ in some books and catalogues.

All the species mentioned below are suitable for a shaded wall, or can be trained up poles or pillars. To obtain fruit, plants of both sexes must be grown. They like a rich loamy soil and plenty of well-rotted compost or manure in the form of mulches. Propagation is by means of half-ripened wood in summer, the cuttings put in a propagating frame.

***Schisandra chinensis** will climb to 9m and has red young shoots with wart-like lenticels. The leaves are elliptic to obovate, sparsely toothed, 5–10cm long. The flowers, borne on slender stalks, in bunches of two to three towards the bottom of the new growths, are fragrant, pale pink and 1.25–2cm across, with six to eight perianth segments. The fruits, scarlet when ripe, are borne in a pendulous spike up to 7.5cm long, which remains on the plant during most of the winter. [Apr–May, H, PS, China, Japan, Korea & neighbouring NE USSR]

A very handsome climber when fruiting. It is not so attractive at the flowering stage because the sepals and petals drop quickly. Its dried wood is pleasantly aromatic.

***Schisandra rubriflora** = *S. grandiflora* var. *rubriflora* (Pl.1) grows to 6m high with reddish young shoots. The leaves are usually obovate, toothed, 6–12.5cm long and hairless. The fragrant flowers are pendulous and solitary in the leaf axils towards the bottom of new shoots, deep crimson and about 2.5cm in diameter, with five to seven perianth segments. The spike of round red fruits hangs on a 7.5–15cm stalk. [Apr–May, H, PS, W China & NE India] ◐

Schisandra sphenanthera reaches 5m in height and has reddish-brown, warty young growth. The leaves are oval to almost round, 5–10cm long, the margins with tiny teeth. The flowers are solitary, hanging on slender stalks and about 1.3cm across. There are usually about nine perianth segments of which the outer are greenish and the inner are orange. The scarlet berries hang in a 5–7cm long spike. [Apr–May, H, PS, China]

Schisandra henryi differs from the other species in that the young stems are triangular with a wing on each angle. The leaves are ovate or heart-shaped, 7.5–10cm long, sparsely toothed, shiny above and rather blue-green beneath. The flowers are white, about 1.25cm across and borne on a stalk 5cm long. The red fruits are borne in a spike 5–7cm long. [Apr–May, H, PS, China]

Schisandra propinqua has young stems which are angled. The leaves are narrowly ovate to oval, 5–12.5cm, hairless and finely toothed or untoothed. Normally the flowers are solitary and the outer perianth segments are greenish-yellow, the inner ones orange. The red berries are carried in a spike up to 15cm long. [Apr–May, HH, PS, Himalaya]

var. **chinensis** = var. *sinensis* has narrower leaves, which are sometimes marked with white, and yellowish flowers which appear in late summer. It is said to be hardier than the type. [China]

SCHIZOPHRAGMA (Hydrangeaceae)

Climbing shrubs related to the climbing *Hydrangea* species but differing mainly in that the sterile flowers possess only one sepal (not three to five). The plants climb by the aerial roots produced on the underside of the stems which cling closely to supports. The leaves are opposite and have long stalks. The flowers are borne in a flat inflorescence, with tiny fertile flowers in the middle and showy sterile flowers round the edge.

Although Schizophragmas flower best on a sunny wall, they can be grown quite successfully on a north-facing or shady wall. They look most attractive when allowed to ascend a large tree, although they may take some years to reach a large size. Most ordinary garden soils will suit them and they should be planted in the autumn, October and November. Cuttings can be rooted in a propagating frame in summer. Sometimes they are slow starters, but usually flower at an earlier age than the climbing Hydrangeas. Young plants need a little help by tying in the stems until they begin to cling by themselves.

***Schizophragma integrifolium**, (Pl.2) will climb to 12m by means of its aerial roots. The leaves are ovate or heart-shaped, 7.5–18cm long, either untoothed or with small teeth. The inflorescences are up to 30cm across and bear creamy-white sterile flowers at the margin. Each sterile flower consists of a white narrow ovate sepal 6–9cm long, with darker veins. [July, H-HH, PN, China]

The initial clinging growth will climb a wall, but the flowers are produced on lateral branches which hang down from the attached stems. Any unwanted growth should be removed during the winter. In the south of England, this species prefers semi-shade to full hot sun. It is one of E.H. Wilson's many introductions from China, slightly less hardy than the following species, but more commonly grown.

Schizophragma hydrangeoides has hairless stems reaching 12m, bearing aerial roots. The young stems are reddish. The leaves are broadly ovate,

10–15cm long, toothed, deep green and hairless above and paler and silky-haired beneath. The inflorescences are 20–25cm in diameter and the marginal sterile flowers have a pale yellow ovate or heart-shaped sepal 2.5–4cm long. [July, H, PN, Japan]

Cultivation is similar to that of *S. integrifolium*. It is sometimes mistaken for *Hydrangea anomala* or *H. petiolaris*, but can easily be told apart by the form of the sterile flowers.

***'Roseum'** — has the sterile flowers tinged with pink; a pretty form.

SINOFRANCHETIA (Lardizabalaceae)

A genus of one species closely related to *Holboellia* but quite hardy and with all the leaves being trifoliate. The genus was named in honour of Andrien Franchet who did a great deal of work on the plants of China and who died in 1900.

Sinofranchetia chinensis is a very vigorous deciduous climber with twining shoots which may attain a height of 15m, covering sizeable trees in its native haunts. The young shoots and slender leaf stalks are covered in a purplish bloom. The leaves are green above but bluish-green beneath, the leaflets oval or elliptic, 6–14cm long, pointed and untoothed. The small, dull, whitish flowers are of no great beauty and are borne in pendent racemes, up to 10cm long, on short leafy shoots. The male and female flowers occur on separate plants. The grape-sized fruits are borne alternately on an elongated axis, each containing many seeds. [May, H, PA, Central & W China]

This is a plant which needs plenty of room and certainly has no place in a small garden. The flowers are of little significance from an ornamental point of view, though the foliage is strikingly handsome. Fruit is often produced on the female plant even in the absence of a male partner which suggests that the plants may not be wholly female. E.H. Wilson introduced *Sinofranchetia* to cultivation in 1907.

SOLANUM (Solanaceae)

The evergreen Solanums, including the popular *S. crispum* and *S. jasminoides*, are dealt with on p.112 but the following species is deciduous.

Solanum valdiviense is a vigorous, more or less climbing shrub reaching about 3m tall, which produces suckers. The young shoots are angular and downy. The ovate-lanceolate, alternate leaves are untoothed and up to 6cm in length. The scented flowers are produced in short two- to seven-flowered racemes in the axils of the leaves. The corolla is mauve or white and about 1.25cm in diameter and there is a central 'beak' of yellow anthers. The fruit is a spherical dull green berry, about 6mm long. [May–June, T, PA, Chile & adjacent Argentine]

Introduced from the Argentine in 1927 by Harold Comber, this tender plant will survive in the south and west of Britain if given as much sun as possible. It is especially beautiful when the flowers first appear because at this stage the leaves are not fully expanded.

VITIS (Vitaceae)

This genus contains amongst its 50 or so species the common grape vine, *Vitis vinifera*, grown by man for many centuries. The species are confined to the Northern Hemisphere, many to the North American Continent. However, it is the Asian species that are the most decorative garden plants. Most are vigorous deciduous vines with large, usually palmate, leaves borne alternately along the stems. They climb by means of simple or branched tendrils borne opposite the leaves, but often missing from every third leaf node. The flowers are small and greenish and of little beauty. They are usually bisexual though they may be male only. The five small petals are joined together at their apices, forming a tiny cap. These are succeeded by loose or dense bunches of small succulent berries – grapes.

These vines are fine subjects for tumbling over old walls and fences, or growing up pergolas, poles or tree stumps. The large-leaved species such as *V. coignetiae* and *V. davidii* are excellent when allowed to scramble into old trees.

Vitis prefer a well-drained loamy soil, particularly a slightly calcareous one, though they will succeed on a wide variety, however, the addition of well-rotted manure is highly beneficial on poorer soils. The best time to plant is during the late winter or early autumn. Mulches of well-rotted manure or compost applied in the spring and summer will help to prevent the soil from drying up too severely around young plants.

Position is quite important. Most *Vitis* species like a warm sunny aspect if they are to produce the best autumn colouring. If grown on walls or fences a south or west aspect is therefore desirable, although not absolutely essential.

Those left to smother a tree stump or to climb into a tree require little pruning, but those on walls, fences and pergolas or poles will require some pruning to keep them in check. Lateral shoots can be cut hard back to one to three buds of the main stem during the winter. This operation should be carried out before the end of January or else the cut surface will bleed badly due to the rise of sap which generally commences in February. Leafy non-fruiting shoots can be pinched out after they have made seven or eight leaves during the summer if desired. For the treatment of cultivated grapes grown as wall fruits see the chapter on Wall Fruits.

The main stems should be tied in carefully as pruning proceeds. Plants grown on pillars or posts look best if the lateral shoots are allowed to hang down all around, indeed they can look very effective trained in such a way.

Most vines can be readily propagated from short lengths of young well ripened wood, one or two node lengths, inserted in a cold frame in the autumn. The majority can also be propagated from 'eyes', short one bud lengths placed horizontally in a sandy compost during the early spring. The buds should be just above the soil surface and gentle bottom heat will greatly assist rooting.

See also the closely related *Ampelopsis* and *Parthenocissus*.

ASIAN SPECIES OF VITIS:

◐ **Vitis vinifera**, the Common Grape Vine, is almost too well known to warrant a description. The vines are vigorous and deciduous reaching 7m or more if left unchecked. The three- or five-lobed leaves are coarsely toothed and bright green in the usual form. [June–July, H, PW]

The common grape has been cultivated for many centuries and today many fine cultivars exist, grown primarily for their fruit. The original home of the grape is a matter for speculation, although it is now believed to be Asia Minor and the Caucasus. In former times grape-vines were cultivated extensively for their fruit in southern England but, through the centuries, a change in climate to cooler wetter summers led to a decline in viticulture. The advent of early ripening clones has enabled a number of vineyards to be re-established in some southern counties. There are also a number of fine cultivars grown for their ornamental value.

Plate 3 Wisterias 1 *Wisteria sinensis* (p.62), 2 *W. venusta* (p.62).

3
1
2

4
1
2
3
4
5

'Apiifolia' = 'Laciniosa', the Parsley Vine or Ciotat, bears handsome dissected leaves, each of the main lobes deeply cut into long narrow divisions. It has been cultivated in Britain since the middle of the seventeenth century.

'Fragola' is a decorative cultivar with pleasant strawberry-flavoured berries.

***'Incana'**, the Dusty Miller Grape, bears handsome grey-felted leaves which are whitish when young. They may be three-lobed or unlobed. The berries are black.

***'Purpurea'** (Pl.4), the Teinturier Grape, is a handsome and very striking plant. The young leaves are whitish downy but they soon become claret or plum-purple, changing in the autumn to an intense deep dark purple. The grapes are purple-black when ripe but unpleasant to taste. One of the very finest ornamental vines.

Vitis amurensis is a vigorous vine similar in habit to the preceding species. The young shoots are downy and reddish and the three- or five-lobed leaves, 12–30cm long, are deep green, turning crimson and purple in the autumn. The berries are small and black, 7–8mm long. [June–July, H, PW, N China, Japan, Korea & E USSR]

***Vitis coignetiae** is an extremely vigorous vine reaching the tops of lofty trees in its native habitats, generally 10–15m in cultivation. The young shoots are ribbed and covered in grey down. The large rough leaves are broadly heart-shaped, 10–30cm long with three to five pointed lobes, coarsely toothed, dark green above, rusty-brown with down beneath. The black berries bear a purplish bloom and are about 12mm long. [June–July, H, PW, Japan]

This handsome vine deserves a place in any garden where space permits. It looks particularly fine grown on a patio wall or draped over a large tree stump or simply allowed to ramble into a suitable tree. The decorative leaves take on glorious rich autumn hues, a mixture of orange, mahogany and scarlet.

The species is named in honour of Mme Coignet, daughter of Jean Sisley the French Rosarian, who collected seed in 1887.

Propagation is difficult and careful layering generally produces the best results.

Vitis pulchra is possibly a hybrid between *V. amurensis* and *V. coignetiae*. It is another vigorous climber reaching 10m or more in height, the young shoots smooth and reddish. The rounded heart-shaped leaves are 7–15cm long and slightly three-lobed, coarsely toothed, deep green above, grey-downy beneath. The leaves turn rich purple and blood red in the autumn, but may also have a reddish tinge when young. [June, H, PW, origin unknown]

Vitis davidii = *Spinovitis davidii, Vitis armata,* is a luxuriant climber attaining 8m or more, the young stems covered in short, slightly curved prickles, a unique feature amongst cultivated vines. The leaves are variable but basically heart-shaped in outline with a slender point, 10–25cm long, shiny dark green above, but bluish- or greyish-green beneath. The berries are black when ripe, 15–17mm long, edible. [June–July, H, PW, China]

Another fine plant introduced from Shensi in 1872 by Père David. The leaves turn a brilliant red during the autumn.

'Veitchii' = *V. armata* var. *cyanocarpa* is a less prickly form with fine bronzy-green leaves which take on rich red autumn tints. The berries have a bluish bloom.

Vitis romanetii is a vigorous climber reaching 8m or more in height, the young shoots downy. The narrow heart-shaped leaves are three-lobed, 15–25cm long, shallowly toothed, dark green above, downy grey beneath. Berries black, 8–12mm long. [June–July, HH, PW, China]

Vitis romanetii is closely allied to *V. davidii* but easily distinguished by the grey-

---

Plate 4 Deciduous and Evergeen Climbers 1 *Passiflora caerulea* (p.109), 2 *Fallopia aubertii* (p.47), 3 *Solanum jasminoides* 'Album' (p.112), 4 *S. crispum* 'Glasnevin' (p.112), 5 *Vitis vinifera* 'Purpurea' (p.57).

felted undersurface to the leaves. Plants are not completely hardy and young growth and thin wood may be cut back by frost. Père David introduced the species to Europe from China in 1872–3.

Vitis flexuosa is one of the most elegant vines with its slender hairless stems reaching 5m or more in height. The leaves are rather thin, heart-shaped or more or less rounded in outline, pointed, 5–10cm long, glossy-green above and downy on the veins beneath. The pea-sized berries are black when ripe. [June, H, PW, China, Japan & Korea]

A dainty species with smaller leaves than most and usually represented in gardens by the following variety.

var. **parvifolia** = *Vitis parvifolia* is a pretty plant with smaller leaves which are green with a bronzy metallic sheen, purple beneath when young. [Central & S China, Taiwan, E Himalaya.] Sometimes regarded as a quite separate species, but generally found in catalogues and lists as a variety of *V. flexuosa*.

Vitis thunbergii = *V. sieboldii* is a slender-stemmed vine of moderate vigour reaching 3m or more. The heart-shaped leaves are three- or five-lobed, 'fig leaf-shaped', 6–15cm long, sharply toothed, dull dark green above but rusty-brown with down beneath. The berries are black when ripe and covered by a purplish bloom, 10mm long. [June–July, HH, PN, Japan & Korea]

A rather rare species in cultivation, possibly because the shoots tend to die back during the winter and the plant is not as vigorous as some of the other species described. The leaves do, however, turn a rich crimson during the autumn.

Vitis wilsoniae is a very vigorous vine with woolly young shoots, reaching 5m or more. Leaves ovate, slightly heart-shaped at the base, wavy-toothed, 7.5–15cm long, woolly when young but becoming deep green and hairless above whilst remaining downy beneath. Berries black with a purple bloom when ripe, 10–12mm long. [June–July, H, PW, Central China]

Another fine vine, but strangely enough an uncommon one in our gardens. It is worth growing for its handsome foliage and striking fiery red autumn coloration. E.H. Wilson, after whom the species is named, discovered this plant in China in 1902.

Vitis piasezkii = *Parthenocissus sinensis, Vitis sinensis,* is a vigorous though rather slender climber reaching 7m or more. The leaves are variable in shape, being three- or five-lobed or composed of three or five separate leaflets. Leaves range in size from 7.5cm to 15cm long, with sharply toothed margins and purplish leaf-stalks. The black, rounded berries are about 8mm across. [June–July, H, PW, Central & W China]

A rather extraordinary vine. The leaves at the base of shoots are generally lobed, whilst those further along the stem consist of distinct leaflets radiating from a central point. The dark green leaves turn bronze and red during the autumn.

var. **pagnuccii** = *Vitis pagnuccii* is a form with practically hairless stems but differs little from the type in other respects.

Vitis betulifolia is closely allied to the preceding species but the leaves are always simple, sometimes faintly lobed, ovate and up to 10cm long. The bluish-black berries bear a slight bloom. [June–July, H, PW, Central & W China]

Vitis quinquangularis = *Vitis pentagona, V. filifolia* var. *pentagona,* is another vigorous climber with the young shoots covered in white-felted hairs. The leaves are ovate or heart-shaped, 7.5–15cm long, usually with three or five shallow lobes, dark green above but white-felted beneath, a striking contrast. The blue-black berries are 7–8mm long. [June, H, PW, Central & W China]

First introduced in 1907 by E.H. Wilson, *V. quinquangularis* deserves to be more widely grown, although its tongue-twisting name may discourage some people.

var. **bellula** has smaller leaves, only 3.5–6cm long.

NORTH AMERICAN SPECIES OF VITIS

Vitis riparia = *Vitis odoratissima*, the River Bank Grape, is a strong growing vine reaching 10m, or more left to its own devices. The broad heart-shaped leaves are poorly three-lobed, and coarsely toothed, 10–22cm long and shiny bright green on both surfaces. The flowers, borne in panicles up to 20cm long, are sweetly scented and, when ripe, the berries that follow turn purplish-black with a pronounced bluish bloom, each 7–8mm long. [June–July, H, PW, Central & E N America]

This fine vine is a common plant particularly in the eastern United States. It is easily rooted from cuttings and is frequently used as a stock on which many French varieties of grape are grafted, due to its 'phylloxera' resistance. Phylloxera is a serious disease of wine-producing vines in Europe. The sweet fragrance of the flowers has been likened to that of mignonette.

***'Brandt'** = *Vitis vinifera* 'Brant' is a superb cultivar remarkable for its autumn colours, the leaves turning bronzy-red, except for the veins which remain green. The berries are delicious and sweet providing there has been enough sun during the late summer and autumn. The origin of this vine is somewhat complex but it is generally believed to be a hybrid between *Vitis* 'Clinton' and *V. vinifera* 'Black St Peters'. *Vitis* 'Clinton' itself is a hybrid probably involving *V. labrusca* and *V. riparia*. Whatever its origins 'Brant' is certainly one of the very best ornamental vines. It has been cultivated in Britain since 1886 having originated in China. Plants generally reach 5–6m high.

Vitis rotundifolia = *Muscadinia rotundifolia* is a vigorous vine reaching as much as 30m tall in its native haunts, 10m or more in cultivation. The bark does not shred as in other vines and the young shoots are warted and bear simple unbranched tendrils. The broad rather rounded heart-shaped leaves are pointed, seldom lobed, 5–11cm long, coarsely toothed, glossy dark green above but glossy yellowish-green beneath. The dull purple berries are 16–25mm long with a pleasant musky flavour. [June–July, HH, PW, S USA]

Vitis rotundifolia is one of the parent species of a number of varieties of vineyard grapes grown in the United States.

Vitis labrusca, the Northern Fox Grape, is another very vigorous vine attaining 10m or more unpruned, with very woolly young shoots. The leaves are thick, heart-shaped to rather rounded, unlobed or three-lobed, 7.5–20cm long, the margin with irregular teeth, dark green above but rusty with down beneath. The rounded berries are dark purplish-black, 15–17mm long. [June–July, H, PW, E North America]

This luxuriant vine is very important in the United States as the source of many varieties of grapes, however, it is of little value as a fruit producer in Britain where it has been cultivated since 1656 for its ornamental value. The fruit is said to have a musky or foxy aroma.

Vitis aestivalis, the Summer Grape, is an extremely vigorous climber reaching 15m or more if allowed, the young stems hairless or slightly downy. The leaves are very large, 10–30cm long, with three or five shallow or deep lobes, dull green above but brown with down beneath. The flowers are borne in long panicles up to 25cm long. Berries black with a blue bloom, about 8mm long, pleasantly flavoured. [June–July, H, PW, Central & E USA]

V. aestivalis resembles *V. labrusca* but the former has a tendril missing at every third node. It has been cultivated in Britain since the seventeenth century.

Vitis argentifolia = *V. aestivalis* var. *argentifolia* is easily distinguished from the previous species by its bluish-white young shoots. This coloration also covers the undersurface of the leaves which are three- or five-lobed, 10–30cm long with rather coarse irregular teeth along the margin. [June–July, H, PW, Central & E USA]

A handsome and most striking vine which well deserves to be more widely known. In the wild it grows in abundance around the Niagara Falls.

Lastly come five rather small-leaved species of vine, all from North America, which are sometimes met with in our gardens.

Vitis californica is a moderately vigorous vine which reaches 10m in height with the young shoots covered at first in a fine grey down. The heart- or kidney-shaped leaves are sometimes three-lobed, 5–10cm long, green above but downy-grey beneath. The small berries are black with a purple bloom when ripe, 7–8mm long. [June–July, H, PW, W North America]

The leaves turn a handsome deep crimson before they fall.

Vitis candicans, often known as the Mustang Grape, is a vigorous vine reaching 10m or more, the young shoots covered in a dense white wool. The leaves are basically heart- or kidney-shaped, unlobed or somewhat three-lobed, 5–12cm long, dull dark green above and woolly at first, but always white-woolly beneath. The rounded berries are purplish, 15–17mm long, unpleasantly flavoured. [June–July, HH, PW, S USA]

Vitis doaniana is closely related to the preceding species but the leaves are always three-lobed, the upper surface bluish-green mottled with whitish wool, the under surface completely woolly. [June–July, HH, PW, S USA]

Vitis cordifolia, the Frost or Chicken Grape, is a very strong growing vine, the main stem becoming thick and trunk-like with age. The leaves are thin and heart-shaped with a slender point, coarsely toothed, sometimes somewhat three-lobed, 7–13cm long, glossy green above but paler and downy on the veins beneath. The rounded berries are black when ripe and quite tasty, 8–12mm long. [June–July, H, PW, E & S USA]

Vitis monticola reaches about 10m tall with slender angled stems. The leaves are heart-shaped, pointed, 5–10cm long, slightly three-lobed and coarsely toothed, dark green above but greyish beneath. The rounded berries are about 12mm long, black, sweet and tasty when ripe. [June–July, HH, PW, S USA (Texas)]

WISTERIA (Leguminosae)

A genus of ten species native to East Asia and eastern North America, of which six are generally cultivated. The leaves are alternate and odd-pinnate. The flowers are borne in terminal and axillary, usually pendulous, racemes and are typical 'pea' flowers. The fruit is a flattened pod, usually with several seeds, though only occasionally produced in cultivation.

Wisterias are some of the most beautiful climbing plants and can be used on walls, or trained on pergolas or up tall trees. They can be grown in any type of soil providing it is well drained but prefer a sunny position, and are a glorious sight when in full flower. Young strong container grown plants should be purchased and planted during the winter or early spring, preferably the latter in colder districts.

The initial shoots should be tied to the structure to be covered and usually so many lateral growths will be produced that some thinning out will be necessary. These lateral growths are normally pruned each year to encourage the formation of flower buds. It is best to prune in two stages; firstly after flowering (usually about July) the long laterals should be cut back to about 15cm; secondly in December or January, these are again shortened, leaving only two or three buds to each lateral shoot.

Wisterias can take a few years to settle down and to start flowering and this can prove a frustrating wait. Plants grown in too much shade or in too rich a soil are the main culprits. On no account should plants receive nitrogenous fertilisers otherwise flowering can be badly delayed. Some form of root restriction together with a regular system of pruning should bring most plants into bloom within four or five years.

★**Wisteria floribunda**, the Japanese Wisteria, will grow to 9m tall. The leaves are 25–35cm long, composed of eleven to nineteen ovate leaflets which are 4–8cm long, downy when young but eventually hairless. The drooping racemes are slender, 12–25cm long, with fragrant flowers. The calyx is about 1–2cm long and downy and the corolla is violet-blue, 1.5–2cm long. The pods measure 7–15cm long and are velvety. [May–June, H, PA-PS, Japan]

This handsome and widely grown species has been cultivated for centuries in Japanese gardens and it was introduced into Europe in the eighteen-thirties. Many cultivars have been selected over the years, both in this country and abroad. The following are generally in cultivation:

'Alba' has white flowers, sometimes tinged with lilac on the keel and borne in racemes 50–60cm long.

'Coelestina' has lavender-blue flowers.

'Geisha' has lavender-blue flowers.

'Multijuga' has the standard mauve, yellow at the base, and the wings and keel bluish-violet. The racemes are about 60cm long. This was sent to Britain in 1874 by van Houtte, the Belgian nurseryman, and was the first cultivar to be introduced.

'Rosea' has the standard a pale pink and the wings and keel purple. The racemes are about 55cm long.

'Russelliana' has the standard deep mauve, the wings and keel deep bluish-violet, while the whole flower has cream markings.

'Violacea' has violet-blue flowers.

'Violacea Plena' has double lilac flowers.

★forma **macrobotrys**. The flowers are lilac, suffused with bluish-purple and carried in racemes 90–120cm long. A truly magnificent form.

The cultivars with long racemes look their best on a pergola or some overhead structure where the flowers can dangle downwards — much of their impact is lost if grown on a wall. The long-racemed forms have only been developed in *W. floribunda*, which is the most hardy species.

☼ ***Wisteria sinensis** = *W. chinensis* (Pl.3), the Chinese Wisteria, is a very vigorous climber which can attain as much as 30m, especially if allowed to grow up a tree with no hindrance. The leaves are 25–30cm long and usually have eleven leaflets which increase in size towards the leaf apex. The dense drooping racemes are 20–30cm long, with mauve or lilac fragrant flowers, each about 2.5cm long. The velvety pods are 12–15cm long and contain one to three seeds. [May, H, PA-PS, C China]

W. sinensis is the most fragrant species in cultivation, the beautiful racemes appearing before the leaves open properly. Although its main time of flowering is May, it often blooms again in August, which is an added bonus.

***'Alba'** has white flowers and is very powerfully scented.

***'Prolific'** = 'Oosthoek's variety' is a cultivar which was originally bred in the Netherlands. It has longer racemes than the type, produced in great abundance.

'Black Dragon' has deep purple double flowers.

'Plena' has lilac double flowers.

☼ **Wisteria × formosa,** *W. sinensis* × *W. floribunda* 'Alba', has leaves with nine to 15 leaflets which are downy at first but in time lose the hair on the upper surface. The racemes of pale violet flowers are about 25cm long. All the flowers open at roughly the same time. The pods usually contain only one seed. [May–June, H, PA-PS, Garden origin]

This hybrid was raised in the USA in 1905 and introduced to Britain 17 years later.

'Issai' has slightly shorter racemes (18–25cm) with lilac-blue flowers.

☼ ***Wisteria venusta** (Pl.3) will climb to 9m or more and has downy young shoots. The leaves are 20–35cm long and made up of nine to thirteen ovate to oblong-elliptic leaflets. The racemes are 10–15cm long. The slightly fragrant flowers are white and the standard has a yellow blotch at the base; they all open at the same time. The velvety pods are 15–20cm long. [May–June, H, PA, PS, Japan (gardens)]

W. venusta is not known in the wild and was first imported to Europe from Japanese gardens in 1912. It has the largest flowers (2.5–3.5cm long) of any cultivated *Wisteria* and they are very long-lasting and borne in great profusion.

forma **violacea** has purplish flowers. Some botanists consider that this may, in fact, be the wild form of the species.

'Alba Plena' = forma *plena* has double white flowers.

☼ **Wisteria frutescens** reaches 9–12m in height and the young branches are hairless or nearly so. The leaves are 18–30cm long with nine to 15 ovate or oblong leaflets. The racemes are 10–15cm long, the shorter ones often standing erect. The scented flowers are rather crowded, each about 2cm long, mauve with a yellow spot. The pods are 5–10cm long and hairless. [June–Aug, H, PA-PS, SE USA]

W. frutescens is not very commonly cultivated in Britain and tends to be less vigorous than the Asian members of the genus.

'Nivea' = forma *nivea* has white flowers.

☼ **Wisteria macrostachys** is similar to *W. frutescens*. It reaches about 8m tall and the young shoots are hairy at first but quickly lose their hairs. The leaves usually have nine ovate to narrowly elliptical leaflets. The racemes are densely-flowered with up to 90 flowers and, at 15–35cm, are longer than those of *W. frutescens*. The flowers are lilac-purple. The pods are hairless, 7–12cm, and slightly constricted between the seeds. [May–June, H, PA-PS, S USA]

***Wisteria japonica** is an almost completely hairless species. The leaves are 15–23cm with nine to 13 bright green, ovate to roundish leaflets. The racemes are 15–30cm and are often branched. The flowers are white or very pale yellow, each 1–1.3cm long. The pods are hairless, 7.5–10cm long, containing six to seven seeds. [July–Aug, H, PA-PS, Japan]

A magnificent plant for growing up a tree. It is such a distinct species (in its branched racemes, small flowers and absence of hair) that some botanists consider that it is not a *Wisteria* at all, being closer to the tropical genus *Milletia*.

Clematis
(Ranunculaceae)

Clematis are among the most popular, colourful and useful of all climbing plants. Go to almost any garden and you are virtually certain to see one or two draped over a fence, or clinging to a wall or tree. There are a large number of species and cultivars on the market, many of which have been grown for years.

There are some two hundred or so species of Clematis in the wild among which we can count our own native 'Old Man's Beard' or 'Travellers' Joy', *Clematis vitalba*. The genus is distributed throughout all the major continents of the world and although some species have small greenish-white flowers of little garden value, there are many beautiful and brightly coloured species well deserving attention. Besides these, there are numerous large-flowered hybrids and cultivars that have been selected over the years. Some of these may be considered by some to be big and blousey, however, they do provide bright splashes of colour in the garden from spring through to the late autumn. One or two species even manage to push forward flowers during the winter.

Clematis are versatile plants. Some are tender and need careful protection if they are to succeed, but many have less exacting requirements and can be grown on a variety of supports. Walls, fences, pergolas, pillars and trees are all suitable. Besides this, many can be successfully grown amongst shrubs or other climbing plants providing an attractive contrast or combination of colours. Indeed many of the large-flowered varieties are better in association with other plants than in isolation on their own, for the lower half of the plant is often devoid of flowers and this can detract from the beauty of the flowers at the top; Roses, Cotoneasters, Ceanothus and wall fruits past their best are all suitable partners, though everyone can enjoy working out new combinations of plants and colours.

Not all Clematis are woody climbers for there are a number of attractive herbaceous species as well as a few shrubby ones, though they mostly do not concern us here. The climbing species cling to supports by means of their twining leaf stalks which grip any support at hand and many soon make a tangled mass of shoots and leaves unless the stems are carefully spaced and trained. Leaves of some remain through a part or all of the winter and may become brown and unsightly unless the plants are in a very sheltered position. The clematis flower is basically rather simple. There are four or more separate sepals. Just to confuse everyone these are coloured and petal-like, though botanically they are sepals in the true sense. They may be held close together or indeed partly fused to one another to form a bell- or urn-shaped flower, though in the majority of species they are quite separate and widely spreading. There are numerous stamens surrounding a group of single-seeded fruits or 'achenes' in the centre of the flower. The tip of each achene, the style, elongates after pollination and in most species is densely hairy, thus giving the fruitheads their fluffy or feathery 'old man's beard' appearance.

CULTURE

Clematis prefer a deep moist loamy soil. Soils that dry out quickly, such as sandy soils or heavy clays, are not generally suitable unless carefully prepared to improve their composition. Although there is no general agreement amongst gardeners it would seem that a calcareous soil is good, though not essential, for most species. Species and cultivars, except for the more tender ones, will thrive equally well in a sunny or partially shaded position, some even flowering well in almost total shade. However, they are best with their roots planted in a shady moist place, for they will not tolerate strong sun drying out the soil around them. A sheltered site is also preferable, for constant buffeting by the wind may cause damage, especially to the large-flowered cultivars. Large vigorous species will need strong supports as they tend to get very heavy with age.

Young specimens can be planted out in the autumn or early spring, although nowadays with the advent of healthy strong container-grown stock they can virtually be planted out at any time except midwinter. Evergreen species, however, are best planted out in March or early April. Young plants, except those of the *C. montana* group, are best pruned back to a strong pair of buds in February or March. This will help to encourage strong young growth. Most clematis, especially the large-flowered cultivars, respond to regular feeding and generous mulches during the growing season.

The only major disease of Clematis is Clematis Wilt which is caused by a fungus. The large-flowered cultivars especially are often struck without warning by this annoying disease, causing a shoot or several shoots to die back. Occasionally the entire plant may be affected. Infected shoots should be cut out from the base leaving only healthy growth. Benlate sprayed regularly can greatly help to hold the fungus in check.

The flowers of many of the large-flowered forms bleach badly in strong sunlight, especially those with blue or pink flowers. Planting in semi-shaded positions is therefore preferable for these, or at least in a position that avoids the direct sun during the midday hours.

PRUNING

Most people find pruning a complex subject and the pruning of clematis impossible. However, the procedure is really quite simple providing a few general rules are obeyed, bearing in mind that the point of pruning is to promote healthy strong growth and a good crop of flowers, whilst at the same time keeping the plant to some extent in check.

Clematis can be grouped according to their pruning requirements. Those that flower early in the year from the previous year's growths, such as *C. montana* and *C. chrysocoma* should be pruned immediately after flowering, although pruning is mainly done to remove old or weak growth or to reduce the size or bulk of the plant. Pruning these later in the year will only remove the following year's flowers. Evergreen species like *C. armandii* should on the whole be pruned lightly and with discretion, though some gardeners appear to 'get away' with a more vigorous assault on such plants.

The second group includes all the species and cultivars that flower from midsummer onwards on the current season's growth. This includes two main types, the herbaceous climbers such as *C. viorna* and *C. viticella* and the vigorous late-flowerers such as *C. flammula*, *C. tangutica* and *C. vitalba*. With the former it is only necessary to remove all dead growth in the spring. The latter, however, after a year or two tend to produce a mass of top growth with bare tangled stems beneath. Some of the larger stems can be pruned hard back in the spring to encourage new growth. Alternatively the whole plant can be cut back to about a metre, leaving a few healthy buds at the top of each stem.

The third group consists of most of the large-flowered cultivars and hybrids with the exception of the *C. viticella* group. Little pruning is required other than to remove dead or old shoots and to train and untangle new growths. Most of these flower from the early summer onwards on short shoots produced from those of the previous season. If a later display is desired early flowering can be sacrificed wholly or in part by pruning back growth in the spring, although care should be taken not to leave this too late. Many of these cultivars will, under normal circumstances, produce a later second crop of flowers, though generally far fewer than the midsummer flush.

GROUP A

Any pruning should be done immediately after flowering and should consist mainly of reducing the size or bulk of the plant, or removing old or dead growth.

CLEMATIS MONTANA AGGREGATE

Mostly vigorous deciduous species with ternate leaves and four-'petalled' flowers, borne solitary or in small groups at the leaf axils.

***Clematis montana** and its allies are amongst the hardiest, most floriferous and vigorous groups of clematis. *Clematis montana* is a deciduous climber reaching 8m high, sometimes more, the stems rather wiry, becoming thick, woody and entangled with age. Leaves deep green, sometimes tinged with red. Flowers white, 5–6.5cm across, borne on long slender stalks at the leaf nodes, in small clusters, usually vanilla-scented. [May–June, H, PA, Himalaya & W China]

One of the most popular garden clematis, easily grown on most garden soils in almost any aspect including total shade. Plants are very floriferous, growing fast and flowering quickly after planting. It is equally at home on a wall, a fence, pergola or sprawled over a tree or tree stump. Plants are easily propagated from cuttings or from seed which, in the southern part of the British Isles, is generally set in abundance. Plants grown from seed can be unpredictable as regards flower size, colour and scent. In a small garden this lovely species needs to be kept in check by judicious pruning and shoot thinning as soon as flowering ceases.

Clematis montana has been cultivated since early in the nineteenth century, the first plants supposedly introduced by Lady Amherst in 1831.

'Alexander' is a fine form with sweetly scented creamy-white flowers. The flowers are variable in size, more or less pure white on a shaded wall.

*'**Elizabeth**' has large pale pink, vanilla-fragrant flowers.

'**Grandiflora**' = forma *grandiflora* has large white flowers, 6.5–7.5cm across. Particularly good on a north wall or fence.

*var. **rubens** (Pl.6) is similar to the type but distinct on account of its reddish-purple young stems and leaf-stalks and purplish foliage. Flowers rose-red, 6–6.5cm across. [W China] One of the very finest clematis.

*'**Tetrarose**' is a superb cultivar with large, rather fleshy flowers of a purplish-pink hue overall, each 6.5–7.5cm across.

'**Percy Picton**' is a less vigorous plant than the others with deep pink flowers.

var. **wilsonii** is like the type but with rather small white flowers borne on downy stalks, strongly scented [June–July, C China] A useful variety which extends the flowering period of the 'montana group' well into summer. The flowers start off greenish-white but soon expand to a glistening white.

Other cultivars such as 'Lilacina' and 'Pink Perfection' are sometimes seen for sale. Most of them are worth growing, though ideally plants should be selected in flower to ensure good colour forms.

Clematis chrysocoma (Pl.5) is a fairly vigorous species reaching 6m tall, often less, the young stems and leaves as well as the flower-stalks covered in a dense brownish-yellow down. Flowers soft pink, 4–5.5cm across, borne in profusion. [May–June, (–Sept), H, PA, SW China]

A charming plant less hardy than *C. montana*, which when young may need a little protection in colder districts. Although its main flowering season is from May until the end of June, plants continue to flower spasmodically through the summer though never in great numbers after the first flush. Pruning should take into account these secondary blossoms. The wild plant which is known from Yunnan in China is a more shrubby form with weaker stems and the cultivated form may not be the true species, but a plant of hybrid origin. *Clematis chrysocoma* was first introduced to Britain round about 1890.

*var. **sericea** = *C. spooneri* is a more vigorous plant reaching 7m tall. Leaves silky with yellowish down, especially when young. Flowers white, 5–7cm across, occasionally with a slight hint of pink, solitary or in pairs.

Hardier than the type but normally does not produce any secondary flowers.

Clematis graciliflora reaches 4m in height with greenish, ribbed, stems. The leaves are usually ternate, but occasionally pinnate with five to seven leaflets. Flowers white, 3.8–5cm across, in clusters of two to four. [May–June, H, PA, W China]

A graceful free-flowering species which deserves to be more extensively grown if plants can be obtained.

Clematis × vedrariensis, *C. chrysocoma* × *C. montana* var. *rubens*, is a vigorous climber to 7m with ribbed, hairy stems. Leaves dull purplish-green, coarsely toothed, densely hairy beneath, particularly when young. Flowers pale rose-pink, 5–6.5cm across, solitary on long slender stems; with four to six 'petals'. [May–June, H, PA]

A plant similar in habit and general features to *C. montana* var. *rubens* but with the hairiness of *C. chrysocoma*. It is a fine plant in full flower.

'**Rosea**' is a particularly good cultivar of this successful hybrid. It was at one time sold under the name *C. spooneri* var. *rosea*.

CLEMATIS ALPINA AGGREGATE (ATRAGENE)

A group of semi-vigorous deciduous species with biternate leaves and nodding flowers with four 'petals' and numerous petaloid stamens, transitional between the 'petals' and the stamens. The species were at one time included in a distinct genus, *Atragene*, due to the presence of the petaloid stamens, known botanically as staminodes. They are amongst the most beautiful and elegant species, ideal mixers amongst other wali shrubs.

Clematis alpina = *Atragene alpina* (Pl.5), the Alpine Clematis, reaches 2–3m in height, rarely more, the young stems often flushed with red or purple. Flowers are pale to deep blue or lilac-blue with a contrasting white centre, solitary, nodding open bells, 2.5–3.7cm long. [Apr–May, H, PA, Central & N Europe, W Asia] ◐

One of the most delightful species which is found in deciduous and coniferous woods in the wild as well as growing over rocks, often preferring calcareous soils. In cultivation it frequently proves one of the less vigorous species, although a good plant in full flower is a very fine sight. It is an ideal plant for the small garden with limited space.

The petaloid stamens (staminodes) are spoon-shaped and white in this species, whereas in the closely related *C. macropetela* they are large and pointed, smaller versions of the 'petals' and similarly coloured.

*__'Frances Rivis'__ = 'Blue Giant' is a particularly fine, deep-coloured and large-flowered form.

'Ruby' is like the type but the flowers are reddish-purple with a white centre.

var. **sibirica** = *Atragene sibirica* is similar in general characteristics to the type but the leaves are paler green and the flowers creamy-white. [N China & E USSR]

'White Moth' is a lovely white-flowered cultivar, flowering mostly in May.

Clematis verticillaris = *Atragene americana* is very similar to *C. alpina*, reaching 2–3m tall with thin hairless stems. Leaves untoothed or with a few coarse teeth. Flowers purple or bluish-purple with a whitish centre, nodding, 5–7.5cm long, solitary rather open bells. [May–June, H, PA, E N America] ◐

Very similar to *C. alpina* but scarcely as good a garden plant, being less easy to cultivate and certainly not as handsome. It is usually represented in gardens by var. *columbiana*.

*__Clematis macropetala__ = *Atragene macropetala* (Pl.6) a semi-vigorous climber reaching 4m tall with slender, slightly angled, stems. Flowers blue or violet-blue, nodding, 6–9cm across, solitary, axillary or terminal, with four spreading 'petals', and with numerous similar, though smaller petal-like structures (staminodes) which grade gradually into the whitish stamens. [May–June, H, PA, W & N China & Siberia] ◐

A very beautiful and free-flowering species which has been cultivated in Europe for more than two hundred years. An excellent plant for a wall or fence, or for tumbling down a bank or retaining wall.

*__'Maidwell Hall'__ has flowers of pure blue.

'Markham's Pink' has rosy-mauve flowers flushed with purple at the base of the 'petals'.

White-flowered forms exist in cultivation, however, these lack the beauty of the others and are scarcely worth growing except perhaps out of curiosity.

CLEMATIS ARMANDII AGGREGATE

Vigorous or semi-vigorous evergreen species usually with ternate leaves, though occasionally pinnate. The leaflets are untoothed. Flowers borne in large lateral clusters, each with between four and seven 'petals' spreading widely apart.

***Clematis armandii** (Pl.5), the finest species in the group, is a vigorous plant reaching 6–10m in mature plants. The leaves are deep glossy green, each with three large oblong or lanceolate leaflets, 7–14cm long, and three-veined. The flowers are borne in rather dense clusters, white or cream sometimes flushed with pale rose-pink, each 5–6cm across with four to seven 'petals'. [Apr–May, HH, PA, W & Central China]

Undoubtedly the best of all the evergreen clematis, a species that needs plenty of room in which to develop. Plants make a heavy tangled mass after a few years unless the shoots are trained carefully each season. Foliage and flowers will be damaged by winter and early spring winds unless plants are given a well sheltered warm wall. Gardening authorities disagree over the pruning of this species and its allies. Some stress the need to prune with care shortly after flowering, but never too severely. However, we have seen plants cut hard back to old wood which have sprouted away quite unaffected and occasionally this may be the remedy for old tangled, heavy, specimens.

Clematis armandii was introduced to cultivation by E.H. Wilson in 1900. Nursery grown plants, particularly those raised from seed, should be selected with care as there are some poor-coloured and small-flowered forms about. Preferably select container grown specimens in flower.

***'Apple Blossom'** is the best cultivar of all with its bronzy-green young leaves and white flowers softly flushed with pink.

'Snowdrift' (Pl.5) has good-sized flowers of pure white.

Clematis finetiana = *C. pavoliniana* reaches about 5m with dark green, leathery leaves which are mostly ternate, though some may be simple. The leaflets are oval, hairless, 5–10cm long and three-veined. The fragrant pure white flowers are suffused with green on the outside, and are borne in small

Clematis finetiana.

lateral clusters, each flower 3.5–4cm across and with four 'petals'. [June, HH, PA, W & Central China]

Rather like a small-flowered version of *C. armandii*, pretty in bloom but inferior as a garden plant. It is suitable for a warm niche in the milder parts of the country.

***Clematis × jeuneana** is said to be a garden hybrid between *C. armandii* and *C. finetiana*, though whatever its origin it is a very fine plant. Plants reach 5m in height bearing leaves rather like *C. armandii*. The silvery-white flowers are flushed with pink on the undersurface, each 2–2.5cm across, with five to six spreading 'petals'. [May–June, HH]

A beautiful plant likened to a small flowered *C. armandii*, though despite this equally worth cultivating.

Clematis meyeriana is a vigorous species reaching 7m tall in some specimens, with purplish-brown wiry hairless stems. The leathery leaves are ternate. Its white flowers are borne in large, loose, drooping clusters, each flower 2.2–2.6cm across with four 'petals' notched at the tips. [Feb–Mar, T, PA, S, & SE China, S Japan & the Philippines]

A beautiful species which is all too rarely seen in cultivation. Its tender nature, combined with a very early-flowering habit, mark it out as a plant for only the mildest districts. *Clematis meyeriana* is most frequently grown as a greenhouse or conservatory plant where its flowers can be more readily appreciated.

Clematis quinquefoliolata is closely related to the previous species and equally rare in cultivation. Plants reach 4–5m tall and have ribbed downy stems. The leaves are pinnate, the leaflets 5–10cm long, hairless except along the midrib above. The white flowers are borne in small lateral clusters, each 3.8–5cm across with four to six narrow 'petals'. [Aug–Sept, HH, PS, Central & W China]

A handsome late-flowering member of the *C. armandii* group which well deserves to be more widely known. The fruits are very striking with their yellowish-brown silky plumes.

CLEMATIS CIRRHOSA AGGREGATE

Two species only are contained here. Both are evergreens bearing small lateral clusters of dainty bell-shaped flowers each made up of four 'petals'. The most characteristic feature of the flowers are the small cup-shaped pair of fused bracts situated midway along the flower stalks.

Clematis cirrhosa, the Virgin's Bower, is a slender-stemmed climber reaching 3m. The attractive green leaves are glossy beneath, simple, oval or heart-shaped, occasionally three-lobed, 2–2.5cm long. Flowers are delicate, drooping, rather wide bells, dull white or creamish, often spotted with reddish-purple inside, 4–7cm across and faintly scented. [Dec–Mar, HH, PS, Mediterranean Europe, Asia Minor & Cyprus]

An attractive winter-flowering species, delicate and pretty in close up but not showy. The flowers are succeeded by silky fruit heads and in the autumn the foliage takes on bronze or purplish hues which last through the winter. Plants do particularly well on a west-facing wall or a sheltered pillar though they are not reliably hardy and may prove shy at flowering, at least when young.

*var. **balearica** = *C. balearica, C. calycina* (Pl.5), the Fern-leaved Clematis, is a taller plant reaching as much as 5m tall. The leaves are more finely divided, rather ferny-looking, green in summer but strikingly bronzy-purple during the autumn and winter. [Nov–Feb, HH, PS, Balearic Islands & Corsica]

A more free-flowering plant than the type and rather hardier. A fine conservatory wall plant for its winter-flowering habit.

Clematis napaulensis = *C. forrestii* (Pl.6) is a vigorous semi-evergreen species reaching 10m with greyish young shoots. Leaves ternate or digitate with three to five leaflets, each 4–9cm long, three-lobed, toothed or untoothed. Flowers are narrow drooping silky bells, 1.2–2.4cm long, creamy-yellow with purple stamens. [Oct–Feb, HH, PS, Himalaya & SW China]

A species rarely seen in cultivation and then only in the mildest districts. It is, however, a good plant for a cool greenhouse or conservatory where its charming winter flowers can be more closely appreciated.

Clematis afoliata = *C. aphylla* is an extraordinary species which stands alone but is best described here. Plants form shrubs up to 1.5m high, sometimes more, with numerous interlacing dark-green rush-like stems. The leaves are absent but are represented by green stalk-like tendrils 2–10cm long. Flowers are greenish-white, fragrant, 2–2.5cm across, in small clusters, the male and female flowers quite distinct and borne on separate plants; 'petals' four to six, spreading. [Mar–Apr, HH, PA, New Zealand]

An unusual species worth growing as a talking point or a botanical curiosity. Plants are rather sprawling and should be tied into the wall or allowed to clamber over a neighbouring shrub. Plants require a sheltered south-facing wall, or in the less mild districts the comfort of a conservatory.

GROUP B(I)

Herbaceous climbing species in which the stems die back partly or wholly to a woody base during the autumn and winter. Pruning should consist of cutting out all dead or weak growth in the early spring — February until early March. The larger-flowered, more vigorous cultivars of *C. viticella* can be treated as under Group B(II) pruning hard back to within 30cm in early spring.

Clematis viticella (Pl.7) is a variable slender semi-woody deciduous climber 2–4m tall. Leaves ternate, the leaflets oval to lanceolate, 2–7cm long, often two- to three-lobed but untoothed. Flowers blue, purple or rose-pink, fragrant, 3.5–4cm across, nodding on long slender stalks; 'petals' four, spoon-shaped and spreading with the margins rolled backwards. [July–Sept, H, PS, S Europe]

This attractive species has been cultivated since the sixteenth century and is certainly one of the finest and most floriferous species for the average garden. A large number of good cultivars have been produced over the years ranging from small- to large-flowered ones. In some the elegance of the species is sacrificed for the larger more colourful blooms.

*'**Abundance**' grows to 5m tall with flowers of delicate lilac-purple with deeper veins.

'**Alba Luxurians**' has white flowers suffused with pale mauve.

'**Ascotiensis**' is a very floriferous cultivar with azure-blue flowers.

*'**Ernest Markham**' grows to 2.5m tall with large velvety petunia-red flowers of great substance. [June–Sept]

'**Etoile Violette**' grows to 5m tall; flowers deep violet-purple, each with four to six 'petals' and a central boss of creamy stamens. [June–Aug]

Clematis afoliata.

***'Kermesina'** grows to 5m tall; flowers wine-crimson. [July–Sept] A fine cultivar for sunny or semi-shaded positions and a prolific flowerer. It is probably the same cultivar as *C. viticella* 'Rubra'.

'Lady Betty Balfour' grows to 5m tall; flowers large rich velvety violet-blue with yellow stamens, each with six 'petals'. [Aug–Oct] A plant for a sunny position.

'Little Nell' has small pale mauve flowers.

'Minuet' has flowers larger than the type and erect, white banded with pale purple.

'Plena' has flowers larger than the type, rosy-purple, double.

'Royal Velours' has deep velvety purple flowers.

'Ville de Lyon' grows to 3m tall; flowers bright carmine-red, deeper at the margins with a central boss of yellow stamens. [June–Sept] Sun or partial shade.

Clematis campaniflora (Pl.5) is closely related to the previous species but often more vigorous, reaching 6m in height with slender stems and pinnate leaves. Flowers small, 2–3cm across, whitish tinted with blue and rather cupped. [July–Sept, H, PS, Portugal & S Spain] ◐

A dainty species which blooms in profusion and should certainly be more widely grown.

CLEMATIS TEXENSIS AGGREGATE

A group of small-flowered herbaceous or deciduous semi-herbaceous species with pinnate leaves. The attractive pendulous flowers are borne on slender stems being generally bell-shaped with four 'petals'. Except for *C. fusca* all the species mentioned here are from North America.

***Clematis texensis** = *C. coccinea* (Pl.5) is a partly herbaceous climber reaching 2–3m in height. Leaves pinnate with four to eight leaflets, often terminating in a sort of tendril, bluish-green. Flowers red, scarlet or purple, 2.3–2.6cm long, solitary, the 'petals' slightly recurved at the tip. [July–Sept, HH, PS, S USA (Texas)] ☼

A fine species well worth cultivating on a sunny sheltered wall. It is slightly un-

Clematis texensis.

predictable in cultivation, only partly dying down in mild winters but right to ground level during more severe weather. Some form of winter protection is generally advisable. It is tolerant of rather drier soils than most clematis but is seen at its best planted amongst wall shrubs and other climbers. The deep red-flowered forms are the finest — a unique colour amongst clematis. Plants tend to be rather difficult to propagate from cuttings.

Clematis texensis has been crossed in the past with *C. patens* and various large-flowered cultivars, to produce a series of beautiful and distinct varieties. These, like *C. texensis* itself require pruning hard back in February or early March as they flower on the current season's growth.

'Countess of Onslow' reaches 3m tall with medium-sized flowers which are pink with a deeper bar of colour down the centre of each 'petal'. Rare in cultivation. [July – Sept]

***'Duchess of Albany'** is a fine plant which reaches 3 – 4m tall with erect bell-shaped deep pink flowers, each 'petal' shading to pale lilac-pink on the margins. [July – Sept] Plants generally die back to ground level each winter.

'Etoile Rose' has cherry-purple flowers, the 'petals' edged in silvery-pink. Plants die back to ground level during the winter. [mid-June – Sept]

***'Gravetye Beauty'** has crimson flowers which are at first narrowly bell-shaped but the four to six 'petals' gradually spread outwards. [July – Sept]

'Sir Trevor Lawrence' is a difficult plant to obtain but a very attractive one with cherry-red flowers, each with four to six 'petals'.

◐ **Clematis pitcheri** = *C. cordata* is the most striking of this group, a partly herbaceous climber reaching up to 4m tall. Leaves pinnate, sometimes ternate with three to seven leaflets, the terminal leaflet sometimes replaced by a tendril.

Flowers purplish-blue, greenish-yellow inside, bell-shaped, 2–3cm long, solitary. [May–Sept, H, PS, Central USA]

A curious and rather beautiful plant with flowers borne over a long season, though never in great profusion. Unlike its allies, *C. pitcheri* dies back only a little during the winter and as a result requires rather lighter pruning.

Clematis viorna (Pl.7) is an herbaceous climber 2–3m tall. Leaves pinnate, with five variously shaped leaflets, 2–5cm long, the lower heart-shaped and often three-lobed, the upper oval. Flowers dull reddish-purple, greenish-yellow or whitish inside, 2.5–3cm long, solitary nodding bells, the 'petals' slightly recurved at the tip. [June–Aug, H, PS, E USA]

Not one of the most attractive of the *C. texensis* association, although the flowers have a certain curiosity value. Plants die right down to a resistant woody base during the winter.

Clematis crispa is a semi-woody climber reaching 2m tall, sometimes more. Leaves ternate or pinnate with three to seven leaflets. Flowers pale bluish-purple, bell-shaped, 3–5cm long, solitary, nodding, the 'petals' strongly recurved near the tip, each 'petal' with a whitish wavy edge. [June–Aug, HH, PS, SE USA]

An attractive but rather delicate species rarely seen in cultivation in Britain. *C. crispa* has been crossed with *C. texensis*.

Clematis fusca is a semi-herbaceous climber to 3m high, though often less; stems angled, downy when young. Leaves pinnate with five to seven oval or heart-shaped leaflets. Flowers reddish-brown, violet inside, bell-shaped, 1.8–2.3cm long, solitary. [June–July, H, PS, NE Asia]

This interesting species is an Asian cousin of *C. viorna*. It is easy to cultivate, although it cannot be rated amongst the most attractive species, however, it has a place in the specialist garden or in the collections of botanic gardens.

GROUP B(II)

Perennial climbers of moderate or vigorous habit flowering on the current season's growth. Plants should be pruned hard back in February or March to about 1m. Alternatively, lighter pruning will promote earlier flowering, however, one or two shoots should be pruned hard back to promote some young growth from the base of the plant.

***Clematis × jackmanii**, *C. lanuginosa* × *C. viticella* (Pl.6), is one of the most superb and best known of all clematis and without doubt the most important hybrid. Plants are of moderate vigour reaching 3m or sometimes 4m tall. The leaves are rather pale green, pinnate, ternate or sometimes simple. Flowers large, rich velvety violet-purple, 10–13cm across, borne mostly in threes and each with four to five rather flat 'petals'. [June–Oct, H, PS]

A glorious and much-loved plant widely grown and, together with *C. montana*, probably the most commonly cultivated clematis. This hybrid was raised in 1860 by the famous nursery firm of Messrs Jackman of Woking and led the way to a vast race of large-flowered hybrid cultivars, many with good dark rich colours. However, this race is of complex origin, involving the European *C. viticella* as well as large-flowered Asian species such as *C. lanuginosa* and *C. patens*. Some of the best 'jackmanii' types are listed below. Although the main flowering season is in midsummer further flowers are often produced right through until the autumn.

***'Comtesse de Bouchard'** reaches 3.5m; flowers soft rose-pink or cyclamen-pink, with yellow stamens, borne freely, each 10–14cm across and with five to seven 'petals'. [June–Aug]
'Gipsy Queen' is a vigorous cultivar with large rich velvety violet-purple flowers with broad rounded 'petals'. [July–Sept]
'Hagley Hybrid' grows to 2.5m tall; flowers in profusion, shell pink with five to six pointed 'petals' and purplish anthers. [June–Sept]
***'Superba'** is a vigorous plant often reaching 5–6m; flowers large deep rich violet-purple, each with five to six broad 'petals'. Not for full shade. A superb plant, probably the same as 'Madame Grange'.
'Madame Edouard André' is less vigorous than most reaching 2.5m in good specimens; flowers rich crimson with yellow stamens, 10–13cm across, each with six 'petals'. [Late May–July and Sept]
***'Perle d'Azur'** reaches 4m tall; flowers large pale blue, 13–15cm across, each with four to six 'petals'. A fine free-flowering plant.

CLEMATIS VITALBA AGGREGATE

Vigorous or very vigorous deciduous species with rather coarse ternate or pinnate leaves and large clusters of generally rather small white, cream or greenish-white flowers with narrow spreading 'petals'. Plants benefit from a hard annual prune and will become bulky and difficult to handle if left unpruned.

Clematis vitalba, the Traveller's Joy or Old Man's Beard of our hedgerows, is the best known species of this association, though certainly not the most attractive. Plants are very vigorous reaching 15m high or more and forming a coarse entanglement, the stems becoming thick and bare below if left unpruned. Leaves pinnate, leaflets usually toothed. Flowers greenish-white, slightly scented of almonds, 1.8–2.2cm across, borne in large clusters; 'petals' four, downy on both sides. [July–Oct, H, PS, most of Europe, except the north, & Asia Minor]

A rapid grower common in the woods and hedgerows of the south of England, where the silky clusters of fruits are often a feature during the autumn and winter. In gardens it is invasive and suitable only for the wilder parts, on large old walls, or scrambling over fences or tree stumps. However, it is scarcely as good a plant as its southern European cousin *C. flammula*. Like that species it should not be planted where it might invade and spoil more precious and less robust climbers or where its roots will penetrate drains or foundations.

In his famous Herbal of 1597, Gerard writes

> " . . . esteemed for pleasure by reason of the goodly shadow and the pleasant scent or savour of its flowers. And because of its decking and adorning waies and hedges where people travel, thereupon have I named it Traveller's Joy"

Clematis virginiana is similar to *C. vitalba* but inferior and seldom seen outside botanic gardens. It comes from North America.

***Clematis flammula**, the Fragrant Clematis, is a vigorous climber 4–5m tall, sometimes more, forming a bushy tangle, bare and woody below if unpruned. Leaves bright dark green, pinnate, leaflets very variable, usually untoothed though often two- or three-lobed. Flowers pure white, beautifully fragrant, produced in abundance in large clusters, 1.8–2.5cm across, the 'petals' hairless inside. [July–Oct, H, PS, S Europe & W Asia]

This species has been cultivated in Britain since the sixteenth century, loved for its vigour and floriferousness as much as for its delightful fragrance. It is especially good for covering low walls and fences, although succeeding best in a warm sheltered site. Plants rarely set fertile seed in this country, but are more easily propagated from seed than from cuttings.

Clematis maximowicziana = *C. flammula* var. *robusta* is more robust than *C. flammula*, a vigorous plant reaching 10m high and forming a thick entanglement. Leaves dark green, ternate or pinnate, untoothed. Flowers white, hawthorn-scented, 2.2–2.8cm across with four 'petals'. [Sept–Oct, H, PS, N China, Japan & Korea]

A magnificent climber for a large sunny south wall, a species widely planted in the United States. It is rather rare in this country and Europe, being generally regarded as a shy flowerer; however, it deserves to be tried more widely in the milder counties.

Clematis grata var. **grandidentata** is a vigorous climber to 10m tall. Leaves greyish, hairy, ternate or pinnate; leaflets three to five, coarsely toothed. Flowers white, 2–2.3cm across, in loose axillary or terminal clusters; 'petals' four to five, downy on the outside. [May–June, H, PS, W China]

A hardy species little seen in gardens and rather similar to *C. vitalba*. Like most of its allies, it is not suitable for small gardens. The typical form of the species which comes from the Himalaya is not in cultivation.

Clematis chinensis is another vigorous climber reaching 8m; stems ribbed. Leaves pinnate; leaflets five, untoothed, practically hairless. Flowers small white, fragrant, 1.2–2cm across, in dense lateral clusters; 'petals' four. [Sept–Oct, H, PS, W & Central China]

Although quite hardy this species, like the one preceding, produces its flowers late in the season and these may be ruined by an early frost. Probably best in the milder counties.

Clematis fargesii var. **souliei** is a strong growing climber reaching 7m tall; shoots ribbed, purplish and downy when young. Leaves dull green, bipinnate with five basic divisions; leaflets coarsely toothed and sometimes three-lobed. Flowers satiny-white tinged with yellow on the outside, 5–6cm across, solitary or several together; 'petals' usually six, relatively broad. [June–Sept, H, PS, W China]

Attractive flowers are produced over a long season, though never in great profusion.

Clematis phlebantha (Pl.7) is a trailing shrub with ribbed stems reaching 2m in length; the young stems are white with wool, although this eventually disappears, and the older stems generally shed their bark after a year or two. Leaves pinnate, 5–10cm long, with five to nine, generally three-lobed, leaflets, deep green and silky above, white-woolly beneath. Flowers usually solitary at the leaf axils towards the shoot tips, 2.5–4.5cm across; 'petals' five to seven, white with reddish veins; anthers yellow. [June–July, HH, PN, C W Nepal]

An interesting species only discovered in 1952 by the Polunin, Sykes and Williams expedition to Nepal. It is a fine plant with its silvery foliage and relatively large flowers. The hardiness of this plant is still questionable, although it is hoped that more people will try growing this unusual Clematis.

Clematis uncinata is an evergreen or semi-evergreen species climbing to a height of some 5m with slender hairless stems. Leaves biternate or bipinnate, green above but bluish-green beneath. Flowers creamy-white, fragrant, 2.5 – 3.5cm across, borne in large lateral or terminal clusters; 'petals' four, rather narrow. [June – Aug, HH, PS, China, including Hong Kong]

A vigorous species for a warm sheltered wall, which may be hardier than is generally supposed. It was first introduced into cultivation in 1901 by E.H. Wilson but is rarely seen in cultivation today.

Clematis paniculata = *C. indivisa* is a vigorous evergreen shrub or climber reaching as much as 10m high. Leaves glossy green, ternate; leaflets oval or slightly heart-shaped, 3.5 – 7cm long, untoothed though sometimes lobed. Flowers white with yellow anthers, unisexual, 3.5 – 7cm across, smaller on female plants, borne in long loose clusters on lateral shoots; 'petals' six to eight. [May – June, T, PS, New Zealand]

Clematis paniculata of gardens is generally the hardy Japanese *C. maximowicziana*. This New Zealand species is unusual in having male and female flowers on separate plants. The flowers are attractive, especially the larger ones of the male plants, and this species is certainly worth trying against a sheltered sunny wall in the warmer counties of the south and west, if it can be obtained.

'Lobata' is a beautiful cultivar with more deeply lobed leaves and more readily available than the type.

CLEMATIS ORIENTALIS AGGREGATE

Moderately vigorous deciduous climbers with slender stems and pinnate or ternate leaves, green or bluish-green. Flowers solitary or in lateral clusters, sometimes terminal, yellow or greenish-yellow, each with four often rather fleshy 'petals'; stamens with hairy stalks or filaments. Fruits showy.

They are strong growers with smallish flowers produced during the summer and autumn, often in large quantities. They are all easily raised from seed and young plants quickly flower.

Clematis orientalis is a moderately vigorous climber 5 – 6m high with slender greyish or whitish-green young stems sometimes tinged with purplish-red. Leaves bluish-green or greyish-green, thick and fleshy, leaflets unlobed or with a few blunt uneven lobes but rarely toothed. Flowers small, in large axillary or terminal branched clusters, yellowish-green, often tinged or spotted with purplish-red on the outside, the 'petals' 10 – 22mm long, downy on both surfaces, recurved in full flower revealing the maroon filaments of the stamens. [July – Oct, H, PS, W Asia, S USSR, Iran, Afghanistan & Pakistan]

This species is seldom seen in cultivation, indeed it is probably the least attractive and desirable of all the species in this association. However, the name *C. orientalis* should not be dismissed in catalogues for quite erroneously several of the other species are to be found under it. It is unfortunate that in the past gardeners and botanists have confused this complex of species and included everything under *C. orientalis* as subspecies, varieties or forms of different kinds. The truth is that most are quite distinct as species in their own right and several, *C. tangutica*, *C. vernayi*, and *C. serratifolia* in particular make excellent and beautiful garden plants. As a consequence of this muddle some of these plants need to be known under new names but it will take some time before the horticultural trade can be expected to use them in earnest. In general *C. tangutica* and

C. serratifolia are usually found under their correct names in catalogues and botanic gardens, although the former is sometimes to be found as *C. orientalis* var. *tangutica. Clematis orientalis* of catalogues and also regretfully of some botanic gardens usually proves to be *C. glauca* or *C. graveolens*, whilst *C. orientalis* 'Orange Peel' is the Himalayan *C. vernayi*. To confuse matters even more, many of the species have been crossed and recrossed to produce a complex selection of fine hybrid cultivars, though only a few have been given names to date.

***Clematis tangutica** = *C. orientalis* var. *tangutica* (Pl.7) is a vigorous quick growing climber reaching 4–5m high, though often less. The green leaves are pinnate, the leaflets sharply toothed except in the upper part. Flowers lemon-yellow, pendent bells or lanterns, 2.5–4.5cm long, borne on long slender stalks. The 'petals' are scarcely spreading, shiny and hairless inside but slightly downy outside generally. [Aug–Oct, H, PS, W China (W & N Tibet & Kansu, S Mongolia)]

The finest of all the yellow-flowered species, a lovely sight with its numerous dainty lanterns borne over a long season, followed by striking silky seed heads borne well into the winter. It will succeed equally well on a sunless or a sunny wall or fence providing it is fairly well sheltered. Some forms in cultivation are very much finer than others and are well worth seeking out.

subsp. **obtusiuscula** = *C. tangutica* var. *obtusiuscula* has deeper yellow flowers tinged on the outside with purplish-brown and the 'petals' are spreading and less pointed than the type. [SW China (W Szechwan)] An uncommon plant in cultivation, not unlike a green-leaved *C. vernayi*.

Clematis serratifolia is a moderately vigorous climber to 4m high though often less. Leaves bright green, ternate or pinnate with three to five sharply toothed leaflets. Flowers pale yellow with brownish-purple filaments, lemon-scented, 4–5.2cm across; 'petals' wide-spreading, giving the flowers a starry appearance. [Aug–Sept, H, PS, NE China & Korea]

A free-flowering species that produces a succession of blooms well into the autumn, followed by attractive fruits. It is certainly one of the best of the yellow species, like *C. tangutica* and *C. vernayi*.

Clematis graveolens = *C. parvifolia, C. orientalis* subsp. *graveolens*, reaches about 3m tall. The bluish-green leaves are bipinnate and rather ferny in appearance, with a few to numerous elliptic or lanceolate leaflets. Flowers yellow with purplish filaments, 2–3.5cm across; 'petals' oval, notched at the apex, widely spreading, densely downy on the inner surface. [Aug–Sept, HH, PS, W Pakistan & W Himalaya]

Allied to *C. orientalis*, and often sold under that name, but with finer foliage and larger flowers with broad 'petals' which are distinctly notched at the apex. *C. graveolens* is well worth trying on a sheltered wall if authentically named plants can be obtained. One of the most attractive members of this association, it has been used in Holland in experiments to try to produce larger-flowered clones.

Clematis vernayi is a rather vigorous species reaching 3–4m in height, the young stems pale greenish-white, sometimes flushed with purple. Leaves bluish-green, rather fleshy, pinnate or more or less bipinnate. Flowers yellow or greenish-yellow, flushed or spotted with bronze or sometimes purple, nodding open bells 1.5–3.5cm across, solitary or two to three together, the 'petals' usually half-spreading, thick and fleshy, velvety-downy inside but quite hairless outside. [Sept–Oct, H, PS, N Nepal & Tibet]

A fine and attractive floriferous species normally sold as *C. orientalis*. The thick fleshy 'petals' have been likened to orange or lemon peel.

*'**Orange Peel**' is the finest cultivar with good-sized open lantern flowers of great substance with their characteristic thick waxy petals. *Clematis orientalis* L & S 13342 is the same or very similar and well worth acquiring. The original collection was made in Tibet by Ludlow & Sherriff, *C. vernayi* being particularly common in the mountains around Lhasa.

'Orange Peel' has been crossed with *Clematis tangutica*, purposefully or inadvertantly and the resultant hybrids are the very finest of all the yellow-flowered clematis of the *C. orientalis*, persuasion:

'Bill MacKenzie' can be likened to a yellower 'Orange Peel' but with rather larger flowers and greener leaves.

*'**Corry**' is a superb cultivar raised in Holland in recent years and just available on the open market. The flowers are large, 3.5–6cm across, clear yellow with thick widely spreading petals. The parents are probably *C. tangutica* subsp. *obtusiuscula* and *C. vernayi*.

Other cultivars are in circulation, these being mainly hybrids between *C. tangutica, C. vernayi* or *C. serratifolia* or *C. graveolens* and some of these are very fine, however, most are unnamed and they should be selected with care, preferably choosing a pot-grown specimen in flower. These hybrid cultivars, like the *C. orientalis* complex itself, have been amazingly muddled and it will take a year or so before they are finally sorted out. The gardener can be forgiven for finding this all a trifle perplexing!

Clematis akebioides = *C. glauca* var. *akebioides, C. orientalis* var. *akebioides*, is a vigorous climber to 5m tall, though often less. Leaves bluish-green, pinnate; leaflets five to seven, oval to oblong with shallow, rounded teeth. Flowers yellow or greenish-yellow, tinged on the outside with green, bronze or purple, pendent bells, 1.5–2.5cm long, several borne at each node on long slender stalks; 'petals' fleshy, hairless except on the margins. [Aug–Oct, H, PS, SW China (Szechwan, N Kansu & N Yunnan)]

An attractive species similar in appearance to *C. tangutica* but with smoother more fleshy flowers and bluish-green foliage. It is a robust grower, flowering profusely on a sheltered wall or pillar, though unfortunately it is now rather rare in cultivation.

Clematis glauca is a rather weak-stemmed climber to 3m with greenish stems. Leaves bluish-green, pinnate. Flowers yellowish or greenish-yellow, 2.5–4cm across, solitary, or two or three together, the four 'petals' widely spreading, rather narrow and thin in texture, downy inside. [Aug–Oct, H, PS, E USSR & NW China]

Another rather rare species in cultivation though inferior as a garden plant and really not deserving attention save in the confines of a specialist collection or botanic garden. There is also a subspecies, *intricata* with more finely cut, rather ferny foliage and smaller flowers which are often flushed with red or purple on the outside. It is a native of N China and S Mongolia.

The remaining species in this group represent a miscellany which, although not particularly closely related, all require hard pruning early in the year, like the preceding species and cultivars.

Clematis aethusifolia is a graceful small deciduous climber to 2m tall, with slender downy young stems. Leaves rather pale green, pinnate with three to seven leaflets, each deeply lobed and toothed. Flowers pale whitish-yellow, narrow bells

1.3–2cm long, nodding in leafy clusters; 'petals' narrow and recurved at the tip. [July–Sept, H, PS, N China & Manchuria]

A delicate and rather lovely species with elegant foliage, which forms a dense tangle if not regularly pruned. Although the flowers are not spectacular they are borne in such a profusion as to make an attractive show. This species is not in general cultivation but it is a good and rather unusual plant for the smaller garden.

***Clematis rehderiana** = *C. nutans* var. *thyrsoidea* (Pl.7) is closely related to the previous species, a very much more vigorous plant reaching as much as 8m tall. Leaves hairy, pinnate, rather bright green; leaflets usually seven to nine, broadly heart-shaped, 4–8cm long, coarsely toothed. Flowers pale primrose-yellow, cowslip-scented, nodding bells 1.2–1.8cm long, borne in profusion in large erect clusters; 'petals' four or five, ribbed and downy with recurved tips. [Aug–Oct, H, PS, W China]

This delightful species has been much confused in gardens with the Himalayan *C. nutans* which does not appear to be in cultivation, although the name might be found in some catalogues. Plants are readily raised from cuttings.

Clematis veitchiana which also comes from W China is very similar but with bipinnate leaves, each with twenty or more smaller leaflets and with smaller yellowish-white flowers. It is not as good a plant as *C. rehderiana* in gardens, but it may also be found erroneously under the name *Clematis nutans*.

Clematis lasiandra is an uncommon species in gardens, a deciduous climber to 5m high with slender stems which are rather sticky when young. Leaves dark green, pale beneath, ternate or biternate. Flowers usually dull purple, sometimes white, bell-shaped, 1.1–1.3cm long, often in threes at each node, the 'petals' recurved at the tip. [Sept–Oct, H, PS, China & Japan]

Clematis lasiandra has been cultivated in Britain since 1900. Although it has never been popular the small flowers are quite attractive at close quarters.

Clematis connata is a vigorous deciduous species to 7m with slightly ribbed stems. The leaves are bright green, ternate or pinnate; leaflets three to five, coarsely toothed and sometimes lobed. The leaf stalks or petioles are flattened at the base and surround the stem forming characteristic flattish disks. Flowers soft yellow, slightly fragrant, bell-shaped, 1.8–2.5cm long, borne in large lateral clusters; 'petals' four, slightly ribbed and recurved at the tip. [Sept–Oct, H, PS, Himalaya & SW China]

A variable plant, some forms in cultivation being very much more downy than others. It is similar to *C. rehderiana* but a coarser plant and scarcely as good a garden plant.

Finally in this group mention must be made of two fine hybrids:

***Clematis × durandii**, *C. integrifolia* × *C.* ×*jackmanii*, is a rather vigorous semi-climber reaching 3m tall, often with stout stems and simple shiny green, oval leaves. Flowers large, dark violet-blue, 7.5–11cm across, with a central boss of yellow stamens; 'petals' four, widely spreading, with wavy margins. [June–Sept, H, PS]

A super hybrid worthy of a place in any garden. It was first raised in France about 1870. Strangely enough it is not seen as much as it deserves. The plant is not a climber in the true sense and the stems need to be tied in carefully to maintain some order to the growths. Plants can be prone to mildew like some of the other large-flowered cultivars and they should be sprayed regularly.

'Pallida' has paler, violet-pink flowers. A highly desirable plant which is rarely available in the gardening trade.

***Clematis × jouiniana,** *C. heracleifolia* var. *davidiana* × *C. vitalba*, is another vigorous hybrid, again only a semi-climber and rather shrubby, but reaching up to 3.5m high eventually. Leaves ternate or pinnate. Flowers yellowish-white at first, later white flushed with lilac on the outside, 2.5–3cm across, produced in profusion in flat-topped clusters; 'petals' four, spreading to slightly recurved. [Aug–Oct, H, PS]

One of the very finest of the small-flowered garden hybrids which is quick-growing and free-flowering, although not a plant for the small garden. It is ideal for covering low walls and fences or tree stumps. The base of the plant is woody to about 1m and from this arise annual stems which need to be tied in against walls or fences. The flowers are not scented but are none-the-less attractive to butterflies. In gardens it is often found under the name *C. grata* but this is quite wrong.

'Côte d'Azur' is a fine cultivar with azure-blue flowers.

'Mrs Robert Brydon' is a form with pale lavender flowers.

'Praecox' has soft lavender-blue flowers that first appear in July.

GROUP C

This group consists of most of the large-flowered species and cultivars with the exception of those belonging to *C.* ×*jackmanii* and *C. viticella*. Indeed they mostly belong to, or are derived from, only two species, *C. lanuginosa* and *C. patens*. Usually no pruning is required, except to remove dead or unwanted or weak growth in the late winter or early spring. However, many gardeners trim back shoots slightly to the first strong pair of buds in the spring, or alternatively the moment flowering ceases. Summer growths need to be spaced and trained carefully as they elongate so as to gain the best effect when flowering commences, and of course this helps to prevent nasty entanglements. Most of the cultivars in this group flower from mid-summer onwards, often with a secondary, smaller flush of blooms in late summer or early autumn. If desired, they may be pruned as in Group B(II) thereby sacrificing the first flush of flowers for a larger late display.

Clematis florida is a deciduous or semi-evergreen climber to 3–4m high with wiry stems and glossy, dark green leaves. The white or cream-coloured flowers have a greenish band down the back of each petal and a large 'eye' of purple-black stamens, each flower some 6–9cm across and borne singly on long stalks with four- to six-pointed 'petals'. [June–July, H, PN, China (Hupeh)]

Cultivars of this lovely species have been grown in Japanese gardens for several centuries and some were introduced to Europe in the latter half of the eighteenth century. The wild form of the species is probably not in cultivation. Some of the cultivars often placed under this species are of complex origin, probably involving both *C. lanuginosa* and *C. patens* in past hybridisations. However, whatever their origins they are best treated as *C. florida*. Most cannot be considered vigorous growers and require more care than most clematis. The main growths are best when spaced apart in the spring, one or two being looped around the lower part of the plant which often becomes rather bare with age.

In the double-flowered forms some, or indeed all, of the stamens are transformed into short narrow petals giving the centre of the flower an 'anemone' or 'rosette' appearance.

'Belle of Woking' reaches 3m tall with double mauve flowers. [May–June]

***'Duchess of Edinburgh'** also reaches about 3m tall when mature; flowers pure white with green shading, double, somewhat scented. [May–June]

'Plena' = 'Alba Plena' has greenish-white flowers, fully double. A very similar plant to 'Duchess of Edinburgh'.

***'Sieboldii'** = *C. florida* var. *bicolor* (Pl.6) is less vigorous than the others, up to 2.5m in good specimens; flowers very beautiful, white with a purple anemone-centre. [June–July] This glorious cultivar deserves to be tried in every garden. However, be warned, it is neither reliable nor very vigorous despite the fact that it has been cultivated in Britain for well over a century and a half. The flowers are long-lasting and generally about 8cm across.

'Vyvyan Pennell' is a rather more vigorous cultivar than most, perhaps reaching 3.5m in height; flowers deep violet-blue, carmine in the centre, double. [May–July] A second crop of single flowers is usually produced in the autumn. This plant is sometimes placed under *C. patens*.

Clematis lanuginosa = *C. standishii* is a deciduous climber to 3m tall. Leaves simple or trifoliate; leaflets heart-shaped. The large flowers are white to pale lilac in the wild species, 10–15cm across, borne at the shoot tips; 'petals' six to eight, spreading and overlapping. [June–Oct, H, PN or PS, China]

C. lanuginosa itself is rare in cultivation, but this species is one of the parents of many of the large-flowered garden hybrids and is therefore very important in this respect. However, as with the other species involved, *C. florida, C. patens* and *C. viticella* in the main, the origins of many of these cultivars is complex and grouping them is mainly a convenient way of prescribing the correct cultural treatment.

Cultivars of this association can be left unpruned as for *C. florida* and *C. patens*, or alternatively, they may be treated as for *C. ×jackmanii* and *C. viticella*.

'Beauty of Worcester' grows to 2.5m tall; flowers deep violet-blue with a central boss of creamy-white stamens, double on old wood but young shoots usually with single, six-'petalled' flowers. [May–July] A fine cultivar but not vigorous.

'Fairy Queen' has very large flesh pink single flowers, each 'petal' with a brighter pink central band. [May–June]

'Henryi' = 'Bangholme Belle' is vigorous to 5m tall; flowers creamy-white, 15–18cm across, with six to eight long pointed 'petals'. The young foliage has an attractive bronzy hue. [June–July]

'King George V' is rather like 'Fairy Queen' but a deeper flesh pink. [July–Aug]

'Lady Northcliffe' grows to 2.5m tall; flowers deep lavender-blue with white stamens. [June–Oct] The flowers will bleach in strong sunlight.

'Lord Nevill' grows to 3.5m tall; flowers large, rich purple-red, 15–18cm across, each 'petal' with a deeper central bar, anthers purple. [June–Aug]

***'Marie Boisselot'** is a vigorous plant to 4.5m tall; flowers pinkish in bud but opening pure white with cream coloured stamens, 15–16cm across, 'petals' seven to ten, broad and overlapping. [June–Aug]

***'Mrs Cholmondeley'** is vigorous, to 4.5m tall; flowers large, wisteria-blue, freely borne, 17–20cm across, 'petals' usually six to seven. [May–June, Aug–Sept] This cultivar also bleaches badly in direct sunlight.

'W.E. Gladstone' is a vigorous and free-flowering variety to 4m tall; flowers very large, lavender with purple anthers. [June–Sept]

'William Kennett' is a vigorous plant 4–5m tall; flowers lavender-blue with a deeper centre and purple anthers, 'petals' usually eight with wavy edges. [June–Aug]

Clematis patens = *C. coerulea* is a deciduous climber with slender stems reaching 3–4m in height, though often less. Leaves ternate or pinnate. Flowers creamy-white to whitish-violet or violet-purple, 10–15cm across, produced on short shoots from the previous year's wood; six to eight pointed 'petals', spreading, but not overlapping. [June–Sept, H, PN, China & Japan]

This species is often regarded by botanists as a variety of *C. florida* but lacks the flower-stalk bracts of that species. Its contribution to the large-flowered garden cultivars has already been stressed. The form generally in cultivation has creamy-white flowers.

'Barbara Dibley' grows to 3.5m tall; flowers violet-blue with purple-magenta bars down each petal, 14–15cm across, 'petals' usually eight. The flowers bleach in strong sunlight. [May–June, Sept]

***'Barbara Jackman'** grows to 3.5m tall; flowers reddish-mauve or purplish with a plum-red bar down each of the eight 'petals' and cream stamens. Bleaches in strong sunlight. [June–July, Sept]

'C.W. Dowman' grows to 3.5m tall; flowers pale pink with a darker bar down the centre of each 'petal' contrasting with the cream coloured stamens, 'petals' usually eight. [June–Sept] A particularly good cultivar for a north-facing wall or fence.

'Daniel Deronda' has large double or single violet-blue flowers with creamy stamens. [June-Sept]

'Lady Londesborough' is a free-flowering cultivar with pale mauve flowers turning to silvery-grey with age and with purplish stamens. [May–June]

***'Lasurstern'** grows to 3.5m tall; flowers large, 15–18cm across, rich purplish-blue, fading to lavender-blue, stamens creamy-yellow, 'petals' seven to nine, with wavy margins. [May–July, Sept] A very beautiful cultivar and without doubt one of the very finest of the large-flowered hybrid clematis. The flowers fade in strong sunlight. The late crop of flowers are generally much smaller than the earlier ones.

'Marcelle Moser' is a weaker plant than the better known and much loved 'Nelly Moser'. The flowers are larger, 18–20cm across, rose-mauve with a carmine bar along each 'petal', stamens reddish-purple. [May–June]

***'Nelly Moser'** grows to 3.5m tall; flowers large, 16–18cm across, pale mauve-pink, each 'petal' with a central carmine-pink bar down the centre, anthers purplish. [May–June, Sept] This is so popular a plant that it scarcely needs a description but plants are often placed in an unsuitable position where strong sun makes the flowers fade almost to white. A shaded north-facing wall or fence is ideal or a position away from direct sunlight. 'Nelly Moser' is sometimes placed under *C. lanuginosa*.

***'The President'** is another popular clematis, fairly vigorous, to 3.5m tall; flowers rich deep violet-purple with a paler bar down each 'petal' and a silvery reverse. [June–July, Sept] A fine cultivar which is suitable in a sunny position as the flowers scarcely fade.

Honeysuckles

The Honeysuckles are amongst the best loved garden plants, grown as much for their beauty and elegance as for their delightful fragrance. Most people are familiar with the Common Honeysuckle or Woodbine, *Lonicera periclymenum*, common in our hedgerows and woodlands, a plant cultivated for many centuries, though few realise that the genus *Lonicera* contains over 200 species. The genus consists of shrubs or twining climbers and many of the latter make ideal plants for training on walls and pillars, for covering trellis work or pergolas and for masking old tree stumps. The leaves are always opposite and untoothed, and in some species the leaves unite together in pairs below the flowers to form a sort of 'cup'. The flowers occur in pairs or in small whorls and may be tubular or bell-shaped, the mouth of the flower with five equal lobes or with four lobes forming an upper lip whilst the remaining lobe forms a distinct lower lip as in the Common Honeysuckle. The small ovary is placed below the flower and develops eventually into a fleshy, often brightly-coloured berry.

Honeysuckles thrive in a moist loamy soil and benefit from mulches and feeds during the summer months. Preferably they should be planted with their roots and lower stems in cool shaded spots whilst the upper stems and flowers enjoy the sunshine — a west wall is ideal. They are readily increased by cuttings or seed. Cuttings can be taken in midsummer of semi-mature young shoots. Many older gardeners prefer to take cuttings of semi-mature shoots, about 7–10cm long with a heel, inserting these in the open garden in a shady position under a cloche or bell jar. The time to do this is July or August. Little pruning is necessary, other than to remove old or straggling shoots; indeed many species suffer badly if pruned too vigorously. New growths should be tied in, otherwise plants can become very untidy. Greenfly (aphids) can be a serious problem, particularly in the spring and early summer, and the annual crop of flowers can be easily ruined unless plants receive a precautionary insecticide at the first sign of an attack.

LONICERA (Caprifoliaceae)

Lonicera periclymenum, the Common Honeysuckle or Woodbine, is almost too well known to warrant description, however, it needs distinguishing from the other deciduous species. In the wild it is a twining and scrambling plant which may occasionally reach 7m in height. The oval or oblong leaves are generally pointed, green above but rather bluish-green beneath, the upper unstalked but not uniting into a cup below the flowers. The deliciously fragrant flowers generally open white but gradually turn yellowish, often with a reddish or pink flush. They are borne in a series of close whorls at the ends of shoots, each two-lipped, 36–50mm long with a slender downy tube. The berries are bright shiny red. [July–Aug, H, PN, Europe & N Africa]

This is certainly one of our most glorious native plants, prized as much for its beauty as for the powerful fragrance of its blooms. The scent is at its finest in the early morning or late evening. The species is at its best in a semi-shaded or shaded position, as much at home on a wall or fence as clambering over tree stumps or other shrubs. The wild form is not often cultivated but has largely been replaced by some fine forms and cultivars, some known for several centuries in English gardens.

*'**Belgica**' (Pl.8), the Early Dutch Honeysuckle, has a bushier habit than the wild type, with purplish stems. The flowers are purplish-red outside fading to yellowish-pink, pale yellow inside. [June–July]

A fine honeysuckle which has been in cultivation since the seventeenth century having originated probably in the Low Countries.

*'**Serotina**', variously known as the Flemish, the Late Dutch or Late Red Honeysuckle, a super plant with flowers which are dark purple on the outside, but paling with age, whilst being pinkish inside. [July–Oct]

A vigorous cultivar which gives very good value in the garden, the flowers often continuing until the first frosts of autumn. This cultivar has also been known under the name *L. periclymenum* var. *semperflorens*.

forma **quercina** is an interesting plant in which the leaves are lobed rather like those of the Common Oak. It was noticed in the wild in Britain during the seventeenth century, but really has more curiosity value than garden merit.

***Lonicera caprifolium** (Pl.8), the Early Cream Honeysuckle, is a vigorous deciduous climber sometimes reaching 7m in height. The oval leaves have a distinctive bluish-green colour, particularly on the underside, the upper two or three pairs uniting below whorls of flowers to form a series of cups around the stem. The flowers are yellowish-white tinged with pink, each two-lipped and 35–50mm long. The berries are shiny orange. [June–July, H, PN, Europe]

This is a magnificent plant, arguably the finest garden honeysuckle. It is a profuse flowerer and the richness of its fragrance will attract the least garden-conscious person. Grown by a window or a doorway where the scent can be wafted about in the early summer sunshine this is surely one of the great joys and rewards of gardening. *L. caprifolium* is sometimes confused with *L. periclymenum*, however the leaves are a distinctive bluish green colour and the uppermost unite in pairs around the stem just below the flowers — this never happens in the latter.

'Pauciflora' has smaller flowers that are tinged with rose-pink on the outside.

***Lonicera tragophylla** is a deciduous climber with hairless young shoots. The oval bluish-green leaves are 5–11cm long, the uppermost pair united into a diamond-shaped cup below the flowers. The bright yellow flowers are produced in terminal heads, up to 20 flowers to a cluster, each two-lipped and downy on the outside. The ripe berries are red. [May–June, H–HH, PN, China (Hupeh)]

One of the largest-flowered and showiest honeysuckles which looks particularly fine on a pergola or trellis. Like most of its cousins it is tolerant of sunny or shaded positions, although preferring its roots in the shade. Well worth growing, although unfortunately the flowers are not scented.

Lonicera etrusca, the Etruscan Honeysuckle, is a moderately vigorous deciduous or semi-evergreen climber, reaching 4m tall, with purplish or reddish young shoots. The oval leaves are green above but bluish-green beneath and slightly downy, the upper unite together in pairs at their bases around the stem. The fragrant flowers start off yellowish, becoming gradually flushed with red, but eventually turning deep yellow with age, each two-lipped and 40–45mm long. [July–Oct, T, PN, Mediterranean Region]

This is certainly one of the most splendid honeysuckles, a vigorous grower and a profuse bloomer with a long flowering season. It could certainly be recommended more widely if it were hardier, however, it rarely does well outdoors in Britain and Ireland, although it makes an admirable conservatory plant grown against a pillar or on a suitable wall. The mild south-western parts of the country are best for it, especially if grown against a sheltered south-facing wall.

'Superba' is a particularly vigorous form with large panicles of flowers.

***Lonicera sempervirens** (Pl.8), the Trumpet Honeysuckle, is a vigorous evergreen or deciduous climber with bluish-green young shoots. The oval leaves are a deep green above, but bluish-green and somewhat downy beneath, the upper one or two pairs uniting around the stem forming oblong or rounded cups. The flowers are borne in three to four close whorls at the shoot tips; they are rich orange-scarlet outside but yellow inside, unscented, each tubular and scarcely two-lipped, 37–50mm long. [June–July, HH, PN, S & E USA]

A beautiful plant which is best grown in the milder parts of the country, however, it is hardier than is generally assumed, surviving outdoors in all but the coldest districts, providing it has a well-sheltered wall. *L. sempervirens* is probably the finest of the North American species having been cultivated since the mid seventeenth century, but it is not as common a garden plant as one might expect, having largely been replaced by hybrids in which it is one of the parents — *L. × brownii* and *L. × heckrottii*.

Unfortunately *L. sempervirens* is not scented although the beauty of the flowers more than makes up for such a deficiency. Although usually an evergreen species, plants may lose some or all of their leaves during a cold winter.

var. **minor** is a more slender, less vigorous variety which has oblong leaves and smaller flowers. Seldom seen in cultivation and probably most suitable for a conservatory wall.
'Superba' is a particularly fine form with broad oval leaves and deep orange-scarlet flowers.
'Sulphurea' has plain yellow flowers.

Lonicera splendida is an evergreen climber closely related to *L. periclymenum* and *L. etrusca*. The oval or oblong leaves are bluish-green, all stalkless and the uppermost fused together in pairs around the stem. The flowers are reddish-purple and glandular outside and yellowish-white inside, 25–38mm long; they are borne in a stalkless glandular head consisting of three to five whorls, one above the other. [June–Aug, HH, PN, Spain]

This beautiful species is seldom seen in cultivation but well deserves to be better known. The flowers are borne in profusion if the plant is given a sunny south-facing wall and it really is a splendid sight in bloom, as its name implies. It is fast growing, often extending up to 2m in a season. For gardeners wishing to distinguish *L. splendida* from its allies they should look at the uppermost leaf pairs and the flowerheads. If the uppermost leaf pairs are not united around the stem then the species is *L. periclymenum*, if they are and the first flower cluster is stalkless, arising directly from the final leaf pair then the species is *L. splendida*. If the first flower cluster is stalked then the species is *L. etrusca*. In *L. caprifolium* the whorls of flowers occur in the cups formed by the uppermost united leaf pairs.

Lonicera implexa is an evergreen climber of only moderate vigour reaching a height of 2.5m, sometimes more. The oval or oblong leaves are strikingly bluish-green beneath, though greener above, the upper pairs forming cups around the

Lonicera splendida.

stem inside which are found the stalkless clusters of flowers. The flowers are yellow flushed with pink outside whilst white turning to yellow inside. [June–Aug, T, PN, Mediterranean Region]

An attractive species, but a slow grower and too tender for most gardens. It requires the warm shelter of a west wall.

Lonicera japonica, the Japanese Honeysuckle, is a well known, delightfully fragrant, evergreen climber of great vigour, reaching as much as 10m tall. The twining stems are hollow, and covered in soft hairs. The bright green leaves vary in shape from elliptic to oval or sometimes lobed. The flowers occur in stalked pairs in the leaf axils and open white, sometimes with a purple tinge, but soon turn yellowish, each two-lipped, 32–50mm long. The small berries are black and shiny. [June–Oct, H, PS, China, Japan & Korea]

This rampant species is less attractive in flower than any of the previous species, but it has a long flowering season and a marvellously powerful fragrance. It is one of the best species for covering large tree stumps, old fences or garden walls, being less suitable against the average house. In cultivation *L. japonica* is widely known having been introduced to our gardens in 1806. The cultivar 'Halliana' is the best known form. In the United States, particularly in the east, *L. japonica* has unfortunately become a widespread and pernicious weed. Plants can be pruned back with care in the spring and will sprout vigorously as a result.

'Aureo-reticulata' is a less vigorous small-leaved form in which the midrib and veins are picked out in bright yellow. Some of the leaves have distinct lobes. This attractive cultivar is commonly grown but it is not as hardy as the type and may be damaged during a cold winter. Flowers are not profusely borne unless plants are grown against a warm sheltered wall.

***'Halliana'** (Pl.8) is a fine form with very fragrant white flowers that age to yellow. This cultivar is almost hardy and is a fine plant for a south- or west-facing wall or fence. The main flowering period is in June and July, though flowers are borne spasmodically through to the autumn.

var. **repens** has leaves quickly becoming hairless, often stained with purple beneath. Flowers white flushed with purple on the outside.

Lonicera confusa is closely allied to the preceding species, but the undersides of the leaves, and the young fruits, are very hairy. The bracts are distinctly awl-shaped. [June–July, T, PN, S China]

Lonicera similis is also closely related to *L. japonica* and is represented in gardens by var. **delavayi**. The leaves are oval-lanceolate, green and hairless above but with a thick felt of grey hairs beneath. The pale yellow flowers are sweetly scented, being borne in stalked pairs in the leaf axils or in loose heads at the shoot tips, each 50–65mm long with a slender tube. [July–Aug, T, PN, SW China]

Lonicera giraldii is an evergreen climber forming a dense entanglement, the young shoots covered with yellowish hairs. The narrowly oblong leaves are hairy on both surfaces. The bright reddish-purple flowers are yellowish and hairy inside, being borne in short panicles at the shoot tips, each flower two-lipped, 23–25mm long. The small berries are purplish-black when ripe. [June–Sept, HH, PN, S China]

An attractive and rather striking plant closely allied to *L. japonica*. *L. giraldii* is more or less hardy on a wall in the southern and western parts of the country, but needs careful protection elsewhere, making a fine plant for a conservatory. The flowers are small but are borne in sufficient quantity to make a pretty display.

The yellowish hairs of the young growths give the plant a distinctive attractiveness.

Lonicera henryi is a vigorous evergreen or semi-deciduous climber reaching as much as 10m tall, the young shoots covered in short bristly hairs. The leaves are deep green above but paler and rather shiny beneath. The flowers are purplish-red, being borne in clusters at the shoot tips, each stalk carries two flowers; each flower is two-lipped and 18–20mm long. The berries are purplish-black when ripe. [June–Oct, H, PS, W China]

This is a vigorous species suitable for a large wall or fence. The foliage is handsome and in autumn the plant is adorned with attractive shiny berries. The flowers are small and do not have the beauty or size of many of the other species here described.

Lonicera alseuosmoides is closely related to the preceding species but less vigorous and with slender hairless young shoots. The elliptic leaves are pointed, 3–5cm long, and with a hairy margin. The purple flowers are yellow inside, being borne in pairs close together at the shoot tips, each flower is tubular, not two-lipped and only about 13mm long. The berries are purplish-black. [July–Oct, H, PS, China]

Like *L. henryi* this species is not spectacular in flower, though the foliage and fruits are quite ornamental. Neither species is as easy to obtain as it was 10–20 years ago.

Lonicera hildebrandiana, the Giant Honeysuckle, is a vigorous evergreen climber, sometimes semi-deciduous, to 20m tall and quite hairless. The large broad oval or rounded leaves are dark green above but paler and glandular beneath. The fragrant flowers start white or cream but gradually become orange or yellow-brown. They are borne in axillary pairs or at the shoot tips, each flower two-lipped, very long and slender, 9–15cm. [June–Aug, T, PN, S China, Burma & Thailand]

This is a giant of a honeysuckle in every respect with large leaves and the biggest flowers of any species. It is unfortunately not hardy and few gardens can boast a good flowering specimen out of doors, however, it does well on a wall as a conservatory plant. Despite this, if plants can be obtained it is worth a try out of doors on a sheltered sunny wall in the mildest parts of Britain and Ireland. Young plants take several years to settle down and are shy flowerers at first. Like most honeysuckles, its roots should be in the shade.

There are several fine hybrids well known in gardens that combine the best qualities of their parent species. These are dealt with in alphabetical sequence.

***Lonicera × americana**, *L. caprifolium* × *L. etrusca*, is a moderately vigorous deciduous climber reaching 7m in height. The leaves are oval and rather pointed, the uppermost united into cups just below the flowers. The flowers are borne in these cups and also above them in branched clusters. They are sweetly scented, yellow flushed with reddish-purple, each two-lipped, and 45–50mm long. [June–July, HH, PN]

A beautiful hybrid with the general growth of *L. caprifolium* with which it is sometimes confused, and the large, branched flower panicles of *L. etrusca*. It is an early and prolific bloomer with a powerful fragrance and is certainly one of the very finest honeysuckles. It deserves to be far more widely grown.

L. ×*americana* is found in the wild in southern Europe in several places but it is rare. The origin of the cultivated plant is unknown and its name 'americana' was given by Philip Miller who mistakenly thought it an American species. Although generally found under this name in nurserymen's catalogues it is sometimes found as *L. ×italica* which unfortunately is a later synonym, though decidedly a more appropriate name.

● ***Lonicera × brownii**, *L. hirsuta* × *L. sempervirens* = *L. etrusca* var. *brownii*, (Pl.8), the Scarlet Trumpet Honeysuckle, is a deciduous or semi-evergreen climber with the general characteristics of *L. sempervirens*. The oval leaves are bluish-green. The flowers are scarlet with an orange throat, each two-lipped, though not pronouncedly so, 38–42mm long. [May–Sept, H, PN]

A beautiful hybrid, well known in gardens, which combines the charm of *L. sempervirens* with the hardiness of *L. hirsuta*. The latter parent is rarely seen in cultivation for it has rather small orange-yellow flowers of little substance compared with some of the other species. *L. ×brownii* would be perfect if it only had a scent but this is a feature sadly lacking from either parent. There are a number of fine cultivars which are all selections of various crosses between the two parent species:

'Dropmore Scarlet' is a fine-coloured form noted for its very long flowering season.
'Fuchsioides' has glowing orange-scarlet flowers borne early and late in the season.
'Plantierensis' is like 'Fuchsioides' but with less strongly two-lipped flowers.
'Punicea' and **'Youngii'** are sometimes seen in catalogues but differ little from 'Fuchsioides'.

◐ **Lonicera × heckrottii**, *L. ×americana* × *L. sempervirens*, is a handsome deciduous weak-stemmed shrub with a loose spreading habit. The oblong or oval leaves are green above and bluish-green beneath, quite hairless and with a very short stalk, the uppermost leaf pairs encircling the stem. The flowers are pink with a yellow throat, 36–40mm long, borne in whorls or in long-stalked clusters at the shoot tips. [June–Aug, H, PN]

A handsome hybrid which is often found in catalogues as *Lonicera* 'Gold Flame'. The plant is a shrub rather than a climber, though the stems are rather weak and generally require the support of a few wires fastened to the wall. *L. ×heckrottii* is a slow grower and dislikes too much direct sunlight. The flowers have a sweet fragrance unlike the previous hybrid. The parentage is not certain though most authorities now seem agreed that both *L. ×americana* and *L. sempervirens* are involved.

◐ ***Lonicera × tellmaniana**, *L. tragophylla* × *L. sempervirens* 'Superba' (Pl.8), a deciduous climber to 5m tall, has oval green leaves, the uppermost pairs of which form 'cups' around the stem below the flowers. The beautiful glowing yellow flowers are borne in clusters at the shoot tips, each two-lipped and 45–50mm long and with attractive protruding stamens. [May–July, H, PN]

A glorious plant and quite the best of all the hybrid climbing honeysuckles. The flowers are large and produced in profusion, the buds usually flushed with bronze. It is a vigorous grower and like most of its allies it dislikes having its roots in the sun, although plants which tumble over walls or fences from the shade into the sun can look very handsome. The flowers are not scented.

There are two winter flowering shrubby honeysuckles that well deserve wall culture if a space can be found for them. Both *L. fragrantissima* and *L. standishii* have strongly fragrant flowers, though the flowers themselves are not showy. However, positioned by a doorway, arch or window where their fragrance can waft around the house they are a sheer delight at a rather bleak time of the year. Both species are hardy in the open garden though the blossoms can be ruined by severe frosts and wall protection is therefore desirable. Walls of west- or north-west-facing aspect are best where morning sunshine can be avoided. They can be a delightful feature of a winter border planted with other subjects such as *Viburnum farreri (= V. fragrans), Jasminum nudiflorum, Helleborus orientalis, Eranthis hyemalis, Galanthus nivalis* and *Cyclamen coum*. Both species have been cultivated since the middle of the nineteenth century having been discovered in 1845 in China by Robert Fortune.

***Lonicera fragrantissima** is an evergreen or semi-deciduous shrub to 3m tall with smooth hairless young stems. The leaves are oval and rather leathery, dull green above but bluish-green beneath, the margin distinctly bristly. The cream flowers are borne in several pairs at each leaf joint, each with a two-lipped corolla, 14–16mm long. [Dec–Mar, H, PS, China]

A delightful fragrant shrub, certainly finer than its cousin *L. standishii*. In a mild winter all the leaves are retained, though in more severe seasons many of the leaves may be shed.

Lonicera standishii is a deciduous or semi-evergreen shrub growing to 4m tall against a wall. The young stems are bristly in contrast to the previous species. The leaves are oblong-lanceolate, bristly along the margin as well as the midrib. The cream flowers are usually borne in two pairs at each leaf joint, each corolla two-lipped, 12–14mm long, bristly on the outside. Red berries fused in pairs are produced in the early summer. [Nov–Mar, H, PS, China]

Lonicera × purpusii is a fine hybrid between the two preceding shrubby species.

Evergreen Climbers

Evergreen climbers, by their very nature, carry leaves throughout the year so that they are excellent for covering unsightly walls or fences or where a permanent curtain of green foliage is desired.

The siting of evergreen climbers is important. Many are not hardy or even if they are the foliage can be easily damaged by biting winter winds and frost. On the whole sheltered sites are preferable, the aspect and the amount of sun depending on the particular plant in question.

Planting time is also important, late winter or early spring being a much better time to plant than the late autumn or early winter. This is because the evergreen leaves lose moisture even during the winter and this can severely weaken or even kill a young plant, especially during spells of cold, dry, windy weather. Autumn planted specimens are best protected by a screen of straw or hessian until the spring arrives, and even then take care not to remove the protective barrier too soon. Indeed, mature evergreen climbers will often benefit from some form of winter protection, especially the tender and half-hardy ones.

Most of these climbers should be pruned in the early spring or as soon as they have finished flowering — if they require any pruning at all. Autumn pruning, except for some *Rubus* species, is best avoided and plants are best overwintered with as much mature growth as possible.

These remarks are not intended to put the gardener off, although it is wise to adhere to these few rules of culture. Amongst the evergreen climbers are to be found some of the most glorious wall plants, the Coral Plant, *Berberidopsis corallina*, the Chilean Bellflower, *Lapageria rosea*, and the Passion Flower, *Passiflora caerulea* for instance. These and many others are well worth a try.

Evergreen species of Clematis, Honeysuckles and Roses will be found in the chapters dealing with these individual groups.

ARAUJIA (Asclepiadaceae)

A small genus of evergreen South American twiners with opposite leaves, having white or pink flowers. The corolla has a tube which is inflated at the base, and there are five corolla lobes. The fruit is a pod containing many seeds, each bearing a tuft of silky hairs.

The latin name is in fact the Brazilian vernacular name.

☼ **Araujia sericofera** = *A. albens, Physianthus albens,* the Cruel Plant, is a vigorous twiner whose stems exude a milky juice when cut. The leaves are ovate-oblong, 5–10cm long, dark green above and whitish-felted beneath. The strongly scented flowers are borne in groups of three to eight in racemes about 5cm long. The corolla is white, often streaked inside with maroon; the tube is about 1.2cm long and has five spreading lobes at the mouth where the diameter is 2.5–3.5cm. The pods are 10–13cm long, grooved and yellowish-green. [Sept, T, PN, S Brazil]

A curious plant which will only survive outdoors in very mild areas. The flowers have a very strong scent which can be almost offensive if the flowers are approached too closely. The common name refers to the fact that visiting insects (usually night flying moths) in their quest for nectar insert their tongues into the slits which are situated between wings on the anthers. These slits become very narrow at one end and as the insects struggle their tongues become firmly jammed in the slits so that they are held fast. Lucky insects may succeed in escaping the following day; the less fortunate die a slow death.

ASTERANTHERA (Gesneriaceae)

There is only one species in this genus, which was introduced from Chile by Harold Comber in 1926.

◐ ***Asteranthera ovata** will attain 4m by producing clinging aerial roots at the stem nodes. The slender stems are covered in white hairs. The leaves are opposite, roundish, toothed, 1–3cm long, and clothed with rather stiff hairs. The flowers are produced in the leaf axils, usually one, occasionally two to a flower stalk. The calyx has five toothed lobes and the tubular corolla is a beautiful reddish-pink, 5.5cm long, expanding at the mouth into five lobes, and somewhat two-lipped. The lower lip is often striped with yellow, and the throat of the flower is whitish inside. The fruit is greenish-purple and fleshy. [June onwards, HH, PS, Chile & W Argentine]

A lovely plant which should be tried more frequently. It is not easy to give it the conditions under which it will flourish: a certain amount of rather damp shade but not excessive shading. Too dry a position will result in stunted growth. A

Asteranthera ovata.

damp, slightly acid or neutral, leafy soil is ideal and it looks beautiful if it can climb a mossy tree trunk. A shaded wall will suit it provided that the site is sufficiently humid. It is sometimes seen creeping over the ground making a charming and unusual ground cover subject.

BERBERIDOPSIS (Flacourtiaceae)

A genus containing a single species only, but one that can be classed amongst the very finest and most spectacular of climbing shrubs. The genus gets its name from the similarity of its flowers to those of the *Berberis*, however they belong to two entirely different families. The affinities of *Berberidopsis* are with such genera as *Azara, Carrierea* and *Xylosma*.

Plants are more or less hardy in many parts of the country, although they resent drying winds and strong sunshine. In districts away from the south and west it is advisable to give some protection to the base of the plant during the winter. In the mildest districts it can be trained on pillars or even up a tree. Plants like a moist loamy soil or sandy loam and will tolerate a slightly alkaline soil, provided that some peat is added, but they succeed best on lime-free soils. Planting is best carried out in March. Newly planted specimens benefit from a peat mulch; this helps to get the roots established. Plants require little pruning other than to remove dead or unwanted growths. The lead shoots should be tied in close to the wall. Propagation is relatively easy by cuttings or layerings. Fruits formed in this country rarely contain viable seeds.

***Berberidopsis corallina** (Pl.9), the Coral Plant, attains a height of 4.5m, rarely more. The alternate, ovate or heart-shaped leaves are leathery and edged with spiny teeth. Flowers are borne in the axils of the uppermost leaves and at the shoot tips and form small drooping clusters of great beauty. Each flower is globular, deep red, 12mm across and made up of nine to fifteen overlapping petal-like segments. [July – Sept, H, PN, Chile]

This species came from the forests of Arauco Province, Chile, where it is now thought to be extinct. It was introduced to cultivation in 1862 by Richard Pearce. Although hardy, it can be badly damaged by buffeting winds. A north sheltered wall is ideal, except in the north of the country where a west-facing wall is preferable.

BIGNONIA (Bignoniaceae)

A genus containing a single species for wall culture in temperate latitudes. *Bignonia* is closely related to the equally lovely *Campsis* but distinguished by the leaf tendrils which enable the plant to climb. For culture see *Campsis* (p.41).

☼ **Bignonia capreolata** = *Doxantha capreolata* (Pl.9), the Cross Vine, is a vigorous evergreen or partly deciduous climber reaching 16m tall in the wild but generally far less in cultivation. The slender stems are practically hairless and bear opposite pairs of leaves, each with two oblong-lanceolate deep green leaflets and a branched tendril. The orange-red funnel-shaped flowers are borne in clusters at the leaf axils, each flower 3.5–5cm long and spreading at the mouth into five rounded lobes. The slender fruit pods reach 15cm in length and are flat and bean-like. [June, HH, PS, SE USA]

This charming climber was introduced into this country as long ago as 1710. It gets its common name from the cross-shaped mark observable on the woody stems when they are cut in half. Plants are generally evergreen but may become partly deciduous during severe weather.

BILLARDIERA (Pittosporaceae)

There are nine species in this Australian genus, of which only one is cultivated in Britain. They are small shrubs with twining stems which bear alternate leaves.

◐ ***Billardiera longiflora** (Pl.9) has slender hairless stems which climb to 2m. The leaves are narrowly lanceolate, untoothed and 2.5–4cm long. The solitary

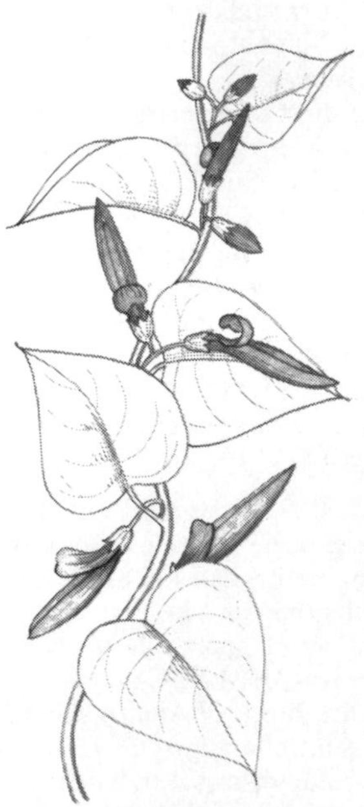

Brachysema latifolium.

flowers are produced in the leaf axils, and hang on slender stalks. They are scented and composed of five petals which are free from one another, although they appear to be united. About 2cm in length, the flowers are greenish-yellow, sometimes becoming tinged with purple. The fruit is a cylindrical to globular dry capsule, 2–2.5cm long and deep blue. [July–Sept, T, PS, Tasmania]

This lovely species grows best on the west coast of Britain and can be trained on a wall, trellis or even up a tree trunk, or left to clamber amongst other shrubs. Plants need a position sheltered from cold winds and strong sunshine, though not complete shade. The flowers are elegant but not showy; it is when the lovely fruits are produced in October and November that it attracts attention.

The generic name commemorates J.J.H. de Labillardière, a French botanist who travelled in Australia.

'Fructu-Albo' = 'Alba' has white fruits.

'Fructu-Coccineo' has red fruits. Uncommon in cultivation.

BRACHYSEMA (Leguminosae)

An Australian genus of climbing and trailing shrubby plants with simple leaves which are silkily-hairy beneath. The flowers are carried in few-flowered terminal and lateral racemes.

Brachysema latifolium has alternate ovate leaves with a sudden sharp apical point. The relatively large flowers are crimson-scarlet, in clusters of one to three. They have an oblong-ovate standard which is much shorter than the wings and keel. The keel is three times as long as the calyx. [Apr–Aug, T, PN, Australia]

A very beautiful but uncommon climber. Most species of *Brachysema* demand greenhouse cultivation but *B. latifolium* can be planted outside once the danger of frost has past.

CISSUS (Vitaceae)

A large genus of tropical and subtropicial plants which are mostly tendrilled climbers. They are related to other vines, *Ampelopsis, Parthenocissus* and *Vitis* in particular. There are a number of fine species for indoor culture, *Cissus discolor* being perhaps the most magnificent. However, the most well-known species is undoubtedly the Kangaroo Vine, *Cissus antarctica*, which is commonly grown as a house plant. Only one species is suitable for outdoor culture.

Cissus striata = *Vitis striata* is a vigorous evergreen climber with tendrils, reaching 5m tall. The digitate leaves are rather leathery, glossy green, the five leaflets obovate and coarsely toothed. The inconspicuous greenish flowers are succeeded by small currant-like reddish-purple berries. [July–Sept, HH, PS, S Brazil & Chile]

DECUMARIA (Hydrangeaceae)

A genus of two species, both of which are cultivated. These woody plants climb by aerial roots and have opposite leaves. The flowers are small and borne in a terminal inflorescence. The fruit is a ribbed, top-shaped capsule which splits between the ribs, releasing many tiny seeds. They grow best in a moist, well-drained, loamy soil.

Decumaria is related to the climbing *Hydrangea* and to *Schizophragma* but is distinguished by the absence of sterile flowers, and by the flowers having more sepals and petals.

Decumaria barbara is a semi-evergreen, or sometimes deciduous, climber which will reach 9m high, its stems slightly hairy when young. The leaves are ovate to oval, 7.5–13cm long, untoothed or with shallow teeth towards the tip. The fragrant white flowers are carried in a round-topped inflorescence which measures 5–7.5cm in length and width, each flower only 6mm across. The fruit is 8mm long, striped white in the lower part. [June–July, T, PA, SE USA]

A rather tender plant which is not commonly grown, although it can be seen in various gardens in Devon and Cornwall. It is best grown on a sheltered wall, but can look very effective when allowed to climb a tree. It has been cultivated in Britain since 1785.

Decumaria sinensis will grow to 2m tall, and sometimes more. The leaves are oval or narrowly obovate, slightly toothed or untoothed, 2.5–8cm long and hairless. The cream flowers smell of honey and are borne in a pyramidal inflorescence 3.5–8cm long and wide. [May–June, HH, PA, C China]

Not such a vigorous species as *D. barbara*, and doing best on an east- or west-facing wall. It has handsome leaves and the plant has the advantage of being one of the few evergreen self-clinging climbers to be grown in Britain. *D. sinensis* was first discovered in the Ichang Gorge in Hupeh by Augustine Henry, the Irish amateur botanist, who found it hanging down the cliff walls.

EUONYMUS (Celastraceae)

A large genus of evergreen or deciduous shrubs or small trees grown for their showy fruits or attractive foliage, or both. The flowers are generally small and greenish and certainly not showy. The best known species is the Common Spindle Tree, *Euonymus europaeus*. Only one species *E. fortunei* is suitable for growing against walls, being generally represented in cultivation by var. *radicans*.

Euonymus fortunei var. **radicans** is a creeping or climbing evergreen shrub reaching 7m high against a wall, the long slender stems self-clinging by means of short roots produced at intervals. The oval or ovate leaves are dark green, short-stalked, 1.5–3.5cm long. The small, rounded fruit capsules are pink when ripe, about 6mm across, and split to reveal small bright orange seeds. [July–Aug, H, PN, China, Japan & Korea]

The normal form of var. *radicans* is the immature one and like ivies, *Hedera* spp., the growth alters at maturity. Only when this phase is reached will plants flower and fruit. Some plants may never reach maturity. Mature growth is much more bushy with larger leaves, looking very similar to another species, *E. japonicus*. The typical form of *E. fortunei*, which comes from China, is rare in cultivation.

Euonymus fortunei var. *radicans* is extremely hardy, indeed in the eastern USA, where ivy is not hardy, this plant is grown on walls as a substitute. Plants are very easily rooted from small sprigs pulled from older plants. The only pruning that is necessary is to remove untidy or excess growth in the spring to keep plants in shape.

***'Coloratus'** grows to 8m tall given some support. The leaves are reddish-purple throughout the winter months especially if plants are grown in rather poor soils. In the spring they change back to the normal green colour.

'Silver Gem' is very similar to 'Silver Queen' but less bushy in habit and has smaller leaves with silver margins which are flushed with red in the best forms. A vigorous climber.

***'Silver Queen'** grows to 3m tall against a wall, and is vigorous, but soon produces bushy mature growth. The leaves, creamy-yellow when young, are green with white variegations when mature. The largest leaves may reach 6.5cm long.

***'Variegatus'** = 'Argenteo-marginata' or 'Gracilis', is rather like var. *radicans* but the greyish leaves have a broad marginal band of white, sometimes flushed with red. A fine cultivar although plants are not always stable and the leaves may revert to plain green. Plants with red-flushed leaves are sometimes referred to as 'Roseo-marginata' though this character is not constant.

'Vegetus' = var. *vegetus* is generally seen in its adult bushy form which is fine for training against a low wall or fence. The mature leaves are broadly elliptic or roundish and rather a dull green. This cultivar, which hails from the north island of Japan, near Sapporo, often produces fruit freely. Growths need to be tied into their supports in order to train plants into a pleasing shape.

FICUS (Moraceae)

A large genus containing over 800 species, most of which are evergreen. The alternate leaves vary considerably in shape. Their flowers, more than any other single character, identify figs. They are unisexual and line the internal walls of a hollow receptacle — the typical edible 'fig'.

Two very different species are included in this book. *F. pumila* is evergreen and climbing and described below. The Common Fig, *F. carica,* is a deciduous shrub and is described on p.132, and as a wall fruit on p.274.

Ficus pumila = *F. stipulata* clings to a suitable support by aerial roots which are produced at the stem nodes. The plant has two stages in its development — juvenile and adult — but the adult stage (which bears the flowers and fruit) is usually attained only when grown under glass and when a height of 3–4m is reached. The juvenile leaves are heart-shaped, 1.8–3cm long, and usually hairless. The adult leaves are 3–8cm long, very leathery, dark green above and paler beneath and with net-veins. The fruits are obovoid, about 6cm long, green at first, becoming bright orange and eventually suffused with purplish-red. [June–July, T, PN, China, Taiwan, Japan] ◐ △

F. pumila is a delightful species which is often seen as a conservatory plant or as a trailing house plant. However, it is hardier than is generally supposed and will survive on a warm sheltered wall or a tree trunk in the extreme southern counties, usually remaining in the juvenile state.

No pruning is required, but to promote branching, the stems can be pinched back.

The species has been cultivated in Britain since 1771.

HARDENBERGIA (Leguminosae)

An Australian genus very similar to *Kennedia* but with numerous smaller flowers which have a blunt keel shorter in length than the wings.

Hardenbergia violacea = *H. monophylla* is an hairless climber which can reach 3m tall. The alternate leathery leaves are ovate to linear, 3.5–12cm long and net-veined. The pea-flowers are borne in racemes 5–12cm long, and are usually violet but may be pink or white. The standard has a yellow blotch and is notched at the apex. The pod is about 3–4cm long. [Mar–Apr, T, PA, E Australia & Tasmania] ☼

An uncommon climber which will survive against a wall in mild districts, except in a severe winter. It can be raised from seed or increased by cuttings.

HEDERA (Araliaceae)

A small group of climbers, the ivies need little introduction. They are all evergreens with alternate leaves. Botanists have not yet been able to agree on how many species should be recognised.

Ivies go through two stages in their growth — a juvenile stage which often lasts a long time, and an adult flowering and fruiting stage. In the juvenile stage the stems produce aerial roots, enabling the plant to cling to a support, and the leaves are usually three- or five-lobed and all arranged in the same plane, forming an often beautiful overlapping pattern. The adult leaves are normally unlobed and arranged in a spiral on the woody non-climbing stem. At both stages, the young shoots have a covering of star-shaped or scale-like hairs — to see these clearly it is necessary to use a hand-lens. The flowers are yellowish-green and borne in globose clusters and the ripe fruits or berries are black or yellowish.

Ivies have for many years been labelled 'Victorian' and considered to be dreary, spider-ridden and suitable only for a dark corner where they will not be noticed. Recently, there has been a considerable revival of interest in the genus; many of the more attractive cultivars are now being grown and are readily obtainable from garden centres and nurseries.

All the species described below can be grown in any aspect and are not fussy about soil. They are best trained on a wall or up a tree and are invaluable for disguising unsightly buildings. Contrary to popular belief, ivy will not harm a wall or building provided it is in a good state of repair, although the clinging roots may spoil the paintwork of window frames, and the vigorous shoots may get under the eaves and lift the roof tiles unless regularly checked.

Annual clipping may be required to remove any outgrowths which might be caught by the wind, or to prevent the adult stage being reached if this is not wanted. It is best undertaken in May and June.

Planting can take place during the autumn or spring and young pot grown plants generally establish themselves fairly quickly, although they may take a while to start clinging to their support. Gardeners recommend various ways of starting them off which include painting the wall with a solution of manure to encourage aerial roots to form. If you are averse to this the young shoots can be tied close to the wall. Alternatively, long shoots can be laid along the ground against the wall. This will encourage side shoots to grow out straight onto the wall.

Plants can be propagated from short firm young shoots taken in midsummer and placed in a propagating frame. Layering can also be undertaken at any time.

Hedera helix, the Common Ivy, will grow to 10m if allowed, and bears three- or five-lobed leaves, 4–6cm long which have a strong smell when crushed. The starry hairs on the young shoots have six to sixteen rays. The fruits are dull black when ripe. [Oct, H, PS, Europe & W Asia]

An enormous number of cultivars, mainly differing in shape, size and colour of leaves, have been produced over the last two or three centuries, and their naming is still somewhat confused, although recent attempts to sort out the muddle have been reasonably successful. A selection is given below:

'Adam' has greenish-purple stems. The three-lobed leaves, 3–4cm long with the central lobe directed somewhat to one side, are pale green, greying as they age and with an irregular creamy-white margin. They develop pinkish edges in cold weather.

***'Buttercup'** has stems which are pale green in the shade, but yellow-green in the sun. The five-lobed leaves are 5–7cm long, with the central lobe longer than the others. Like

Plate 5 Clematis 1 *Clematis alpina* (p.67), 2 *C. armandii* 'Snowdrift' (p.68), 3 *C. campaniflora* (p.71), 4 *C. chrysocoma* (p.66), 5 *C. cirrhosa* var. *balearica* (p.70), 6 *C. texensis* (p.71).

5
1
2
3
4
6
5

6
1
2
3
4
5

the stems, the leaves are green in the shade, but a rich yellow-green in a sunny spot. A bright attractive cultivar.

'Cavendishii' has light green stems bearing three-lobed leaves which are 5–6cm long and medium green in the centre with an irregular pale yellow margin which often develops a pink flush in winter. This is one of the quickest cultivars to reach the adult (fruiting) stage.

'Deltoidea' has stems which are green, rather stiff and bear dark green, shallowly three-lobed leaves 6–10cm long, their bases strongly heart-shaped with overlapping lobes. In autumn they often become coloured purplish-brown.

'Digitata' has greenish-purple stems. The leaves, are five-lobed with a long central lobe and reduced basal lobes, 7–9cm long, and dark green with lighter veins. One of the earliest cultivars and extremely hardy, 'Digitata's' leaves are larger than in the other cultivars.

***'Glacier'** (Pl.10) has purplish-green stems. The leaves, 3–6cm long, have three or five lobes, with the basal lobes reduced, and are greyish-green with patches of a lighter silvery-grey and a narrow cream margin. A lovely ivy which makes strong growth and provides a cool accompaniment for colourful neighbours.

'Glymii' has green stems in summer which turn purple in winter. The leaves are very shallowly three-lobed and 4–5cm long. In the summer they are a glossy deep green but in winter they turn purple.

***'Goldheart'** = 'Jubilee' (Pl.10), has deep pink stems which turn brown with age. The three-lobed leaves are 4–6cm long and the central lobe is longer than the lateral ones. Their colour is dark green, with an irregular splash of bright yellow in the centre. This ivy can be slow to establish itself, but its attractively coloured leaves make it well worth waiting for.

'Gracilis' has purplish-red stems and dark green leaves with lighter veins. The leaves are three- or five-lobed, the central lobe being only slightly longer than the others. The leaves are 2–4cm long and turn purplish-red in the autumn.

'Green Ripple' has greenish-purple stems. The five-lobed leaves, 5–9cm long are heart-shaped at the base. The lobes all point forward and the sinuses between them are twisted. The leaves are bright green, turning coppery in the autumn. A vigorous ivy with elegant leaves.

***'Heron'** has greyish-green stems and purplish leaf-stalks. The leaves have five lobes, measure 3–5cm long and their basal lobes point backwards; they are deep greyish-green with whitish veins.

'Hibernica', Irish Ivy, has green stems. The five-lobed leaves have a heart-shaped base, a large central lobe and are 5–9cm long. They are a dull green with greyish-green veins. Common in cultivation and very vigorous. There is a variegated form whose leaves have irregular yellow markings.

***'Ivalace'** has purplish-green stems. The shallowly five-lobed leaves, 4–6cm long, have margins which are very wavy. They are dark shiny green with paler veins. This cultivar is particularly happy on a north-facing wall. The leaves turn a coppery colour in winter.

'Minor Marmorata' has dull purplish stems and its young shoots are tinged with pink. The three-lobed leaves are 3–5cm long, dark green with spots and splashes of whitish-cream. Like the previous cultivar, it does well on a north-facing wall. The older leaves lose some of their whitish markings.

***'Parsley Crested'** = 'Cristata' has greenish-purple stems. The leaves are unlobed or slightly three-lobed, ovate to roundish, 4–6cm long, and with margins strongly waved and crimped. In colour they are bright green with paler veins, and in winter turn reddish.

'Pedata' = 'Caernwoodiana' has green stems. The leaves have five lobes, the central one being narrow and long, the two basal ones pointing backwards. The leaves measure 4–5cm in length and are dark green with whitish veins.

'Sagittifolia' has greenish-purple stems. The dark green leaves 3–5cm long are spear-shaped with horizontal or backward-pointing, sometimes overlapping, basal lobes.

Plate 6 Clematis 1 *Clematis florida* 'Sieboldii' (p.81), 2 *C.×jackmanii* (p.73), 3 *C. napaulensis* (p.70), 4 *C. montana* var. *rubens* (p.66), 5 *C. macropetala* (p.67).

Hedera helix.

var. **poetica**, often known as Italian Ivy, has pinkish stems. The five-lobed, bright green leaves, 5–7cm long, have very small basal lobes. The fruits are pale yellowish-orange and the plant has rather a stiff habit. [Greece, North Africa & Turkey]

☀ **Hedera canariensis** = *H. algeriensis, H. maderensis*, the Canary Island or African Ivy, has smooth dark red stems and leaf stalks. The hairs on the young shoots are scale-like, with 13–16 rays. The leaves are unlobed, ovate with a heart-shaped base and 10–15cm in length. They are green in the summer, turning bronze in the winter. [H, PS, Canary Is, Azores & NW Africa]

H. canariensis is not quite so hardy as *H. helix* but will succeed in most areas.

'Azorica' has green stems. When young, both stems and leaves are thickly covered with a brownish-red felt. The leaves are bright green and five- or seven-lobed, 9–11cm long.

***'Gloire de Marengo'** = 'Variegata' (Pl.10) has smooth dark red stems. The leaves, usually unlobed and 9–11cm long, are green with patchy areas of silver-grey between the veins and an irregular cream margin. A very decorative fast-growing cultivar which, although hardy enough, does best on a sheltered wall.

***'Margino-maculata'** (Pl.10) is a mutation from 'Gloire de Marengo'. The leaves are light green, with cream mottling and often with patches of cream.

'Striata' = 'Gold Leaf', 'Golden Leaf' has dark red stems which bear unlobed leaves 8–14cm long, dark green with a light green or yellow centre.

☀ **Hedera colchica** (Pl.10) the Persian Ivy, has green stems and generally unlobed ovate leaves with a heart-shaped base, usually 6–15cm long but sometimes up to 25cm long. The scale-like hairs on the young shoots have 15–25 rays. The dark green leaves are thick and leathery and the fruits black when ripe. [H, PS, N Turkey, Caucasus & N Iran]

***'Dentata'** has purplish-brown stems with leaves produced at intervals of 6–10cm. The unlobed, ovate leaves are 15–20cm long with tiny widely spaced teeth on the margins. A vigorous plant.

'Dentata Variegata' has leaves which are unlobed, untoothed or with a few scattered teeth, and often with the margins curling under. They are green with irregular patches of greyish-green and a very irregular deep cream margin. It is the most hardy of the variegated ivies.

***'Sulphur Heart'** = 'Paddy's Pride', 'Gold Leaf' (Pl.10), has green stems turning brown when old. The unlobed leaves have a few marginal teeth and measure 10–13cm in length. They are light green with irregular paler green or yellow splashes towards the centre, or with yellow veins.

Hedera pastuchovii has greenish-brown stems, the leaves a dark glossy green, leathery, narrowly ovate, 4–6cm long and sometimes with marginal teeth. The fruits are black when ripe. [H, PS, W Caucasus]

Similar to *H. colchica* but with smaller less leathery leaves. It was only introduced to this country in 1972, by Roy Lancaster. Not yet widely grown and probably of interest only to the ivy specialist.

Hedera nepalensis = *H. himalaica, H. helix* var. *chrysocarpa*, the Himalayan Ivy, has green stems which are reddish-brown when young and clothed in yellowish-brown scale-like hairs with 12–15 rays. The ovate to lanceolate leaves are 5–10cm long, occasionally with very shallow lobes or teeth, and shining green. The fruits are yellow or orange. [Nov–Jan, H-HH, Afghanistan and Himalaya to W China and N Burma]

Slightly less hardy than *H. helix* and *H. colchica* but it will still grow in almost any position.

Hedera rhombea, the Japanese Ivy, produces purplish-green stems. The young shoots have scale-like hairs with 10–18 rays. The leaves are ovate or triangular and usually unlobed. They grow 2–4cm long and are dark green with the veins on the upper surface slightly recessed. [Nov–Dec, H, PS, Japan & Korea]

'Variegata' — the leaves have a regular, narrow cream margin. It is more commonly cultivated than *H. rhombea* itself.

HOLBOELLIA (Lardizabalaceae)

A genus of evergreen twining shrubs with digitately-lobed leaves and male and female flowers separate but borne on the same plant. There are five species, all native to Asia, although only two are in cultivation. The genus is named after F.L. Holboell, one-time Superintendent of the Copenhagen Botanic Garden.

The flowers are small and egg-shaped with fleshy sepals but without true petals. The male flowers possess six separate stamens and the female three carpels which develop into fleshy 'pod-like' structures. The genus is related to *Stauntonia* which differs in its thin sepals and united stamens.

Holboellias thrive on most average garden soils and have the added merit of succeeding in sunny or shaded positions. Hand-pollination may encourage fruit formation.

Holboellia coriacea is a vigorous climber of luxuriant character reaching 7m, sometimes more, the young shoots twining, purplish and hairless. Leaves glossy dark green, rather leathery with three large leaflets. Male flowers purplish-white, 11–13mm long, borne at the shoot tips or in the leaf axils in small, stalked, clusters. Female flowers rather larger, greenish-white flushed with purple, in clusters of three to four, usually in the lower axils of young shoots. Fleshy, purple fruits, rarely produced in cultivation, are sausage-shaped, 4.5–6cm long, and contain rows of jet-black seeds. [Apr–May, H, PA, Central China (Hupeh)]

A good plant for a tall wall, but it is equally at home on an old tree. Flowers, and occasionally fruits, are produced most freely on specimens grown against a sunny wall. However, it is for the handsome foliage that this species is usually grown.

Holboellia latifolia = *Stauntonia latifolia* (Pl.9) is similar to the previous species but the leaves have three to seven leaflets. The flowers are very fragrant, the male greenish-white and the female purplish. [Mar–Apr, HH, PA, Himalaya]

Holboellia latifolia is very little different from *H. coriacea*. Some botanists believe they are variations of the same species, but they are fairly readily distinguished in the forms in cultivation. *H. latifolia* was the first to be described, indeed it has been in cultivation since 1840. This species is more tender than its cousin, and flowers earlier. It does particularly well in the southwest of Britain.

HYDRANGEA (Hydrangeaceae)

The genus has been described on p.47 under deciduous climbers, where the common climbing Hydrangea, *H. petiolaris* can be found.

Hydrangea serratifolia = *H. integerrima, Cornidia serratifolia*, like the other climbing hydrangeas, attaches itself to supports by aerial roots, reaching 4m or more high. Its leathery leaves are elliptic or obovate, 5–15cm long, with or without distantly-spaced teeth. The flowers are produced in small clusters, several of which make up a panicle 7.5–15cm long. Each cluster, when at the bud stage, is enclosed in four papery bracts which fall as the flowers expand. The white flowers are usually all fertile and have four petals and eight stamens; the stamens are about 6mm long and much more conspicuous than the petals. Sterile flowers are only occasionally produced. [Aug, HH-H, PS, Chile & adjacent Argentina]

The lack of sterile flowers makes it the least decorative of the climbing hydrangeas, although it has the advantage of being evergreen. It is hardy enough in a sheltered position. The original introduction from Chile was made by Harold Comber in the mid nineteen twenties.

JASMINUM (Oleaceae)

A delightful group containing the ever-popular winter-flowering *J. nudiflorum* and the exquisitely scented summer-flowering *J. officinale.*

There are about three hundred species of jasmine, native to the Old World tropics and subtropics. They are woody plants, shrubs or climbers, evergreen or deciduous. The leaves can be opposite or alternate, simple, ternate or pinnate. The flowers are solitary or borne in terminal or lateral clusters, the calyx five-lobed, whilst the corolla has four to nine spreading lobes which fuse together below to form a narrow tube. There are only two stamens, usually hidden inside the corolla tube. The fruit is a small berry, black when ripe.

Most of the cultivated species grown out-of-doors in Britain are evergreen scramblers or climbers, though *J. nudiflorum*, perhaps the most widely grown is a deciduous species dealt with on p.137. The shrubby evergreen Jasmines are included below for convenience. Jasmines prefer a sunny position; although most can tolerate shade they will not flower well. They can be grown in any soil, but do not like conditions that are too dry. A well drained moist loam is most suitable with the addition of summer mulches. Propagation is by layering at any time or cuttings taken in the late summer and placed in a propagating frame.

The Latin name *Jasminum* comes from the Arabic name of the plant 'Yasmin'. From the flowers of several white species an essential oil is extracted and much prized in the perfumery trade, especially in southern Europe.

YELLOW-FLOWERED SPECIES

***Jasminum floridum** is an evergreen or semi-evergreen scrambling or semi-climbing shrub with angled shoots, reaching 2.5m high. The leaves are alternate with three or sometimes five ovate or broad oval leaflets. The yellow flowers are small but borne in great profusion in terminal clusters on long arching stems, each with a corolla 12–20mm long and five-lobed. [July–Sept, T, PS, W China]

A fine plant for a warm, sheltered, nook in the full sun, although unfortunately far less grown today than in former times. Young plants are rather shy to flower but older plants do better, especially during hot summers.

Jasminum fruticans, the Shrubby Jasmine, is a lax shrub, not climbing but included here for convenience. It is evergreen or semi-deciduous, reaching 4m high. The deep green leaves are alternate and composed of three blunt oval leaflets. The small bright yellow flowers are faintly fragrant, being borne in terminal clusters of one to eight, the corolla tube 10–15mm long with five lobes. The pea-sized black berries are sometimes produced in abundance. [June–July, H-HH, PS, S Europe, N Africa & Asia Minor]

A lovely plant cultivated for over 400 years and referred to in Gerard's Herbal of 1597.

Jasminum humile, the Italian Yellow Jasmine, is an almost evergreen hairless loosely branched shrub to 3m. The deep green leaves bear three to seven leaflets, 1.5–5cm long. Flowers yellow, borne in small clusters at the shoot tips, each 18–20mm across, sometimes fragrant. [June–Aug, H, PA, W Asia to C China]

'Revolutum' = *J. revolutum* (Pl.21) is a stouter plant with bigger clusters of fragrant flowers, each up to 25mm across.

Jasminum subhumile = *J. diversifolium, J. heterophyllum*, is an evergreen or semi-evergreen scrambling shrub 1–2m tall, although deciduous in northern localities, or during a severe winter. The hairy young shoots are often purplish and the alternate leaves are glossy with one to three 'privet-like' leaflets. The small yellow flowers are scented, borne in dense many-flowered clusters at the shoot tips; the corolla tube about 10mm long, generally with five lobes. [May–July, T, PA, Central & E Himalaya, Burma & S China]

Jasminum mesnyi = *J. primulinum*, the Primrose Jasmine, is a strong growing rambling evergreen or semi-evergreen shrub which will climb to 3m high. The leaves are opposite, each with three elliptical deep green leaflets. The soft yellow flowers are solitary and semi-double, 30–40mm across, with six to ten lobes. [Mar–May, T, PA, W China]

A fine species, but most often seen as a conservatory plant, however, it will succeed outdoors in mild areas given a warm sheltered wall. The flowers are similar, though larger than, the Winter Jasmine, to which it is closely related. It is disputably the finest yellow Jasmine in cultivation — a shame that it is not hardier! Plants get bulky with age and need careful pruning to keep them in order.

WHITE- OR RED-FLOWERED SPECIES

Jasminum azoricum = *J. trifoliatum* is an evergreen climber with twining shoots. The opposite leaves have three leaflets. The sweetly-scented flowers are white, flushed with purple in bud, and borne in clusters of 5–25 at the shoot tips, each flower 20–30mm across. [July–Sept, T, PS, Madeira]

A pretty species which like the next is suitable only for the very mildest districts. In mild seasons flowers will be produced into the early part of the winter.

Jasminum angulare is another evergreen climber with opposite dark green leaves, each composed of three leaflets. The fragrant white flowers are borne in small clusters of three to seven, which make up handsome broad panicles, the individual flowers larger than those of *J. azoricum*. [Aug–Sept, T, PS, S Africa]

A lovely plant but, alas, a tender one. It makes a fine conservatory subject.

***Jasminum polyanthum** is an evergreen twining climber reaching 3m or more high. The opposite leaves are pinnate, each with five or seven leaflets, the terminal one longer than the others. The deliciously fragrant flowers are borne in large terminal clusters, white although often flushed with pink or red on the outside, especially in bud, each flower 10–20mm across, with five lobes and a corolla tube 20–22mm long. [May–Sept, T, PS, S China]

A beautiful and extremely floriferous jasmine, again one for a warm sheltered wall in milder districts. Elsewhere it is a marvellous plant for a conservatory wall or pillar and it is often seen today as a house plant, although it needs to be pruned vigorously to keep it in check. In exceptionally mild maritime areas *J. polyanthum* can be grown up a pergola or shrub. On conservatory walls plants have been known to reach 7.5m in height. In such places it will often commence flowering shortly after Christmas.

This delightful plant was discovered by the French missionary Père Delavay in Yunnan during 1883, though it was not introduced to Britain until some fifty years later.

Jasminum dispermum is similar to the preceding but is semi-evergreen or even deciduous in all but the warmest districts. The leaves have only three or five leaflets which have wavy margins. The flowers are smaller, white flushed with pink, only 12–16mm across. [June–July, T, PS, E Himalaya]

***Jasminum officinale**, the Common Jasmine or Jessamine, is a lovely deciduous twining climber, semi-evergreen in milder districts. It will climb to 12m if allowed. The opposite leaves usually have seven or nine leaflets, each 1.2–6cm long. The buds are usually tinged with pink and open to fragrant white flowers which are carried in terminal clusters of five to twelve. The corolla is 19–21mm across, with four or five spreading lobes. [June–Oct, H-HH, PA, Himalaya & S China]

The most commonly cultivated white jasmine in Britain and a favourite climber for growing near a house door or window, or over an archway where its fragrance can be readily appreciated.

The Common Jasmine is one of our oldest garden plants, certainly going back as long ago as 1548 and it is deservedly popular. In mild districts it can be grown in more open situations and is equally fine draped over an old wall, pergola or tree stump. Elsewhere it is best against a sheltered wall or fence where it will often grow up to 2m in a season. Young plants are shy at flowering and too drastic pruning may reduce flowers on established plants. Indeed if possible it is best left unpruned and allowed to romp, only removing old or dead growth when necessary.

Jasminum officinale is commonly naturalised in southern Europe and western Asia.

***'Affine'** = forma *affine* has larger flowers which are suffused with pink on the outside.
'Aureum' = 'Aureomarginatum' has leaves with yellow blotches. Said to be less hardy than the typical form, though a handsome plant.

Jasminum beesianum is an evergreen climber to 3–5m, often deciduous in colder districts. The opposite leaves are simple, lanceolate, 2.5–5cm long, often downy when young. The fragrant flowers terminate side shoots in groups of one to three. They are rose-red, 8–10mm across and usually with six lobes. [May–June, H-HH, PA, W China]

This is the only cultivated jasmine with red or carmine flowers. It is one of the few species to produce fruits regularly, the glossy black berries persisting on the plant well into winter in hanging clusters. *J. beesianum* is one of the many introductions of George Forrest, and it was named in honour of the seed firm of Bees Ltd for whom Forrest worked at the time.

***Jasminum × stephanense** is a fine hybrid between *J. beesianum* and *J. officinale.* It is a vigorous climber, evergreen in mild districts, reaching 7.5m in height. The leaves vary from simple to pinnate with up to five leaflets. The fragrant pink flowers are borne in terminal clusters of three to ten, each 14–16mm across. [June–July, HH, PA, S China]

This beautiful hybrid was put into commerce about 1921 from a garden cross at Nancy, France, though it is also known to occur in the wild. It is the only hybrid known in the genus. Shiny black berries are produced in the autumn making a pretty display. The leaves of young shoots can often be variegated with white or pale yellow.

***Jasminum grandiflorum**, sometimes known as Royal or Spanish Jasmine, is an evergreen scrambler with opposite leaves composed of seven or nine hairless leaflets. The fragrant flowers are borne in terminal clusters of up to fifty. The corolla is white, occasionally tinged with red, 30–40mm across, with five or six lobes. [June–Oct, T, PS, SW Arabia]; A lovely species, sometimes confused with *J. officinale* but with larger flowers. It is a tender plant, suitable only for a sheltered position. It was introduced to southern Europe by the Arabs, where it was used for perfume extraction, the area around Grasse in the south of France being the main region for this industry today. (See illustration p.104).

KADSURA (Schisandraceae)

Very similar to *Schisandra* (p.53), but bearing its fruit in a globose head instead of a long spike.

Kadsura japonica has slender twining stems which reach about 3.7m tall. The alternate dark green leaves are oval or lanceolate, 5–10cm long. The flowers are unisexual, solitary in the leaf axils of the current year's shoots, cream with six to nine petals, fragrant and about 2cm in diameter. The scarlet berries, up to 6mm long, are borne in a pendulous globose cluster 2.5–3cm wide. [June–Sept, HH, PN, China, Taiwan & Japan]

Jasminum grandiflorum

Not commonly grown, *K. japonica* needs the shelter of a warm wall to grow well. If fruits are required, it is necessary to grow both male and female plants. The leaves take on rich red and purple colours during the autumn, making a handsome show.

'Variegata' has leaves with an irregular cream border.

KENNEDIA (Leguminosae)

A genus of 15 Australian climbers with alternate leaves each composed of three leaflets. The pea-flowers have the keel curved and longer than the wing petals.

☼ **Kennedia macrophylla** is a twiner with the young shoots clothed in silky hairs. The leaflets are roundish to broadly obovate, 2.5–8cm long and silky-hairy. The red flowers are about 1.8cm long and carried in clusters of two to six on long stalks up to 15cm in length. The pods are linear, about 3–4cm long and hairless. [July–Aug, T, PS, W Australia]

Propagation is by seed. A plant not often seen in this country, but worth trying in a warm sheltered position.

LAPAGERIA (Philesiaceae)

This genus is named in honour of the Empress Joséphine, first wife of Napoleon Bonaparte. The basis of the name is found in Joséphine's maiden name — de la Pagerie. There is only one species, but it is quite one of the most glorious of all climbers. The family Philesiaceae, to which it belongs, is confined to South America and is distantly related to the large and widespread Lily Family, Liliaceae.

● ***Lapageria rosea** (Pl.11), the Chilean Bellflower, is an evergreen climber reaching 5m in height, though often less, with thin twining hairless stems. The leaves are leathery, alternate, heart-shaped or ovate with three or five veins, 3–10cm long, glossy rather dull green above but paler beneath. The flowers are the true glory of the plant, pendulous waxy narrow bells 7–8cm long, borne singly or two or three together at or near the shoot tips. The fleshy tepals are six in number, rich crimson flecked with rose. The fruit is an oblong three-sided berry, which is sometimes set in cultivation. [June–Sept, HH, PN, Argentina & Chile]

The Chilean Bellflower has been prized as one of the very finest greenhouse climbers since the middle of the last century when it was introduced to Kew Gardens (in 1847). However, it will succeed on a shady wall in mild districts and is probably hardier than is generally supposed. Ideally a shaded sheltered wall, even a south-facing wall if shaded, will suit it. The soil must be a deep moist loam where plants will never be allowed to dry out. Hot dry summers and biting winter winds are the chief dangers, so some winter protection is a wise precaution, together with copious mulches around the base of the plant during the spring and summer. The plant has a rather rambling habit sending up shoots rather randomly from the root system. Lapagerias are propagated from seed or from layers taken during the summer. Plants are best placed outside during late March and old or dead wood should be removed at the same time annually. There are various colour forms and cultivars available and it is wise to select a good form carefully before spending one's money.

var. **albiflora** is a beautiful variety with glistening white flowers; the national flower of Chile.

'Nash Court' is a fine cultivar with soft pink bells which have a faint marbling.

LARDIZABALA (Lardizabalaceae)

A small genus of climbing evergreens with two species only, restricted to South America. The flowers are either male or female, though both occur on the same plant. They have six rather fleshy sepals and the female flowers possess three to six carpels, one of which develops into a sausage-shaped fleshy fruit.

Lardizabala biternata (Pl.11) is a vigorous climber reaching 3–4m in height with slender twining stems. The leaves are ternate to triternate consisting of three to nine leathery quite large dark green leaflets. The flowers are dark chocolate-brown with small whitish petals, the male ones 8–12mm long, borne in long drooping spikes. The female flowers are rather longer, 15–18mm long, being borne singly in the leaf axils on slender stalks. The fleshy purple fruits are oblong in outline, 5–7.5cm long. [Nov–Dec, T, PN, Chile] 

This handsome plant has been in cultivation since 1844, however, it is rare in Britain where it only succeeds in the mildest districts on a warm sheltered wall. Elsewhere it is a fine plant for a conservatory wall or trellis and it certainly deserves to be more widely known. *L. biternata* can perhaps be seen at its best in Mediterranean regions, especially the south of France, where flowers and fruits are freely produced. The sweet pulpy fruits which contain many seeds are edible and apparently greatly relished by the people of Chile, though the authors have not had the good fortune to try them.

MITRARIA (Gesneriaceae)

Mitraria contains only one species which was introduced by William Lobb (who collected for the famous nursery of Messrs Veitch) in 1846.

◐ △ ***Mitraria coccinea** (Pl.11) has slender stems which will attain 2m. The opposite somewhat leathery leaves are ovate, up to 2.5cm long, toothed and with short hairs on both sides. The flowers are produced singly in the leaf axils, on a drooping slender stalk 2.5–3.5cm long. The downy corolla is orange-scarlet, 2.5–3.5cm long, tubular and slightly inflated and with four exserted stamens. The fruit is an egg-shaped berry about 1cm long. [May–Sept, T-HH, PN, Chile & adjacent Argentina]

A lovely plant which dislikes hot sunshine and dry conditions, and does best on a partially shady wall or tree trunk, although it will succeed on a north-facing wall. It does particularly well in the milder coastal areas of western Britain and elsewhere makes a fine conservatory plant, flowering mainly in May and June. Plants are best placed out-of-doors in the early spring. A moist loamy soil with added peat suits it best.

MUTISIA (Compositae)

A charming and distinctive South American genus of some 60 species, only five of which are generally cultivated. They climb with the aid of tendrils produced at the ends of the alternate leaves, which are simple or pinnate. The flowers are in typical 'daisy' heads and are solitary, usually borne on long stalks, and have attractively coloured, petal-like, marginal ray florets.

These magnificent climbers appreciate a well-drained soil and do best with their roots and main stems in the shade, and their top parts in the sun. A plant in full flower always attracts attention, and the brilliant flower-heads are long-lasting. Mutisias have a reputation for being tender, but this is not borne out and they should be tried much more often. They also have a reputation for not living long and certainly the plants can suddenly die with no obvious cause, although *M. clematis* is very amenable to cultivation. However, in some gardens they have been known to live for many years.

They can be grown against a wall or fence but are perhaps best when allowed to climb up other wall shrubs, especially old or unwanted ones. Propagation is easiest from seed if it can be obtained.

The genus is named in honour of the Spaniard José Celestino Mutis who directed the Spanish royal botanical expeditions in Colombia in the 1760s.

☼ ***Mutisia oligodon** will reach 1.5m. Its young shoots are ribbed and clothed in pale woolly hairs. Stalkless leaves, 2.5–3.5cm long, are oblong with toothed margins, dark green above but with pale woolly hairs beneath. The leaf tendril is unbranched. The flower-heads are borne on a stalk 2.5–7.5cm long; they have six to twelve shiny pink ray florets, about 3cm long and a central yellow disk. At the base of the flower-heads are a number of overlapping ovate, pointed bracts which have hairy margins. [June–July and sporadically until autumn, HH, PN, Chile & Argentina]

A lovely plant for a low wall or trellis or for growing through a shrub. Introduced from Chile in 1927 by Harold Comber.

☼ **Mutisia spinosa** = *M. retusa* grows to 6m tall. The leaves are 2.5–6cm long, stalkless and elliptic to oblong, variable in the amount of toothing, sometimes untoothed. They are hairless and dark green above, and either hairless or woolly beneath. The flower-heads have about eight pink ray florets 3cm long, the disk being yellow. [July–Aug, HH, PN, Chile & Argentina]

This species was first introduced by Richard Pearce who sent it to the nursery of Messrs Veitch of Chelsea in 1868. It looks very well growing through a bush, and is said to set fertile seed more readily than the other species.

Mutisia ilicifolia has slender stems which will climb to 4.5m. Young shoots have toothed wings. Stalkless leaves, 2.5–6cm long, are ovate-oblong with strong spiny teeth on the margin looking very like a holly, dark green above and with woolly hairs below. Tendrils unbranched, 2.5–10cm long. The flower-heads have shorter stalks than the other species, 1.25cm or less, eight to twelve pale mauvish or pink ray florets and a yellow disk; the whole head is 5–7.5cm in diameter. [June–Aug, and intermittently throughout the year, H, PN, Chile]

M. ilicifolia, the first *Mutisia* to be brought to Britain, was introduced in 1832.

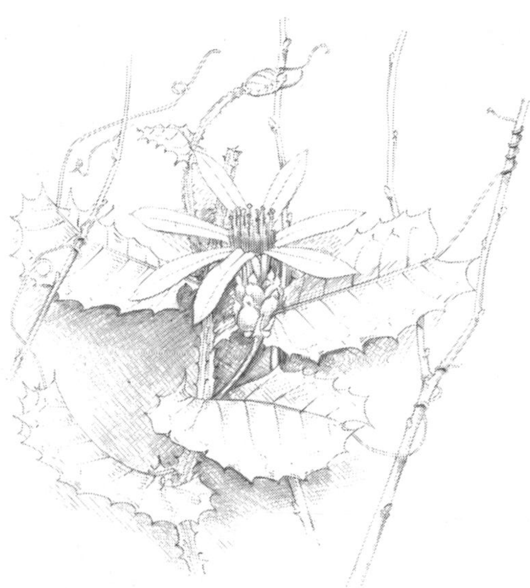

Mutisia ilicifolia.

***Mutisia decurrens** (Pl.11) has slender hairless stems which reach 3m tall. Leaves narrowly oblong are stalkless, 7.5–13cm long, the base of the blade running down each side of the stem to form a couple of narrow wings. The leaf tendril is forked. The flower-heads are 10–13cm across, with a yellow disk and orange or scarlet ray florets, usually about 15 in number. [June–Aug, H, PN, Chile & Argentina]

Another of Richard Pearce's introductions. A difficult plant to establish, and therefore not very often seen in our gardens, but worth the trouble as it is a most glorious sight when in full bloom. It is best on a south- or west-facing wall but one which is slightly shaded.

***Mutisia clematis** is the tallest-growing cultivated species, climbing to 9m or more. The leaves are pinnate with six to ten oblong-ovate leaflets which are 1.5–3.5cm long, white-woolly on both surfaces when young, becoming hairless above when older. The leaf tendril has 2–3 branches. The flower-heads hang downwards and are 5–6cm across, with nine or ten bright scarlet-orange ray florets which spread horizontally or are somewhat recurved. [May–Oct, T, PS, Andes of Colombia & Ecuador]

A very vigorous species which may require pruning. This is best done in the early spring. *M. clematis* is the easiest species to cultivate.

PANDOREA (Bignoniaceae)

A small genus of evergreen twining climbers native to Australia. One species *P. jasminoides* is obtainable in this country, a plant for the mildest localities on a sunny sheltered wall. Elsewhere it is best confined to a conservatory. Plants can be propagated from semi-mature wood placed in a propagating frame in midsummer, or from seed.

☼ **Pandorea jasminoides** = *Bignonia* or *Tecoma jasminoides*, the Bower Plant of Australia, is a beautiful climber reaching 4–5m high with pinnate, glossy green leaves composed of five to nine slender pointed elliptic leaflets, each 2.5–6cm long. The funnel-shaped flowers are white, flushed with crimson, 4–5cm long, borne in small branched clusters. [July–Sept, T, PN, Australia]

var. **alba** has white flowers.

PARSONIA (Apocynaceae)

A southern hemisphere Old World genus of about an hundred species. The cultivated species come mainly from Australia and New Zealand. They have opposite leaves and bear small flowers in terminal and axillary panicles.

☼ **Parsonia heterophylla** is an hairless slender climber producing leaves which are very variable in size and shape. The leaves of young plants are linear, oblong or spoon-shaped, 2.5–12cm long, and unlobed or with four to eight lobes. The leaves of mature plants are linear, ovate or obovate, 3.5–8cm long and unlobed. The creamy-white fragrant flowers are borne in panicles up to 10cm long; each flower, about 6mm long, has a bell-shaped corolla with recurved lobes. In the centre of the flower is a 'cone' formed from the five stamens. The fruits contain many seeds, each bearing a tuft of silky hairs. [May–June, T, PN, New Zealand]

This species is normally grown under glass, but in the mildest parts of Britain will survive outside.

PASSIFLORA (Passifloraceae)

The Passion Flower is a widely known plant, though few realise that there are probably more than 500 species in the genus *Passiflora*. Most are woody climbers, the majority coming from Central and South America, although a few come from the Old World tropics. The species most commonly seen in this country is *P. caerulea*, the Blue Passion Flower, but the fruits sold by greengrocers come from *P. edulis*, the Granadilla.

The blooms of the Passion Flowers are very beautiful, although complex. They consist of a tubular calyx with five sepals on the outside followed by a whorl of five petals which often closely resemble the sepals. Within these there is a ring of threads or 'filaments', which are usually coloured, called the 'corona'. Five conspicuous stamens are carried on an elongated central column which also supports the ovary and three stigmas.

The Passion Flower gets its name from the resemblance which Spanish priests in South America saw between the flower parts and the instruments of Christ's

Passion. The ten tepals (sepals + petals) thus represented ten apostles, the 'corona' the crown of thorns, the five stamens the five wounds and the three stigmas the three nails.

The climbing species have coiling tendrils which cling to all sorts of support. Many have lobed, hand-like leaves, but they vary greatly from species to species.

In Britain fruits are produced generally only during particularly hot summers, although some fortunate growers seem to get a regular crop each year. Both *P. caerulea* and *P. edulis* produce large egg-shaped fruits containing numerous seeds embedded in an edible jelly-like pulp.

Unfortunately only a few species can tolerate outdoor conditions in Britain, none being completely hardy. They require a sunny sheltered south or west-facing wall or a tall fence.

***Passiflora caerulea** (Pl.4), the Blue Passion Flower, is a more or less evergreen vigorous climber forming a tangled growth up to 5m tall, sometimes more. The palmate leaves have five or seven blunt oblong lobes, deep green above but bluish-green beneath, quite hairless. The slightly fragrant solitary flowers are 7–10cm across when fully open, the tepals greenish-white and the corona banded with purple, white and blue. The egg-shaped fruits are tough-skinned, orange when ripe, and 4–8cm long. [June–Sept, HH, PS, S Brazil]

The best species for general cultivation, though sadly suitable only outdoors in the south of the country or in the mildest corners of the west coast. The flowers open in the sunshine and remain closed on dull cloudy days. Plants grow rapidly but require extra protection for the first year or two. Plants are easily propagated from seed or cuttings struck in midsummer from semi-mature growth. Pruning should be fairly selective, removing only excessive, weak or dead growth in the early spring.

'Constance Elliott' is a fine cultivar with ivory-white flowers.

***Passiflora 'Allardii'**, *P. caerulea* 'Constance Elliott' × *P. quadrangularis*, is a vigorous evergreen climber with three-lobed leaves. The flowers have white tepals flushed with pink and a corona banded with white and cobalt-blue. A fine hybrid suitable for milder districts, especially in the south-western counties. [July–Sept]

Treat as *P. caerulea*.

Passiflora racemosa, the Red Passion Flower, is a climber with three-lobed leaves and flowers of vivid scarlet with a purple and white-banded corona which are borne in pendulous racemes of great beauty. This outstanding species is not suitable for growing outside in Britain, though it makes a fine plant for a sunny conservatory wall, but it has been crossed with *P. caerulea* to produce the fine hybrid described next which has greater hardiness.

Passiflora × caerulea-racemosa, *P. caerulea* × *P. racemosa*, is a vigorous climber with deeply five-lobed leaves. The flowers are borne singly at the leaf axils, the tepals are greenish flushed with deep violet and the corona violet-purple. [July–Sept, HH, PS]

A fine free-flowering hybrid suitable for the milder counties if given a sunny sheltered wall.

***Passiflora umbilicata** = *Tacsonia umbilicata*, is a vigorous hairless climber reaching 8m tall on favoured sites. The deeply three-lobed leaves are 3–5cm long. The fairly small flowers, 5–6.5cm across, are rich mauve-purple or amethyst with a stout broad tube. [July–Aug, HH, PS, Bolivia & adjacent parts of Paraguay & N Argentina]

A fine plant that deserves to be more widely grown. *Passiflora umbilicata* is probably as hardy as *P. caerulea*, coming as it does from a wild habitat in the mountains at altitudes of 2,500–3,000m. The flowers are smaller than the latter species but brilliantly coloured and freely borne. Some fine specimens can be seen in the south-west of Britain.

☼ **Passiflora edulis**, the Granadilla, is a vigorous evergreen climber with angular stems and hairless, deeply three-lobed, shiny green, leaves. The large flowers are 5–6cm across with whitish tepals and a corona of curly filaments which are banded with white and purple. The egg-shaped fruits are yellow or purplish when ripe, 4.5–5cm long. [July–Sept, T, PS, Tropical S America]

An attractive plant, but only suitable for growing outdoors in the very mildest districts. Fruit is sometimes produced but rarely in profusion. In Southern Europe it is a splendid sight in full flower, and the delicious fruits are especially good to eat on a hot day.

☼ **Passiflora antioquiensis** = *Tacsonia vanvolxemii* a fine plant growing to 4m with slender downy stems. The leaves can be unlobed and lanceolate or deeply three-lobed, downy beneath. The large pendulous flowers are exquisite, 10–13cm across, deep rose-red with a violet corona and a stout perianth tube. [Aug–Oct, T, PS, Colombia]

A very beautiful species which will succeed in very mild districts only but makes a fine conservatory subject elsewhere, though a rather rampant one. Fruits are seldom set in Britain.

PERIPLOCA (Asclepiadaceae)

The genus has been described on p.52 together with the deciduous species.

☼ **Periploca laevigata** is an evergreen or semi-evergreen woody plant whose stems can reach 3m tall, twining at the ends. The hairless leaves are elliptic or lanceolate, 2.5–5cm long. The flowers are borne in almost stalkless terminal and lateral clusters of up to 15 blossoms. The corolla is greenish outside and purplish-brown and white inside, about 1.2cm across. The spreading fruit-pods are 5–10cm long. [May–Nov, T, PN, Canary Is & N Africa]

PILEOSTEGIA (Hydrangeaceae)

A small genus related to *Schizophragma*, and like that genus, climbing by means of aerial roots. The leaves are opposite and the flowers (all fertile) are carried in terminal clusters. There are four or five sepals and petals and eight to ten stamens.

☀ ***Pileostegia viburnoides** = *Schizophragma viburnoides* is a slow-growing climber ultimately reaching 6m tall. The young shoots and leaves are scurfy and the opposite leaves are oblong or obovate, 6–15cm long, leathery, untoothed, hairless and dull green. The white or cream flowers are borne in dense pyramidal clusters 10–15cm long, each flower about 9mm across, its long stamens the most obvious feature. [Aug–Oct, H, PS, India, China & Taiwan]

An excellent plant which will grow in any soil and any aspect but most useful for a north-facing wall. It is one of E.H. Wilson's many introductions from

China. In addition to spring pruning, unwanted growths can be removed as they are produced in summer.

PROUSTIA (Compositae)

A genus of 15 species native to the West Indies, temperate South America and the Andes. Somewhat similar to *Mutisia* but with the flower-heads undifferentiated into disk and ray florets.

Proustia pyrifolia grows up to 3m tall in the wild, having slender downy stems armed with hooked spines. The alternate leaves are roundish or oval with a heart-shaped base and a finely-pointed tip, rather leathery, and densely hairy beneath. The flower-heads are white or purple and borne in terminal or axillary panicles. Each individual flower is two-lipped with recurved corolla segments. The fruits bear a tuft of purple hairs. [Aug–Sept, HH, PS, Chile]

SEMELE (Liliaceae)

A strange genus related to the Butcher's Broom *Ruscus* and to *Asparagus*. They all have strange flattened stems or 'cladodes' which look, and function, like leaves. In *Ruscus* and *Semele* the small flowers are produced from the middle of the 'cladode'.

Semele androgyna = *Ruscus androgynus*, the Climbing Butcher's Broom, is a vigorous scrambling climber reaching as much as 30m. The evergreen branching stems bear alternate, oval or lanceolate, leathery cladodes which are 7.5–10cm long. The small greenish-yellow flowers are borne in clusters of up to 20 followed by rounded, rather pulpy, berries. [May–June, HH, PS, Canary Is]

A curiosity rather than a plant of ornamental value. In the wild it is a rampant and smothering climber, clambering over quite large trees as well as bushes and rocks. In cultivation it needs a rich soil and is easily propagated by division of the much-branched rootstock.

SENECIO (Compositae)

An enormous genus containing 2,000–3,000 species world-wide. A number of species are grown in herbaceous borders or in dampish situations, but only one climber is in general cultivation.

Senecio scandens is a moderately vigorous climber reaching 5m tall. The leaves are ovate or long-triangular, 5–10cm long, toothed, often with lobes at the base, greyish-green and downy on both surfaces. The daisy-like flower-heads are borne in terminal and lateral clusters, each about 1.25cm across, and usually with eight yellow ray florets, sometimes up to twelve. [July–Oct, HH, PS, E Asia]

A useful climber which will scramble over hedges or shrubs, or can be trained on a sheltered wall. In cold parts of the country the stems may be cut to the ground, but the stock will sprout again in the spring after all but the severest winters. In mild weather plants may still be in flower in November.

SOLANUM (Solanaceae)

A large genus of some seventeen hundred world-wide tropical and temperate species, which has given us the potato *(S. tuberosum)* and the aubergine *(S. melongena)*. The leaves are alternate and both calyx and corolla are five-lobed.

The five stamens have short filaments and the long anthers lean towards one another to form a 'cone'. The fruit is a berry containing many seeds.

The two species described below climb by their twining leaf stalks. Both will thrive on most average garden soils and at midsummer can be propagated from firm young shoots in a propagating frame. The deciduous *S. valdiviense* is described on p.55.

Solanum crispum is a quick-growing, scrambling semi-evergreen, reaching up to 6m tall. Its ovate leaves are 6–13cm long. Slightly fragrant flowers are carried in clusters 7.5–15cm across, each 2.5–3cm in diameter, the corolla bluish-purple with a yellow cone of anthers. The berries are globose, 4–6mm across and creamy-coloured when ripe. [June–Sept, H, PS, Chile & Peru]

A lovely plant, requiring full sun and preferring a south- or west-facing wall. Although hardy, it grows best in the milder parts of Britain and does particularly well on a chalky soil. In addition to wall culture, it can be used on a fence, or to cover unsightly structures. Care should be taken in pruning this plant as it gives some people a rash.

***'Glasnevin'** = 'Autumnale' (Pl.4) is a vigorous and lovely cultivar with a longer flowering period — in a mild winter a few flowers will often still be produced. It originated in the Glasnevin Botanic Garden, Dublin, and is said to be hardier than the type. One of the finest of all wall plants.

Solanum jasminoides, the Potato Vine, also climbs to 6m and usually is semi-evergreen. The ovate to lanceolate leaves are 2.5–5cm long, with a slightly wavy margin, sometimes lobed at the base, or even with separate leaflets. The flowers are pale blue with a greyish tinge, 2–2.5cm across, and have a yellow 'beak' of anthers. [July–Nov, T, PS, S Brazil & Paraguay]

Less hardy than *S. crispum* and needing the protection of a south- or west-facing wall. In bad winters, or cold parts of the country it can be cut to ground level. It is not known to have produced fruit in Britain; in the wild, purple berries about 1.3cm in diameter follow the flowers.

***'Album'** (Pl.4) has white flowers. More commonly grown than *S. jasminoides* itself for it is considered by many to be a more beautiful plant.

SOLLYA (Pittosporaceae)

Sollya contains only two species and both are in cultivation. They have alternate, simple leaves. The flowers have five sepals and petals and the five anthers join together to form a 'cone' in the centre of each bloom.

Sollya species are rather tender and need a sunny wall and a well-drained peaty soil. They will grow well only in the milder areas of Britain. Their beautiful blue flowers always attract attention and they deserve to be more widely known and grown. Some form of winter protection is advisable for these delightful plants.

***Sollya heterophylla** = *S. fusiformis*, the Bluebell Creeper, has slender twining stems up to 3m tall. Its leaves vary from ovate to narrowly lanceolate and are 2.5–6cm long. The wide, bell-shaped flowers are borne in nodding clusters of four to nine; the corolla, 12–13mm across, is a lovely sky-blue. [June–Oct, T, PN, W Australia]

Introduced into England in 1830 and most often seen as a greenhouse climber.

Sollya parviflora = *S. drummondii* has a more slender habit than *S. heterophylla*. The leaves are linear and the flowers are smaller and a darker blue, borne singly or two together. [June–Oct, T, PN, W Australia]

This species inhabits the Swan River region of New South Wales and is rare in cultivation in this country, being generally seen as a greenhouse subject. Like *S. heterophylla* plants can be propagated from cuttings of firm young growths inserted in sand in a propagating frame in midsummer. Young plants of both species should not be placed out of doors until spring has arrived.

STAUNTONIA (Lardizabalaceae)

Another genus which, like *Sinofranchetia*, finds a close ally in the better known *Holboellia*. The two are readily distinguished because the stamens of *Stauntonia* are joined together whilst those of *Holboellia* are quite separate. The genus contains some 15 species from east and south-east Asia, although only one is in general cultivation. The generic name commemorates Sir George Staunton who was a member of the famous Macartney embassy to China in 1792.

Stauntonia hexaphylla = *Rajania hexaphylla* is an evergreen twining climber reaching 10m tall or more and forming a dense tangled growth. The long-stalked leaves are composed of between three and seven oval or elliptic, sharply pointed leaflets, each 5–13cm long. Borne in few-flowered racemes, the fragrant white-flushed violet flowers are each about 18mm across, with six fleshy sepals but no petals. Male and female flowers are produced on separate plants. The fleshy plum-shaped fruits are purple and juicy when ripe, 2.5–5cm long. [Apr–May, HH, PA, S Korea, Japan & Ryukyus Is]

An handsome vigorous climber suitable for a warm sheltered spot in milder districts, succeeding on most ordinary garden soils. Elsewhere it makes a good cool greenhouse or conservatory subject. The fruits are sweet and succulent when ripe and are eaten in Japan, however, they are seldom set in quantity in Britain, except during a hot summer. Like *Sinofranchetia, Stauntonia* will set some fruit occasionally even in the absence of a male plant. Plants are sometimes found under the name *Holboellia hexaphylla* in books and catalogues.

TECOMARIA (Bignoniaceae)

A beautiful genus containing a few species of evergreen climbers and shrubs native to southern Africa. They are related to *Campsis* and *Bignonia* and other tropical and subtropical climbers which all possess showy trumpet-shaped flowers of great beauty.

Tecomaria capensis, the Cape Honeysuckle, is a moderately vigorous self-clinging twining climber up to 4.5cm tall. Leaves pinnate with five to nine leaflets. Flowers borne in terminal racemes, brilliant scarlet, each trumpet-shaped with five rounded lobes, 4.5–5cm long. [Aug–Oct, T, PS, S Africa]

A fine plant, glorious in full bloom but only at its best in a hot sunny corner against a sheltered south-facing wall in the very mildest districts of the south west. It is commonly grown in the Mediterranean area and in subtropical gardens where it is a grand sight for a number of weeks. Occasionally *Tecomaria capensis* is seen as a cool greenhouse or conservatory plant in Britain, where it is more likely to survive longer.

TRACHELOSPERMUM (Apocynaceae)

Twining shrubs whose stems produce milky sap when cut. The leaves are opposite, leathery and untoothed. The jasmine-like flowers have a five-lobed calyx and a five-lobed corolla whose lobes all overlap one another to the right. The fruit is a pair of cylindrical pods, which contain seeds each of which bears a tuft of hairs.

The two species cultivated in British gardens are hardy in all but the coldest districts, provided they have wall protection. They can put up with partial shade, although they grow better in a sunny position. They can be easily trained on a south- or west-facing wall and produce their delightfully scented flowers on the old wood. This should be borne in mind when pruning — which is done mainly to remove dead wood or weak growth, or to control unwanted extension growth. Cuttings of firm young shoots can be made in August using a propagating frame.

***Trachelospermum jasminoides**, the Star Jasmine, has stems which if permitted will climb to 9m tall. The dark shining leaves are elliptic, oblong or oblanceolate, up to 10cm long. The very fragrant flowers are borne in terminal and lateral clusters, and the calyx lobes are recurved. The corolla is white, about 2.5cm across the lobes. The pods are up to 15cm in length. [July–Aug, H, PS, China]

'Variegatum' (Pl.11) has wider, shorter leaves margined and splashed with white, flushed crimson in winter. It is possibly hardier than the type.

'Wilsoni' has bronze leaves with pale green veins, which usually turn a beautiful deep red in winter.

Trachelospermum asiaticum = *T. majus, T. japonicum*, grows to a height of 6m. Its much-branched habit and neat growth produce a dense cover of dark glossy leaves, which are oval and 2-5cm long. The scented flowers have a calyx with erect lobes. The corolla, about 2cm across, is cream, deeper in the throat, and changes to yellow as it ages. Seed pods are 12–22cm long. [July–Aug, H, PS, Japan & Korea]

Hardier than *T. jasminoides* but with flowers less powerfully scented.

WATTAKAKA (Asclepiadaceae)

Similar to *Cionura* but the corolla lobes are ovate or oval.

Wattakaka sinensis = *Dregea sinensis* is a twining shrub reaching 3m tall, with very downy young shoots. The opposite leaves are ovate, heart-shaped at the base, long-pointed at the tips, 3–10cm long and densely greyish-downy on the lower surface. The fragrant flowers are borne in a lateral hanging umbel of 10–25 blossoms. The corolla is star-shaped, 1.3–1.5cm across, white or creamy and dotted and streaked with red. The pods, borne in pairs, are 5–7cm long, and downy. [June–July, HH, PA, China]

A botanically interesting plant with dainty, but not especially showy, flowers. It is available in commerce, but is not often found in our gardens. It was introduced into cultivation by E.H. Wilson in 1907, some 20 years after its discovery by Augustine Henry, an Irishman who collected many plants while working for the Imperial Chinese Customs Service.

Deciduous Wall Shrubs

A good proportion of our finest garden shrubs are deciduous species. Many are completely hardy and a number half-hardy or tender, although there are more tender species in the evergreen shrubs. Nonetheless, this section includes a wide range of beautiful shrubs for growing against walls and fences; the *Forsythia* and pretty Winter Jasmine, *Jasminum nudiflorum*, the beautifully fragrant Winter Sweet, *Chimonanthus praecox*, the Japanese or Flowering Quinces, *Chaenomeles* and the lovely Rose Acacia, *Robinia hispida,* are all to be found here.

Except for the more tender species, most deciduous shrubs can be planted in the late autumn or early winter, or indeed anytime up until spring, the weather permitting. On the whole they require more in the way of regular pruning than their evergreen cousins, especially the Forsythias, Winter Jasmine and the Flowering Quinces; this not only to keep them in check but to encourage as many flowers as possible.

Since deciduous species do not have a continuous cover of leaves, if an unsightly wall or fence is to be masked evergreen species are probably a wiser choice. However, on average walls most gardeners will want to grow a range of both evergreen and deciduous shrubs and climbers and it can be great fun choosing different plants to associate with one another. A lot can be done by simple trial and error, however, you can learn by observing plantings in different gardens but beware — what grows in one garden may not necessarily grow in another.

Many more hardy deciduous shrubs could have been included here. We have described as many as space permits, especially those which look well on a wall.

ABELIA (Caprifoliaceae)

The Abelias are beautiful shrubby cousins of the honeysuckles. Most of the species are tender and are therefore ideal subjects to grow within the protection of walls and fences. They are rather easy to grow, though fairly slow, and thrive in moist loamy soils which must not be allowed to dry out during the summer months. Liberal mulches will help to prevent excessive drying. South- and west-facing walls are most suitable, especially in southern and western districts. Plants flower on new wood and pruning should consist of cutting back weak or untidy growths shortly after flowering. Most of the species are readily propagated from cuttings of half-ripened wood taken in midsummer.

The leaves are opposite or in threes and the flowers tubular or bell-shaped, being usually borne in pairs which are often clustered close together. The calyx can have two to five sepals which persist after the corolla has fallen.

Abelia chinensis = *A. rupestris*, the Chinese Abelia, is a deciduous shrub, 1–1.5m tall, of rather sprawling habit. The oval leaves are slightly toothed and pointed, 2–3.5cm long. The charming funnel-shaped flowers are white, each about 12mm long. The rose-coloured calyx has five narrow lobes. [July–Oct, HH, PA, China]

The Chinese Abelia is not common in cultivation though it is sometimes sold by nurserymen disguised under the name *A. rupestris*, however, such plants may prove to be *A.* ×*grandiflora* so they need to be chosen with some care. It is worth growing for its haunting fragrance.

Abelia chinensis was discovered by Dr Clarke Abel in the early part of the nineteenth century and it is in his honour that the genus was named by Robert Brown.

◐ **Abelia engleriana** is also deciduous, reaching a maximum height of some 2m. Its stems become shiny and peel as they age. The oval-lanceolate leaves are bright green above and glossy beneath, 0.8–1.5cm long. The rose-pink flowers are mostly borne in pairs, the corolla funnel-shaped, 15mm long, with the stamens not protruding from the mouth. The calyx has two sepals only. [June–Sept, HH, PA, China (Szechwan)]

◐ **Abelia graebneriana** is closely related to the preceding species but a coarser plant with larger, more markedly toothed leaves, up to 5.5cm long. The solitary flowers are bell-shaped, pink with a yellow throat, 22–25mm long. [June–July, HH, PA, Central China]

'Vedrariensis' is a particularly fine form with deeper green leaves and larger flowers which are more conspicuously yellowed in the throat.

☼ **Abelia schumannii** is a rather graceful deciduous shrub rarely exceeding 1.5m tall in cultivation, with slender arching shoots which have a pleasing purplish colour when young. The leaves are oval, scarcely toothed, 1.5–3.2cm long. The solitary rose-pink flowers are funnel-shaped, about 25mm long; the calyx has two sepals only. [June–early Nov, T, PA, Central China]

A fine species allied to *A. engleriana* but with larger flowers. Unfortunately it is not as hardy and may be cut back severely in a hard winter, although established plants will generally sprout anew in the spring.

◐ **Abelia triflora** (Pl.18) is an erect deciduous shrub of vigorous habit reaching 3m tall or more, the stems greyish and rather brittle when young. The oval-lanceolate leaves are 3–7cm long, the leaf margin untoothed to deeply toothed or lobed. The delicate whitish-rose flowers are borne in erect clusters, often in threes, the corolla is bell-shaped; the reddish calyx has five lobes. [June–July, H, PA, NW Himalaya]

Abelia triflora is one of the hardiest, and certainly the most vigorous species in cultivation, some specimens having been known to reach 6m in height. In many districts it is hardy in the open garden, however, it can be a sulky plant when it comes to flowering, only occasionally producing a dense show of blooms. In this respect it is certainly more reliable when grown against a high wall. The flowers have a pleasing fragrance and the persistent calyces give interest to the plant well after flowering has ceased.

◐ **Abelia spathulata** is another hardy deciduous species, a rather densely-branched shrub to 1.5m tall. The oval-lanceolate or rhomboidal leaves are 2.5–5cm long with a toothed margin. The flowers occur in pairs at the end of short shoots, the corolla funnel-shaped, pink with a yellow throat, 20–25mm long. The pink calyx has five lobes. [June–July, HH, PA, Japan]

This plant is more or less hardy in milder districts but only half-hardy elsewhere.

Another Japanese species, *A. serrata*, is sometimes seen in cultivation, but it has small pale flowers of little merit and is certainly an inferior as a garden plant to those described above.

The evergreen species, *A. floribunda* and *A. uniflora* as well as the hybrid *A.* ×*grandiflora* are to be found on p.165.

ABELIOPHYLLUM (Oleaceae)

This genus contains only one species which is a deciduous shrub with simple opposite leaves. Both the calyx and corolla are four-lobed and there are only two stamens.

***Abeliophyllum distichum** grows 1–3m tall and has four-angled branches. The leaves are ovate, 2–5cm long, untoothed and downy. The fragrant flowers are whitish, orange in the centre and often tinged with a very pale pink. They appear before the leaves unfold, in clusters on the twigs of the previous year, each 6–12mm in diameter. The fruit is roundish, flattened, about 2.5cm across and with a wing all the way round. [Jan–Apr, H, PA, Korea]

Abeliophyllum distichum.

A slow-growing plant but its early flowering makes it a pretty addition to any garden. It is in the same family as *Forsythia* and at first glance looks like a whitish-flowered member of that genus. It is best grown against a south-facing wall or fence where the flowers are less likely to suffer from frost damage. The lower branches often hang down to touch the ground, where they will root; it is sensible to remove them, otherwise they will develop into competitive young plants. Propagation is by cuttings of half-ripened wood taken in midsummer, or by layering. *Abeliophyllum distichum* has been cultivated since 1924.

ABUTILON (Malvaceae)

The beautiful semi-evergreen, or sometimes deciduous, Abutilons, *A. ochsenii*, *A.* ×*suntense* and *A. vitifolium* are to be found in the chapter on Evergreen Wall Shrubs.

ADENOCARPUS (Leguminosae)

This genus contains both deciduous and evergreen shrubs: there are some 20 species growing in the Mediterranean area and the Canary Islands. The leaves have three leaflets and are alternate, or borne in clusters.

☼ **Adenocarpus decorticans** grows up to 3m tall and has a whitish bark which tends to peel off in long strips. The leaves are very crowded and have narrow hairy leaflets with inrolled margins. The slightly fragrant golden-yellow pea-flowers are borne in racemes 3–6cm long. The fruit pods are 3.5–5cm long. [May–June, T-HH, PA, Spain]

A handsome and floriferous shrub seldom seen in our gardens. It is only hardy in the mildest parts of Britain and elsewhere needs wall protection. It is not a long-lived shrub, but it can easily be propagated from seeds which are often set in large numbers.

Adenocarpus foliolosus is an evergreen species and is described on p.169.

ALBIZIA (Leguminosae)

A mainly Old World genus of some 100 species often erroneously spelt 'Albizzia'. They are deciduous trees or shrubs with alternate bipinnate leaves. The leaflets are numerous and small. The flowers are borne in axillary globose heads or spikes. The calyx and corolla are relatively small, the most attractive feature of the flowers being the many long stamens. The fruit is a flattened pod.

There are two species cultivated in Britain and both are very beautiful but tender, needing to be grown in the protection of a warm wall in full sun. Any pruning should be done in the spring, either to restrict the vigorous growth or to encourage growth at the base of the plant which has a tendency to become bare.

☼ **Albizia julibrissin** (Pl.12), the Pink Siris, grows 9–12m tall with rather angular hairless young branches. The leaves have 6–12 primary divisions, each with 20–30 pairs of leaflets. The flowers are carried in dense clusters, with conspicuous pink stamens 2.5cm or more long. The pods are 12–13cm long, constricted between each seed. [July–Aug, T, PS, Near East]

Albizia julibrissin has been cultivated in Britain since 1745, and was certainly grown in China long before then. The base of the plant becomes bare with age and it is often a good idea to plant lower shrubs in front as a mask to these bare stems. They may also aid in protecting this lovely, though tender, beauty.

***'Rosea'** has stamens of a brighter pink. It is said to be more hardy.

☼ **Albizia lophantha** can reach 13m against a house wall. The young branches are velvety and the leaves have 8–11 primary divisions, each with 20–30 pairs of leaflets. The yellow flowers are borne in brush-like heads, which form spikes 2.5–7.5cm long, often carried in pairs. They are scented. [Apr–May, T, PS, W Australia]

ANAGYRIS (Leguminosae)

There are two species of *Anagyris*, but only the one described below is cultivated in our gardens.

☼ **Anagyris foetida** has alternate leaves with three leaflets which are downy beneath and 2.5–6cm long. The yellow pea-flowers are 2–2.5cm long and borne in racemes 3–8cm long. The fruit is a curved pod. [May–June, T, PN, Mediterranean area]

A tender shrub which only grows well in the warmest parts of Britain, and even there it requires a south-facing wall. The flowers have no scent, but when the leaves are crushed they emit a rather unpleasant smell — hence the Latin specific name *foetida*. Plants are readily raised from seed.

ANTHYLLIS (Leguminosae)

Two species are cultivated — the evergreen *Anthyllis barba-jovis* is described on p.169.

Anthyllis hermanniae is a bushy shrub which grows about 1m tall, and has crooked branches which end in a spine. The leaves are simple or sometimes with three leaflets, narrowly obovate, 1.25–2.5cm long and covered in silky hairs. The flowers are yellow marked with orange on the standard, 7–8mm long, and borne in small axillary clusters. [June–July, HH, PA, Mediterranean area]

A good plant for a low wall or for planting at the foot of taller-growing plants. It needs a sunny position to flower well. Seed is rarely set in Britain, although plants can be increased by cuttings struck in midsummer and overwintered in a frost-free place.

ARISTOTELIA (Elaeocarpaceae)

A small genus of deciduous or evergreen trees or shrubs native to South America, Australia, New Zealand and the New Hebrides. Four species are cultivated but they are all tender and suitable only for the mildest parts of the country — favoured places being the moist mild areas of south-western England and Ireland and the western coast of Scotland swept by the warming Gulf Stream.

If cut back by frosts they generally have the capacity to sprout anew from the sturdier branches. Plants can be propagated by cuttings taken in midsummer from half-ripened wood.

Aristotelia serrata = *A. racemosa, Dicera serrata,* is a deciduous species, making a bush or small tree up to 8m. The leaves are opposite or subopposite, heart-shaped, toothed, 5–10cm long. The rose pink flowers, borne in downy panicles from the leaf axils are small, only 4mm across, but they are numerous. The male and female flowers are produced on separate plants. The pea-sized fruits are dark red, blackening when ripe. [May, T, PN, New Zealand]

Fine specimens can be seen in western Scotland, especially at Inverewe and in County Down, Northern Ireland. The flowers are small but produced in sufficient quantity to compensate for size.

Aristotelia fruticosa is like the previous species but does not exceed 4.5m in height. The leaves are rather leathery and never more than 2.5cm long and the flowers are borne singly or in few-flowered clusters. [May–June, T, PN, New Zealand]

Both *A. serrata* and *A. fruticosa* colonise cleared forest or waste areas in the wild, often hybridising where they come in close contact with one another. *A.* ×*colensoi* is the name generally applied to such offspring.

BUDDLEIA (Loganiaceae)

The genus is too well known to need much introduction, although few realise how many fine species there are in cultivation. The common Buddleia, *B. davidii* is widely grown and has become naturalised in many places, relishing waste areas, building sites or railway embankments and often growing in the cracks of walls and buildings, however, it is far too hardy to require wall culture in the average garden.

The genus is named in honour of the Rev. Adam Buddle, once vicar of Farnbridge in Essex, who died in 1715. The species are shrubs or small trees with angled stems and opposite leaves which are often woolly. The individual flowers are generally small, the corolla half-tubular. They occur in large, rather dense, racemes or panicles. Each flower has four rounded lobes and four stamens. The flowers of most species are very attractive to butterflies.

Buddleias are easily cultivated, growing on most soil types but relishing a rich loamy soil in a sunny position. They can be propagated by cuttings of short side-growths in the late summer, or by seed. Those that flower on the current season's shoots need to be pruned back in the spring, whilst the remainder should be pruned immediately flowering ceases.

Both evergreen and deciduous species are described here for convenience.

☼ **Buddleia asiatica** is a slender, rather graceful evergreen shrub growing to 6m tall, the stems and leaves covered in whitish or yellowish down, the leaves narrowly lanceolate, 10–20cm long and generally slightly toothed. The white flowers are deliciously fragrant and occur in long drooping spike-like panicles, up to 15cm long. [Feb–Apr, T, PA, India, SE Asia & Java]

☼ **Buddleia auriculata** is another evergreen species with white flowers. The shrub reaches 3–5m tall. The leaves are lanceolate or oblong, 5–10cm long, white with down beneath. The base of each leaf stalk has a pair of rounded auricles which clasp the stem and which give the plant its name. The very fragrant flowers are borne in panicles 2.5–5cm long, the corollas white or creamy-white with a yellow eye, each only 6–8mm long. [Sept–Jan, HH, PA, S Africa]

This species is almost hardy in the mildest parts of the country but needs protection even there during severe weather. Pruning is best carried out in the early spring.

☼ **Buddleia fallowiana**, is more commonly seen than the two preceding species. It is a deciduous shrub growing to 3m tall or rather more with white-felted shoots. The leaves are lanceolate, 6–24cm long, dark green above but white-downy beneath. The lavender flowers are very fragrant and occur in long spike-like panicles 20–30cm long. Each flower, only about 9mm long, is covered in white down on the outside. [June–Sept, HH, PS, China]

This beautiful species may be cut right back during a severe winter but generally sprouts again from the base to produce flowers in the same year. There is a particularly fine form, var. *alba*, with beautiful milky-white flowers, which was collected by George Forrest in Yunnan.

Several fine hybrids exist between this species and *B. davidii* and have the merit of being hardier than *B. fallowiana*.

☼ ***Buddleia crispa** = *B. paniculata* (Pl.12) is a deciduous shrub growing to about 4m tall with downy white branches. The attractive lanceolate leaves are coarsely toothed, 5–7cm long, and white with down on both surfaces. The fragrant flowers are lilac with a white eye, each only 8mm long but occurring in a broad panicle about 8cm long overall. [June–Sept, HH, PS, E Afghanistan, N Pakistan & N India]

This attractive W Himalayan shrub is one of the finest Buddleias for wall culture, flowering often from midsummer onwards until the first frosts of autumn. It is still quite frequently sold under its synonym, *B. paniculata*.

☼ **Buddleia forrestii**. Another deciduous shrub which may reach 4m in height but generally less. The shoots, like the undersurface of the leaves, are clothed in reddish-brown down. The leaves are lanceolate, 20–30cm long and toothed. The flowers are fragrant and vary in colour from maroon to lavender or pale mauve, or even white, each about 8mm long but occurring in large panicles up to 20cm long. [Aug–Sept, HH, PS, SW China]

This attractive species was discovered by George Forrest in 1903, although live plants were not introduced until some ten years later. It is sometimes confused with the next species.

Buddleia farreri = *B. tibetica* var. *farreri*. A deciduous shrub to 3m tall, the young shoots covered with white down. The leaves are ovate with a heart-shaped base, toothed, 8–30cm long. The rosy-lilac flowers occur in broad branched clusters up to 20cm long, borne from the terminal joints of shoots of the previous year; each flower is about 8mm long. [Apr–May, T, PA, China]

A little-known species that was first introduced from Kansu in China during 1915. Plants survive outdoors on a warm sheltered wall in the mildest districts but because the flower buds are formed late in the year they are very susceptible to frosts. As a result it is probably best grown as a pot plant given the protection of a glasshouse or conservatory during the winter but plunged outside under a sunny wall in the spring.

***Buddleia colvilei**. This magnificent shrub is perhaps the best species of all for wall culture. Plants grow as tall as 14m, though often less. Young shoots are arching and vigorous, covered at first in reddish-brown hairs. The leaves are more or less oval or lanceolate, 8–25cm long. Flowers rose or crimson with a white eye, in drooping clusters 15–20cm long, borne on the previous year's wood,

Buddleia colvilei.

each flower rather large, about 20mm long and with slightly recurved lobes. [June, HH, PA, Himalaya]

A beautiful plant that often forms a small tree in the wild. It was first discovered by Joseph Dalton Hooker in Sikkim during 1849, but not introduced into cultivation until 1892. In cultivation young plants are rather tender but become hardier with age. It generally flowers best following hot summers during which the wood can ripen adequately. Although it flowers on the previous year's wood, it is probably best not to prune plants annually, rather cut away superfluous wood once flowering has finished. *Buddleia colvilei* is the largest-flowered of all cultivated Buddleias.

★**'Kewensis'** is the finest cultivar with flowers of a richer red. It comes from Bhutan and is perhaps hardier than the type.

CAESALPINIA (Leguminosae)

There are about 100 species of *Caesalpinia* which grow primarily in the tropics and subtropics, and are therefore rather tender when cultivated in Britain. They have alternate bipinnate leaves and bear their flowers in racemes. The flowers are not the usual pea-flowers which are generally characteristic of the Leguminosae, but have a rather cup-shaped corolla of five petals which are more or less equal in shape and size. There are ten conspicuous separate stamens and the fruit is a flattened pod. Both species (below) have delicate ferny foliage. Propagation is usually by seed.

The genus is named after the sixteenth-century Italian botanist, Andreas Caesalpini.

☼ **Caesalpinia japonica** can reach 5m on a wall and has almost hairless stems which have strong thorns 6–8mm long. The leaves have three to eight main divisions. The flowers are in erect racemes up to 30cm long, each raceme with 20–30 flowers. The petals are yellow, the upper one striped with red and slightly smaller than the others; the stamens are bright red. The pods are about 7.5cm long and contain six to nine seeds. [May–July, T, PS, China & Japan]

A beautiful species which requires good warm weather to flower well. It should be carefully tied into the supporting wall and should be handled gently otherwise the brittle twigs can easily be snapped. Pruning in spring should aim at training and restricting the growth.

☼ ★**Caesalpinia gilliesii** = *Poinciana gilliesii* (Pl.12) differs from *C. japonica* in lacking thorns. The young growth is clothed in gland-tipped hairs. The leaves have nine to eleven main divisions. The erect racemes are 30–40cm long and bear up to 40 flowers. The flowers have yellow petals and scarlet stamens which protrude 3–4cm. The pods are 7.5–10cm long. [July–Aug, T, PS, Argentine & Uruguay]

Caesalpinia gilliesii needs the protection of a south-facing wall, and is a lovely sight in full flower.

CASSIA (Leguminosae)

A very large genus of some 500–600 species which are native in all the tropical and warm temperate regions of the world except Europe. They have even-pinnate leaves, borne alternately along the stems. The flowers are not typical pea-flowers, but have five petals which are of more or less equal size and shape. There are usually ten stamens, but sometimes three or five of them are reduced to staminodes or are absent.

Senna is a product of the pods and dried leaves of *C. senna* and *C. angustifolia*.

***Cassia corymbosa** is an hairless shrub which attains about 1.8m in height. The leaves are 3.5–8.5cm long and have two to three pairs of oblong-ovate or lanceolate leaflets, each 2–3.5cm long. The flowers are golden-yellow and carried in small clusters at the ends of lateral shoots, each corolla 2.5–3cm wide. [Aug–Sept, T, PS, tropical S America] ☼

This shrub is a lovely sight when flowering, but unfortunately it can only be grown in the mildest areas, though even there it requires a warm sunny wall. Propagation is by seed or cuttings of half-ripe wood taken during midsummer.

CEANOTHUS (Rhamnaceae)

Ceanothus coeruleus, C. integerrimus and *C.* 'Indigo' are deciduous, although the last two may be semi-evergreen in a mild winter. These species are described on p.183 with the evergreen species of *Ceanothus*.

CESTRUM (Solanaceae)

Cestrum parqui, a usually deciduous species, is described on p.188 with the other species of the genus.

CHAENOMELES (Rosaceae)

A very popular group containing four species and numerous cultivars for the general garden, but well suited to wall culture. They are popularly called 'Flowering Quinces' or 'Japonicas', but although closely related to the Common Quince, *Cydonia oblonga*, they are at once distinguished by their finely-toothed, rather than untoothed, leaves. Indeed the species were at one time all included in the same genus, *Cydonia*, and botanists are not generally agreed on the best way to treat the various species. *Chaenomeles sinensis* is now generally accepted as belonging to a distinct genus, *Pseudocydonia*, but is included here for convenience.

The Flowering Quinces are perfectly hardy and succeed in most average garden soils, in sun or partial shade. The lower growing cultivars are particularly good subjects for growing under windows. They all require a methodic and regular pruning once they have filled their allotted space, indeed flowering is greatly improved by pruning. Shoots should be cut back to within two or three buds of the base after flowering and unwanted or crowded growths should be removed entirely. In addition outward-directed growths can be shortened in the late summer. Plants can be propagated in June or July from half-ripe wood by cuttings or layers, or by the removal of suckers if they are produced. The species can be grown from seed.

Chaenomeles have deciduous alternate leaves and large leafy stipules at the base of each leaf; the stipules are smaller on old growths but considerably larger on young vigorous shoots. Except in *C. sinensis* the flowers occur in leafless clusters along the old wood or as solitary individuals at the ends of leafy shoots. They are like apple blossom with five separate petals (except in double forms) and numerous stamens. The fruits are apple-like but hard, fragrant when ripe and edible when cooked. Like the true Quince they are the basis for making excellent jellies and conserves.

Chaenomeles speciosa = *C. lagenaria*, the true Japanese Quince, makes a wide-spreading rather tangled shrub up to 3.5m tall. The branches are smooth and more or less spiny. The leaves are oval and finely toothed, 4–9cm long, glossy green above. The scarlet or blood-red flowers occur in clusters generally of two to four, each 4–4.5cm across. The apple or pear-shaped fruits are greenish-yellow when ripe, speckled and dotted, 5–6.5cm long. [Mar–May, H, PA, China]

This glorious shrub was introduced to England in 1796 by Sir Joseph Banks. However, it has been cultivated in Chinese and Japanese gardens for many centuries and at one time there were many more varieties available than there are today. Although the main flowering season is from March until May the odd flower may be produced at almost any time and plants may even commence flowering before Christmas in some seasons. The species and its cultivars all love a lot of sun, but will at the same time tolerate a certain amount of shade so that walls or fences of most aspects except north will suffice.

The following cultivars are a selection that are fairly readily obtainable.

***'Cardinalis'** has crimson-scarlet flowers, 4cm across. A good old variety.

'Falconnet Charlet' = 'Rosea plena' is a vigorous variety with double salmon-pink flowers.

'Moerloosii' has large, white flowers flushed with pink or carmine. This cultivar is sometimes sold incorrectly as 'Apple Blossom'.

***'Nivalis'** (Pl.12) is a vigorous variety with single pure white flowers. The finest of all white *Chaenomeles*.

'Phylis Moore' has double salmon-rose flowers.

'Rubra Grandiflora' is a shrub of low spreading habit with large crimson flowers. Good for a low wall.

'Simonii' is a low growing variety like the previous one, but with rather flat semi-double flowers that are deep red.

'Umbilicata' is a vigorous variety with deep pink flowers.

Chaenomeles japonica = *Cydonia japonica, C. maulei, Pyrus japonica*, Maule's Quince, is a low spreading spiny shrub generally less than 1m tall, but much wider. The oval or rather rounded leaves are toothed and hairless, 2.5–5cm long. The stipules on the young shoots are large and leaf-like. The flowers range in colour from orange-red to scarlet or blood-red and are borne in clusters from the nodes of one year old shoots, each about 4cm across. The apple-shaped fruits are about the same size as the flowers, yellow flushed with red when ripe and pleasantly fragrant. [Apr–June, H, PA, China]

This is certainly one of the finest of all red-flowered shrubs. Unfortunately some confusion exists in gardens where the species, *C. speciosa*, has long been known under the name *Cydonia japonica*. The two are easily separated. The true *C. japonica* is a much more dwarf plant with finely warty twigs and more coarsely toothed leaves. However, so many forms, hybrids and cultivars exist that even the most astute botanists can be forgiven for getting in a muddle.

forma or var. **alba** is a good white form which should not be confused with 'Alba' of gardens which is a hybrid in the *C. × superba* group.

Chaenomeles × superba is a variable low growing shrub generally 1–1.5m tall, the shoots rather like *C. japonica*, being downy at first but later finely warty. The flowers vary from white through various shades of pink to crimson, orange, or scarlet. [Mar–June, H, PA]

This hybrid, which arose spontaneously in the first instance between *C. japonica* and *C. speciosa*, has given rise to a host of exciting cultivars. Formerly its hybrid origin was not suspected and in old catalogues it was placed under *Cydonia maulei* (at one time *Chaenomeles japonica* was sold under this name). A few of the finest cultivars are listed here.

'Alba' has glistening white flowers.

***'Boule de Feu'** (Pl.12) has orange-scarlet flowers followed by bright yellow fruits of good size.

'Coral Sea' is a dwarf cultivar rarely 1m tall, with pretty coral pink flowers. ('Yaegaki' is similar but the flowers are double.)

'Crimson and Gold' is a dense shrub 1m tall with deep red flowers with a central boss of golden anthers. This fine plant unfortunately suckers in some gardens.

***'Knap Hill Scarlet'** is a good old variety with a spreading habit and a profusion of brilliant deep red flowers.

'Perfecta' has scarlet flowers.

***'Rowallane'** is low spreading with brilliant crimson flowers of great substance.

'Vermilion' has flowers of orange-scarlet, a plant not unlike 'Boule de Feu'.

Chaenomeles cathayensis = *Cydonia cathayensis, Chaenomeles lagenaria* var. *cathayensis* (Pl.12), is a rather open spiny shrub up to 5m tall with somewhat tortuous branches. The long-stalked leaves are lanceolate and finely toothed. The young shoots bear large leafy stipules, but old shoots have leaf clusters and small stipules. The flowers are 4cm across, white often flushed with pink. The fruits are large and pear-shaped, 10–15cm long, dull green flushed with yellow and pink when ripe. [Apr–May, H, PA, Central China]

This is a rather coarse plant with attractive apple-like blossoms and a fascinating crop of large fruits set close on the stems in the late summer and autumn. The fruits only ripen out-of-doors properly during hot summers.

var. **wilsonii** is a taller plant, often reaching 7m with pretty salmon-pink flowers.

Chaenomeles × vilmoriniana = *C. vedranensis* of horticulture, is a hybrid raised at the Vilmorin Nurseries in 1921 between *C. cathayensis* and *C. speciosa*. The shrub is very spiny and up to 2.5m tall with sharp-toothed leaves and white, pink-flushed flowers. Two cultivars of this cross are available, 'Afterglow' and 'Mount Everest'.

Chaenomeles × californica. This interesting cross is a complex hybrid between *C. cathayensis* and *C. × superba* which includes characters of all the three species so far described; an erect spiny shrub of rather stiff habit, with lanceolate, toothed leaves and large flowers, 4–5cm across, in shades of pink and rose-red. The handsome fruits are bright yellow when ripe.

***'Cardinal'** is a fine clone which should not be confused with 'Cardinalis' which is a cultivar of *C. speciosa*.

Chaenomeles sinensis = *Cydonia sinensis, Pseudocydonia sinensis,* is a small deciduous or semi-evergreen spineless bush or tree to 15m tall with flaking bark, like a small plane tree. The obovate or oval leaves are finely toothed, 6.5–11cm long. The carmine-pink flowers are solitary in contrast to the other species, being borne at the nodes of the one-year-old shoots or on short lateral spurs, each flower 2.5–3.8cm across. The egg-shaped fruits, 12–18cm long, are pale lemon-yellow when ripe. [Apr–May, HH, PA, China]

This attractive tree is seen at its best on the Italian Riviera where the branches are hung with large ripe fruits in the autumn. It was first introduced to Britain at the end of the eighteenth century but was later lost and reintroduced from Italy in 1898. In Britain it is suitable only for the mildest districts and then only on a high sheltered sunny south-facing wall where it can be allowed to develop to a good size. Plants are best raised from seed if it can be obtained, and it is certainly worth a try. Fruits seldom ripen in Britain.

CHIMONANTHUS (Calycanthaceae)

A Chinese genus of four species, evergreen and deciduous, with opposite untoothed leaves. The flowers are borne in the leaf axils and have many perianth segments which are not differentiated into sepals and petals. There are five or six stamens which remain attached to the top of the many-seeded fruit.

Only the following species is cultivated.

☼ ***Chimonanthus praecox** = *C. fragrans* (Pl.13), Winter Sweet, is a deciduous shrub growing to 3.5m tall. The leaves are lanceolate to narrowly oval, deep green and 5–12cm long. The translucent fringed bell-flowers are beautifully fragrant, solitary or two together and 2–2.5cm across. The outer perianth segments are yellowish-green, the inner ones purplish and smaller. The fruit is about 3.5cm in length. [Nov–Mar, H, PA, China]

A lovely and popular shrub deserving a place in any garden, especially by a window or doorway where its fragrance can waft around the house. The flowers are borne on leafless shoots at a time when little is in flower. It flowers most profusely if left unpruned, but if pruning is necessary to control the growth or to remove weak shoots, it should be carried out immediately after flowering. When young, *C. praecox* only flowers sparsely, but once established it should flower freely. It is best propagated by seed or layers, and will grow in any soil although it seems to be especially happy on chalky ones. Winter Sweet is a fine shrub for cutting, the buds opening readily in water.

'Grandiflorus' grows taller, to 5m and has larger leaves and flowers. The flowers are deeper yellow than the type, but less heavily scented.

'Luteus' has flowers which are completely yellow. A really lovely cultivar.

CHORDOSPARTIUM (Leguminosae)

Chordospartium contains a single species which is related to *Notospartium*, differing in its pod which contains only one seed, and does not split open.

☼ **Chordospartium stevensonii** is an almost leafless shrub or small tree up to 9m tall in the wild, but seldom attaining 3m in cultivation. The leaves last only for three or four months and are produced only on young plants. The racemes are solitary or in bunches of two to five, 3.5–8cm long and densely-flowered. The flowers are about 8mm long, pale lilac or pinkish-lavender, with darker lines on the reflexed standard. The pods are about 5mm long. [May–July, T, PN, New Zealand (South Island)]

An unusual shrub which looks like a small weeping willow. It does best in sunny, warm areas, but is not very long-lived in Britain.

CLETHRA (Clethraceae)

A genus of about 70 deciduous and evergreen trees and shrubs with alternate leaves. The fragrant flowers are borne in racemes or panicles, and have five sepals and petals and ten stamens. The fruit is a three-valved capsule.

The deciduous species are somewhat hardier than the evergreen ones. None of the species likes chalk or limestone. Propagation is by seed, by layers in spring or by half-ripe cuttings taken in late summer.

Clethra delavayi can reach 12m in height and has the young growth covered with starry down. The lanceolate or narrowly ovate leaves are 5–15cm long, velvety below and with a toothed margin. The flowers are borne in a terminal single-sided raceme, 10–15cm long. The calyx is covered with short hairs and turns red when the petals have dropped. The fragrant cup-shaped flowers are white, usually flushed with yellow. [July–Aug, HH, PN, SW China (Yunnan)]

One of the many fine introductions of George Forrest who brought it to Britain in 1913.

Clethra arborea is evergreen and described on p.189.

COLQUHOUNIA (Labiatae)

The Labiate family is well known because it contains a large number of aromatic herbs such as the mints, thymes and marjorams. Indeed, most of the species are herbs, only a few being shrubs or trees. The family gets its name from the flowers which are usually two-lipped (Latin *labium*, a lip), the corolla with an upper lip which protects the stamens and style and a lower lip, often three-lobed, which acts as a landing stage for visiting insects.

Colquhounia is an Asian genus containing two or three species of deciduous shrubs. The genus is named in honour of Sir Robert Colquhoun, a patron of the Calcutta Botanic Garden in the nineteenth century.

Colquhounia coccinea is a rather lax shrub of straggling habit to 6m tall. The stems are downy when young, becoming woody with age. The opposite leaves are heart-shaped to lanceolate, 5–20cm long, dull green above, but felted with grey or whitish hairs beneath. The scarlet or orange-red flowers are borne in whorls or panicles at the tips of the current year's shoots, the corolla funnel-shaped and clearly two-lipped. [Aug–Oct, HH, PS, Himalaya, SW China & SE Asia]

This is a fine shrub when grown well, though it can become rather straggly and the stems may need a little support. It is certainly a magnificent sight in Himalayan valleys where it often borders streams and pathways. There are various clones in cultivation, some less hardy and some less colourful, so choose a stock with care. Container grown young specimens are best and they should be planted in the spring as growth commences. A sheltered south- or west-facing wall and a well-drained loamy soil are its chief requirements. Pruning consists mainly of shortening back or removing weak or overstraggling growths. The crushed leaves have an apple fragrance.

var. **vestita** is a fairly reliable hardier variety, though scarcely distinguishable from the type.

CORNUS (Cornaceae)

Cornus chinensis although a deciduous shrub is described on p.190 along with several evergreen relatives.

COTONEASTER (Rosaceae)

Few genera have provided the gardener with as many glorious berried shrubs as has *Cotoneaster*. The heavy displays of red, orange or sometimes yellowish berries are a feature of autumn and winter in our gardens. Most of the species are quite hardy in the open garden, however, they can look magnificent trained against a wall or fence. Although many of the cultivated species and cultivars could be grown in this way if desired, only a few of the finest are included here.

Cotoneasters can be shrubs or trees, evergreen or deciduous. The whitish flowers are often rather dull, though attractive enough *en masse* and are borne in small or large clusters on short lateral spurs in the early summer.

Most Cotoneasters will grow on average garden soils, or indeed often on rather poor soils, providing they are well-drained. Plants are best propagated from cuttings of half-ripened wood taken in July. Seed may not come true to type.

Cotoneaster frigidus is a large deciduous fast-growing shrub to 6.5m tall in mature specimens, less if trained against a wall. The narrow oval leaves are 8–13cm long, deep dull green above but paler and woolly beneath, especially when young. White flowers, 8mm across, are borne in flattish clusters about 5cm across. Bright red, pea-sized fruits are borne in abundance. [May–June, H, PA, Himalaya]

Cotoneaster frigidus is one of the very finest berrying shrubs, though the true species has been largely replaced in gardens by hybrids between it and *C. henryanus* or *C. salicifolius*. These are generally referred to as the *C.* ×*watereri* Group.

'Fructuluteo' = *Xanthocarpus* is a fine cultivar with yellowish or creamy-white fruits.

Cotoneaster affinis is similar to *C. frigidus* but has smaller leaves, 3–8cm long and dark purplish-brown or nearly black fruits. [May–June, H, PA, Himalaya]

This species is generally represented in cultivation by var. *bacillaris* which bears handsome jet black fruits.

***Cotoneaster horizontalis** (Pl.13) is one of the best-loved and most widely planted Cotoneasters. It is a deciduous shrub forming wide flat fans of branches with a characteristic herring-bone pattern. The growths normally fan out over the ground but will equally well fan the base of a wall to a height of 2–3m in many instances. The tiny shiny green leaves are rounded or oval, 8–12mm long. Flowers are white tinged with pink, solitary or in pairs, 6mm across. Berries are globose, bright red, 5–6mm in diameter and borne in large numbers. [May, H, PA, China]

A very lovely plant which makes an ideal specimen for a low wall or beneath a window, or it can look equally good against a fence. The leaves fall late in the autumn having turned a striking mixture of orange and red. *Cotoneaster horizontalis* makes a very pleasing association planted next to *Jasminum nudiflorum*. Plants can be easily kept within bounds by judicious pruning. Stems need no support and are usually held stiffly away from the wall or fence.

'Variegatus' has leaves edged with white.

For evergreen species, *C. franchetii*, *C. henryanus*, *C. microphyllus*, *C. salicifolius* and *C.* ×*watereri*, see p.191.

CYDONIA (Rosaceae)

The name Cydonia is as perplexing to the average gardener as is Syringa. *Syringa* botanically speaking is the Latin name for the genus that contains the common lilac, *Syringa vulgaris*, however it is also the common garden name for Mock Orange or *Philadelphus*. Cydonia is a common name often applied to the Flowering or Japanese Quinces whose correct botanical name is *Chaenomeles*. The genus *Cydonia* contains only a single species *C. oblonga*, the Common Quince, whose

---

Plate 7 Clematis 1 *Clematis phlebantha* (p.75), 2 *C. rehderiana* (p.79), 3 *C. tangutica* (p.77), 4 *C. viorna* (p.73), 5 *C. viticella* (p.70).

1
2
3
4
5

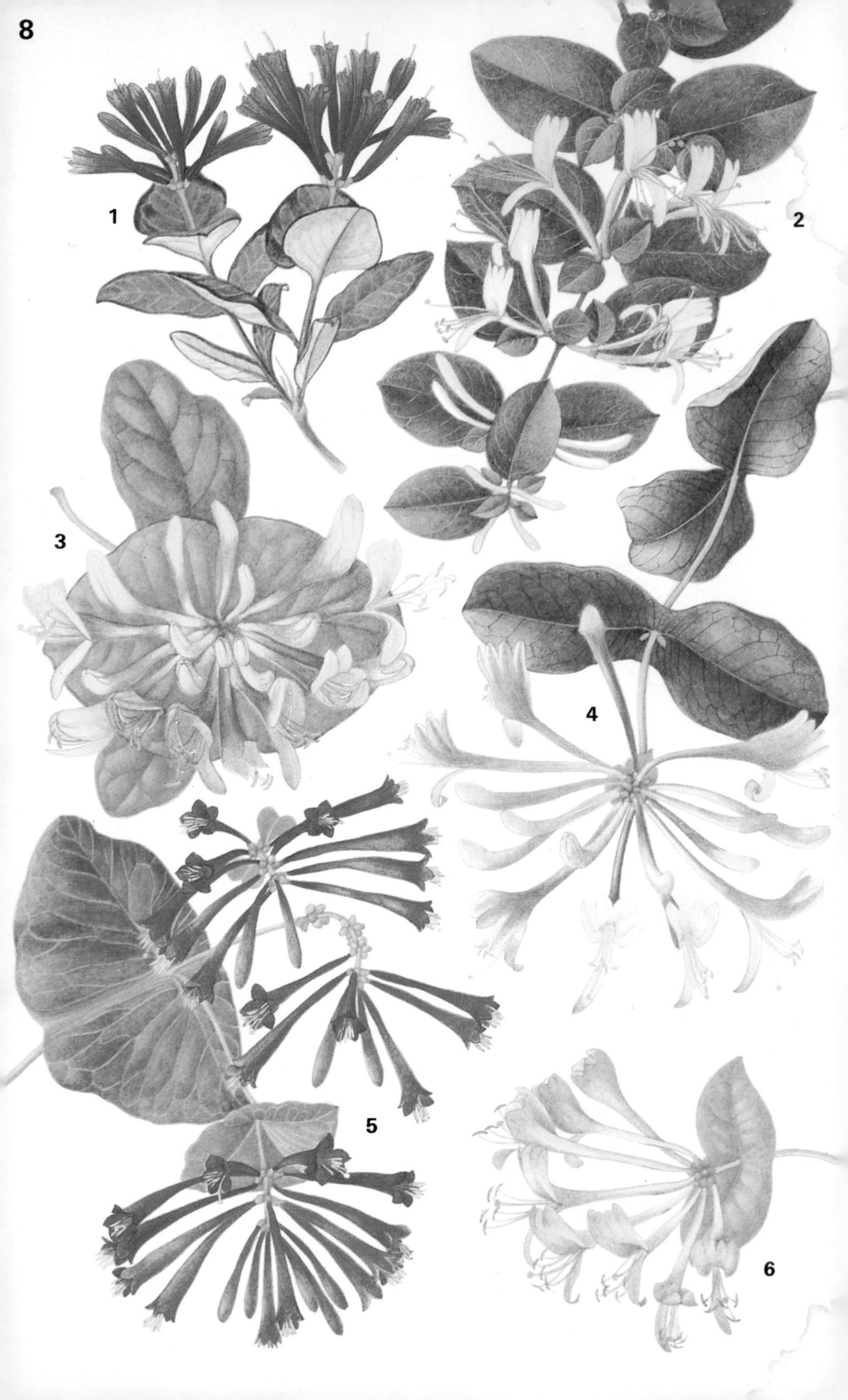
8
1
2
3
4
5
6

large golden fruits are used widely in this country for various preserves, jellies and for flavouring apple pies. If this is not confusing enough one has to add that the fruits of *Chaenomeles*, which are like small quinces can be used in the same way. Before final confusion overwhelms the reader it is probably wise to point out that botanists are not generally agreed on how to treat all the quinces, some throwing them all into one genus, *Cydonia*, whilst others will not recognise less than three or four distinct genera. Despite this the Common Quince, *Cydonia oblonga* can be at once distinguished from all *Chaenomeles* by possessing untoothed, not toothed, leaves.

Cydonia oblonga = *Pyrus cydonia, Cydonia vulgaris*, the Common Quince, is a deciduous, thornless, tree or shrub growing to 6m tall. The ovate or elliptic leaves are 6.5–10cm long, untoothed. The solitary pink or white flowers are 4–5cm across, being borne at the ends of short twigs or spurs. The large golden-yellow fruits, are broadly pear-shaped and deliciously fragrant. [May, H, PA, ?Near East & C Asia]

The origin of the Common Quince is imperfectly known. Like many plants that have been cultivated for many centuries it is difficult to find an exact wild counterpart. Certainly the species has been cultivated in the countries bordering the Mediterranean for many years, prized for its fine crop of fruits. The fruits are unfit to eat being very astringent, though at the same time are beautifully fragrant when ripe. However, they can be cooked easily and are a delightful addition to preserves and pies of various sorts.

C. oblonga is more often seen as a free standing tree than as a wall subject. On a wall it will need careful training, pruning carefully each year after flowering and again in the late autumn once the framework of the plant has been established. General treatment is the same as for the Japanese Quinces (see p.124). The Common Quince is used widely in the horticultural trade as a stock on to which to graft many varieties of pear.

'Lusitanica', the Portuguese Quince, has large pale rose flowers. It is a more vigorous plant than the common form, but not quite hardy except in the mildest districts.

'Maliformis' has apple-shaped fruits, otherwise very similar to the normal form.

***'Vranja'** is a beautiful form with very fragrant pure shiny golden fruits. The name is derived from Vranja in Yugoslavia (Serbia) where this form has been long cultivated.

CYTISUS (Leguminosae)

Cytisus battandieri, the Pineapple Broom, which is often semi-deciduous, is described on p.194 with the other species of *Cytisus*.

DESMODIUM (Leguminosae)

A large genus of some 450 tropical and subtropical species with leaves which are odd-pinnate or reduced to a single leaflet. The typical pea-flowers are borne in racemes or panicles, and eventually produce a jointed pod containing several seeds.

The following species can be grown against a wall, but are uncommon.

Desmodium praestans will grow to 5m and, although usually deciduous, can retain its leaves through the winter in favoured districts. The leaves usually consist of one broadly ovate leaflet, 10-22cm long, pale green above and white downy below. The purplish-pink or magenta flowers are carried in downy terminal

---

Plate 8 Honeysuckles 1 *Lonicera* × *brownii* (p.88), 2 *L. japonica* 'Halliana' (p.86), 3 *L. caprifolium* (p.83), 4 *L. periclymenum* 'Belgica' (p.83), 5 *L. sempvirens* (p.84), 6 *L.* × *tellmaniana* (p.88).

racemes up to 40cm long which vary considerably in width and density of flowers. [Aug–Nov, T, PS, SW China]

Desmodium praestans will bloom until frosts put a stop to flowering, but is not hardy and will only succeed on a sheltered south-facing wall. It was introduced by George Forrest in 1914.

☼ **Desmodium tiliifolium** is shorter than the previous species, reaching only about 2m. The leaves have three leaflets, the terminal one being 5–10cm long, obovate and larger than the others. The flowers vary from deep pink to pale lilac and are borne in panicles 20–30cm in length. [Aug–Nov, H, PS, Himalaya]

A good hot summer is necessary for the flowers to open properly. Seeds were first introduced to Britain from Kashmir in 1879.

DIOSPYROS (Ebenaceae)

A genus primarily of tropical trees including the well-known ebony, *Diospyros ebenum*. Only three species are cultivated in the open garden but a fourth, *D.kaki*, is suitable for wall culture. The species have alternate untoothed leaves and shoots that do not form terminal buds. The male and female flowers are borne on separate plants and are small and of little beauty. The attractive fruits are large with a conspicuous persistent calyx that expands rapidly as the fruits develop. The Persimmon, *D. virginiana*, which is a native of the eastern USA, has the best-known fruits, which many find delicious, however, the Persimmons sold in Europe are usually those of *D. kaki*.

☼ **Diospyros kaki,** the Kaki or Chinese Persimmon, is a deciduous tree growing to 12m tall. Leaves oval, 7–20cm long, are glossy green and strongly veined above,

Diospyros kaki, flowers and fruit.

downy beneath. Flowers are greenish-white, the corolla with four recurved lobes and a ruff-like calyx at the base. Fruits globose, yellow or orange-red, variable in size but generally 6–9cm in diameter. [June, HH, PS, China]

This species has long been cultivated in Japan where there are numerous forms and varieties. Today it is extensively cultivated in Southern Europe, whence most of the fruits seen in our shops derive. The Chinese Persimmon is perfectly hardy in mild districts and can be grown as a free-standing tree, however, in most places it can be cut back by frosts and is therefore best planted against a sunny south-facing wall in a good loamy soil. Most forms of *D. kaki* obtainable are grafted on to seedlings.

ERYTHRINA (Leguminosae)

Erythrinas are natives of tropical and subtropical areas. Of the 100 or more species only a couple are grown in Britain, as wall shrubs.

They are shrubs or trees with large leaves divided into three leaflets. The large coral-red flowers are borne in dense racemes and have a large standard and a two-lipped calyx. The fruit is a narrow pod, constricted between the seeds.

***Erythrina crista-galli**, the Common Coral Tree, produces semi-woody stems up to 2m high. The leaflets are oval or ovate, leathery and blunt-ended, with prickly stalks. The flowers are bright coral-scarlet and carried in large terminal racemes. [Aug–Sept, T–HH, PS, Brazil]

A splendid plant most often seen as a conservatory or pot plant, but deserving to be tried on a warm sheltered wall.

Erythrina herbacea is smaller with non-prickly leaf-stalks and deep scarlet flowers about 3.5cm long. [June–Sept, T, PS, USA (Carolina)]

Both species need a sunny wall and plenty of water during the growing season. In most areas, some form of winter protection is advisable.

FALLUGIA (Rosaceae)

An interesting genus containing only a single species which is closely related to *Cowania*. Both have beautiful flowers with distinctive feathery styles in the centre of the corolla and are native to the south-western USA and northern Mexico.

Fallugia paradoxa = *Sieversia paradoxa*. A slender deciduous shrub to 2.5m though generally less, the young branches white with down. Leaves cut into 3–7 linear lobes, 12–15mm long. Flowers white, 2.5–3cm across, solitary or several together borne at the shoot tips. Fruits are handsome with a cluster of feathery persistent styles. [July, T, PN, SW USA & N Mexico]

A very rare plant in cultivation but well deserving attention if you can find a source. In the wild *Fallugia* comes from sunbaked rocky areas, which are about the worst conditions to simulate in Britain. A well-drained soil at the base of a south-facing wall, completely sheltered from the wind, is ideal, otherwise it is best treated as a conservatory plant. (Illustration on p.132).

FENDLERA (Philadelphaceae)

There are four deciduous species in this small genus, all native to the south-western USA and Mexico. They have untoothed opposite leaves and the flowers have four sepals and petals and eight stamens. The fruit is a capsule containing many seeds.

Fallugia paradoxa

☼ **Fendlera rupicola** var. **wrightii** = *F. wrightii* has a straggling habit and reaches 2m in height. The leaves are lanceolate, 1.25–3cm long on the sterile branches and smaller on the flowering shoots; they have three prominent nerves and are somewhat bristly on the upper surface. The flowers are solitary or in small clusters in the leaf axils and have white or pink petals. [May–June, T, PN, SW USA & N Mexico]

A tender and difficult plant which needs a sunny sheltered wall to succeed, and appreciates a well-drained soil. Propagation is by soft cuttings taken in the early summer and placed in gentle heat.

FICUS (Moraceae)

☼ **Ficus carica**, the Common Fig, is a deciduous tree or shrub reaching 6m, sometimes more. The alternate leaves are three- or five-lobed, 10–20cm wide and long, and roughly hairy on both sides. The flowers are produced inside a pear-shaped structure which matures to become the 'fig' which is eaten. [May–Oct, H–HH, PA, W Asia and E Mediterranean]

The Common Fig needs the protection of a sunny south-facing wall except in the warmest areas of Britain. See also the treatment of *F. carica* in the chapter on Wall Fruits.

FORSYTHIA (Oleaceae)

Forsythias are amongst the best known, most colourful of all spring-flowering shrubs and are widely grown. Most are grown in the open, but *F. suspensa* responds well to wall-training. Plants need to be pruned judiciously to keep them within bounds and the main shoots are best tied into horizontal wall wires.

Forsythia suspensa (Pl.13), the Golden Bell, can reach 9m when trained on a wall. The young branches are hairless, often pendulous. The leaves are 5–10cm long, can be two- or three-lobed or even divided into three separate leaflets. Small clusters of golden-yellow flowers are produced on the wood of the previous year. The flowers are 2.5–3cm in diameter and have four petals. [Mar–Apr, H, PA, China]

Pruning when flowering has finished will encourage new growth which will bear the next season's flowers. *Forsythia suspensa* can be grown on a north-facing wall. Propagation is usually by layers.

var. **sieboldii** has slender, rather drooping branches and is especially suited to an east or north aspect.

var. **fortunei** is the most vigorous variety, with erect or arching branches.

forma **atrocaulis** has young stems and leaves of very dark purple and its large flowers are lemon-yellow.

'Nymans' is a sport of forma *atrocaulis* with bronzy-purple branches and large pale yellow flowers which nod pleasantly.

Forsythia × intermedia, an hybrid between *F. suspensa* and *F. viridissmia* is sometimes grown as a wall or fence shrub, though it is less effective than *F. suspensa* in such a position. Plants have a stiffer more erect habit.

FUCHSIA (Onagraceae)

The Fuchsia is almost too well known to need a description here. However, most people know the large-flowered conservatory varieties which are also widely sold as pot plants. There are two small-flowered species and a number of cultivars that can be grown outside in our climate. Anyone who lives in the milder parts of Devon and Cornwall or who has visited those parts will have seen the dainty *Fuchsia magellanica* growing against the stone walls or actually growing in wall crevices. In the very mildest districts some of the large-flowered cultivars such as 'Ballet Girl' can be grown against a sunny sheltered wall and will last there until a bad winter strikes, making thick woody branches which sprout anew each season.

The Fuchsias described here are half-hardy in most places, but practically hardy in the mildest parts of the country. They will do equally well in a sunny or a shaded spot at the base of a sheltered wall. Even if killed to the ground during the winter, in established plants at least they will sprout from the 'stool' the following spring. They prefer a moist loamy soil, particularly a calcareous one, but are not too fussy.

The genus *Fuchsia* contains about one hundred species in all, most of them natives of Central and South America, but a handful coming from New Zealand. They may be creeping plants, shrubs or small trees. The flowers often nod on slender stems, each with four sepals and four petals and with conspicuous protruding stamens and style. The fruit is a small fleshy berry.

Propagation is relatively straightforward. Soft cuttings can be taken during August using a propagating frame, or alternatively cuttings of hard well-ripened wood can be secured in the late autumn. In either case cuttings should be overwintered in a frost-free place before they are planted out the following spring.

Fuchsia excorticata = *Skinnera excorticata* (Pl.14) is a deciduous shrub or small tree reaching 8m or more in height sometimes, the main branches becoming thick and woody with age and with thin peeling bark. The alternate leaves are ovate or lanceolate, 4–10cm long, dark green above but white with down beneath. The pendulous flowers, 20–28mm long, are greenish, often marked or flushed with purple or dull red, with small purplish petals. The berry is purplish-black when ripe, about 12mm long. [Apr–May, HH, PN, New Zealand]

This species is more fascinating than beautiful, although its peeling bark and small fuchsia flowers provide interest early in the year.

Fuchsia magellanica (Pl.14) is a deciduous shrub reaching 3m high, sometimes more, especially in mild shaded places. The leaves are in pairs or more often in threes, ovate or elliptic, 1.5–3cm long. Flowers, borne singly or two together, 28–36mm long, are dainty, drooping on long slender stalks and bright red with purple or bluish-violet petals. Berries are oblong, red or reddish-black when ripe. [July–Oct, HH, PS, Chile & Argentina]

A charming species frequently grown, although most often represented by an hybrid under the cultivars name 'Riccartonii' which is similar, though with more brightly coloured flowers. *Fuchsia magellanica* is a moisture-loving plant, growing frequently along riverbanks in its native haunts, often in association with *Berberis darwinii*.

'Thompsonii' is a bushy rather erect shrub with shorter narrower leaves than the typical plant and smaller flowers borne in great profusion.

'Variegata' = *F. gracilis* 'Variegata' has attractive leaves edged with creamy-white and often flushed with pink. The flowers have scarlet sepals and purple petals.

*var. **gracilis** is a graceful form with arching densely downy stems, and leaves up to 4cm long. The flowers are more slender than the type with scarlet sepals and deep violet petals. A fine plant, but a little less hardy than typical *F. magellanica*.

There are a number of hardy or half-hardy cultivars derived from crosses between *F. coccinea* and *F. magellanica* which are good wall shrubs in all but the coldest districts. In severe winters they may be cut to the ground although established plants will sprout as soon as milder weather arrives. Plants can be kept small, as with *F. magellanica*, by cutting the growths back close to ground level in the early spring. Alternatively the more vigorous ones, especially 'Corallina' and 'Riccartonii', can be trained up a wall to 3 or 4m.

***'Corallina'** is a vigorous semi-climbing shrub reaching 4m in height. The ovate or oblong leaves are borne in twos, threes or fours, bronzy-green above but purplish beneath. Flowers, with spreading scarlet sepals and deep purple petals, are 32–35mm long. A fine wall shrub, but unfortunately not widely grown today, it has been wrongly named *Fuchsia* 'Exonensis', which is not in cultivation.

'Dr. Foster' has reddish stems and ovate leaves. The large flowers have scarlet sepals and violet-mauve petals, 35–38mm long. Well worth growing for its large bright flowers.

***'Madame Cornelissen'** will reach 1.5m tall, bearing handsome dark green foliage. Flowers soft scarlet with white petals, 30–34mm long.

***'Margaret'** will grow 2m high against a suitable wall. Leaves pale green, the flowers semi-double, scarlet with violet petals stained with white at the base, about 30mm long.

'Mrs. Popple' grows to 1.5m and is of bushy habit. Flowers crimson-scarlet with violet-blue petals which gradually turn crimson-purple, 33–35mm long.

'Mrs. W.P. Wood' is like *F. magellanica* but flowers pinkish-white. Less hardy.

***'Riccartonii'** = *F. magellanica* 'Riccartonii' is the hardiest cultivar reaching 2m tall, or 3m plus in favoured localities. The young stems and leaf-stalks are flushed with red. The flowers are more substantial than *F. magellanica* with scarlet sepals and deep violet petals.

This is a commonly grown and deservedly popular plant. In the milder counties it will even make a hedge, though it is seen at its best grown against a wall or fence.

HIBISCUS (Malvaceae)

There are over 200 species of *Hibiscus*, mostly inhabiting tropical and subtropical regions. They usually have simple alternate leaves and the flowers have five petals and numerous stamens. Only three shrubby species are cultivated out-of-doors in Britain. Unfortunately *Hibiscus rosa-sinensis*, the hibiscus traditionally associated with girls of the Pacific islands, with its magnificent scarlet blooms can only be grown under glass in Britain.

Hibiscus syriacus (Pl.14) grows to 3m or more. The leaves are usually three-lobed with coarse teeth, 5–10cm long and more or less hairless. The broad trumpet-shaped flowers are produced singly in the leaf-axils and measure 6–10cm across. The calyx has five unequal lobes, below which are a number of linear bracts, shorter than the calyx. The corolla may be single or double and various colour forms have been selected, the best of which are described below. [July–Oct, H, PN, India & China] ☼

H. syriacus rarely needs pruning in Britain, but if pruning should become necessary it is best done in April or immediately after flowering. Propagation is by semi-hardwood or hardwood cuttings or layers. It is one of the loveliest flowering shrubs for the early autumn, the flowers opening only in sunshine.

***'Blue Bird'** 'Oiseau Bleu' has single mauve-blue flowers with a deeper centre.

'Coelestis' has single flowers of light mauve-blue with a crimson centre, slightly smaller than 'Blue Bird'.

'Duc de Brabant' has double flowers of a deep purplish-pink with maroon buds.

'Hamabo' has single flowers of very pale pink with a brownish-crimson centre. Often confused with *H. hamabo* (see below).

'Lady Stanley' has semi-double white flowers, flushed pink and with a crimson centre.

'Snow Drift' has single white flowers.

***'Violet Claire Double'** has double or semi-double blue-purple flowers, reddish-purple at the base within.

'William R. Smith' has single flowers, white with crimped petals. Sometimes in catalogues as 'W.R. Smith'.

***'Woodbridge'** has single flowers of a deep rich pink with a darker centre.

Hibiscus sinosyriacus is similar to the last species, but has broader, more finely toothed leaves and the bracts below the calyx are equal in length to the calyx or longer. The flowers are 8–10cm wide at the mouth, with lilac petals blotched crimson at the base. [Sept–Oct, H, PN, China] ☼

The following cultivars all with single flowers are commercially available.

'Autumn Surprise' is white with a feathered pink base.

'Lilac Queen' is white, flushed lilac and with a deep red base.

***'Ruby Glow'** is white with a bright pink base.

The flowers do not open as widely as those of *H. syriacus* and it needs a sheltered sunny site to flower well.

Hibiscus hamabo reaches 5m and has elliptic to rounded leaves 6-8m long. The flowers are solitary in the axils of the upper leaves and measure about 7.5cm in diameter. The petals are yellow, with a dark red blotch at the base. [July-Aug, T, PN, Japan & Korea] ☼

Only suitable for the mildest areas. It should not be confused with *H. syriacus* 'Hamabo'.

HOHERIA (Malvaceae)

Most of the species are evergreen; these and the genus are described on p.204. There are two fine deciduous species.

☼ ***Hoheria glabrata** = *Plagianthus glabrata* is a beautiful large shrub, sometimes a small tree reaching 5–6m tall. The ovate leaves are 5–12cm long, pointed, simply toothed. The white, almost translucent, flowers are borne in profusion along the young boughs, each flower 2.5–4cm across. [June–July, HH, PN, New Zealand]

This is the more commonly seen of the two species described here and perhaps a hardier subject. It is certainly a very beautiful shrub, well deserving a space on a sunny sheltered wall.

☼ **Hoheria lyallii** = *Plagianthus lyallii* is an equally lovely plant reaching 5m tall. The young shoots are covered with dense starry down. The adult leaves are ovate, 5–12cm long and doubly- or trebly-toothed, downy even when mature. The white, cherry-like, flowers have purple anthers. [July, HH, PN, New Zealand]

INDIGOFERA (Leguminosae)

A large genus of about 700 species only a few of which are cultivated. They have alternate odd-pinnate leaves and bear slender racemes of pea-flowers in the leaf axils. Some species, especially *Indigofera tinctoria*, yield the dark blue dye, indigo.

◐ **Indigofera heterantha** = *I. gerardiana* will grow to 3m if trained against a wall. The greyish leaves are 5–10cm long, composed of 13–21 leaflets. The racemes are 7–13cm long, produced in succession up the branches, and carry up to 30 scented flowers which are about 1.25cm long and rosy-purple. The pods are 3.5–5cm long with six to ten seeds and hang downwards when mature. [June–Sept, H, PS, NW Himalaya]

An attractive shrub which produces flowers over a long period, although it is late to start into growth. In a really cold winter it can be cut to the ground, but will send up new stems in the spring. It appreciates a sunny position and should not be grown on a north-facing wall. It is often known in gardens under the name *Indigofera gerardiana* and indeed it is still sometimes found in catalogues under that name.

◐ **Indigofera pendula** is a shrub of spreading habit, reaching about 3m. The leaves are 20–25cm long, made up of 19–27 oblong to oval leaflets which are 1.8–3cm long and hairless above when mature. The slender pendulous racemes are up to 45cm long, with many rosy-purple flowers which are 0.8–1.3cm long. The sparsely hairy pods are about 5cm long. [Aug–Sept, H, PS, China (Yunnan)]

Like *I. heterantha*, this species can be cut to ground level in a bad winter. It differs from *I. heterantha* in having longer leaves with more leaflets, and much longer racemes. It can be grown on an east, south or west-facing wall and is one of the many introductions of George Forrest.

Plate 9 Evergreen and Herbaceous Climbers 1 *Berberidopsis corallina* (p.91), 2 *Bignonia capreolata* (p.92), 3 *Billardiera longiflora* (p.92), 4 *Cobaea scandens* (p.238), 5 *Holboellia latifolia* (p.100), 6 *Eccremocarpus scaber* 'Aurea' (p.241).

9
1
2
3
4
5
6

10
1
2
3
4
5
6

JASMINUM (Oleaceae)

General remarks about jasmines can be found on p.100. Most of the species are evergreen climbers, although the most widely planted of all, *Jasminum nudiflorum*, the Winter Jasmine, belongs here amongst the deciduous shrubs. It is a valuable and much-loved species flowering as it does in the depths of winter and tolerating a wide variety of soils and walls and fences of any aspect, even due north.

***Jasminum nudiflorum** (Pl.14), the Winter Jasmine, is a deciduous shrub of straggling habit which can reach 5m. The shoots are four-angled and bear opposite ternate leaves. The solitary or paired, clear yellow flowers are borne along the arching green stems when they are leafless, or practically so. Each flower is 18–20mm across with a long slender tube and five or six lobes. [Nov–Mar, H, PA, SW China]

What a valuable and lovely shrub this is, certainly one of the most widely planted of all wall plants. It is the hardiest jasmine cultivated in Britain and was first introduced in 1844 by Robert Fortune, a plant collector sent out by the Horticultural Society. It is especially valued for its cheerful display of flowers when little else is in bloom and is a popular plant for winter gardens, besides making a good cut flower if the sprays are cut in bud. Old plants become woody and matted with dead stems and a regular system of pruning is desirable. The leading shoots need to be secured to the wall or fence and lateral shoots will be produced which will hang downwards. These laterals should be pruned immediately flowering ceases, cutting them hard back to a suitable pair of buds. These will give rise to new strong shoots which will bear the following winter's blooms. Very old and gnarled main stems can be cut out from time to time and replaced by young healthy stems.

'Aureum' has the leaves marked with yellow blotches.

LAGERSTROEMIA (Lythraceae)

A genus of tropical and subtropical trees and shrubs distantly related to our native Purple Loosestrife, *Lythrum salicaria*.

Lagerstroemia indica, the Crape Myrtle, is a deciduous shrub or small tree growing to 4m tall, rarely more in Britain. The young shoots are four-angled and smooth and bear privet-like leaves which are alternate, opposite, or in whorls of three, 2.5–6.5cm long. The flowers are borne in broad panicles at the tips of the current year's shoots and vary in colour from deep red to pink or white, each 2.5–4cm across with six crinkly, clawed petals and numerous stamens. [July–Sept, HH, PS, China & Korea]

A commonly grown species, often seen as a park or street tree in Mediterranean countries where it may attain a height of up to 10m. In Britain it is mostly seen as a cool greenhouse or conservatory plant, however, it is hardier than is generally supposed succeeding on a sheltered sunny wall in the south and south-west. Young plants are best planted in the spring and will grow quickly, often flowering in the same year. *Lagerstroemia indica* is a sun-loving species, flowering well during hot summers, but it may not do its best if subjected to a cool wet summer. The leaves often produce good autumn colour. Plants can be propagated from leafy cuttings taken in midsummer, or raised from imported seed.

Plate 10 Ivies 1 *Hedera canariensis* 'Margino-maculata' (p.98), 2 *M. canariensis* 'Gloire de Marengo' (p.98), 3 *H. helix* 'Goldheart' (p.97), 4 *H. helix* 'Glacier' (p.97), 5 *H. colchica* (p.98), 6 *H. colchica* 'Sulphur Heart' (p.99).

LINDERA (Lauraceae)

A genus containing about 80 species of evergreen or deciduous shrubs or small trees. Several are in cultivation but only one is suitable for wall culture. The species mostly come from eastern and south-eastern Asia, though several hail from the eastern states of North America. The alternate leaves are often aromatic. Male and female flowers are borne on separate plants in small dense clusters at the nodes. Each flower cluster is surrounded at the base by four bracts or scales which enfold the young buds before they emerge. There are usually six sepals but no true petals. Fruits are rarely produced in cultivated species.

◐ △ ***Lindera praecox*** = *Benzoin praecox, Parabenzoin praecox,* is a deciduous shrub of bushy habit reaching 7–8m in height, with dark brown, shiny young shoots. The thin light green leaves are ovate or oval, pointed, 2.5–9cm long and generally hairless. Small, greenish-yellow flowers form small rounded clusters about 13mm across. Fruits about 2cm long, reddish-brown, with 5–6 lobes, splitting when mature to reveal a single stone. [Mar–Apr, H, PA, Japan & Korea]

A charming plant worthy of greater attention from gardeners. Although it is more or less hardy it flowers better given the protection of a wall in a semi-shaded position away from early morning sunshine. The flowers are borne on the bare branches before the leaves appear. However, they are laid down in small rounded buds the previous summer. The leaves turn a striking yellow in the autumn just before they fall.

Plants prefer a light well-drained soil, which must be neutral or slightly acid if they are to thrive.

Some authorities place this species in the genus *Parabenzoin* and as such it may be found in catalogues or books under the name *Parabenzoin praecox*. The dry lobed fruits distinguish this genus from *Lindera*, but the differences are admittedly slight.

LIPPIA (Verbenaceae)

There are about 220 species of *Lippia*, native to tropical America and Africa. They have opposite leaves, or leaves in threes and the small flowers are borne in slender spikes or panicles. The tubular corolla is two-lipped, each lip itself with two lobes.

☼ ***Lippia citriodora*** = *Aloysia triphylla*, the Lemon-scented Verbena, is a shrub or small tree up to 3m tall, sometimes higher. The leaves are 7.5–10cm long, lanceolate and mostly in threes. The panicles are 7–12cm long and the flowers are light purple, c. 4mm long. [Aug, HH, PS, Chile]

A popular deciduous shrub much beloved by herbalists in the past. It is only hardy in the milder areas of the country, although it will survive on walls in colder areas if given winter protection. Plants thrive best on a south- or west-facing wall, particularly on light soils. The leaves are delightfully lemon-scented when crushed. Plants are best placed outdoors in the spring once the danger of late frosts has passed. Pruning consists mainly of removing dead or frost-damaged stems. Plants can be propagated by semi-hardwood cuttings during the summer and these should be overwintered in a frost-free site.

The dried leaves are often used to make a herbal tea.

LYCIUM (Solanaceae)

Loose rambling shrubs usually with spiny branches and untoothed leaves which are alternate or in clusters. The flowers are usually violet and have five united petals forming a funnel-shaped corolla. The five stamens usually protrude beyond the corolla mouth. The fruit is a fleshy berry.

There are 80–90 species native to temperate and subtropical areas but only three species are suitable for wall cultivation. They are best propagated from seed, although cuttings can also be used. An annual winter or spring pruning will become necessary to prevent the mass of shoots becoming entangled and too thick. They are good plants for coastal gardens.

Lycium barbarum = *L. chinense, L. europaeum, L. halimifolium, L. vulgare*, the Duke of Argyll's Tea Tree or Chinese Box Thorn, is a deciduous hairless shrub which grows to 4m against a wall, with arching branches which may or may not bear spines. The leaves vary considerably in size and shape, but are usually 2.5–6cm long. The flowers are produced at the leaf-axils, two or three together, 0.9–1.25cm long. The corolla is purple, fading to buff with age. The berries are up to 2.5cm long, egg-shaped or oblong and orange or scarlet when ripe. [May-July, H, PS, China] ☼

The Chinese Box Thorn is often seen as a hedging plant in mild coastal areas. The attractive fruits ripen in August and September.

'Carnosum' has pink flowers.

Lycium barbarum, flowers and fruit.

Lycium chilense is a glandular-hairy spineless shrub reaching 1.8m tall. The young shoots are pale and usually downy. The leaves are 1.2–5cm long, obovate to oblanceolate and with hairy margins. One or two flowers are borne in the leaf-axils and are yellowish outside and purple inside. The fruits are globular, about 8mm long and orange-red when ripe. [June–Sept, HH–T, PS, Chile & Argentina] ☼

Lycium afrum is a much-branched spiny shrub with pale hairless shoots, which will reach 3m tall. The hairless, greyish-green leaves, 1.25–2.5cm long are in clusters. The flowers are very deep purple, fragrant, 2–2.5cm long. The berries ☼

are egg-shaped, about 8mm long, reddish at first, purplish-black when mature; the calyx persists at the base of the berry. [May–June, HH, PS, S Africa]

MAGNOLIA (Magnoliaceae)

The genus is described on p.208, with the evergreen species.

☼ △ **Magnolia liliiflora** = *M. quinquepeta* is a bushy species growing to about 6m tall. The young wood is aromatic and the leaves are ovate to obovate, 7.5–20cm long, deep green above and downy beneath. The fragrant flowers are reminiscent of slender tulips and are white inside and purple and white outside, about 7.5cm long. [Apr–June and intermittently through the summer, H–HH, PN, China]

Hardy in the mildest areas but requiring wall-protection in northerly counties. It cannot be grown on limy or chalky soils.

'Nigra' is a more compact plant with larger flowers (10–12cm long) which are deep purple outside.

MELIA (Meliaceae)

A small tropical and subtropical genus. *Melia azedarach*, the only species cultivated in Britain, is grown throughout the warm temperate and subtropical regions of the world as an ornamental, and is frequently planted there as a street tree.

☼ **Melia azedarach**, the Bead Tree or Persian Lilac, is a deciduous tree up to 12m tall in warm countries, but less when grown as a wall shrub in Britain. It has alternate bipinnate leaves 30–60cm long. The fragrant flowers are borne in loose panicles 10–20cm long and are produced on the young shoots. The corolla is 2cm across, made up of five lilac narrowly-oblong petals which are spreading or somewhat reflexed. There are ten to twelve violet stamens which are joined together to form a tube. The fruit is about 1.25cm long, roundish and yellow-brown, containing a single seed. [June–July, T, PN, N India & Central & W China]

A graceful plant which is easily raised from seed, or from cuttings under glass. In this country it needs the protection of a warm wall. The common name of 'Bead Tree' refers to the use of its fruits in necklaces or rosaries.

NOTOSPARTIUM (Leguminosae)

There are only three species of *Notospartium* and all are cultivated in this country. They look rather similar to the Common Broom, *Cytisus scoparius*, and are leafless, except on the juvenile shoots. All require wall-protection. Pruning is not usually necessary, although untidy growth or dead wood is best removed after flowering.

☼ **Notospartium carmichaeliae** will reach 3–7m in height and has slender hanging lateral branches. The tiny leaves which are present only on young plants, are roundish and 5–6mm long. Flower purplish-pink, about 8mm long; there are up to twenty flowers per raceme. The fruit pods are 2–2.5cm long. [July, HH, PN, New Zealand]

☼ **Notospartium glabrescens** is taller than the previous species, growing up to 9m in strong specimens. The young shoots are ribbed. The leaves, present on young plants, are very small, being nothing more than triangular scales. The racemes are less dense than those of *N. carmichaeliae*, and carry up to 25 flowers. The flowers, 8–13mm long, are rose-pink, the standard with deeper veins and a purplish basal blotch. The calyx is nearly hairless. The pods are 2–2.5cm long and the seeds red marked with black dots. [May–June, HH, PN, New Zealand]

Notospartium torulosum is only rarely seen in gardens. It has purple flowers in racemes which are less dense than those of *N. carmichaeliae* and contain fewer flowers. The calyx is hairless and the pods are narrow and constricted between the seeds. [June, HH, PN, New Zealand]

PHILADELPHUS (Philadelphaceae)

This genus contains the ever-popular Mock Orange or Syringa, *Philadelphus coronarius*. There are a number of other species of Mock Orange which are all shrubby and mostly hardy in the open garden but one, *P. mexicanus*, requires wall-protection in Britain. All the species have opposite leaves and flowers with four sepals and petals and 20-24 stamens. They are noted for their strong and delightful fragrance. The fruit is a dry woody capsule which splits into four parts, exposing numerous seeds.

Philadelphus mexicanus reaches 1.8m in height and has hairy young shoots. The ovate-lanceolate leaves are 1.2–6cm long. The creamy-white flowers are usually solitary, occasionally two or three together, cup-shaped, 3.5–5cm across. [June–July, T, PA, Mexico]

A beautiful shrub needing a sunny sheltered wall where its fragrance will fill the air. It should be pruned immediately after flowering, the amount of pruning consistent with the vigour of the plant.

*'**Rose Syringa**' has petals with a purplish-pink blotch at the base. This cultivar is more commonly cultivated than *P. mexicanus* itself.

PRUNUS (Rosaceae)

This genus is too well known to warrant a description here. Apart from the flowering and fruiting cherries the genus, as understood by most gardeners and botanists today, also includes the Apricot, *Prunus armeniaca*, and Peach, *Prunus persica*. Species and cultivars grown primarily for their fruits are dealt with in the chapter on wall fruits. The evergreen *P. ilicifolia* is described on p.221.

Prunus triloba (Pl.15) is by far the finest flowering cherry for wall culture, making a deciduous shrub 3–5m tall. The midgreen leaves are ovate or obovate, often three-lobed and generally coarsely toothed, 2.5–5cm long. The double rosette-like flowers are pale pinkish-white, 20–25mm across, borne in clusters of two to three or solitary along one-year-old branches. [Late Mar–Apr, HH, PA, China]

This splendid plant is a delight in any garden and seen at its best against a warm sunny wall, where the young branches are festooned with flowers during the early spring. In the open garden it is neither a free bloomer nor reliably hardy. Plants should be pruned hard back the moment the flowers fade in order to produce a good amount of strong new growth to bear the flowers the following year. Plants thrive in a deep moist loamy soil and are readily propagated from firm young shoots struck in July and early August. When buying plants care should be taken to ensure that they are growing on their own roots for grafted plants may sucker tiresomely.

The wild Chinese species which has single flowers has little ornamental value and is seldom seen. The double form common in gardens and as a 'forced spring shrub' in conservatories was collected in China, where it had long been cultivated, by Robert Fortune in 1855.

***'Multiplex'** = *Prunus triloba* var. *multiplex* is the finest cultivar with very double peach-pink flowers, larger than the type, 25–40mm across.

☼ **Prunus argentea** = *Amygdalus argentea, A. orientalis,* is a rarely seen but handsome deciduous shrub to 2m tall. The elliptic or ovate leaves are covered in silvery down, 2–4cm long. The rose-pink flowers are borne singly or in pairs, each 18–20mm across. The egg-shaped almond fruits are rather flattened, about 14–16mm long and covered in whitish down. [Mar–Apr, HH, PA, Asia Minor, Iran and adjacent areas]

A plant for a sunny wall which is easily recognised by its attractive silvery leaves. Unfortunately the flowers are not borne very freely and even if they are, do not last very long.

PUNICA (Punicaceae)

The Pomegranate, *Punica granatum,* has been cultivated for its delicious fruit for many hundreds of years. In Britain it is a tender plant and needs the protection of a sunny wall. It grows best in a rich heavy soil and should bear fruit in its third or fourth year, given a good hot summer.

☼ **Punica granatum** (Pl.21), the Pomegranate, is a shrub or small tree growing up to 6m, although generally less in this country. Usually opposite, glossy, deep green leaves are narrowly oblong, untoothed, up to 7.5cm long, and copper-coloured when young. Flowers up to 3.5cm across are solitary or in clusters at the ends of the branches, with five to seven crumpled orange-red petals and numerous stamens. Fruit 5–12.5cm across, a brownish-yellow or purplish-red thick-skinned berry with many seeds embedded in the pinkish edible pulp.[Aug–Sept, T, PN, probably SW Asia]

The Pomegranate is thought to have originated in south-west Asia, but is now extensively cultivated in the tropics and subtropics as well as being naturalised in the Mediterranean area and parts of South America. The flowers are produced in late summer, so the fruit ripen only rarely in Britain. The leaves turn bright yellow in autumn, before they fall. Propagation can be from seed, or by hard-wood cuttings taken in spring, or softwood cuttings taken in summer.

'Alba-plena' = 'Multiplex' has double creamy-white flowers. The young leaves are green.

'Flore Pleno' has double orange-red flowers.

RIBES (Grossulariaceae)

Ribes speciosum may be deciduous or semi-evergreen and is described on p.226.

RUBUS (Rosaceae)

The deciduous R. laciniatus and several semi-evergreen species are found on p.227.

ROBINIA (Leguminosae)

This genus contains amongst its 20 or so species the widely grown false Acacia, *Robinia pseudacacia*. All of them hail from North and Central America. Two, *R.*

hispida and *R. kelseyi*, although hardy in many districts, have brittle boughs and the shelter of a sunny wall suits them admirably. Indeed they do best if the main branches are secured to the wall for extra support. Robinias revel in dry soils and care must be taken not to enrich the soil too much, otherwise the branches become even more brittle.

Both species mentioned below are suckering plants and, even if one or two of the main branches are lost, others will generally be produced from below ground, especially in established plants. Some stocks are grafted on to ordinary false Acacia, *R. pseudacacia* and any suckers must be removed with care.

***Robinia hispida** (Pl.15), the Rose Acacia, is a lovely shrub reaching 2.5m tall, sometimes more, the rather lax branches covered with gland-tipped bristles. The odd-pinnate leaves are deep green. The deep rose-pink pea-flowers, each 28–32mm long, are borne in short racemes in the leaf axils of young shoots. The fruit pods are extremely rare on cultivated plants. [May–June, H, PA, SE USA]

A beautiful plant worthy of a space on any sunny wall. It has been cultivated since the middle of the eighteenth century.

'Macrophylla' has less bristly branches and larger leaves. Its flowers are sometimes likened to a rose-pink Wisteria.

Robinia kelseyi is an equally beautiful shrub, again one of lax habit, but with smooth stems. The bright lilac-pink flowers are 18-24mm long, borne in small, sometimes branched clusters, at the base of young shoots. The slender fruit pods reach 5cm long and are covered with gland-tipped bristles. [June, H, PA, origin unknown, possibly the southern Allegheny Mts, USA]

SOPHORA (Leguminosae)

Sophora davidii is a deciduous species, but is described along with the evergreen species on p.231.

SPARTOCYTISUS (Leguminosae)

Erect shrubs with small trifoliate leaves and white pea-flowers which have a two-lipped calyx with very short teeth.

Spartocytisus supranubius = *Cytisus supranubius, Spartocytisus nubigenus*, the Tenerife Broom, is a much-branched shrub with stiff erect, rather bluish-green stems up to 3m tall. The leaves, which fall early, have three narrow leaflets, 4–8mm long which are densely covered with short hairs. The flowers are borne in dense clusters on the wood of the previous year; they are white, flushed with pink and up to 1.25cm long. The pods are 2.5–3cm long, hairy, black when ripe. [May, T, PA, Canary Is]

STYRAX (Styracaceae)

Shrubs or small trees with alternate simple leaves. The white flowers are borne in clusters, and usually have five to eight petals and twice as many stamens. The fruit is fleshy or dry and contains one or two seeds.

Styrax species can be propagated by seed, or cuttings taken in mid-summer and placed in a propagating frame. They will not grow on chalk or limestone soils.

Styrax officinalis, the Storax, will reach 5m high and has branches covered with starry hairs. The leaves are ovate or oval, usually untoothed, 5–9cm long,

Styrax officinalis.

hairless above and white-hairy below. The fragrant white flowers are about 3cm wide and borne three to eight together in drooping terminal clusters. [June, H–HH, PN, E Mediterranean & Near East]

Storax needs a warm sheltered position to grow satisfactorily in Britain. In its native countries it is a source of gum storax, which is used for incense. The seeds are used in rosaries. An attractive shrub which deserves to be grown more often.

Styrax wilsonii is a much-branched shrub growing to 3m, the young shoots covered with starry hairs. The leaves are ovate, three-lobed or toothed towards the tip, 1–2.5cm long. The white flowers are 1.3–2cm in diameter, nodding and in clusters of one to four. [June, T, PN, W China]

Best on a south-east or west-facing wall. It may be necessary occasionally to prune it to control the growth.

Styrax dasyantha is larger than the two previous species and can grow to 8m tall. It has obovate to broadly ovate, finely toothed leaves 5–10cm long. The flowers are borne in slender terminal racemes, 5–10cm long. The corolla lobes are white, lanceolate, 1–2cm long and downy outside. [July, T, PN, C & W China]

This species was introduced by E.H. Wilson in 1900.

SUTHERLANDIA (Leguminosae)

A small South African genus of shrubs with alternate, odd-pinnate leaves. The following species can be grown on a sunny sheltered wall in the warmer parts of Britain.

Sutherlandia frutescens grows to 4–5m and has shoots which are greyish-downy. The leaves have 13–21 lanceolate leaflets. The pea-flowers are about 2–5cm long, coral-scarlet and borne in axillary racemes 2–5cm long. The pods are 5cm long and inflated. [June, T, PN, S Africa]

A beautiful shrub which is not often seen, but which certainly deserves to be grown more widely. Dead or unwanted growths can be cut out in the spring once the danger of frosts has passed, although little in the way of an annual prune is generally required.

Sutherlandia frutescens.

VIBURNUM (Caprifoliaceae)

For general remarks see p.233, where the evergreen species, *V.* × *burkwoodii, V. japonicum, V. macrocephalum, V. odoratissimum, V. rhytidophyllum, V. rigidum* and *V. suspensum*, can be found.

***Viburnum farreri** = *V. fragrans* is a deciduous shrub growing to 3m tall, or higher against a wall. The leaves are oval, short-stalked, 4–10cm long, deep-green and often bronzy when young. The flowers are pink in bud but open white with a delightful fragrance of heliotrope. They are borne in small terminal and lateral clusters 3–4cm across, each flower funnel-shaped, 9–14mm across. The red berries are only rarely set in cultivation. [Nov–Feb, H, PS, W China] ◐

Viburnum farreri is one of the most widely grown of all garden shrubs. Surprisingly it was not introduced to Europe for cultivation until 1910 when William Purdom collected it for Messrs Veitch, although it had apparently been grown all over northern China for many centuries. It is one of the loveliest and most pleasing sights to see in flower on a cold sunny winter's day. Plants grown against a sheltered wall will commence flowering well in advance of those in the more open garden. Walls or fences of east or west aspect are ideal. Little pruning is required except to encourage strong new growth or to remove dead wood. Sprigs are excellent as cut flowers picked in young bud.

'Candidissimum' has paler green leaves and pure white flowers.

Viburnum × bodnantense, *V.farreri* × *V.grandiflorum*, can be treated in the same way as *V. farreri* and many gardeners favour it for its larger flowers and more vigorous habit. Like *V. farreri* it is quite hardy in the open garden. ◐

VITEX (Verbenaceae)

There are some 250 species of *Vitex* which occur both in tropical and temperate regions. They can be evergreen or deciduous, but the species we grow in our gardens are deciduous. They have opposite leaves which are palmately divided and small flowers in clusters of spikes or racemes. The corolla is tubular and two-lipped.

☼ **Vitex agnus-castus**, the Chaste Tree, grows to 3–8m and the young shoots are grey-downy. The leaves have five or seven radiating leaflets which are 5–15cm long, dark green above and grey-hairy beneath. The fragrant flowers are borne in whorls on narrow racemes 7.5–15cm long. The corolla is violet and about 8mm long. [Sept–Oct, T, PS, Mediterranean area, SW & Central Asia]

The stems and leaves are aromatic when crushed. In a warm summer it will flower profusely, but is happiest with wall-protection even in the south; in the north a wall is always necessary. In the spring, dead wood should be cut out and the flowering branches of the previous year should be shortened. This plant was symbolic of chastity in ancient Greece, hence its common name.

'Alba' has white flowers.

'Latifolia' is a more vigorous plant with broader leaflets.

☼ **Vitex negundo** will reach 3–4m and has square stems. The leaves have three, five or seven leaflets which are 6–10cm long, oblong to lanceolate, toothed or not, deep green above and grey-hairy beneath. The flowers are borne in spikes 15–22cm long, in terminal clusters. The fragrant flowers are violet-blue, smaller than those of *V. agnus-castus*. [Aug–Sept, T, PS, India, Sri Lanka to China and Taiwan]

Like the preceding species this requires the protection of a south-facing wall to flower satisfactorily.

var. **heterophylla** = *V. negundo* var. *incisa* has leaflets which are deeply toothed and smaller than the more typical plant.

Roses
(Rosaceae)

In Britain, the rose is the most popular and widely grown of all garden plants. In gardens old and new, large and small, private and public, the many colours and forms of roses brighten the scene. Britain has traditionally produced innumerable specialist plant societies concerned with everything from heathers or ivy, to cacti and gladioli, but of all of them the Royal National Rose Society boasts by far the largest number of members.

Roses have been cultivated for as long as any garden plant (there is evidence that the Greeks were growing them about 300 *B.C.*) and inevitably, the influence of hybridisation and breeding has produced vast numbers of cultivars. It is neither possible nor desirable, in this book, to enumerate all those which are presently available. Anyone who wishes to specialise in roses should consult relevant books as well as keeping a keen eye on current rose nursery catalogues to see which new cultivars are being offered.

The genus *Rosa* is native throughout the northern temperate region, but by far the largest number of cultivated species come from the Far East. Historically, it was the introduction to Europe of forms of the Chinese *R.* ×*odorata* at the end of the eighteenth and the beginning of the nineteenth centuries which provided the important repeat-flowering character which was bred into their derivatives.

There are no truly climbing roses; they use their thorns to attach themselves lightly to supports, but in wind the stems will be blown down unless they are tied carefully. They are best regarded as scramblers rather like brambles, in contrast to the free standing bushy types so commonly seen in our gardens. The only scrambling roses which do not need tying are those grown into trees, where the branches and twigs usually give enough support to prevent the rose from falling.

In general, roses like a sunny position, although a small number will tolerate semi-shade. Very few will flower in permanent shade. Roses can be planted with their roots in the shade provided that their stems can grow into the sun. When planted against a wall they should be at least 30cm away from it; if too close the roots will become very dry as the wall tends to keep the rain off. Many make splendid subjects for fences, pergolas and pillars. If a rose is to be trained into a tree it is best planted on the side towards the prevailing wind so that the stems will be blown towards the tree rather than away from it.

Air circulation is important, especially for those varieties subject to mildew. A position in a very hot sheltered wall-bounded corner can result in the plant transpiring excessively and becoming dehydrated. On the other hand, roses do not appreciate being planted in draughty places such as exposed wind-tunnels between buildings — they may survive but they will not flower well.

Good drainage is essential. Roses will not tolerate water-logged soils. The type of soil does not matter so much, although roses appreciate a rich well-balanced soil. They will grow on sandy or clay soils, as long as the latter are not really wet. It is a myth that they will only grow well on clay soils. Any average soil that has been well prepared with the addition of composts and mulches will suit them. Acidity and alkalinity only become a problem when they are extreme.

The pruning of roses depends primarily on the type of rose. However, as many an expert gardener will tell you, when to prune is a subject of much debate. Some will insist that autumn is the time for such action, others will not touch a bush before Christmas. However, the different groups covered in this book do require rather differing treatments. The species, the shrubs and the climbing miniatures need only as much pruning as is necessary to keep them within required limits, or to remove dead, weak or diseased growths. This is best carried out after flowering unless the plants are wanted for their decorative hips. Pruning is then best deferred until late winter. Species which are trained into trees are rarely pruned as it can be almost impossible to reach the branches.

Rambler roses, with the exception of the few repeat-flowering cultivars, are best pruned after flowering. Old or dead stems can be cut away at ground level.

The other groups, bourbon, noisette, climbing teas, kordesii and the large-flowered, are best pruned in late winter. This should aim at controlling their growth as well as the removal of old or dead wood.

One word of advice on pruning. Cut long stems that are to be removed into short lengths as pruning proceeds, otherwise the young growths can be badly damaged as the old thorny stems are dragged out of the plant.

Roses are susceptible to a number of pests and diseases including aphids, caterpillars, red spider mites, capsid bugs, scale insects, grey mould, powdery mildew and honey fungus, for which the section on pests and diseases should be consulted. In addition, the following may affect rose plants.

Black spot is probably the commonest rose disease and shows itself on the leaves as blackish-brown spots surrounded by yellowing tissue. Badly affected leaves fall early, and a really bad attack of this fungus can result in the plant losing all its leaves. Any fallen leaves must be burned because the fungus overwinters on them, and the plants should be sprayed with Captan, Maneb, Zineb, Triforine or Dichlofluanid every two weeks through the growing season. Black spot tends to be less prevalent in industrial areas; in rural districts it is best to choose roses which have resistance to the disease.

Rust is another fungus disease which occurs as orange patches on the stems and leaf stalks in spring and yellow spots on the tops of the leaves in summer, accompanied by orange spore-masses on the leaf undersides. Badly affected plants should be burned, taking care to destroy any fallen leaves. The fungicides Maneb, Zineb and Thiram will help to control rust, but the best chemical to use is Oxycarboxin which at the time of writing, can only be bought in commercial quantities.

Leaf-rolling sawfly is a small black insect which lays its eggs on rose leaves in early summer. The leaves roll up tightly and the eggs hatch into green caterpillars which eat the rolled leaves. If possible, rolled leaves should be removed and burned before the caterpillars appear, but if the infestation is extensive, the plants should be sprayed with HCH. Plants growing in sheltered positions are most prone to attack.

Rose Leafhoppers are sap-sucking yellow or greyish insects about 3mm in length, whose activities produce colourless spots and areas of mottling. Disturbed adults will jump off the leaves — hence their name. Roses on sheltered walls are particularly likely to be attacked, and badly infested plants can lose all their leaves. Affected plants should be treated with a systemic insecticide such as Dimethoate or Formothion.

A little should be said about the botany of roses. Most species have thorny stems although by no means all are thorny. The thorns or prickles may be large or small, straight or curved and they are sometimes mixed with various bristles and hairs, especially in the young state. The leaves are alternate and pinnate, the leaflets toothed and often shiny-green. The flowers are usually borne in branched clusters at the branch tips, though they can sometimes be solitary. Basically they consist of five green sepals, five broad prominent petals and a large number of stamens and a cluster of short styles fused together. The flowers are often fragrant, although not always so. The fruit is the familiar rose hip but it can vary greatly in shape and size. Globose, pumpkin-shaped or urn-shaped are the most common forms and their colour varies from green to brown, red or black. Many cultivars have semi- or fully-double flowers in which the stamens are replaced by a profusion of petals.

The following account is divided into two main sections. In the first section some 27 'climbing' species are discussed whilst the second part deals with garden hybrids and cultivars suitable for wall culture, or indeed for trellises, pergolas, pillars or trees.

Scrambling Species

Rosa hemisphaerica = *R. sulphurea,* the Sulphur Rose, is a rather loose growing shrub reaching 2m tall. The leaves are bluish-green, each with five to nine leaflets. The solitary double flowers are sulphur-yellow, about 5cm across and sweetly scented. [July–Aug, HH, PN, Asia Minor, the Caucasus, N & W Iran]

This lovely plant is rare in cultivation. It does best on a warm south-west-facing sheltered wall and even there only flowers well in warm sunny summers. The flowers are rather heavy and tend to droop and in a bad season they often die before they open properly. A plant for the mildest districts of the country, often failing to do well even near London.

Rosa corymbulosa is a deciduous shrub reaching 2m tall, the stems usually having only a few scattered prickles. The leaves are deep green above but bluish-green and downy beneath. Flowers single, deep pink with a white 'eye', 2–2.5cm across, borne in dense clusters. Hips globose, scarlet, 1–1.5cm long. [June–July, H, PN, Central & W China]

This pretty rose is related to the following species but rarely grown in our gardens. It was introduced in 1907 by E.H. Wilson who collected it in Hupeh. The leaves turn reddish in the autumn.

Rosa beggeriana = *R. anserinaefolia* is a rather dense-growing bush 2–3m high eventually, with stems armed with hooked prickles which are often in pairs. The grey-green leaves have five to nine elliptic or oval leaflets. The single flowers are white, sometimes pink, 2.5–3cm across, usually borne in small clusters. Hips globose, red turning purplish, 0.7–1.3cm long. [June–July, H, PN, Central & SW Asia]

The flowers have a rather nasty scent but the attractive leaves have the fragrance of sweet briars.

***Rosa multiflora** is a spreading shrub, 3–5m tall, which sends out long arching stems which produce the following season's blooms. The stems are clothed in small prickles. The leaves have seven to nine obovate to lanceolate leaflets, often downy beneath. Flowers white, occasionally pinkish, single and fragrant, 2–3cm across, in many-flowered trusses. Hips small globose, bright red, 5mm. [June–July, H, PN, E Asia]

This rose can be trained on a wall or fence or allowed to clamber into a tree where it may reach 6m high. It is quite one of the most beautiful of all the wild roses and one of the most vigorous in cultivation. Propagation is often made easy by the self-layering habit of branches that touch the soil. It is widely planted along motorways in the United States and frequently used as a stock on to which garden roses, especially ramblers, are grafted; indeed it is an ancestor of many ramblers.

'Carnea' bears light pink double flowers. It is a rare plant in cultivation, although it was the first form of *R. multiflora* introduced to the west from China where it had long been cultivated.

'Grevillei' = *'Platyphylla'*, the Seven Sisters Rose, is a very vigorous rose with larger leaves than the type, the flowers varying in colour from white to pink, red or purplish. Its name refers to an early description which listed flowers of seven shades. [China & Japan] This cultivar needs a sheltered position as the new growths can be cut back by frost or cutting winds.

var. **cathayensis** has larger flowers, 2–4cm across.

Rosa watsoniana = *P. multiflora* var. *watsoniana*, the Bamboo Rose, is a trailing shrub with slender stems bearing scattered small prickles. Leaves have three to five linear leaflets. Flowers single, pale pink or white, 1–1.2cm across are borne in broad clusters. Hips red, globose, 6mm. [June, T, PN, Japan (garden origin)]

A rather curious plant cultivated for many years in Japan before it was introduced to the West at the end of the last century. It succeeds fairly well in some southern gardens but undoubtedly does best in Southern Europe. *R. watsoniana* is closely related to *R. multiflora* though it can easily be distinguished on account of its narrow untoothed leaflets and narrow petals.

Rosa setigera, the Prairie Rose, is a vigorous scrambling shrub with long slender stems reaching 4–5m, covered with straight prickles. Leaves deep green with three large oval leaflets. Flowers, 5–6cm across, are single, deep, rosy-pink fading to whitish, and almost scentless, borne in few-flowered clusters. Hips globose, red or brownish, 1cm long. [June–Aug, H, PN, Central & E N America]

Perhaps the finest wild rose from North America, this attractive species makes a fine sight when left to scramble over a tree or trellis. One of its chief values lies in its late-flowering habit. It is a parent of the famous rambler 'American Pillar', so often seen in gardens.

Rosa anemoniflora is a rambling shrub whose stems bear small scattered prickles. The leaves, dark green above, paler beneath, have three or sometimes five lanceolate or oval leaflets. Flowers double, 2.5–4cm across, are borne in loose clusters, pinkish in bud but opening white, the inner petals narrow. [June–July, T, PN, E China (Garden origin)]

R. anemoniflora was originally introduced to Europe in 1844 by Robert Fortune, who found it growing in a Shanghai garden. This plant is now assumed to be of hybrid origin, perhaps with *R. laevigata* or *R. multiflora* as one of the parents. *R. anemoniflora* is not very hardy, indeed shoots may be cut back by frosts. It is essential to give it a sunny sheltered wall. The flowers are unscented.

Rosa helenae is a large vigorous rambling species reaching 6m or more, with strong stems armed with hooked thorns. The leaves have seven to nine lanceolate oval leaflets. Single white flowers, 2–4cm across are borne in many-flowered, flat-topped clusters. The hips are egg-shaped 1–1.5cm long, scarlet when ripe, in drooping clusters. [June–July,H, PN, C & W China]

This fine rose is suitable for a tall wall or trellis, or better still left to scramble into a tree. It was introduced by E.H. Wilson in 1907 and named after his wife, Helen. It is a parent of the rambler roses 'Lykkefund' and 'Patricia Macoun'.

Rosa rubus = *R. ernestii*, the Blackberry Rose, is a big scrambling climber attaining 9m in a suitable position, the stems armed with hooked prickles. There are usually five leaflets to each leaf. The flowers are single, pinkish in bud but opening to white, 2.5–3.5cm across, borne in dense clusters, which are succeeded by globular dark red hips, about 1cm long. [June–Aug, H, PN, C & W China]

Although available in the horticultural trade *R. rubus* is rare in our gardens. The species has been cultivated in Europe since about 1886.

Rosa mulliganii is closely related to the previous species, a vigorous rambling shrub to 6m, the stems adorned with wide-based reddish prickles. Leaflets five to seven, elliptic. Flowers fragrant, white, single, 4–5cm across, in loose clusters. The orange-red hips are egg-shaped, 1–1.3cm long. [June–July, H, PN, W China]

A rose which produces an abundance of flowers. The young growth has an attractive purplish flush. Seeds were first sent back to Britain by George Forrest who collected it in Yunnan during his 1917–19 expedition.

Rosa brunonii = *R. moschata* var. *nepalensis*, the Himalayan Musk Rose, is a rampant deciduous or semi-evergreen rose reaching as much as 12m high. The stems bear large hooked thorns. The leaves have five to nine elliptic, greyish-green leaflets. Flowers beautifully fragrant, pale yellow in bud, opening white, 2.5–5cm across, borne in tight clusters up to 30cm across. Hips up to 1.5cm long, egg-shaped, brown. [June-July, HH, PN, Himalaya, & S W China]

R. brunonii is reasonably hardy once established, but young plants or young shoots may be cut back by frost. However, it is a fine plant for a lofty south- or west-facing wall or for scrambling up a suitable tree in a warm sheltered nook. It is characterised by having rather limp drooping leaves, which may be dull or shiny above.

At the end of the nineteenth century *R. brunonii* was thought to be synonymous with *R. moschata*, and even to this day many plants sold as *R. moschata* turn out to be *R. brunonii*.

'La Mortola' is a selection with larger leaves and flowers with pointed, not notched, tips to the petals. This cultivar is slightly more hardy. A fine plant raised at La Mortola in Italy.

Rosa moschata, the Musk Rose, is a strong-growing, rather loose, shrub up to 4m tall, the stems with hooked prickles. The dark shiny green leaves have five to seven elliptic or oval leaflets. Flowers white or cream, single, 3–5cm across, carried in loose clusters and sweetly musk-scented; the pointed petals quickly reflex at the tip. Hips small, egg-shaped, orange-red. [Aug–Nov, H, PN, Himalaya & Iran, naturalised in the Mediterranean region]

This lovely rose is seldom seen in our gardens today, although it was certainly cultivated during the reign of Henry VIII. It was introduced for the purgative properties of the flowers, much sought by medieval herbalists, rather than their musk fragrance. Today the Musk Rose has been largely superseded by some of its hybrids. It is an ancestor of the modern Large-flowered (Hybrid Tea) group of roses.

Rosa longicuspis is a handsome vigorous semi-evergreen rambler growing to 6m, its stems armed with hooked thorns. Leaves dark glossy green, leathery, have five to seven lanceolate-oval leaflets. Flowers single, cream in bud, but white when fully open, 3–5cm across, borne in loose clusters, scented of bananas; the petals are densely silky on the back. Hips egg-shaped, scarlet, 13–18mm long. [July–Aug, H, PN, NE India]

R. longicuspis is closely related to *R. sinowilsonii* which has rounded, rather than long-pointed, flower buds. Although not so fine a plant in flower it is remarkably handsome in leaf.

Rosa sinowilsonii is another semi-evergreen, reaching as much as 15m. The stems are reddish-brown and bear sparse short thorns. The large leaves are handsomely flushed with red when young, and usually have seven, sometimes five oblong or elliptic leaflets, purplish beneath. Flowers single, white, the petals silky on the outside, 3.5–4cm across, are borne in loose, many-flowered clusters. Hips red, rounded, 1–1.25cm long. [June–July, HH, PN, W China]

This handsome rose is more striking in leaf than in flower. Unfortunately now rarely seen in cultivation, but worth growing for its attractive foliage alone; the large leaves sometimes reach 30cm in length. Less hardy than *R. longicuspis* it needs a warm sheltered lofty wall, though in the mildest districts it can scramble up a tree with effect. It is a parent of the rambler 'Wedding Day'. The Latin name is a direct translation of the nickname of E.H. Wilson who introduced it in 1904. Wilson introduced a vast number of plants to the United States and Europe and became known as 'Chinese Wilson'.

Rosa filipes (Pl.16) is another striking vigorous shrubby climber, reaching 10–12m, the stems armed with hooked thorns. Leaflets five to seven, coppery when young. Flowers single, fragrant, cream in bud but opening white, 2–2.5cm across, borne in enormous loose clusters. Hips scarlet, globose, 1–1.25cm long. [June–July, H, PN, W China]

This is another of Chinese Wilson's introductions (1908) and a grand plant.

***'Kiftsgate'** is a particularly vigorous cultivar producing even larger flower clusters with up to 100 flowers. It is more readily available than the species.

R. filipes, R. sinowilsonii and *R. longicuspis* are ideal plants to grow up through a large tree (preferably an old decrepit one). They take time to establish, usually forming a tangled mound below the tree before starting to climb. *Rosa filipes* is probably the slowest, being apparently the least tolerant of shade, but it is well worth waiting for. These species are a wonderful sight when in flower with their great cascades of white flowers.

Rosa soulieana is a strong-growing shrub reaching 4–5m in height, the stems armed with yellowish thorns. The grey-green leaves have seven to nine oblong-elliptic leaflets. The single white flowers, creamy-yellow in bud, 2.5–4cm across, are borne few to a cluster. Hips roundish or egg-shaped, 1–2cm long, orange-red. [June–July, H–HH, PN, W China]

Rosa soulieana.

This is one of the most vigorous roses, best suited to the wild garden where it can be left to spread at will. It can be trained on a wall which can offer protection to the long stems. However, even when cut to the ground by frost, *R. soulieana* will usually sprout again. It was first collected by the French Missionary Soulié in Szechwan towards the end of the nineteenth century.

Plate 11 Evergreen Climbers 1 *Lardizabala biternata* (p.105), 2 *Lapageria rosea* (p.104), 3 *Mitraria coccinea* (p.106), 4 *Mutisia decurrens* (p.107), 5 *Trachelospermum jasminoides* 'Variegata' (p.114).

11
1
2
3
4
5

1
2
3
4
5
6

Rosa wichuraiana is a semi-evergreen shrub with trailing stems that can be trained to 6m high in good specimens. The dark glossy green leaves have seven to nine leaflets. Single white flowers, 3–5cm across, are borne in few-flowered clusters. Hips red, egg-shaped 1–1.5cm long. [July–Sept, H, PN, E Asia, including Japan]

This fine plant is more or less evergreen in milder districts. Like many species described here it is increasingly rare in our gardens, being largely superceded by more flambuoyant hybrids and selected cultivars. *R. wichuraiana* deserves a place in the larger garden trained against a sunny wall or better still over a large tree stump. Shoots that rest on the ground often root so that propagation is no problem. A great advantage of this rose is its resistance to mildew, a factor that has made it popular amongst rose breeders. It is a parent of a number of ramblers — 'Albéric Barbier', 'Dorothy Perkins' and 'Albertine' for instance. In the United States it is known as the Memorial Rose because it is often planted in cemeteries.

Rosa sempervirens, the Evergreen Rose, is an evergreen scrambling species with thorny stems reaching as much as 7m tall. The rather leathery leaves are usually glossy deep green, with five to seven elliptic leaflets. The fragrant flowers are single, white, 3–5cm across, in few-flowered clusters. Hips orange-red, globose or egg-shaped, 9–15mm long. [June-July, HH-T, PN, S Europe & N Africa]

R. sempervirens has been cultivated for a long time, although it has never become common. Its main contribution is as the parent of such ramblers as 'Félicité et Perpétue' and 'Adélaide d'Orléans'. It is closely related to the next species *R. arvensis* but the latter is deciduous and much hardier in Britain.

Rosa arvensis, the Field Rose, is a somewhat trailing or rambling shrub reaching 3–5m against a wall. Leaves with five to seven oval or elliptic leaflets often bluish-green beneath. Flowers single, white or sometimes pale pink, 3–5cm across, solitary or several in small clusters, generally scentless. Hips rounded to egg-shaped, dark red when ripe, 10–20mm long. [June–July, H, PN, Europe including Britain, & Asia Minor]

The British wild form is seldom grown in our gardens, except where it has crept into a hedge or wild area. However, it is particularly valuable in being completely shade-tolerant and in this respect it is a good species for scrambling into trees or up a north-facing wall or fence. It is a parent of the Ayrshire ramblers, the best and most commonly grown of which is 'Splendens'.

Rosa gigantea = *R.* × *odorata* var. *gigantea* is a very vigorous rose as its name implies, with strong growths reaching up to 15m. Leaves have five to seven lanceolate to oval leaflets. Flowers large, single, creamy-white, 8–14cm across, solitary or two or three together, slightly fragrant. Hips globose to lemon-shaped, 20–25mm long, yellowish or orange-red. [May–June, T, PN, SW China, Burma & NE India]

This fine deciduous or semi-evergreen plant is perhaps the most vigorous of all species roses, indeed in warmer countries it has been known to reach about 25m in height. It is also the largest-flowered of all wild roses. Unfortunately not hardy in this country, it will often be killed in a cold winter.

Rosa × odorata, the Tea Rose, is a name which covers a group of variable hybrids between *R. chinensis* and *R. gigantea*. They are more or less evergreen, reaching 3–6m tall, or more under favourable conditions, the stems with scattered hooked prickles. The leaves have five or seven elliptic or oval leaflets. The

---

Plate 12 Deciduous shrubs 1 *Albizia julibrissen* (p.118), 2 *Buddleia crispa* (p.120), 3 *Chaenomeles speciosa* 'Nivalis' (p.124), 4 *C. cathayensis* (p.125), 5 *Caesalpinia gilliesii* (p.122), 6 *Chaenomeles* × *superba* 'Boule de Feu' (p.125).

flowers are single or double, white, pink or yellow, 5–7.5cm across, solitary or several together. [June–Sept, T, PS, W China (garden origin)]

This is a tender group of roses, needing the protection of sunny sheltered walls. They require some pruning in the early spring, cutting out part of the old wood and weak growth to encourage strong new growths. *R. ×odorata* was of immense historical importance in the development of modern garden roses.

'Pseudindica' = 'Fortune's Double Yellow' is a vigorous climber with semi-double pinkish-yellow flowers flushed with copper. It was introduced to Europe by Robert Fortune in 1845.

☼ **Rosa × noisettiana**, the Noisette Rose, climbs to about 3m tall, the stems bearing hooked red thorns. The leaves have five or seven leaflets which are generally hairless. The fragrant flowers are semi-double, white, pink, red or yellow, borne in many-flowered trusses. [July–Oct, H, PN, Garden Origin]

Often grown as a shrub rose, but quite happy when trained up a support. The original cross, probably between *R. ×odorata* and *R. moschata*, gave rise to the Noisette group of roses, some of which can be grown on walls.

☼ **Rosa banksiae**, the Banksian Rose or Lady Banks' Rose, is a vigorous semi-evergreen attaining 7.5m tall with thornless or very sparsely thorny slender stems. Bright shiny green leaves have three or five leaflets. Flowers, single or double borne in dense clusters, white or yellow, 2.5–3cm across. [May–June, HH, PN, China, but of cultivated origin]

This well-known rose exists in a number of forms both white and yellow-flowered, single, or double. They are rather tender and all do best on a sunny sheltered wall. Even in the most favoured places Banksian Roses take some time to settle down and flowers are not freely produced during the first few years. This should in no way discourage people from growing this rose for it is a most delightful sight in full flower. Plants should be pruned with care for they flower mostly on growths which are two or three years old. Annual pruning should be avoided, but every two or three years a few of the older stems can be cut out to encourage some new replacement growth.

R. banksiae was named in honour of Lady Banks, wife of the famous Sir Joseph Banks, one time President of the Royal Society and Director of the Royal Botanic Gardens, Kew.

'Alba Plena' has double white flowers which smell of violets.
***'Lutea'** (Pl.16) the Yellow Banksian, has lovely clear yellow double flowers similar to the type, although not as fragrant. It is the form most often seen in gardens, being slightly more hardy than the others and flowering more freely.
'Lutescens' has single yellow, fragrant, flowers.
var. **normalis** is the wild form of the species which bears single creamy-white flowers. [C & W China]

☼ **Rosa × fortuniana** is a scrambling shrub, usually with thornless stems, reaching 12m tall. It is very similar to *R. banksiae* but bears larger leaflets and larger, double, white flowers. [May–June, HH, PN, China (garden origin)]

This attractive rose needs a south-facing sunny wall. Unfortunately it is not known to be free-flowering anywhere in Britain. It is generally thought to be a hybrid between *R. banksiae* and *R. laevigata*, being first introduced from a Chinese garden by Robert Fortune in 1850.

☼ **Rosa laevigata**, the Cherokee Rose, is a semi-evergreen, fairly vigorous climber, reaching 4.5m tall, the stems bearing numerous hooked prickles. The handsome

Rosa laevigata.

dark glossy leaves usually have three, occasionally five, leaflets. Flowers are single, white, 5–8cm across, solitary. Hips large and bristly, orange-red, 3.5–4cm long. [May–June, HH–T, PN, Burma & S China]

A beautiful rose, but rather tender and suitable only for the milder districts of the country, preferring a sunny sheltered position. It has been in cultivation for a long time and is widely naturalised in the south-eastern USA; it is the state flower of Georgia. Any pruning that is necessary should be carried out the moment the plants cease flowering.

R. laevigata is the parent of several modern garden roses such as 'Anemone' and 'Silver Moon'.

'Cooperi', Cooper's Burma Rose, is a beautiful rose reaching up to 12m in height with glossy green leaves like those of *R. laevigata*. The large pure white flowers are sometimes flushed with pink. A delightful rose, hardier than *R. laevigata* and possibly an hybrid between it and *R. gigantea*. It is often found in catalogues as *R. gigantea* 'Cooperi'.

***Rosa bracteata** (Pl.16), the Macartney Rose, is an evergreen or semi-evergreen scrambling shrub, its stout stems up to 6m tall, armed with prickles and covered with dense brownish down. Leaves with five to eleven shiny leaflets. Flowers single, white, 6-10cm across, with a delightful lemon-fragrance, are usually solitary, each surrounded by leaf-like bracts which give the plant its name. Hips globose, orange-red, 2.5–3cm long. [June–Oct, HH–T, PN, SE China & Taiwan]

R. bracteata is really hardy only in the south-west of Britain, although it does fairly well in many parts of the south provided that there are no severe winters and it is given a sunny sheltered south- or west-facing wall. A fine rose with a long flowering season, said to be resistant to black spot. Like *R. laevigata* it has become naturalised in the south-eastern United States. The English name commemorates its introduction to Britain by Lord Macartney in 1793. *R. bracteata* is one of the parents of the beautiful and well known 'Mermaid' rose.

Some of the *R. bracteata* offered by the trade is misnamed and generally turns out to be *R. wichuraiana*.

Garden Hybrids and Cultivars

RAMBLERS

These are strong-growing roses, mostly derived from *R. moschata, R. multiflora, R. sempervirens* and *R. wichuraiana*. Stems are supple and easy to train and flowers usually small (less than 5cm across) and carried in dense clusters. Non-repeat flowering, they generally flower around midsummer, although there are exceptions.

Ramblers are especially suitable for growing on fences, trellises and arches, climbing into hedges or rambling into trees. A disadvantage of many is their susceptibility to mildew, so growing them against a wall where air circulation is often restricted is not generally recommended, although cultivars like 'Albertine' will succeed well on an airy sunny wall.

Ramblers are best pruned immediately after flowering, removing old, dead or diseased wood, cutting them back close to ground level or to a strong young growth. This does not apply to the handful of repeat-flowerers in this group — 'Albéric Barbier' for instance. These should be pruned during the winter instead.

'Adélaide d'Orléans', *R. sempervirens* hybrid. Semi-evergreen to 5m. Flowers creamy-pink in bud but opening to whitish, loosely double, scented. [June – July]

'Aimée Vibert' grows to 5.5m high. Flowers double, pink-tipped in bud but opening white, borne in small clusters, faintly scented. [mid-July – Oct] The longest-flowering rambler.

'Albéric Barbier', *R. wichuraiana* hybrid, grows to 6m, being practically evergreen in a favourable position. Flowers double, pale yellow fading to creamy-white, sweetly-scented, rather flat and often quartered. [June-July, repeating at intervals until autumn]

***'Albertine'** (Pl.17), *R. wichuraiana* hybrid, is a vigorous thorny rose reaching 5 – 6m tall. The loosely double flowers are red in bud but open a delightful coppery-pink, richly fragrant. [June – July] A popular and beautiful rose, bred in 1921 and still grown in many gardens.

'Alexandre Girault', *R. wichuraiana* hybrid. Up to 6m tall, the branches with few thorns. The double flowers are carmine-red with a yellowish-salmon base, ageing to lilac-carmine, fragrant. [June – July]

'American Pillar' is a very vigorous rambler, sometimes 6 – 7.5m tall. Flowers single, carmine with a large white 'eye', borne in large clusters. [June-July with a few flowers later on] This popular rambler needs careful placing in the garden in relation to other colours as its flowers are a strident shocking pink. Despite this and its susceptibility to mildew it is widely grown.

'Blush Rambler' is almost thornless, reaching 3 – 4.5m. Flowers semi-double, pale pink, fragrant. [June – Sept]

'Bobbie James' grows to 7.5m, vigorous with attractive glossy-green leaves. Flowers freely borne in large clusters, single or with a few extra petals, creamy-white. [June – July]

'Breeze Hill', *R. wichuraiana* hybrid, 3 – 5m tall with rather large flowers for a rambler, 6 – 7cm across, which are double, pink tinged with apricot, fading to buff-cream, fragrant. [June – July]

***'Crimson Shower'** reaches 3 – 4.5m tall. Flowers semi-double, crimson, borne in large clusters. [Aug – Oct] A popular rambler because it flowers rather late in the season and the colour does not fade, but it has no scent.

'Débutante', *R. wichuraiana* hybrid, 2.5 – 4.5m tall. Flowers double, mid-pink, cupped at first but petals reflexed with age and quilled, slightly fragrant. [June – Aug] Similar to 'Dorothy Perkins' but unaffected by mildew.

'Dorothy Perkins', *R. wichuraiana* hybrid, up to 5.5m high. Flowers double pink in large and small clusters, almost scentless. [Aug–Sept] One of the most commonly-grown ramblers, popular since its introduction in 1901. It is at its best grown in an airy place on a trellis or arch as it is subject to mildew.

'Evangeline', *R. wichuraiana* hybrid, up to 5.5m high. Flowers single, bright pink, sweetly scented. [June–July]

***'Félicité et Perpétue'**, *R. sempervirens* hybrid. An almost evergreen rambler, especially in mild winters, reaching 4.5m. Flowers double, white, but stained with crimson in bud, delicately perfumed. [June–July] An attractive rose which is very easy to grow and extremely hardy, succeeding even on a shady north-facing wall. It flowers most prolifically when left unpruned.

***'Francis E. Lester'** grows to about 4.5m, bearing reddish young growths. Flowers single in clusters of up to 30, pink in bud but opening white with a fruity scent. [June–July] A hardy rambler which doesn't ramble too much and is easily controlled.

***'Franfois Juranville'**, *R. wichuraiana* hybrid, a vigorous rambler to 7.5m. Flowers double, coral-pink fading to light pink, yellow at the base, flat and often quartered. The flowers are larger than those of most ramblers, 6–7cm across, and fragrant. [June–July] This is a fine rambler, especially good grown on a trellis or arch or trained up a pole. On a wall it is susceptible to mildew.

'Fräulein Oktavia Hesse', *R. wichuraiana* hybrid. Flowers double, pale yellow with a darker centre, fragrant. [June–July but repeating later]

'Gardenia', *R. wichuraiana* hybrid. A vigorous rambler to 5.5m. Flowers double, yellow in bud but opening to creamy-white with a yellow quartered centre, fragrant. [June–July with a few later flowers]

'Goldfinch' has almost thornless stems reaching 4.5m tall. Flowers semi-double, yellow in bud, gradually changing to white as the flowers open, with dark yellow stamens and a fruity fragrance. [June–Aug]

'Hiawatha' grows to 4.5–6m tall. Flowers single, deep crimson with a white centre, scentless. [Aug–Sept]

'Jersey Beauty', *R. wichuraiana* hybrid. Up to 5.5m tall. Flowers single, pale yellow fading to white, strongly perfumed. [June–Aug with a few later blooms]

'Kew Rambler', *R. soulieana* hybrid, 4.5–5.5m high with greyish-green leaves. Flowers single, pale pink with a white centre, fragrant. [June–Sept] A fine rambler particularly effective when allowed to ramble in a tree.

'La Perle', *R. wichuraiana* hybrid, a vigorous rose reaching as much as 9m tall, with reddish-brown young foliage. Flowers double, white with a yellow centre, scented. [June–Aug]

'Lauré Davoust' reaches 3–4m tall. Flowers double, white to pale lilac-pink, free flowering. [June–Aug]

'Lykkefund', *R. helenae* hybrid, a thornless rambler to 6m tall. Flowers semi-double, creamy-yellow tinged with salmon, fading with age. [June–July]

'Madame Alice Garnier', *R. wichuraiana* hybrid. Stems up to 3m tall. Flowers double, bright pink with a yellow centre, flattening with age and fading to pale pink, quartered, sweetly scented. [June-Aug] A free blooming rambler.

'Patricia Macoun', *R. helenae* hybrid. Stems up to 6m tall. Flowers white, double, slightly fragrant [June–July] A free-flowering, very hardy rambler which survives well under cold northerly conditions.

***'Paul Transon'**, *R. wichuriana* hybrid, up to 3–4.5m high. Flowers double, coppery-orange in bud, but opening salmon-orange, fading in turn to yellowish salmon-cream, fragrant, freely borne. [June–July, with some later flowers]

***'Paul's Himalayan Musk Rambler'**, is a vigorous rose to 9m. Flowers small, double, lilac-pink, scented, borne on slender stems. [June–July] A pretty rose which looks especially charming when grown up an old tree.

'Phyllis Bide' grows to 3.5m tall. Flowers double, yellow flushed with salmon-pink, sweetly scented. [June–Sept]

'Rambling Rector', *R. multiflora* hybrid, a very thorny rose growing to 6m high. Flowers semi-double, cream fading to white, borne in large trusses, fragrant, very free flowering. [June–Aug]

'Russelliana', *R. multiflora* hybrid. Stems densely thorny reaching 3–6m tall. Flowers small, double, magenta-crimson, fading to mauvish, fragrant. [June–July]
***'Sander's White Rambler'**, *R. wichuraiana* hybrid. Stems almost thornless reaching 5.5m high. Flowers double, white and sweetly scented. [Aug–Sept] An attractive rose closely related to 'Dorothy Perkins', but with white flowers and not affected by mildew. It is similar to 'Patricia Macoun' but less hardy.

'Seagull' grows to 4.5m tall. Flowers single or semi-double, white with bright yellow stamens, borne in large clusters, scented. [June–Aug]
'Silver Moon', *R. laevigata* hybrid, a very vigorous rambler up to 9m tall. Flowers almost single, yellow in bud opening to creamy-white, scented. [June–Aug] A good cultivar for the warmer areas of Britain where it flowers best.
'Spectabilis', *R. sempervirens* hybrid, a small rambler reaching only 2m high. Flowers double, creamy-pink, fragrant. [June-July, sometimes with later flowers]
'Splendens' = 'Ayrshire Splendens', *R. arvensis* hybrid, a vigorous rose 5–7.5m high. Flowers semi-double, cream-tinged with red along the petal margins, solitary or in small groups, smelling of myrrh. [June-July] This rambler is able to grow in shady places and is particularly happy left to scramble over a tree.
'Thalia', *R. multiflora* hybrid. Stems to 4m high. Flowers double, white, very fragrant, borne in large clusters. [June–early July] Rather earlier-flowering than most ramblers.
***'The Garland'**, *R. moschata* × *R. multiflora*, reaches 4.5m tall with purplish thorns set on green stems. Flowers semi-double, salmon in bud, opening cream, flat with quilled petals and a scent of oranges. [June–July]
'Veilchenblau' has almost thornless stems 3.5–4.5m long. Flowers semi-double, violet with white streaks on the petals and a white centre, darkening later to maroon and then fading to lilac-grey, sweetly scented. [June–early July] Another rather early-flowering rambler. The flowers fade less if plants are grown in a partially shaded spot.
'Violette' is a vigorous rambler to 4–5m with practically thornless stems. Flowers semi-double to double, deep crimson-purple with occasional white streaks, deepening to maroon-purple and then fading to greyish-maroon, scarcely scented. [June–July]
***'Wedding Day'**, *R. sinowilsonii* hybrid, a very vigorous rambler attaining 11.5m. Flowers single, yellow in bud, opening to creamy white with orange stamens and rather pointed petals; scent reminiscent of oranges. [Late June–Aug] A fine rambler for a lofty wall. 'Wedding Day' is not very hardy and needs a sheltered south-facing aspect. The flowers are long-lasting but the petals are liable to become marked with pink spots after rain which some people consider to be a disadvantage.

LARGE-FLOWERED CLIMBERS

A term of convenience to cover those roses whose stems are stiffer than those of the ramblers and whose flowers are larger (usually more than 5cm across). The flowers can be borne singly or in loose clusters. This group includes climbing hybrid tea roses (in the new nomenclature known as 'large-flowered') and climbing floribundas (now known as 'cluster-flowered'), many of which are sports from original hybrid teas and floribundas. Many of these have the value of being repeat-flowerers so that blooms are produced from the first flush of summer (late June–July) right through until the autumn.

Pruning is best done in late winter, the aim being to shorten back and control strong healthy growth and to remove excess, dead or diseased wood.

For convenience these are divided into groups according to their colour. R=repeat flowerer, NR=non-repeat flowerer.

WHITE OR CREAM

***'Climbing McGredy's Ivory'** has large double, creamy-white flowers, fragrant [R]
'Climbing Mrs. Herbert Stevens' has double, white flowers tinged with lemon or

pale green, fragrant. [R] A vigorous rose growing to 6m tall that does well even on poor soils, but its flowers tend to suffer in extreme wet weather.
'Swan Lake' grows to 2.5–3m tall, with double white flowers tinged with pink in the centre, fragrant. [R] The flowers stand up well to wet weather but plants need protecting from black spot.
'White Cockade' grows to 2.5m high with double white, slightly fragrant flowers. [R]

YELLOW

***'Casino'** grows to 2.5–3m tall. Flowers double, soft yellow, fragrant. [R] A free-flowering and disease-resistant cultivar.
'Climbing Golden Dawn' grows to 3m tall with double, pale yellow flowers that are flushed red on the outside, fragrant. [Partial R]
***'Easlea's Golden Rambler'** reaches 3.5–4m high. Flowers double, yellow with red marks on the outer petals, sweetly scented. [NR] In nurserymen's catalogues this is often classified as a rambler rose.
'Elegance' grows to 4.5m tall with double, yellow blooms which fade to whitish along the petal margins, fragrant. [NR — but sometimes a few blooms later] Best on a south- or west-facing wall.
'Emily Gray' is a vigorous rose to 6m. Flowers double, buff-yellow, fragrant. [NR] Often slow to establish, it is worth waiting for the freely-produced flowers. The leaves are semi-evergreen. Often classified as a rambler rose in catalogues.
'Gloire de Dijon' grows to 5.5m with large double, buff-yellow flowers suffused with pink and apricot, fragrant. [R] A good rose for sunny or shady aspects.
***'Golden Showers'** grows only 2.5–3m tall. The semi-double bright yellow flowers fade to cream, fragrant. [R] A profuse bloomer, weather resistant and suitable even for a north-facing wall.
'Paul's Lemon Pillar' grows to 6m with large double, lemon-yellow flowers paling with age, fragrant. [NR] A cultivar favouring a south- or west-facing wall or fence.
'Royal Gold' reaches 2.5–3m tall, bearing double, golden-yellow fragrant flowers. [R] This rose does best on a south- or west-facing wall.

ORANGE, APRICOT OR COPPER

'Auguste Gervais' reaches 6m tall. Flowers semi-double, pale apricot with a coppery-salmon reverse, borne in large clusters, fragrant. [NR — though a few flowers are usually produced later in the season] This cultivar is often classified as a rambler rose in catalogues.
***'Compassion'** grows to 2.5–3m with double, pale salmon blooms shaded orange, very fragrant. [R]
***'Meg'** reaches 3–4m, the flowers almost single, salmon-apricot with red-gold stamens, fragrant. [R]
***'Schoolgirl'** reaches 3–4.5m tall. The double flowers are orange-apricot with a pinkish reverse, fragrant. [R] This is a good cultivar in northern parts of the country where the colour will not fade so much as in southern districts.
'Vicomtesse Pierre de Fou' is a vigorous rose to 6m tall even on rather poor soils. Flowers double, quartered, copper-orange changing to copper-pink, very fragrant. [R]

SCARLET OR CRIMSON

'Allen Chandler' is a vigorous cultivar often reaching 9m. Flowers semi-double, crimson with golden stamens, fragrant. [R] Often producing a good crop of orange hips, which should be removed if later flowers are wanted.
'Altissimo' grows to 3–4.5m tall. Flowers single, blood-red, scarcely scented. [R] The flowers are not affected by either sun or rain.
'Amadis' grows to 3m with thornless stems and semi-double deep crimson flowers, sometimes streaked with white, scarcely scented. [NR]

'Climbing Crimson Glory' reaches 3–3.5m tall. Flowers double, deep velvety-crimson, very fragrant. [R] In strong sunlight the flowers turn purplish.
***'Climbing Ena Harkness'** reaches 2.5–3.5m high. Flowers double crimson-scarlet, moderately scented. [R]
'Climbing Etoile de Hollande' reaches 4–6m tall, flowers double, dark-red, very fragrant. [R]
***'Danse de Feu'** grows to 2.5–3m tall. Flowers double or semi-double, fiery scarlet, fragrant. [R] A fine free-flowering rose which will grow well on a north-facing wall.
'Guinée' reaches 3–6m tall with double dark red-maroon flowers, fragrant. [NR but a few blooms later]
***'Paul's Scarlet Climber'** is a vigorous rose, 3–6m tall. Flowers semi-double, bright scarlet shaded with crimson, slightly fragrant. [usually NR — though sometimes repeat-flowering] A very popular rose often classified as a rambler rose in catalogues.
'Souvenir de Claudius Denoyel' grows to 5.5m high. Flowers double, rich crimson, very fragrant. [R] The flowers do not fade in strong sunshine.

PINK

'Allen's Fragrant Pillar' reaches only 2.5–3m tall. Flowers loosely double, cerise-pink flushed with yellow at the base, scented. [R]
***'Aloha'** reaches 2.5–3m tall. Flowers double, pink suffused with orange in the centre when young, fragrant. [R] Will flower on a north-facing wall.
'Bantry Bay' grows to 3m with semi-double, pale pink flowers tinged with salmon, only slightly scented. [R]
***'Chaplin's Pink Climber'** (Pl.16) grows to 3m tall. Flowers semi-double, bright pink, revealing yellow stamens. [NR]
***'Climbing Blessings'** is a vigorous rose up to 6m tall, with double soft coral-pink flowers, fragrant. [R]
'Climbing Madame Butterfly' reaches 3–6m tall. Flowers double, pale pink, tinged with yellowish, very fragrant. [R]
'Climbing Mrs. Sam McGredy' grows 3–4.5m high. Flowers double, deep salmon-pink tinged reddish, slightly scented. [R] This cultivar needs protection from black spot.
***'Climbing Shot Silk'** reaches 2.5–3.5m tall. Flowers double, cherry-pink, yellow at the base, very fragrant. [R]
***'Cupid'** grows to 4.5m tall with single flesh-pink flowers with pretty crinkly petals. [NR] The flowers are succeeded by large orange hips which persist into the winter.
'Dr. W. van Fleet' reaches 3.5–6m tall, bearing double, pink flowers that fade on ageing, fragrant. [NR]
'Lady Waterlow' grows to about 3.5m. Flowers double, petals salmon-pink edged with carmine, attractively veined, fragrant. [R]
'Madame de Sancy de Parabère' is a vigorous rose 3–6m tall. Flowers semi-double, pale violet-pink, scarcely scented. [NR — coming into flower early]
'Madame Grégoire Staechelin' (Pl.17) will grow to 6m tall. Flowers semi-double, pink with darker reverse, fragrant. [NR] An early-flowering rose, producing blooms on a north-facing wall.
'Morning Jewel' reaches only 3m high bearing semi-double pink, fragrant flowers. [R] A free-flowering cultivar.
***'New Dawn'** grows 4.5–6m tall. Flowers double, silvery-pink, slightly fragrant. [R — over a long flowering season] This rose is a sport of Dr. W. van Fleet. The flowers withstand rain well.
'Pink Perpétue' reaches 2.5–3.5m tall with double, bright pink flowers deeper on the reverse, fragrant. [R]

BI- OR MULTI-COLOURED

'Climbing Masquerade' is a vigorous grower 5–6m tall. Flowers semi-double, yellow in bud opening bright yellow but changing to salmon-pink and later dark red, slightly fragrant, borne in large clusters. [NR — but producing a few flowers during later summer] A well-known, though somewhat gaudy rose.

'Climbing Peace' is a strong grower reaching 6m tall. Flowers large, double, golden-yellow, the petals edged with pale pink, slightly fragrant. [R] A very fine rose which is a shy flowerer until well established.

***'Handel'** (Pl.17) reaches 2.5–3.5m tall, bearing double cream flowers, the petals edged with deep pink, slightly fragrant. [R] The flowers withstand rain well.

'Joseph's Coat' grows to 3m tall. Flowers double, yellow and orange, the petals edged with cherry-red. [R]

Climbing Tea

A rather tender group of repeat-flowering roses which grow best in the warmer parts of the country and need a sunny position. Their soft wood is susceptible to frost damage so that pruning should be delayed for as long as possible, the aim being to cut out weak, diseased or frost-damaged growths in late February or March. The climbing tea roses grow best on a rich loamy soil, this ensuring a good crop of flowers. Flowers are produced from about late June until the autumn.

'Climbing Devonensis' grows to 3.5m tall. Flowers double, the buds tinged with deep-pink but opening cream, often pinkish-apricot in the centre, fragrant. [R]

***'Climbing Lady Hillingdon'** is a vigorous rose to 6m tall with nodding semi-double flowers, apricot-yellow, fragrant. [R] This cultivar will bloom even on rather poor soils.

***'Marie van Houtte'** reaches only 2m high. Flowers double, the petals deep pink tinged with cream towards the edge, fragrant. [R]

'Sombreuil' grows 4–6m high. Flowers large, double but rather flat, creamy-white tinged with pink in the centre, quartered, with quilled petals, fragrant. [R]

'Souvenir de Madame Léonie Viennot' grows to 6m. Flowers very fully double, yellow shaded with pink. [R]

Noisette

A group of shrubby roses originating from a cross between *R. moschata* and a pink form of *R.* ×*odorata*. They are mostly repeat-flowering. The early cultivars in this group bore whitish or pink flowers. Later, yellow was introduced into the group by further crosses with a yellow form of *R.* ×*odorata*.

Noisette roses are best pruned in late winter (mid February to March). Pruning should be limited to removing old, weak or diseased growths or to shortening back excessively long shoots. The majority are not completely hardy and thrive best on a sunny sheltered south- or west-facing wall.

***'Alister Stella Gray'** grows up to 4m against a wall. The long-pointed buds open to yellow flowers with an orange centre, sweetly scented. [R] A very fine noisette blooming freely from July to October.

***'Blush Noisette'** reaches 3–4m with almost thornless stems. Flowers almost double, deep pink fading with age to lilac-pink, clove-scented, borne in small or large clusters. [R] A well-known cultivar, commonly seen in old gardens.

'Céline Forestier' is less vigorous than the previous two cultivars, seldom exceeding 3m in height. Flowers double, pale yellow becoming whitish towards the margin, quartered, fragrant. [R] A slightly tender rose which requires a warm sunny wall. It often takes time to become established, but once settled it generally flowers freely.

'Claire Jacquier' is similar to 'Alister Stella Gray' but much more vigorous, attaining as much as 9m. The double, yellow, scented flowers fade somewhat with age. [NR] The flowers are produced mainly in late June and July though a few are produced later on.

'Desprez à Fleur Jaune' = 'Jaune Desprez' grows to 5.5m tall. Flowers double, borne in clusters, rather flat, very pale yellowish shaded peach, with a powerful scent.

[R] An historic hybrid formed when 'Blush Noisette' was crossed with 'Park's Yellow Tea-scented China'. It was probably the earliest yellow climbing rose to be produced. This fine old rose needs a sunny sheltered position.

'Lamarque' grows 3–4m high. Flowers fully double, nodding, white tinted with lemon in the centre, fragrant; the flowers are rather flat and quartered, the outer petals quilled. [NR — though with a few flowers borne later in the season] This cultivar is slightly tender and requires a sheltered sunny wall.

'Maréchal Niel' grows to 3–4m. Flowers double, large (10–12cm across), clear yellow, quartered, richly fragrant, nodding on rather weak stems. [NR — though with a few flowers later in the season] Like the previous cultivar this one is slightly tender and requires the protection of a sunny south-facing wall.

***'Madame Alfred Carrière'** is a vigorous rose 6–7.5m tall. The globular flowers are creamy-pink fading to whitish, fragrant, often with a quartered centre, borne singly or in small clusters. [R] This rose will flower successfully on a north-facing wall.

'Rêve d'Or' is a vigorous rose 5–6m tall. Flowers double or semi-double, buff-yellow fading with age, fragrant. [R] Another rose for a warm sheltered niche.

***'Solfaterre'** is a vigorous rose 5–6m tall. Flowers double, sulphur-yellow, scented. [R] The flowers are freely produced.

'William Allen Richardson' reaches 4m tall, the young shoots and leaves flushed with dark red. Flowers double, orange-yellow, deeper in the centre, slightly fragrant, solitary or two to three together. [R] A fine sport of 'Rêve d'Or' which is not completely hardy and needs a warm sheltered wall. In hot sun the flowers tend to fade almost to white.

Bourbon

A rather mixed group of roses derived from a cross made in 1817 between the Autumn Damask Rose, *R.* ×*bifera* and a pink form of *R.* ×*odorata*, which occurred on the island of Réunion, at that time known as the Ile de Bourbon.

'Blairii Number Two' is a vigorous climber up to 4.5m tall, the young leaves the colour of mahogany. Flowers double, pale pink but deeper in the centre, sweetly fragrant [late June–July]

'Climbing Souvenir de la Malmaison' grows 3–4.5m tall. Flowers large double, creamy-pink, flat and quartered, fragrant. [late June–July, but also a few again in Sept] Suitable for sunny or shady walls. Plants can be pruned after the first crop of flowers if desired.

***'Zéphirine Drouhin'** (Pl.17) is a semi-vigorous thornless rose 1.5–4.5m with brownish-purple young leaves. Flowers semi-double, cerise-pink, solitary or in small clusters, fragrant. [R — late June–Oct] A fine well-known rose that is widely grown. It is especially valuable by doorways or arches as it is quite thornless. 'Kathleen Harrop' is a shell-pink sport, less vigorous but well worth growing.

Kordesii Hybrids

'Rosa kordesii' was raised by the German breeder Wilhelm Kordes from a hybrid between *R. rugosa* and *R. wichuraiana* called 'Max Graf'. This hybrid is normally sterile, but a chance seedling was found to be fertile and given the name *'R. kordesii'*. This plant was then used in a breeding programme which resulted in the Kordesii hybrids. These roses have clusters of flowers and are repeat-flowering. The glossy foliage is disease-resistant. Like the other repeat-flowering roses these hybrids are best pruned in late winter, February or March.

***'Dortmund'** grows to 3m tall. Flowers single, bright crimson-red with a white eye, borne in large clusters. [R] A fine free-flowering rose which makes a pretty sight on a pillar or trellis, though it does equally well on a wall.

'Hamburger Phoenix' reaches 2.5–3m tall. Flowers semi-double, rich crimson, slightly fragrant. [R — providing the hips from the first flowering are removed]

'Karlsruhe' grows to 3m tall. Flowers double, large, deep pink, freely borne. [R]
***'Leverkusen'** is 2.5–3m tall. Flowers double pale yellow with a lemon fragrance. [R]
***'Morgengruss'** is fairly vigorous reaching 4m high. Flowers double, pale pink suffused with yellow, scented, profusely borne. [R]
***'Parkdirektor Riggers'** produces strong stems up to 4m tall. Flowers semi-double, velvety-crimson, borne in large clusters, scarcely scented. [R]
'Ritter von Barmstede' grows to 3–4m tall. Flowers semi-double, deep pink, produced in large trusses. [R]
'Sympathie' grows to 3.5m tall. Flowers double, dark velvety-red, fragrant. [R]

Climbing Miniatures

Miniature roses are smaller in all their parts than other roses and may be repeat-flowering or not. They are generally derived from *R. chinensis* 'Minima' and 'Rouletii', both of which are tiny cultivars less than 30cm in height. So far only a few climbing miniatures have been produced in Britain, although a larger number is available in the United States.

'Climbing Jackie' grows to 2m tall. Flowers double, cream to pale yellow, slightly fragrant. [R — late June–Oct]
'Climbing Pompon de Paris' grows to 2m tall. Flowers double, bright pink. [NR — early June–July]
***'Nozomi'** grows about 1.5m tall, although somewhat taller on rich soils. Flowers single, pearly-pink fading to white, borne in large clusters. [NR — June & July]
***'Pink Cameo'** is up to 2m tall. Flowers double, rich pink with a darker centre, fragrant. [R — late June–Oct]

Shrubs

A rather mixed group of roses brought together for convenience and containing all those roses not covered in the previous groupings. They are best pruned in late winter, February or March.

***'Anemone'** = 'Anemonoides', R.×anemonoides. A vigorous climber to 4m tall. Flowers single, pale pink with deeper pink veins on the petals, large, 8–10cm across, fragrant. [May–June] This fine rose is thought to be an hybrid between *R. laevigata* and a Tea Rose. In most districts it requires a warm sunny wall, where it will continue to flower for several weeks.
'Climbing Cécile Brunner'. A strong rose climbing to about 6m. Flowers double, clear pink, fragrant. [May–Oct]
***'Complicata'** A beautiful shrub with long arching stems up to 3m long. Flowers single, pink, paler in the centre and with golden stamens, large, 10–12cm across, fragrant. [Mid-June–July] This rose is thought to be an hybrid of *R. gallica* or *R. macrantha*. It is especially fine when trained into a tree or over a trellis.
***'Constance Spry'** A shrubby rose reaching 2m against a wall. Flowers globular, soft pink, 7.5–12cm across, borne singly or a few together on stems produced the previous year; smelling of myrrh. [Late June–July]
'Gruss an Teplitz' grows to 2m high. Flowers double, crimson, in small clusters, fragrant. [R — July–Oct]
***'Lawrence Johnston'** (Pl.16) is a vigorous climber reaching as much as 9m tall. Flowers semi-double, canary yellow, fragrant. [June, but intermittently onwards until Oct]
'Maigold' is an extremely prickly rose growing to 3.5m tall with beautifully glossy-leaves. Flowers semi-double, reddish-orange in bud opening bronze-yellow, very fragrant. [R — late June–Oct]
***'Mermaid'** (Pl.17) is a vigorous rose to 6m tall, the stems with large hooked thorns and the glossy leaves almost evergreen. Flowers single, clear yellow with orange stamens which persist after the petals have fallen, large, 9–10cm across, fragrant. [Late

June–Oct] This beautiful and well known rose was derived from a cross between *R. bracteata* and a yellow Tea Rose. It is not very hardy so it is best grown on a sunny sheltered west- or south-facing wall. 'Mermaid' makes thick woody stems in time and greatly resents harsh pruning. Pruning should therefore consist solely of removing dead or diseased wood or shortening back a few growths in order to encourage some new shoots.

'Ramona' reaches 4–5m tall. Flowers single, crimson, paler on the reverse, large, 8–10cm across. [June–Aug] A sport of 'Anemone'.

***'Souvenir du Docteur Jamain'**. This cultivar will reach 3m against a suitable wall. The large double flowers are plum-coloured shaded with crimson and fragrant. [Late June–July and again in autumn] A west-facing wall suits it best, as too much sun turns the flowers brownish. Plants appreciate a rich soil.

***'William Lobb'**. A fine rose which will attain about 2.5m high against a wall. The flowers are dark crimson-purple, the petals with a lighter pink reverse and tending to fade with age, semi-double with a 'muddled' centre, fragrant. [Late June–July] A fine moss rose, often grown as a free-standing shrub in gardens but very lovely grown against a wall. The 'mossy' outgrowths of the calyx and flowerstalks, typical of moss roses, are pale green.

Evergreen Wall Shrubs

Evergreen shrubs provide the largest group of plants included in this book. Many evergreen shrubs are half-hardy or tender and need the protection provided by a sheltering wall or fence. Some of the most beautiful wall shrubs are evergreen, the Camellias, Ceanothus and Acacias being amongst the most desirable.

Evergreen subjects are best planted in the early spring once the worst of the winter has past. This will allow them to produce new roots as soon as possible. Young plants, especially of tender species, benefit from some form of protection, a straw or wattle screen, during their first winter or two. Evergreens are particularly prone to suffer from cold dry winds and the foliage can be badly damaged if the site is not sheltered enough. Wind can cause more damage than frost.

Most require little regular pruning, though winter-damaged or diseased growths should be carefully cut out in the spring. Autumn pruning should be avoided, the principle being to overwinter plants with as much mature growth as is possible.

Evergreens are often thought of as rather dull, but many have attractive and distinctive foliage, ideal for masking an unsightly wall. A solid 'wall' of evergreen can in some instances be rather depressing, although careful interplanting with deciduous species, shrub or climbers, contrasting foliage and flower colours can produce a most striking effect. Endless hours of pleasure can be spent working out different planting combinations.

ABELIA (Caprifoliaceae)

General remarks are to be found on p.115, together with the deciduous species, *A. chinensis, A. engleriana, A. graebneriana, A. schumannii, A. spathulata* and *A. triflora*.

Abelia uniflora is a spreading evergreen species 1–2m tall, with arching branches. The oval pointed leaves are glossy dark green above but paler beneath, 2.5–5cm long. The funnel-shaped white flowers, 22–25mm long, are tinged with pink and marked with orange in the throat; they are solitary or borne in twos or threes. The calyx consists of two sepals only. [June, HH, PA, China]

A beautiful plant which has the largest flowers of any cultivated species but is rare in cultivation, having largely been displaced by *A.* ×*grandiflora*, which combines the best of *A. chinensis* and *A. uniflora* with increased vigour and greater hardiness. *A. uniflora* is more or less hardy in the mildest districts, but even there it will be cut back in a severe winter. It generally flowers in profusion.

***A. × grandiflora** = *A. rupestris* var. *grandiflora*, *A. chinensis*×*A. uniflora*. A graceful evergreen shrub 1–2m tall with slender arching stems. The bright glossy, dark green leaves are oval. The funnel-shaped white flowers, about 18mm long, are flushed with pink, solitary or in clusters of two to four, and have a slight fragrance. The calyx has two to five sepals which are tinged with purple. [July–Oct, HH, PA, Garden origin]

This hybrid is a fine plant, well worth growing and flowers prolifically. It is hardier than either of its parents, but only reliably so in milder districts. There is a form with leaves variegated with pale and dark green streaks. *A.* ×*grandiflora* is often to be found under the name *A. rupestris* in nurseries, though this name really applies to a synonym of *A. chinensis*.

'Edward Goucher', *A.* ×*grandiflora* ×*A. schumannii* is not unlike *A.* ×*grandiflora* but has dark purplish-pink flowers. The vigorous vegetative shoots generally have leaves in groups of three. An interesting hybrid which is certainly hardier than either of its parents.

***Abelia floribunda** is a magnificent evergreen species, generally 2–3.5m tall, with downy-reddish young shoots. The oval or rather roundish leaves are pointed and slightly toothed. The beautiful funnel-shaped flowers, 35–50mm long, droop in clusters of two or three, ranging in colour from rose-red to magenta. The calyx consists of five short lobes. [June–July, HH, PA, Mexico]

This superb plant deserves a place in all gardens where there is a warm south- or west-facing wall. Specimens have been known to reach 6m tall, although half the height is more normal. Plants are generally cut back in a cold winter but will generally sprout anew when warmer weather arrives, however, during the severe

Abelia floribunda.

winter of 1962–63, and again in 1981–82, many fine plants were killed. Despite this it is well worth a try provided that new plants are propagated regularly to maintain stock.

ABUTILON (Malvaceae)

There are about 100 species of *Abutilon* which are native to the warm temperate and tropical regions of the world. They are mostly shrubs with simple, alternate, lobed leaves. The flowers have five sepals and petals and many stamens which are united into a tubular column. The style is branched, the number of branches equalling the number of sections in the fruit. The fruit splits into five to many sections which are arranged in a single whorl.

These beautiful shrubs, related to Hibiscus, always attract attention when flowering. Propagation is affected by cuttings or seed which is often produced in quantity.

Some species of *Abutilon* are deciduous; they are described below, together with the evergreen species.

☼ ***Abutilon vitifolium** = *Corynabutilon vitifolium* is a semi-evergreen or sometimes deciduous shrub growing to about 2m tall, occasionally taller. The leaves are 10–15cm long, covered with white starry hairs. The pale to deep mauve flowers, 7–8cm across, are borne up to six together at the leaf axils. The stamens are yellow and the purple style has nine or ten branches. [May–July, H–HH, PN, Chile]

A lovely species which in a mild winter or in a very protected place, can retain most of its leaves. It is best against a south or west wall. It is not long-lived and liable to die suddenly, but plants can be easily propagated from cuttings or seed as an insurance. The dead flower-heads should be removed.

'Album' = var.*album* has white flowers.

'Veronica Tennant' has especially large freely-produced flowers.

Abutilon ochsenii = *Corynabutilon ochsenii* is usually deciduous and will reach 2–4m in height. The leaves are three-lobed, 8–10cm long. The flowers, 4–5cm in diameter, are deep mauvish-blue, each petal with a darker basal patch. One to three are borne at the leaf axils. The stamens are yellow and the deep mauve style has seven to nine branches. [May–June, HH–T, PN, Chile]

Similar to *A. vitifolium* but a less hairy plant with smaller flowers, and less often seen in our gardens.

☼ ***Abutilon × suntense** (Pl.18) is a splendid semi-evergreen garden hybrid produced between *A. vitifolium* and *A. ochsenii* and possessing characters intermediate between the parents. It can be distinguished from both by having a mixture of starry and simple hairs on the leaves. It was raised in 1967 and may well be more hardy than its parents; certainly it is very free-flowering. [May–June, H, PN, Garden origin]

'Jermyns' has *A. vitifolium* 'Veronica Tennant' as one of its parents. The flowers are a beautiful dark mauve. A very beautiful hybrid.

☼ ***Abutilon megapotamicum** = *A. vexillarium* (Pl.18) is a hairless slender-stemmed semi-evergreen shrub growing to 2m. The narrowly-ovate leaves are 5–10cm long with toothed margins. The flowers are pendulous, solitary, borne at the leaf-axils and bell-shaped. The calyx is about 2.5cm long, red, five-ribbed and inflated. The petals are 3–4cm long, yellow, becoming darker as they age. [Apr–Sept, HH, PN, Brazil]

A very attractive shrub for a south- or west-facing wall, although perhaps more often seen as a conservatory plant. The rather weak stems need more support than most wall shrubs if the plant is to be seen at its best. The flowers are borne over a very long season.

'Variegatum' has leaves mottled with yellow.

Abutilon × milleri is a semi-evergreen hybrid between *A. megapotamicum* and *A. pictum*. It has narrowly ovate leaves 7–15cm long with toothed margins, occasionally they are three-lobed. The bell-shaped flowers are produced singly or in pairs in the leaf axils. The calyx is greenish, flushed with pink, the petals 3.5–4cm long, yellow with red veins. [May–Aug, HH–T, PN, Garden origin] ☼

The following tender hybrids are probably hybrids between *A. darwinii* and *A. striatum*, with *A. insigne* possibly being involved in 'Boule de Neige'. They can only be grown in the mildest parts of the country against a sunny sheltered wall or fence.

'Ashford Red' has large pinky-red flowers
'Boule de Neige' has white flowers.
'Golden Fleece' has rich yellow flowers.

ACACIA (Leguminosae)

A very large tropical and subtropical genus, characterised by the Mimosas and Wattles, with some 800 species, the greatest concentration being in Australia. They have alternate leaves which are bipinnate, or reduced to leaf-like petioles (phyllodes) which look like simple leaves. The flowers are not the pea-flowers typical of the family but have a regular corolla with four to five yellow petals; they are borne in dense globose heads or spikes, often arranged in panicles or racemes. Each flower has numerous stamens which are its most conspicuous feature. The pods are ovate or linear, usually sickle-shaped and sometimes constricted between the seeds.

Acacias are only suitable for the mildest localities and require a sunny sheltered wall. Any necessary pruning should be carried out immediately after flowering in late spring or early summer. They are not very happy on chalky soils where they tend to become chlorotic. Young container-grown plants should be planted out preferably in the late spring and may need some winter protection when young.

Acacia dealbata *A. decurrens* var. *dealbata* (Pl.18), the Silver Wattle or Mimosa, is a tall-growing species reaching 30m in the wild. The silvery-downy bipinnate leaves are 7.5–13cm long. The fragrant canary-yellow flowers are borne in globose heads each about 4mm wide, arranged in panicles up to 10cm long. The flat bluish-white pods are 5–8cm long. [Jan–Mar, T, PA, SE Australia] ☼

A. dealbata is the 'Mimosa' generally sold in florist's shops, which comes mainly from the south of France shortly after Christmas. It is rather hardier than is generally supposed and quick growing, however, it will be cut back, or worst killed, during a severe winter in all but the mildest districts.

Acacia baileyana, the Cootamundra Wattle, is a large shrub or small tree, usually with pendulous branches and glaucous young shoots. The blue-green bipinnate leaves are 2–5cm long. The yellow flowers are scented and aggregated into globose heads about 6mm wide, borne in racemes 5–10cm long. The pods are 5–8cm long. [Jan–Apr, T, PA, Australia (New South Wales)] ☼

This is one of the loveliest species of *Acacia* with its delicate feathery leaves and abundant flowers, very similar in general appearance to the common Mimosa.

☼ ***Acacia armata** (Pl.18), the Kangaroo Thorn, grows 3m or more high and the young branches are ridged and usually bristly. The phyllodes are 1.2–5cm long, oblong with a curved point, deep green and hairless. Some of the cultivated plants bear pairs of needle-shaped spines up to 1.3cm in length. The slightly fragrant flowers are yellow and borne in globose heads about 8mm wide, solitary or in pairs. The 3–5cm pods are covered in soft silky hairs. [Mar–Apr, T, PA, Australia]

The Kangaroo Thorn is a beautiful sight in full bloom with the rich yellow flowers carried along the entire length of the stems. This shrub has a dense bushy habit.

☼ **Acacia diffusa** has stiff rather angled branches growing to 1.8m tall. The rigid phyllodes are up to 4cm long, linear, straight or sickle-shaped. The bright yellow flower-heads 6mm across, are usually produced in pairs in the leaf-axils. [Mar–Apr, T, PA, SE Australia]

There is a hardier, lower-growing form of this species, introduced from Tasmania by Harold Comber, which is probably the hardiest of the Acacias grown in Britain.

☼ **Acacia longifolia**, the Sidney Golden Wattle, is a large shrub or small tree reaching 9m tall. The young shoots are angular and usually hairless. The dark green oblong-lanceolate phyllodes are 7–15cm long. The scented flowers are bright yellow, the flower-heads borne in cylindrical spikes 4–8cm long. The pods are 7.5–10cm long. [Mar–Apr, HH–T, PA, Australia]

Tender, like all Acacias, but slightly less so than most of the other species, and with the advantage of being more tolerant of limy and chalky soils than most Acacias cultivated in this country.

var. **sophorae** has shorter broader phyllodes and is reasonably hardy in mild areas.
var. **floribunda** has very narrow phyllodes.

☼ **Acacia podalyriifolia**, the Queensland Silver Wattle, grows to 3m or more tall. The phyllodes are 2.5–3.5cm long, oval to ovate, downy and a silvery-green colour. The golden-yellow flowers are packed into globose heads, borne in racemes 5–10cm long. [Jan–Mar, T, PA, Australia (Queensland)]

Acacia rhetinodes, a small tree attaining 6m in height, is completely hairless. The grey-green, linear phyllodes are 3.5–13cm long. Pale-yellow, scented

Acacia riceana

Plate 13 Deciduous and Semi-Evergreen Shrubs 1 *Chimonanthus praecox* (p.126), 2 *Cotoneaster horizontalis* (p.128), 3 *Cornus capitata* and fruit (p.190), 4 *Forsythia suspensa* (p.133), 5 *Dendromecon rigida* (p.195).

1
2
3
4
5

14
1
2
3
4
5

flowers, in globose heads about 6mm across are borne six to twelve together in lax panicles. The pods may grow up to 18cm. [Feb – Mar, and sporadically until autumn, T – HH, PA, SE Australia]

Like *A. longifolia* this species is fairly lime-tolerant. It is reasonably hardy in the warmest localities.

Acacia riceana will grow to 9m and has pendulous young shoots. The phyllodes are needle-shaped, and curved, 2.5 – 5cm long, dark green, in clusters of one to four. The pale yellow flowers are clustered into globose heads, borne in slender spikes 2.5 – 5cm long. The downy pods are 5 – 8cm long. [Mar – Apr, T, PA, Tasmania]. (Illustration p.168).

Acacia verticillata, Prickly Moses, is a large shrub or small tree with a dense habit, growing to 6m in height. The young shoots are ridged and downy. The needle-shaped hairless phyllodes are 0.8 – 2cm long, deep green and usually in whorls of six. The bright yellow flowers are borne in cylindrical spikes 1.2 – 3.5cm in length. The pods are up to 5cm, usually curved or sickle-shaped and with pale scattered hairs. [Apr – May, T, PA, SE Australia]

Distinguished from the other species of *Acacia* described here, by the distinct whorls of phyllodes.

ACRADENIA (Rutaceae)

A genus containing a single species native to Tasmania.

Acradenia frankliniae is an evergreen shrub to 2 – 3m tall when mature, with greyish-downy young shoots. The leaves are trifoliate, borne in opposite pairs, the surface dotted with tiny dark oil glands. The white flowers are small, 10 – 13mm across, borne in flat-topped clusters up to 5cm across. Each flower has five oval petals and ten stamens. The fruit consists of five felted carpels each topped by a prominent gland. [May, HH, PN, Tasmania]

An interesting shrub suitable for a southwest-, west- or northwest-facing wall in mild districts. The plant gets its specific name from the Franklin River near Macquarie Harbour, along whose banks it is found.

ADENOCARPUS (Leguminosae)

Adenocarpus foliolosus is a densely-branched shrub 1 – 1.8m tall, with hairy young shoots. The small crowded leaves have three lanceolate or obovate leaflets. The flowers are yellow, in dense terminal racemes, and have a woolly calyx and a downy standard. The young pods are glandular, becoming smooth when mature. [May – June, T – HH, PA, Canary Is]

In catalogues this species is often listed under the erroneous name of *A. foliosus.*

ANTHYLLIS (Leguminosae)

There are some 50 species of *Anthyllis,* native to Europe, North Africa and Western Asia. They have alternate, odd-pinnate, leaves, or the leaves may be simple or composed of three leaflets. The typical pea-flowers are borne in dense heads and the pods do not usually split open.

Two species are cultivated in Britain as wall shrubs. *A. barba-jovis* is evergreen and is described below and *A. hermanniae* is deciduous and found on p.119.

Anthyllis barba-jovis, Jupiter's Beard, will grow up to 3.5m against a wall, the branches covered in silky hairs. The leaves are composed of nine to nineteen

---

Plate 14 Deciduous and Semi-Evergreen Shrubs 1 *Fuchsia excorticata* (p.133), 2 *F. magellanica* (p.134), 3 *Jasminum nudiflorum* (p.137), 4 *Hibiscus syriacus* (p.135), 5 *Fremontodendron californicum* 'Californian Glory' (p.201).

leaflets. The flowers are cream to pale yellow, borne in rounded heads 2–2.5cm in diameter, at the ends of short twigs. [Apr–June, T, PN, SW Europe and Mediterranean]

A tender shrub which may be injured in a bad winter, even with wall-protection. In Britain the seeds ripen only rarely, so propagation is mainly by cuttings.

ARISTOTELIA (Elaeocarpaceae)

For a general description see p.119; *Aristotelia serrata* and *A. fruticosa* are deciduous species.

Aristotelia chilensis = *A. marqui, Cornus chilensis,* is an evergreen, rather spreading, shrub 2–3m tall, sometimes more. The ovate leaves are opposite or alternate, 5–12cm long, toothed, a dark rather shiny green. The greenish-white flowers are small, only 6mm across, but occur in small clusters. The male and female flowers are borne on separate plants. The small, pea-sized fruits are purplish at first but turn black when ripe. [May–June, T, PN, Argentina & Chile]

This is the commonest species in cultivation, well known in gardens since the nineteenth century. When cut back by winter frosts plants usually put up a crowd of vigorous shoots with extra large leaves and these will require some thinning. In Chile a wine is made from the fruit.

'Variegata' is a handsome form with leaves variegated with yellow. Unfortunately this plant is considered even more tender than the normal form.

Aristotelia peduncularis = *Elaeocarpus peduncularis* is also evergreen, 2m tall and quite hairless in all its parts. The ovate or lanceolate leaves are opposite or in threes, 2.5–7.5cm long and toothed. The flowers are white, 12–14mm long, borne singly usually on slender drooping stalks, each petal distinctly three-lobed. The attractive heart-shaped fruits are pink or red, darkening to black as they ripen, each 13–15mm long. [May, T, PN, Tasmania]

An attractive plant but a rare one in cultivation, being as tender as the previous species.

AZARA (Flacourtiaceae)

A small genus of tender and half-hardy evergreen shrubs or small trees from temperate South America which deserve to be more widely grown. In the wild they are plants of moist mild areas and in cultivation most of the species thrive best in mild western and south-western districts in moist loamy soils shielded from cold drying winds. A west- or south-facing wall is most suitable. They require little pruning other than to remove dead or untidy growths. Propagation can be by striking firm young shoots in gentle heat during the late summer.

Azaras have small leaves which are usually alternate, though at the base of each there is a leaf-like structure, or stipule, generally about one third the size of the true leaf. This often gives the shoots the appearance of possessing opposite leaves. The small flowers are unusual in being petal-less and most of the colour and character is provided by the prominent stamens.

Azara lanceolata is an elegant shrub, up to 7m tall, although generally less. The leaves, 2–6cm long, are lanceolate, bright green and coarsely toothed. The slightly fragrant soft yellow flowers, are borne in small loose clusters from the leaf axils of the previous year's shoots. Fruits are small pale mauve or whitish berries, 8mm across. [Apr, T, PN, Chile and bordering areas of Argentina]

This is probably the finest species in cultivation and when grown well flowers in profusion. It was originally discovered by Charles Darwin on the Tres Montes Peninsula during the voyage of the Beagle in 1834, although it was not introduced to cultivation until almost a century later.

*__Azara petiolaris__ = *A. gilliesii* is a shrub 3–4m tall. The hairless leaves are rather holly-like, ovate or oval, with distant sharp teeth, shiny green above but pale beneath, 4–8cm long. The pale yellow flowers, borne in short dense racemes in the leaf axils, have a sweet fragrance reminiscent of vanilla. [Feb–Apr, T, PN, Chile]

A lovely little shrub which is one of the finest species in flower. Probably the most commonly planted but it deserves to be even more widely grown.

Azara dentata is a shrub 2–4m tall with downy young stems. The leaves are ovate or oval, shiny deep green above contrasting with the downy lower surface, toothed, 2.5–4cm long. The fragrant yellow flowers are borne in short branched clusters. [Mar–Apr, T, PN, Chile]

A species seldom seen in cultivation and not one of the more attractive.

*__Azara serrata__ is similar to the previous species and the two are often confused. However, the leaves are larger and lack down beneath, whilst the flowers occur in rounded clusters borne on delicate downy stalks. [Mar–Apr, T, PN, Chile]

Azara integrifolia is the largest species reaching as high as 12–13m, a shrub or small tree with downy young stems. The leathery leaves are oval or almost diamond-shaped, usually untoothed and with a recurved margin, glossy-green on both surfaces, 2.5–5cm long. The mildly fragrant flowers are borne in small clusters in the leaf axils of the previous year's wood; four tiny purplish sepals are more or less obscured by deep yellow stamens. Berries white flushed with mauve, 6mm across. [Jan–Mar, HH, PN, Chile and neighbouring areas of Argentina]

As the name implies this species has entire (untoothed) leaves, although the leaves of young plants may be slightly toothed. Established plants generally flower profusely.

var. **browneae** = *Azara browneae*, which is rather rare in cultivation, has larger leaves, each with two to eight small teeth near the apex.

'Variegata' is a fine cultivar with more rounded leaves that are edged with pale pink, changing to creamy-white.

Azara microphylla is a shrub or small tree up to 7m tall, the young shoots with dense darkish down forming two opposite rows. The shiny dark green leaves are rounded, generally toothed, 1.25–2.5cm long. The tiny yellow flowers, borne in clusters, have a delightful vanilla-like fragrance. Fruit a small red berry, 5mm across. [Feb–Mar, HH, PN, Chile and neighbouring areas of Argentina]

This species is the hardiest in cultivation, tolerant of drier areas than other species, and can be grown successfully in eastern and south-eastern parts of the country. Once established it survives most winters fairly readily.

'Variegata' is a dainty shrub, the leaves broadly margined with creamy-white.

BERBERIS (Berberidaceae)

The genus *Berberis*, or the Barberries as they are commonly called, are popular spiny garden shrubs. There are many fine species and cultivars available; perhaps 200 species widespread in Europe, Central Asia and the Americas. They can be mainly classed as easy garden shrubs succeeding on most average soils with the minimum of attention. They neither need the protection of a wall nor are generally suited to wall culture, however, *B. darwinii* and *B.* ×*stenophylla* look so fine against an old stone or brick wall that we have included them here. A number of species can be used with great effect planted in front of wall climbers and other wall shrubs. *Berberis thunbergii* for instance with its brilliant orange and crimson autumn colours, can make a glorious combination with *Parthenocissus henryana*.

Berberis darwinii is a dense spiny evergreen shrub 2–4m tall. Glossy dark green oval leaves, usually with three spiny teeth at the top and several along the sides, grow in tufts along the stems. Golden or orange flowers flushed with red are borne in drooping racemes 3.5–5cm long. Berries plum-red, oval in outline, 5–6mm long. [Apr–May, H, PN, Chile]

One of the very finest and most floriferous garden shrubs which is also valuable for its heavy crop of fruits in the autumn. The flowers are greatly loved by bees.

Berberis darwinii was first discovered by Charles Darwin in 1835, during the famous voyage of the Beagle around South America. However, it was introduced to cultivation some 14 years later from the island of Chiloe and collected there by William Lobb.

Berberis × stenophylla is a graceful spreading evergreen bush 2–3.5m tall with dense arching growths and slender interlacing stems. Leaves spine-tipped, deep shiny-green above, grey-green beneath. Golden-yellow flowers are borne in great profusion in small clusters or short semi-drooping racemes. Berries globose, pea-sized, covered in a bluish-white bloom when ripe. [Apr–May, H, PA]

Perhaps the finest of all hybrid barberries, *B.* ×*stenophylla*, was raised in 1860 between *B. darwinii* and *B. empetrifolia*. Plants can be clipped back shortly after flowering in order to keep them in shape, indeed they take well to clipping and are often used as a hedging plants.

BIGELOWIA (Compositae)

Shrubs and herbs native to North America south to Ecuador where there are about 40 species. The leaves are usually alternate, entire and linear. The flowers are yellow, in heads of up to 20.

Propagation is by cuttings. The genus is named after Dr. John Bigelow, a Boston physician who collected plants while visiting his patients and who took part in the United States–Mexican boundary mission.

Bigelowia graveolens = *Chrysothamnus graveolens* (Pl.19) is a much-branched shrub growing to 2m tall with white-downy shoots. The leaves are linear, up to 7.5cm long and hairless. The yellow flower-heads are borne in flattened clusters 3–10cm across. [Sept–Oct, HH, PN, USA]

The leaves and stems are aromatic when crushed. This species appreciates a well-drained soil and grows best against a sheltered south-facing wall.

Bigelowia douglasii = *Chrysothamnus viscidiflorus* is a shrub with erect, sometimes sticky branches, reaching 1.8m tall. The hairless leaves are narrowly linear. There are about five yellow flowers in a head. [Aug-Oct, HH, PN, C & W USA]

BOWKERIA (Scrophulariaceae)

A genus containing five species of evergreen shrubs from South Africa, of which only one is in general cultivation.

Bowkeria gerardiana = *B. triphylla*, is a shrub reaching 2–3m tall. The stalkless leaves occur in threes and are more or less ovate-lanceolate, 10–18cm long, toothed and slightly downy. The flowers occur in a loose cluster at the shoot tips and are very sticky. Individual flowers are pure white and rather like a calceolaria in general appearance, each about 18mm across. [Aug, T, PS, S Africa (Natal)]

A tender shrub, rather rare in cultivation, which needs the warmest niche that can be provided even in the mildest districts. It is frequently found under the name *B. triphylla*, although this is a quite distinct species, not in cultivation.

Bowkeria gerrardiana.

BUDDLEIA (Loganiaceae)

There are two evergreen species of *Buddleia*, *B. asiatica* and *B. auriculata*. They can be found on p.120.

BURSARIA (Pittosporaceae)

There are three species of *Bursaria*, all Australian. They have alternate simple leaves and small flowers in terminal panicles. The fruit is a flattened capsule containing one or two seeds.

Bursaria spinosa is an hairless shrub 2–5m tall with both spiny and spineless branches. The leaves are 2–3.5cm long, obovate, rounded or notched at the

Bursaria spinosa.

apex. The small fragrant flowers are borne in many-flowered panicles. They are white, each less than 1cm across. The fruit is a dry reddish-brown capsule about 1cm wide. [July–Aug, T, PS, Australia (New South Wales and Tasmania)]

This species, which is especially attractive in fruit, will only grow in the milder parts of the country and is best on a south-facing wall. Propagation is by cuttings of half-ripened wood placed in gentle heat during midsummer.

CALLISTEMON (Myrtaceae)

A genus of evergreen shrubs or small trees native to Australia and Tasmania, popularly known as 'Bottlebrushes' because of their brushlike inflorescences. Most species have red flowers but some are yellow. They are related to the Myrtles (*Myrtus*), *Leptospermum* and *Eucalyptus*. In most of these genera the petals are tiny, much of the flower consisting of a prominent brush of long-stalked stamens. The fruits are small globose woody capsules that cling closely to the stem and they may remain thus for many years.

Only a few species can be cultivated out-of-doors in Britain and Ireland, even they are only hardy in the very mildest districts, and generally require the shelter of a sunny wall in other places. They are easily propagated from midsummer cuttings. Plants are best placed outdoors in the spring.

☼ **Callistemon salignus** (Pl.19) is perhaps the commonest species, making a rather erect shrub 2–4m tall, the young stems covered in silky hairs. The alternate leaves are thin but firm, linear to linear-lanceolate, 5–11cm long with a prominent midrib. The 'bottlebrushes' are 5–8cm long, the flowers with red, whitish or more often cream or pale pink stamens. [June–July, HH, PN, SE Australia]

In the wild *C. salignus* is a plant of coastal areas and swampy places, sometimes making a small tree to 10m tall, however, the forms we see in cultivation are much smaller. It is hardy on a warm sheltered wall in all but the coldest gardens.

☼ **Callistemon pallidus** is similar to the preceding but with leaves elliptic to oblanceolate, 3–5.5cm long. The 'bottlebrushes' are cream, 4–6.5cm long. [June–July, HH, PN, SE Australia (Victoria & Tasmania)]

The young leaves are covered at first in silky hairs, turning pinkish before finally becoming green.

☼ ***Callistemon citrinus** = *C. lanceolatus* is a straggling shrub to 3m tall, more in the wild. The leaves are linear to elliptic, 4–9cm long and pointed, the upper surface with prominent veins. The 'bottlebrushes' are 7–10cm long, the flowers with mid to deep red stamens. [July–Sept, T, PN, E & SE Australia]

Probably the finest Bottlebrush, often grown as a greenhouse or conservatory plant where its red flowers can be admired throughout the summer. The leaves have a pleasing aromatic fragrance when crushed, from this the species derives its name. *C. citrinus* was introduced to cultivation by Sir Joseph Banks as long ago as 1788. Some forms sold as *C. speciosus* often prove to be *C. citrinus* so they should be selected with care.

'Splendens' is a particularly fine form with deep crimson 'bottlebrushes'.

☼ ***Callistemon sieberi** = *C. pithoides*, the Alpine Bottlebrush, is a shrub of rather dense habit to 3m tall, often less. The glossy-green leaves are dense, linear, rigid and rather needle-like, usually 2–2.5cm long. The 'bottlebrushes' are narrow, 2–4cm long, the flowers with pale yellow stamens. [June–Aug, HH, PN, SE Australia]

This attractive plant comes from mountainous habitats and in this country it is probably the hardiest species. Despite this it still requires the protection of a wall in most districts.

Callistemon viridiflorus = *C. salignus* var. *viridiflorus* is very similar to the preceding species, the leaves being sharply pointed and closely clustered on the stems. The 'bottlebrushes' are greenish-yellow. [June–Aug, HH, PN, Tasmania]

***Callistemon subulatus** is a small rather spreading shrub to 1.5m tall with shiny reddish-brown young stems. The narrow leaves are awl-shaped, 1.5–4cm long and shiny green on both surfaces. The 'bottlebrushes' are 5–7.5cm long, the flowers with crimson stamens. [June–July, HH, PN, SE Australia (Victoria & New South Wales)]

A handsome species, probably the hardiest of the red bottlebrushes in Britain. The plants are less tall than the other species and very suitable for a lower wall or at the base of other wall plants. *C. rigidus* of the nursery trade often proves to be *C. subulatus*. Certainly the former is less hardy — a taller shrub with linear-lanceolate leaves up to 15cm long and not channelled as in *C. subulatus*. Furthermore, the 'bottlebrushes' are rather longer, red with brown anthers.

Callistemon speciosus is a large shrub up to 5m tall, often less, with reddish-brown branches. The grey- or bluish-green leaves are linear-elliptic, 7.5–12cm long, leathery, with distinct veins above. The large 'bottlebrushes' are dense, 10–15cm long, the flowers with deep crimson stamens flecked with yellow pollen. [June–July, T, PN, W Australia]

A beautiful species, at least as good as *C. citrinus*, but unfortunately more tender. It has the largest 'bottlebrushes' of any of the cultivated species.

Callistemon phoenicus is similar to the preceding species but smaller, only 2m tall and with a looser habit and more slender branches. The leaves are smaller, only 4–9cm long. The 'bottlebrushes' are only 5–6.5cm long and deep crimson, with hairless calyces. [June–July, HH, PN, W Australia]

A smaller species than *C. speciosus* in all respects but hardier, surviving out-of-doors in all but the coldest districts.

CAMELLIA (Theaceae)

The Camellias need very little introduction for they are among the best loved of all shrubs, indeed some of the most exotic of our garden plants. The hardiness of the species was questioned for many years, though it is now generally recognised that many are completely hardy in a sheltered spot. However, the flowers appear early in the year and can be easily spoilt by a late frost or a strong wind. For many of the earliest flowering species and cultivars, or the more tender ones, a wall environment is absolutely ideal and a plant in full bloom is a most glorious sight. Having said this, a word of warning. Camellias hate light dry soils, or calcareous soils, especially close to a wall. A soil that is too dry will result in bud drop and all the flowers may be lost as a result. What they like is a good moist loam with plenty of added peat and leaf mould topped up with generous mulches throughout the summer. They prefer semi-shaded positions and many will thrive against a north-facing wall or fence, though south-west or west aspects are to be preferred. Young specimens are best planted in late March or April taking great care to see that they are watered adequately during the first season. Little pruning is required save to remove weak or unduly overcrowded growths. Young shoots should be tied in close to the wall to train the plants initially.

Camellias are propagated from stem and leaf bud cuttings of semi-mature wood during midsummer, although *C. reticulata* and its cultivars are usually grafted onto *C. japonica* stock.

The genus is named in honour of George Joseph Kamel, one time native of Moravia and contains some 80 species, widely distributed in Asia from the Himalaya to Japan. The most well-known species is the Tea Plant, *Camellia sinensis*, though it is probably the dullest of all in flower.

The one snag about Camellias is the vast number of named cultivars available, a bewildering variety for those choosing perhaps only one or two to grow. In this account we have concentrated on the species, and on the more important, or more popular cultivars. It is advisable to go to a nursery when choosing plants and see them actually in flower so that a good form can be obtained. *Camellias* are expensive and it can be very infuriating to buy a plant out of flower only to discover later that it is a poor form or the wrong variety.

Camellia japonica, the Common Camellia, is a variable shrub up to 13m tall, though generally far less, making a densely-branched bush. The deep glossy green leaves are finely toothed, 7–10cm long, usually speckled with brown dots beneath. The waxy-red flowers are solitary, being borne at the stem tips, each usually with five petals and 65–100mm across, with a boss of yellow anthers in the centre. [Feb–May, H, PN, Japan & Korea]

This is a really wonderful species worthy of a space in any garden provided the conditions are right. Like most species it requires a position sheltered from north and east winds and early morning sunshine.

C. japonica was an extremely important and exotic plant in nineteenth century gardens, although its hardiness had not then been established and it was most often grown as a greenhouse or conservatory subject. Surprisingly, the species is not found wild in China although cultivated there for many centuries. In Japan oil obtained from the seeds was long used by women for their hair. It was not until the beginning of the eighteenth century that plants first reached Europe. Choice of varieties is a matter of preference, though the single and semi-double forms are generally far finer than the fully double ones in which the flowers sometimes fail to open fully, or remain attached to the plant and turn brown once they are over — this can badly detract from the overall effect. Although some cultivars will reach a good height after a few years, many are rather slow growing so that walls or fences 2–3m high are generally suitable.

WHITE-FLOWERED CULTIVARS

*'**Alba-Plena**' = 'Alba Grandiflora' has large double white flowers on a rather erect bush.

'**Alba Simplex**' has large single white flowers.

'**Compton's Brow White**' has medium single white flowers.

*'**Devonia**' has medium single cup-shaped white flowers on a vigorous bush.

'**Imura**' has large semi-double white flowers on a vigorous, rather open, bush.

'**Lady Ardilaun**' (Pl.19) has small double white flowers, the centre tinged with green.

'**Madame Victor de Bisschop**' has medium semi-double white flowers on an open bush.

'**Morning Glow**' has large fully double white flowers on a rather erect dense bush.

*'**Nobilissima**' is early flowering, with medium white or creamish flowers, double with an anemone centre.
'**Royal White**' has large double or semi-double white flowers on a bush of spreading habit.
'**Virgin's Blush**' has medium semi-double white flowers faintly flushed with pink. A vigorous grower.

PINK-FLOWERED CULTIVARS

'**Apple Blossom**' = 'Joy Sander' has medium semi-double flowers, bluish-pink, deeper along the petal margins.
'**Augusto Pinto**' = 'Augusto Lealde Gouveia Pinto' has large double or semi-double lavender-pink flowers, the petals edged white.
'**C.M. Wilson**' has large pink flowers, double with an anemone centre. Rather slow growing.
'**Coquetti**' has medium double bluish-pink flowers. Slow growing and of compact habit.
'**Daitairin**' = 'Hatsu-zakura' has large single pale rose flowers.
'**Drama Girl**' has large semi-double salmon pink flowers on a rather open bush.
*'**Elegans**' = 'Chandleri Elegans' has large deep peach flowers, double with an anemone centre.
'**Furo-an**' has single, pale pink flowers.
*'**Gloire de Nantes**' has semi-double rose-pink flowers on a compact erect bush.
'**Guest of Honour**' has large semi-double salmon-pink flowers on a vigorous rather dense bush.
'**Guilio Nuccio**' has large semi-double deep rose flowers, a bush of vigorous habit.
'**Hano-fuki**' has large semi-double pale pink flowers on a compact bush. The flowers are sometimes flecked with white.
*'**Lady Clare**' has large semi-double deep peach flowers on a vigorous spreading bush.
'**Magnoliiflora**' has medium semi-double pale pink flowers with forward pointing petals, 'shuttlecock'-shaped.
'**Marguerite Gouillon**' = 'General Lamorciére' has medium pale pink flowers with deeper flecking, double with an anemone centre. A vigorous grower.
*'**Mrs. D.W. Davis**' has large semi-double pale pink flowers on a compact bush.
'**Peach Blossom**' has medium semi-double pale peach-pink flowers.
'**Pink Champagne**' has large semi-double pale pink flowers, petals irregular.
'**Preston Rose**' = 'Duchesse de Rohan' has medium salmon-pink flowers with rather irregular petals. A vigorous grower.
'**R.L. Wheeler**' has large rose-pink flowers, semi-double or double on an anemone centre.
'**Tomorrow**' has large rose-pink semi-double or double flowers with rather irregular petals. A bush of spreading habit.
'**Tomorrow's Dawn**' has similar flowers to the previous cultivar but with their centre and petal margins white.
'**Yours Truly**' has medium semi-double pink flowers, the petals streaked with deep pink and edged with white.

RED-FLOWERED CULTIVARS

*'**Adolphe Audusson**' has large semi-double blood-red flowers on a vigorous rather dense bush.
'**Anemoniflora**' has medium double crimson flowers with an anemone centre.
*'**Apollo**' has medium semi-double rose-red flowers, occasionally spotted with white.
'**C.M. Hovey**' has medium double carmine flowers on a vigorous dense bush.
'**Fred Sander**' = 'Fimbriata Superba' has medium semi-double crimson flowers with fringed petals.

*'**Kimberley**' (Pl.19) has medium single carmine flowers, on a vigorous rather erect bush.
*'**Kouron-jura**' has very dark red double flowers on a dense bush. One of the darkest of all Camellias.
'**Lanarth**' has more or less single medium bright red flowers on an erect bush.
'**Mercury**' has large semi-double pale crimson flowers, the petals with deeper crimson veins.
'**Quercifolia**' has large single crimson flowers.
'**Rubescens Major**' has large double crimson flowers, the petals with deeper veining.

BICOLOURED CULTIVARS

'**Betty Sheffield Supreme**' has large semi-double flowers, petals white edged with pink or red.
'**Contessa Lavinia Maggi**' has large double flowers, petals white or pale pink bordered with cerise-pink.
'**Donckelarii**' has large semi-double flowers, red, usually mottled with white.
*'**Kelvingtoniana**' has large semi-double flowers, red mottled with white, borne on a spreading bush.
'**Lady de Saumerez**' has medium semi-double flowers, red spotted white.
'**Lallarook**' = 'Laurel Leaf' has large double flowers, pink mottled with white. A rather dense bush with laurel-like leaves.
*'**Nagasaki**' = 'Lady Buller' has large semi-double flowers, rose mottled with white. The leaves are often marbled with yellow.
'**Prince Albert**' = 'Albertii' has medium double flowers, the petals pink striped with carmine and sometimes white also. A vigorous grower.
*'**Tricolor**' = 'Sieboldii' has medium semi-double flowers, white streaked with carmine-red.

☀ **C. japonica** subsp. **rusticana** = *C. rusticana*, the Snow Camellia, is a hardy northern Japanese subspecies inhabiting mountainous places where it withstands the long snowy winters. The small red flowers open widely; they are almost flat with a central ring of rather short yellow stamens which are scarcely united together. The typical *C. japonica* is a plant of low altitudes with more cup-shaped flowers and longer stamens which have either cream or white filaments.

◐ △ **Camellia saluenensis** is a shrub 3–5m tall forming a luxuriant bushy plant with hairy young shoots. The elliptic or somewhat lanceolate leaves are dark green above but paler beneath, 4–6.5cm long, and finely toothed. Each tooth is tipped by a small blackish gland which is quite distinct. The flowers, 75–90mm across with five notched petals, are pale bluish-pink with deeper veining and borne singly or in pairs, at the shoot tips of the previous year's growths. [Mar–Apr, HH, PN, SW China (Yunnan)]

A splendid plant introduced from Yunnan in 1917 by George Forrest. Not reliably hardy, it needs the protection of a sheltered wall in most districts. Walls of west, north-west or even one of north aspect will suit it well. There is a form, *macrophylla*, with similar flowers but larger leaves than the type.

Camellia saluenensis is not seen nearly as much as the hybrids between it and *C. japonica* which go under the general name *C.* × *williamsii*. These hybrids combine the greater hardiness of *C. japonica* with blooms as beautifully formed as those of *C. saluenensis* but borne in greater profusion.

◐ △ **Camellia × williamsii,** *C. japonica* × *C. saluenensis,* forms a dense bush 2–3m tall, sometimes more, with hairless branches and elliptic leaves 7–10cm long, rather like those of *C. japonica*. The undersurface is often dotted with brown.

Camellia × williamsii 'Donation'.

The funnel-shaped flowers may be single or semi-double, varying in colour from white flushed with pink to pale or deep rose. [Feb–May, H, PN]

'Citation' is a vigorous bush of rather open habit bearing large semi-double silvery-pink flowers.

'C.F. Coates' has attractively pointed leaves and medium single rose flowers.

***'Donation'** has an upright habit and exquisite large semi-double pink flowers. A really glorious Camellia.

'E.G. Waterhouse' has an upright habit with double pink flowers.

'Francis Hanger' has an erect habit with wavy leaves and single white flowers.

'George Blandford' is of lower more spreading habit than the type. The flowers, semi-double and rose-red, are borne over a long season.

***'J.C. Williams'** has rather horizontal branching and single, flat, bluish-pink flowers of great charm.

'Lady Gowrie' is of compact vigorous habit, but with large semi-double pink flowers.

'Mary Christian' bears small single clear pink flowers.

'November Pink' forms a bush of lax open habit which bears single pink flowers over a long season from November to May.

'Parkside' forms a rather open spreading bush with single or semi-double pure pink flowers.

'Pink Wave' has semi-double deep pink flowers.

'St. Ewe' has an erect habit with single rose-red flowers.

***Camellia 'Leonard Messel'**, *C. × williamsii 'Mary Christian' × C. reticulata*. A fine hybrid, raised at Nymans in Sussex, which possesses the hardiness of *C. × williamsii* and the large flowers and long flowering season of *C. reticulata*. Like *C. × williamsii* and its cultivars 'Leonard Messel' is easily raised from cuttings. ◐ △

Camellia reticulata is a strong-growing shrub up to 10m tall. Young shoots are rather greyish but quite hairless. Leaves broad elliptic, abruptly pointed, finely toothed, 5–11cm long, are net-veined on the upper surface. Solitary rose-red flowers, 70–80mm across occur in single, semi-double or double forms. [Jan–Apr, HH, PN, SW China (Yunnan)]

Cultivated in Chinese gardens for many centuries, the first *C. reticulata* plants brought back from China were introduced by Capt. Rawes of the East India Company in 1820. Further introductions were subsequently made though it was not until the present century that the true wild plant with solitary flowers was brought back to the English garden by George Forrest. This species is easily recognised by its broad, abruptly pointed leaves which have a characteristic network of veins on the upper surface. There are several cultivars:

'Buddha' has large semi-double rose-pink flowers on a vigorous erect bush.

*__'Captain Rawes'__ = 'Semi-plena' has very large semi-double carmine-rose flowers. A very fine shrub, the original form of the species introduced to cultivation in this country in 1820 by Robert Fortune.

'Crimson Robe' has large semi-double carmine flowers which have rather wavy petals.

*__'Mary Williams'__ has large single rose-crimson flowers on a vigorous bush. Hardier than most cultivars of *C. reticulata*.

'Noble Pearl' = 'Paochucha' has large semi-double oriental-red flowers. A fine cultivar.

'Purple Gown' = 'Tzepao' has large double flowers of dark reddish-purple streaked with wine red or white.

'Robert Fortune' = 'Pagoda', 'Flore Pleno' has large double crimson flowers on a dense bush.

'Shot Silk' has large semi-double vivid pink rather loose flowers.

*__'Trewithen Pink'__ has semi-double rose-pink flowers of great charm on a vigorous bush as hardy as 'Mary Williams'.

There are several fine cultivars which have been raised by crossing *C. reticulata* with *C. saluenensis*. They combine the very best features of both species. Three are listed here:

'Inamorata' inherits the handsome leaves and habit of *C. reticulata* combined with the beautifully formed rose-pink flowers of *C. saluenensis*.

'Inspiration' is a fairly vigorous shrub with large semi-double deep pink flowers.

*__'Salutation'__ is a very beautiful cultivar with matt green leaves and large semi-double silvery-pink flowers of great substance, produced from December to March.

Camellia maliflora is a bushy shrub 2–3m tall with downy young shoots. The leaves are thinner than most species, tapered to the tip, 3.5–5cm long and a striking deep shiny blackish-green. Solitary terminal flowers, 25–38mm across, of soft rose-pink are double with numerous petals. [Dec–Mar, H, PN, ?China]

The origin of this species is unknown although it is believed to come from China. Plants are hardy but they flower early, starting even before Christmas in a mild year, and for this reason they require the protection of a wall. The flowers fall off when they start to wither, unlike many of the double cultivars. *Camellia maliflora* tends to be a rather shy flowerer.

Camellia rosiflora is similar to the previous species but with single flowers and rather larger leaves.

Camellia sasanqua is a shrub or small tree up to 6.5m although generally far less. The dark, shiny green leaves are narrowly oval, 3.5–5cm long, the margin with fine rounded teeth. The single flowers range in colour from white to pale or deep pink, each 38–50mm across and often scented. [Oct–Apr, H, PN, Japan]

This delightful species has long been grown in Japan where many cultivars have been raised including numerous double and semi-double forms. It was not introduced to Europe until 1896, although plants occurred in Britain under the name *C. sasanqua* at an earlier date. These were in fact a distinct species *C. oleifera* described next.

C. sasanqua is almost as hardy as *C. japonica* although its winter flowering habit makes it particularly prone to frost damage, some varieties even starting to flower in October. Plants are therefore best protected by a wall, indeed *C. sasanqua* will tolerate a sunnier wall than most other Camellias.

'Blanchette' has single white flowers.
'Briar Rose' has single soft pink flowers.
'Crimson King' bears attractive bright red flowers.
'Fukuzu-tsumi' is like 'Narumi-gata' but rather earlier flowering.
'Hiryu' has single or semi-double crimson flowers.
'Momozono-nishiki' has semi-double flowers that shade from rose to white.
***'Narumi-gata'** is a fine cultivar with pleasantly fragrant single white flowers, the petals flushed with pink towards the margin. [Oct–Dec]
'Rosea-Plena' has double pink flowers.
'Tricolor' has single, white flowers streaked with pink and red.
'Usubeni' has semi-double pale pink flowers, sometimes marbled white.
'Variegata' bears white flowers flushed with pink and grey-green leaves bordered with white.

There is also a var. *fragrans* which has large flowers 70–80mm across that are pleasantly scented.

Camellia oleifera is an evergreen shrub, occasionally a small tree, to 4m tall. ◐
The stiff, leathery leaves are obovate, edged with small regular teeth, hairless, except for the short stalk. The fragrant flowers are white and single, 50–62mm across. [Nov–Feb, H, PN, China] △

Another delightful species for a sheltered partially shaded wall where its flowers, which appear in midwinter, can be seen to the best advantage. Like other species that flower during such an inclement time of the year, *C. oleifera* also makes a fine conservatory plant. In cultivation *C. oleifera* is often confused with *C. sasanqua*, however, the latter has smaller flowers and thinner blunter leaves. *C. oleifera* has been cultivated for centuries in China where tea oil is extracted from the seeds, tea oil cake being used in cooking and various toiletries.

Camellia tsaii forms a graceful shrub up to 4–5m tall when mature, its lateral ◐
branches with a rather weeping habit. The young branches are densely hairy. △
The leaves are shiny deep green above, paler and finely hairy along the midrib beneath. The white flowers are borne in profusion along the year-old branches, each about 25mm across with five petals and borne on a short green stalk. [Dec–Feb, T, PN, SW China & neighbouring parts of Burma & Thailand]

Another winter-flowering species delightful when in full flower, the small flowers and drooping branches give a dainty appearance. It was introduced to Britain by George Forrest as late as 1917.

Camellia taliensis is a shrub up to 3m tall with hairless stems and large bright ◐
green leaves which are more or less oval, 8–16cm long. The flowers are white, △
globular in bud, with a central ring of yellow anthers, each flower 50–64mm across with between eight and eleven petals. [Sept–Dec, HH, PN, SW China (Yunnan)]

A species which is particularly attractive in bud and closely related to the tea, *C.*

sinensis. *C. taliensis* is more or less hardy against a sheltered wall in southern parts of Britain but elsewhere needs extra protection.

◐ △ **Camellia cuspidata** = *Thea cuspidata*, forms a bush 2–3m tall with hairless slender, more or less erect young shoots. The shiny dark green leaves are sometimes flushed with purple above, often tinted with copper when young, but pale and dotted beneath. Flowers solitary, about 40mm across when fully open, pure white. [Mar-Apr, HH, PN, W China]

Like the true tea, *C. sinensis*, this species is one of the least attractive species although pleasant enough in full flower. It is usually grown out of curiosity or to complete a collection of species. It cannot be regarded as a good garden plant on the same level as other white-flowered species such as *C. oleifera* or *C. tsaii*. However, there is a hybrid between *C. cuspidata* and *C. saluenensis* that is well worth growing: known as 'Cornish Snow', its flowers are larger and borne in profusion from March onwards.

◐ △ **Camellia sinensis** = *Thea sinensis*, the Tea Plant, is a variable species particularly as regards leaf-shape and size. The plant makes a small compact, rather densely branched bush to 1.5m, rarely more, in forms cultivated in this country. The dull green leaves are lanceolate, 4–12cm long. The fragrant single nodding flowers are white, 25–40mm across with yellow anthers. [Mar–May, HH, PN, S China and SE Asia]

The form generally grown in this country is rather compact, slow growing and only hardy in mild districts. In the wild, however, it is very variable and one variety, var. *assamica*, makes a sizeable tree 16m or more high. The tea of commerce was introduced from China to Java, India and later Ceylon (now Sri Lanka) about 1835. Black and green tea are produced from the same plants but undergo different factory processes.

The fragrant flowers of the Tea Plant are greatly attractive to insects, particularly moths. Perhaps the least attractive Camellia in cultivation, it is grown as a curiosity or in collections of economically important plants.

CANTUA (Polemoniaceae)

Cantua is one of the few woody genera in the Phlox family (Polemoniaceae) and contains some eleven species which grow in the Andes from Ecuador to Chile. Of the few cultivated species, only *C. buxifolia* can be grown out-of-doors in Britain.

☼ ***Cantua buxifolia** is a hairless or downy shrub up to 3m tall. The alternate dull green leaves are oval to obovate, up to 2.5cm long, untoothed or with a few teeth or lobes. The flowers are in small terminal clusters, at first erect but eventually drooping. The corolla is pinkish-red with a yellow-striped tube and five spreading lobes at the mouth, which is 2.5–3.5cm wide; the anthers are deep purple. [Apr–May, T, PN, Peru, Bolivia & N Chile]

A beautiful shrub which deserves to be grown more often. It is only really hardy in mild areas, and in marginal localities it is semi-evergreen. Propagation is by cuttings placed in a sandy compost during the summer.

CARPENTERIA (Philadelphaceae)

A genus containing only a single species related to the Mock Oranges, *Philadelphus*, but differing in its evergreen habit and five- to seven-petaled flowers.

Cantua buxifolia.

***Carpenteria californica** grows to 1.8m tall or more, with minutely downy young shoots. The leaves are opposite and up to 10cm long, oblong or lanceolate, leathery, green and hairless above, grey-hairy below. The fragrant white flowers are occasionally solitary, but are usually borne in terminal clusters of three to seven; each 5–8cm across and with numerous golden-yellow stamens. The fruit is a five- to seven-valved capsule containing many seeds. [June–July, HH, PN, USA (California)]

This very beautiful shrub requires wall-protection but should not be planted very close to the wall. It will grow in any well-drained soil and prefers a southerly aspect. Propagation is best by cuttings or layers.

'Ladham's Variety' is a vigorous selection with larger flowers, 8–10cm across.

CEANOTHUS (Rhamnaceae)

A splendid group of plants containing some of the finest and most popular blue-flowered shrubs in our gardens.

There are about 55 species of *Ceanothus* many of which are native to North America, especially the west coast, which partly explains their common collective name of 'Californian Lilac'. They are shrubs or small trees and there are both deciduous and evergreen species. The leaves are opposite or alternate, often three-veined at the base. The flowers, normally blue or white, are small, but borne densely in panicles which are conspicuous. Each flower has five, often coloured, sepals and petals which are hooded. The fruit is a capsule with three apical lobes.

Many of these lovely shrubs are rather tender and need wall protection. They mostly revel in light well-drained loamy soils. The blue-flowered species are especially useful in the creation of striking or unusual colour combinations in the garden. Both the evergreen and deciduous species are treated here. The deciduous species should be pruned in early spring, and the evergreen ones lightly when flowering has finished. Propagation is by cuttings taken in late summer, placed in a suitable frame with a little heat. They have usually rooted by the following spring.

Ceanothus coeruleus is a deciduous shrub which will reach 2.5m tall. The young shoots are downy. The alternate toothed leaves are narrowly oblong to ovate, 2.5–8cm long, one- to three-veined, brown-downy beneath. The flowers are deep blue, or occasionally whitish, in panicles 8–15cm long. [July–Oct, T, PS, Mexico & Guatemala]

Ceanothus integerrimus, the Deer Brush, is deciduous or semi-evergreen, growing to 3m in height. The leaves are alternate, very variable in shape from lanceolate to ovate or broadly oval, 2.5–7.5cm long, three-veined, untoothed or with teeth towards the apex, usually downy beneath. The flowers are white to pale blue, borne in racemes 7.5–15cm long, a number of which form a large panicle up to 25cm long. [June, T, PS, USA (California)]

Ceanothus crassifolius is evergreen, 1–3.5m tall, and has downy young shoots. The leaves are opposite, 1.25–3cm long, sharply toothed and white-downy beneath. The flowers are white. [Mar–Apr, T, PA, USA (S California) & Mexico (Baja California)]

This species is uncommon in gardens.

Ceanothus rigidus is an evergreen shrub with dense stiff branches, reaching about 3.7m tall. The opposite leaves are rounded to obovate, 0.3–1.25cm long, single-veined, usually toothed, at least towards the apex, grey-downy beneath. The purplish-blue flowers cluster in the leaf axils. [Apr–June, T, PA, USA (California)]

var. **pallens.** The leaves are narrower and the flowers are paler.

Ceanothus purpureus is an evergreen shrub growing to 1.2m tall, with reddish-brown, rather stiff young shoots. The opposite leaves are oval or rounded, up to 2cm long, dark and glossy above, pale and with sparse down on the undersurface, the margin wavy and furnished with sharp teeth. The flowers are deep blue or lavender-purple, in clusters up to 5cm wide. [Apr–May, T, PA, USA (California)]

Ceanothus divergens is related to the last species and differs in having a less stiff habit and leaves up to 2.5cm long with less wavy margins. [Mar–Apr, T, PA, USA (California)]

Ceanothus verrucosus is evergreen and reaches 1–2.5m tall with rigid warty stems. The leathery alternate leaves are single-veined, 0.6–1.2cm long, untoothed or toothed and often notched at the apex. The flowers are white. [Mar–May, T, PA, USA (California)]

This species is only rarely grown.

Ceanothus megacarpus is an evergreen shrub up to 3.7cm tall, with downy young branches. The alternate leaves are up to 3cm long, obovate to oval, single-veined, untoothed and finely downy beneath. The white flowers are borne in clusters about 1.25cm wide. [Mar–May, T, PA, USA (California)]

Ceanothus velutinus is an evergreen shrub 3m tall with hairless young shoots. The leaves are alternate, oval or roundish, 4–7cm long, three-veined, finely toothed, dark green and very glossy above and pale-downy beneath. The white flowers are borne in large clusters 8–12cm long. [June–July, HH, PA, W N America (California to British Columbia)]

var. **laevigatus**. This variety has completely hairless leaves, which are glandular and aromatic. It flowers very late. [Oct & Nov]

***Ceanothus thyrsiflorus** is an evergreen shrub or small tree attaining 7m. The young shoots may be downy or hairless. The alternate leaves are oblong to ovate, 1.8–3.5cm long, three-veined, hairless or downy beneath, and with small glan-

---

Plate 15 Deciduous and Semi-Evergreen Shrubs 1 *Piptanthus laburnifolius* (p.217), 2 *Prunus triloba* (p.141), 3 *Ribes speciosum* (p.226), 4 *Robinia hispida* (p.143), 5 *Romneya coulteri* (p.226).

1
2
3
4
5

16
1
2
3
4
5

dular teeth along the margin. The pale powder-blue flowers are borne in clusters 2.5–7.5cm long, produced in the leaf axils. [May–June, H, PA, USA (California to Oregon)]

A beautiful free-flowering species which can be grown anywhere in Britain, indeed it is the finest species for northern gardens given a suitable wall.

'Cascade' is usually considered to be a form of *C. thyrsiflorus*, but is slightly less hardy. It has bright blue or lilac-blue flowers in elongated clusters.

Ceanothus griseus = *C. thyrsiflorus* var. *griseus* is very similar to the preceding species. It has broader leaves which are hairy beneath, and the leaf margin is rather wavy as well as toothed. It is not quite as hardy as *C. thyrsiflorus*.

***Ceanothus × veitchianus** probably *C. griseus* × *C. rigidus*. An evergreen shrub 3m tall. The opposite leaves are obovate, up to 3cm long, single-veined, whitish beneath and with marginal glandular teeth. Deep-blue flowers are borne in dense clusters up to 5cm in length. [May–June, H, PA, USA (California)]

There is some confusion surrounding the identification of this species; in gardens it is often grown under the name *C. dentatus*. If this were not bad enough, many plants grown as *C.* ×*veitchianus* are in fact *C.* ×*lobbianus*.

Ceanothus spinosus is an evergreen shrub 2.5–6m tall and despite its name the leaves are only rarely spiny in cultivation. They are alternate, 1.25–3cm long, leathery, single-veined and hairless on both surfaces. The flowers are rich blue. [Apr–May, T, PA, USA (California)]

C. spinosus is not often seen in gardens.

***Ceanothus parryi** is an evergreen shrub or small tree reaching 5m tall, with angled downy young shoots. The leaves are alternate, oblong, up to 3cm long, single-veined, toothed, and white-hairy beneath. The deep blue flowers are borne in often branched panicles up to 12cm long. [May–June, H–HH, PA, USA (California)]

A beautiful species which is very free-flowering.

Ceanothus papillosus is an evergreen shrub reaching 4.8m tall in the wild with young stems which are densely downy. The alternate leaves are oblong, oval or linear, 1.2–5cm long with glandular teeth and the margin often rolled under. They are single-veined, glossy above and warty, and downy beneath. The deep or mid-blue flowers are produced in racemes 2.5–3.5cm long. [May, T, PA, USA (California)]

This species can be short-lived and is distinct in having warty leaves. It is a glorious sight in full flower.

***'Delight'**, *C. papillosus* × *C. rigidus*, has rich blue flowers borne in long racemes. It is an hardy and beautiful plant.

Ceanothus impressus is an evergreen shrub 1.5–3m tall. The alternate leaves are broadly oval to almost round, one-veined, 0.6–1.2cm long, slightly hairy above and on the veins beneath. The margins are rolled under. The deep blue flowers are borne in rounded clusters about 2.5cm long. [Apr–June, HH, PA, USA (California)]

'Burtonensis', *C. impressus* × ?*C. thyrsiflorus*, has rounded glossy leaves and flowers of a rich blue.

***Ceanothus dentatus** (Pl.19) is an evergreen densely branched shrub growing to 1.5m tall. The alternate leaves are oval to linear, up to 2cm long, single-veined,

---

Plate 16 Roses 1 *Rosa banksiae* 'Lutea' (p.154), 2 *R.* 'Chaplin's Pink Climber' (p.160), 3 *R. fillipes* (p.152), 4 *R. bracteata* (p.155), 5 *R.* 'Lawrence Johnston' (p.163).

shiny green above and grey-felted beneath. The margin is glandular-toothed and often rolled under. The flowers are bright blue in rounded clusters up to 2.5cm long. [May–June, HH, PA, USA (California)]

This is the most commonly grown species. It is related to *C. papillosus*, but the leaves are not warty and are smaller.

var. **floribundus.** The leaves are broader, with a flat margin and the flowers are carried in denser clusters.

☼ **Ceanothus × lobbianus,** *C. griseus* × *C. dentatus,* is an evergreen shrub reaching 3m with alternate, oblong, three-veined leaves up to 2.5cm and whitish on the lower surface. The margin is somewhat under-rolled and bears a few glandular teeth. The flowers are bright blue. [May–June, T, PA, USA (California)]

Introduced in the 1850's by W. Lobb, a plant collector who introduced several of the *Ceanothus* species which we grow today. *C.* ×*lobbianus* is often grown in gardens erroneously as *'C. dentatus'* or *C.* ×*veitchianus.*

'Russellianus' is thought to be an hybrid of similar parentage, but has smaller glossy leaves and long-stalked flower heads. It is very free-flowering.

'Southmead' has a rather dense habit and small leaves.

☼ ***Ceanothus foliosus** is a small densely branched evergreen shrub up to 1.2m tall, with slender downy shoots. The leaves are alternate, ovate or oval, one to three-veined, 0.6–1.8cm long, usually wavy on the somewhat recurved margin and toothed. The upper surface is dark glossy green, and the lower surface hairless or downy on the veins. The flowers are dark blue or bright blue, borne in rounded terminal clusters up to 1.25cm wide, occasionally aggregated into a panicle up to 10cm long. [May, T, PA, USA (California)]

A lovely, usually rather compact *Ceanothus* which appreciates a slightly less dry position than the other species.

'Edinburgh' = 'Edinensis' is an hybrid between *C. foliosus* and *C. griseus* and has rich blue flowers and leaves of a dark olive-green.

'Italian Skies' is a cross between *C. foliosus* and an unknown species. The deep brilliant-blue flowers are borne in dense clusters up to 7.5cm long. It forms a bush of more spreading habit than *C. foliosus.*

☼ **Ceanothus cyaneus** is an evergreen shrub or small tree which can reach 6m. The young shoots are bright green. The alternate ovate to oval leaves are 2.5–6.5cm long, three-veined, usually toothed, glossy above, rather dull beneath, and hairless. The bright blue flowers are borne in rather narrow panicles 5–12cm long. [May–June, T, PA, USA (California)]

☼ **Ceanothus arboreus**, the Catalina Ceanothus, is an evergreen tree growing to 9m with a rather flaky bark, and thickly downy young shoots. The alternate, ovate or broadly oval leaves are 5–10cm long, prominently three-veined, shallowly toothed, minutely downy above and usually grey-hairy beneath. The flowers are usually pale blue, borne in panicles 7.5–10cm in length. [Apr–May, T, PA, USA (Californian islands)]

Native islands include Santa Catalina, hence its popular name, It is long-lived: plants at least 30 years old are known.

***'Trewithen Blue'** is a selection with slightly scented deeper blue flowers carried in very large clusters up to 13cm long.

☼ **Ceanothus sorediatus**, the Jim Brush, is a dense evergreen shrub up to 3m in the wild, with rigid hairy, often spiny branches. The alternate leaves are oval to ovate, three-veined, up to 2.5cm long, glossy dark green above, greyish-hairy beneath, margined with glandular teeth. The pale to deep blue flowers are produced in small clusters. [Mar–May, T, PA, USA(California)]

In addition to spring flowering, *C. sorediatus* often flowers again in autumn.

The following cultivars are well worth growing; they are put after the preceding descriptions because other species are involved in their ancestry, or because their parentage is unknown.

'A.T. Johnson' bears bright blue flowers in summer and autumn and is very free-flowering.

'Autumnal Blue' has deep blue flowers in summer and autumn and is hardy. It has *C. thyrsiflorus* in its parentage.

'Burkwoodii' *C. floribundus* × 'Indigo' has rich blue flowers in summer and autumn and is tender.

'Indigo' is derived from *C.* ×*delilianus*, itself an hybrid between *C. coeruleus* and *C. americanus*. The flowers are a dark, almost indigo-blue. It is summer-flowering, fairly tender and deciduous.

CESTRUM (Solanaceae)

A New World genus of about 150 species. They have alternate untoothed leaves and the flowers are borne in terminal and axillary racemes. The bell-shaped calyx has five teeth and the five-lobed corolla is tubular. There are five stamens which arise on the wall of the corolla tube and do not protrude from the mouth. The fruit is a berry.

Cestrums are tender shrubs which will only grow outside in the south and west. Any good soil suits them and they can easily be propagated by cuttings of half-ripened shoots. Any pruning should be carried out in the spring when some of the older stems may be removed to encourage strong new growths.

The deciduous *Cestrum parqui* is included here convenience.

***Cestrum elegans** = *C. purpureum* grows to a height of 3–5m. The leaves are ovate or narrowly ovate, up to 13cm long and covered with tiny hairs. The crimson to reddish-purple flowers, about 25mm long are borne at the ends of drooping shoots. The egg-shaped berry, 10–13mm long, is red to reddish-purple. [June–Sept, T, PS, Mexico]

In really sheltered and mild localities *C. elegans* can flower in January or February.

'Smithii' has mid to pale pink flowers.

Cestrum fasciculatum is very similar to *C. elegans* but has larger flowers which are about 30mm long. It only grows 1–3m tall, and both the calyx and corolla are downy. The crimson berry is 9–10mm long. [Apr–May, T, PS, Mexico]

***Cestrum newellii** is thought to be an hybrid between *C. elegans* and *C. fasciculatum* and has brighter flowers than either of them — bright crimson to scarlet. The calyx and corolla are hairless. [June–Sept, T, PS, Garden origin]

This is sometimes found in catalogues as *C.* 'Newellii'.

Cestrum aurantiacum is evergreen or semi-evergreen with a somewhat climbing habit and will grow to 6.5m under favourable conditions. The leaves are 7–14cm long and are ovate to lanceolate. The flowers are carried in small clusters, fragrant at night, the corolla up to 25mm long, bright orange. The berry is round and white. [Aug–Nov but often sporadically throughout the year, T, PS, Guatemala]

Easily distinguished from the other cultivated species by its bright orange flowers. Despite its taller ultimate height, it has a more compact habit than the other species.

☼ **Cestrum parqui** is usually deciduous and reaches 2.5m tall. The leaves are up to 12cm long, narrowly lanceolate and hairless. The greenish-yellow flowers are produced all along the shoots, in small clusters, each 20mm long. The berry is about 10mm long and blackish. [June–July, HH-T, PS, Chile]

C. parqui is the least colourful of the cultivated *Cestrum* species, but is worth growing for its fragrance which is especially powerful at night.

CHAMAECYTISUS (Leguminosae)

There are some 20 species of *Chamaecytisus* closely related to the Brooms *Cytisus*, growing mainly in the Mediterranean area and the Atlantic Islands: only one species is grown as a wall shrub in Britain.

☼ **Chamaecytisus proliferus** = *Cytisus proliferus* is a shrub with a rather loose habit, reaching 5m in height. The slender stems are downy. The leaves are composed of three lanceolate untoothed leaflets with silky hairs on the undersides. The flowers are 2.5cm long and borne in small axillary clusters towards the ends of short lateral shoots. The calyx is downy to densely silky and the corolla is white. The pods are compressed, black when mature. [Apr, T, PA, Canary Is]

A lovely sight when in full flower. In the Canaries it is known as 'Escabon'.

'Miss Wingfield's Variety' is an improved form.

CHOISYA (Rutaceae)

A genus of the Citrus Family which contains some seven species native to Central America and the south-western USA. The widely grown *C. ternata* is the only species commonly cultivated in our gardens.

Choisya ternata.

***Choisya ternata**, the Mexican Orange Blossom, forms a rather dense evergreen shrub of rounded habit, 2–3m tall. The opposite leaves are ternate, each leaflet oval, untoothed, shiny deep green above, paler beneath, aromatic when crushed. The sweetly fragrant white flowers, 25–30mm across, are borne in rounded clusters at the shoot tips. [May–Sept, HH, PN, Mexico]

The Mexican Orange Blossom is among the most accommodating of shrubs. This and its extended flowering season have made it deservedly popular in our gardens. Although the main flowering season is the late spring, blossoms are borne intermittently thereafter and in a very mild winter may even appear during December.

A loamy soil is preferable but this species is not over fussy, however, cold biting winds can prove harmful. *Choisya ternata* will survive most winters. Pruning is generally unnecessary save to remove frost-damaged growth, but if desired shoots can be shortened back immediately the first flush of flowers finishes, in the early summer.

Cuttings of half-ripened wood struck in June in gentle heat, or of ripened wood in a cold frame in the late summer, will generally root with ease.

CLETHRA (Clethraceae)

The genus is described on p.126 together with *C. delavayi*, which is deciduous.

Clethra arborea, the Lily-of-the-Valley Tree, will grow to 7.5m and has young shoots covered with rusty-coloured down. The leaves are 7.5–13cm long, oblanceolate. The fragrant, cup-shaped nodding white flowers are borne in slender racemes clustered into panicles up to 15cm long. [Aug–Oct, T, PN, Madeira]

CLIANTHUS (Leguminosae)

A small but beautiful genus from Australia and New Zealand with alternate odd-pinnate leaves. The large flowers are produced in drooping racemes and although they are of the pea-type of flower expected in this family, they are atypical in having the standard reflexed over the calyx. The fruit is an inflated cylindrical pod.

***Clianthus puniceus** (Pl.19), the Glory Pea or Parrot's Bill, is an evergreen or semi-evergreen shrub which reaches 3.8m. The leaves, 7.5–15cm long, have 13–25 oblong leaflets, dark green above and paler beneath. Hanging racemes, produced in the leaf-axils, are composed of 6–15 brilliant red flowers 5–6cm long. The pods are about 7.5cm long. [May–June, T, PN, New Zealand]

An extremely beautiful plant which deserves to be grown more often. Best on a south- or west-facing wall although it will only grow in mild districts, and even there is rather short-lived. However, it is easily raised from seed. No pruning is necessary, but the plant will develop a bushier habit if some of the growing tips are pinched out. Dead wood should be cut out in the spring.

'Albus' has white flowers. Said not to be as free-flowering as the red-flowered plant.

var. **maximus** = var. *magnificus* is a taller plant with bigger leaflets and flowers of a deeper red.

COCCULUS (Menispermaceae)

See p.46 for the genus description and the other species.

Cocculus laurifolius is an erect, hairless, evergreen shrub, reaching 3m more in height. The leaves are 12–20cm long, lanceolate to oblong, three-veined and

dark shiny green. Small yellow flowers are produced in axillary panicles about 5cm long. The fruits are globose and black. [June-July, T, PN, Himalaya to S Japan]

CORNUS (Cornaceae)

About 45 species of shrubs or small trees originating in the temperate regions of the northern hemisphere. They usually have opposite leaves which are simple and untoothed. The flowers are white, yellowish or greenish and have four sepals and petals; sometimes they are surrounded by an involucre of conspicuous bracts which are often mistaken for petals. The fruit is fleshy and contains two seeds. *Cornus* species are best propagated by layers or by cuttings of mature wood.

The deciduous *C. chinensis* is treated here for convenience.

◐ ***Cornus capitata** = *Benthamia fragifera* (Pl.13) is an evergreen or semi-evergreen shrub which can reach 12m high. The dull greyish-green leaves, 5–13cm long, are narrowly ovate to oval, rather leathery. Flowers small, surrounded by four to six pale yellow bracts 3.5–5cm long, are clustered into a dense dome-shaped bunch 1–2cm across. The fleshy red fruit, 2.5–3.5cm in diameter, looks rather like a strawberry. [June–July, T, PN, Himalaya & S China]

A beautiful shrub when in flower and also again in October and November when the fruits are ripe.

◐ **Cornus oblonga** is evergreen and grows to 6m. The young shoots are angled and thickly covered in down. The leaves are 3.5–12cm long, narrowly oval, shiny above and grey-downy beneath. The white, scented flowers, 4mm across, are borne in terminal clusters about 7.5cm long. [Sept–Oct, T, PN, Himalaya & W China]

C. oblonga is uncommon in gardens although it is available commercially.

◐ **Cornus chinensis** is a deciduous shrub with green young shoots. The leaves, up to 25cm long, are whitish-grey, hairy beneath with prominent veins. Yellow flowers are carried in large stemless clusters and the fruit is black. [Jan–Feb, T, PN, N Assam, W China]

Related to *C. mas*, the Cornelian Cherry, *C. chinensis* was one of the introductions of Frank Kingdon-Ward, but has never been particularly common in cultivation. It should not be confused with *C. kousa* var. *chinensis*.

COROKIA (Escalloniaceae)

Six species of *Corokia* are known, which come from Australia, New Zealand and Polynesia. They have leaves which are alternate or in clusters and untoothed. The flowers are yellow with five sepals and petals, borne in axillary or terminal clusters, racemes or panicles. The fruit is fleshy, red or orange.

Propagation is by seed or cuttings taken in late summer. No pruning is necessary, except to keep the plants tidy.

☀ **Corokia cotoneaster**, the Wire-netting Bush, grows to 2.5m, and has thin rigid, interlaced young branches, white-downy when young, almost black when old. Leaves rather sparse, 1.25–2.5cm long, are ovate to obovate, dark green and hairless above, white-felted beneath. Yellow, star-shaped flowers, about 1.25cm across are produced one to four together in the leaf axils. Fruit round or oblong, 6–8mm long is orange or red. [May–June, HH, PN, New Zealand]

Corokia buddleioides reaches 1.8 – 2.5m tall. Young shoots are clothed with a greyish-white felt which disappears after a couple of years. Leaves linear-lanceolate, 3.5 – 13cm long, shiny deep green above, white-felty beneath. Star-shaped yellow flowers are borne in panicles 2.5 – 5cm long. The fruit is about 8mm long, globose and dark red. [May, T, PN, New Zealand (North Island)]

***Corokia x virgata,** *C. buddleioides* x *C. cotoneaster,* reaches about 4.8m tall. Its somewhat zig-zag shoots are white-downy when young. Oblanceolate to spoon-shaped leaves, 0.5 – 4.5cm long, are deep shining green above, white-hairy beneath. Yellow flowers are produced in threes, towards the ends of the shoots. The egg-shaped fruit, about 6mm long, is orange-yellow. [May – June, T, PN, New Zealand]

This hybrid is especially free-flowering and produces copious fruit.

Corokia macrocarpa grows to 6m and has stouter, stiffer shoots than the other species. The leaves are 5 – 10cm long, narrowly oval, white-hairy beneath. Yellow flowers 8 – 12mm across are borne in racemes 1.2 – 4cm long which arise in the leaf-axils. The deep red fruit, about 8mm long, is broadly oblong. [June, T, PN, Chatham Island]

CORONILLA (Leguminosae)

A genus of about 20 species native to Europe and the Mediterranean. They have alternate odd-pinnate leaves and the flowers are borne in umbellate clusters on long stalks. The flowers are the pea-type typical of the family, and have a roundish reflexed standard petal. The fruit is a slender pod which is constricted between the seeds; when ripe it breaks into single-seeded parts.

Both the following species can be raised from seed, or propagated by cuttings.

***Coronilla glauca** is a dense shrub which grows to 3m and has hairless young shoots. The glaucous leaves are 2.5 – 3.5cm long with five or seven leaflets. The fragrant yellow flowers are about 11 – 12mm long. Pods, about 3 – 5cm long, contain two to four seeds. [Apr – June, T, PN, S Europe]

An attractive plant which may bear some flowers in autumn in addition to the earlier display. Any dead wood can be removed in spring, and although pruning is not generally necessary, the plant can be trimmed after flowering if it becomes untidy. It is closely related to the following species *C. valentina*, and is sometimes treated as a subspecies of it.

'Variegata' has leaves variegated with creamy-white.

Coronilla valentina is a smaller shrub than *C. glauca*, reaching only 1.5m. The leaves are 3.5 – 5cm long, with seven, nine or eleven leaflets, bright green above, glaucous beneath. The sweet-smelling yellow flowers are 7 – 12mm long. The pods, 2.5 – 3.5cm long are three- to seven-seeded. [May – July, T, PN, S Europe]

Slightly less hardy than *C. glauca*, it has been cultivated in Britain since the end of the sixteenth century.

COTONEASTER (Rosaceae)

For general remarks and deciduous species *Cotoneaster affinis, C. frigidus* and *C. horizontalis* see p.127-8.

Cotoneaster salicifolius is a graceful evergreen or semi-evergreen shrub of rather spreading habit up to 5m tall, with downy young shoots. The ovate or lanceolate leaves are rough, deep green above, blue-green and downy beneath. Small whitish flowers, 6 – 8mm across are borne in woolly rounded clusters up to

5cm across. Berries, bright red, rounded, 6mm across, borne in abundance. [May–June, H, PA, W China]

An invaluable shrub well-known in gardens and important as one of the parents of a number of fine cultivars.

'Autumn Fire' = 'Herbstfeuer' is a smaller shrub, more graceful and somewhat pendulous in habit. The berries are orange-red and borne in large quantities.

var. **flocossus** has narrow, shiny leaves which are white with wool beneath. Berries smaller than the type, red [W. China] A particularly fine variety first introduced to cultivation by E.H. Wilson in 1908.

◐ ***Cotoneaster × watereri** is a very fine hybrid raised accidentally by the nursery of John Waterer & Sons at Bagshot between *C. frigidus* and *C. henryanus*. The plant is an evergreen or semi-evergreen shrub with narrow elliptic leaves 4–8cm long. White flowers are followed by large clusters of scarlet berries, each 7–8mm in diameter.

The treatment of this hybrid is the same as for *C. frigidus*. The original cross is often given the cultivar name 'John Waterer' in catalogues to distinguish it from other hybrids raised from the same parent species.

'Exburiensis' is another fine plant of hybrid origin with *C. frigidus* and *C. salicifolius* as the parent species. It has the same habit and general characters though the leaves are rather narrower. The berries are a charming pale yellow.

◐ **Cotoneaster henryanus** is a vigorous evergreen or semi-evergreen species reaching 3–4m tall, the stems becoming dark purplish-brown in the second year. Narrow oval leaves, 5–11cm long are rough and dark green above, greyish-woolly beneath when young. White flowers in dense rounded clusters, 5–6.5cm across are followed by brownish-crimson, egg-shaped berries about 7mm long. [June, H, PA, Central China]

An attractive species closely allied to *C. salicifolius* but distinguished in gardens by its larger, rather longer and broader leaves which are rough and somewhat hairy above, especially when young.

◐ **Cotoneaster franchetii** is a graceful evergreen shrub up to 3.5m tall with slender arching branches which are pale brown-downy at first. Small oval leaves, 2–3cm long are shiny sage-green above, white or grey with down beneath. Flowers white tinged with pink. Berries orange-scarlet, oblong in outline, 6–8mm long. [May–June, H, PA, W China & E Tibet]

This fine and popular species was introduced to cultivation by Abbé Soulie in the late nineteenth century, being first raised in France by the famous nursery of Maurice de Vilmorin.

*var. **sternianus** is one of the very best of all Cotoneasters. It differs mainly in its more globose berries which are borne in great abundance. This plant has been wrongly called *C. wardii* in the past and may still be found as such in some gardens. The true *C. wardii* is a distinct species, apparently not in cultivation.

☀ **Cotoneaster microphyllus** is a low-growing evergreen shrub with slender arching stems reaching 1m high or more if carefully trained against a wall. The branches are covered in small, deep glossy green, leathery leaves, 7–12mm long and greyish-downy beneath. Flowers white, 8mm across, often solitary. Berries rounded, scarlet-red, 6mm diameter. [May–June, H, PA, SW China & Himalaya]

This is an attractive small species that can be trained against a low wall, or better still left to trail from the top of a retaining wall. Shoots often root where they trail along the ground. The flowers like those of *C. horizontalis* are greatly loved by honeybees and bumblebees which visit them in large numbers, thus ensuring a good fruit set. Seedlings often occur around the parent plants.

Plate 17 Roses 1 *Rosa* 'Albertine' (p.156), 2 *R.* 'Handel' (p.161), 3 *R.* 'Madame Grégoire Staechelin' (p.160), 4 *R.* 'Zéphirine Drouhin (p.162), 5 *R.* 'Mermaid' (p.163).

1
2
3
4
5

18
1
2
3
4
5

COWANIA (Rosaceae)

A handsome genus of evergreen shrubs from the southern United States centred on New Mexico. They are notable for their feathery styles which are reminiscent of *Clematis*, although in no way related.

Cowania plicata = *C. purpurea* is a rather stiff, densely branched shrub to 2m tall, with peeling bark and reddish, densely glandular young shoots which are at first covered in a white felt of hairs. The small oblong or obovate leaves are 1–2.5cm long, pinnately divided, usually into five to nine lobes, the lower surface white felted. The solitary rose-pink flowers are borne on short leafy twigs, each 2.5–4cm across with five petals and a central boss of yellow anthers surrounding the feathery styles. [June–July, T, PN, USA (New Mexico).

Certainly the finest species of *Cowania*. Although more commonly grown in the last century it has never really received the popularity it perhaps deserves and is now sadly rare in our gardens. In the wild *C. plicata* is a plant of dry limestone hills and in cultivation a well- drained calcareous soil or a loam to which mortar rubble has been added is best. A sunny sheltered south-facing wall is essential.

Cowania stansburiana = *C. mexicana* var.*stansburiana* has a more sparsely branched habit and an attractive aromatic fragrance, the young shoots being densely glandular. The leaves, 0.5–1.3cm long, have three to five narrow lobes, white with down beneath. Solitary fragrant flowers about 2cm across are white or pale yellow. The feathery styles may reach 4cm in length as the fruits mature and are a handsome addition to the flowers. [June, T, PN, SW USA]

CRINODENDRON (Elaeocarpaceae)

A beautiful genus from Chile which contains two species of evergreen shrubs or small trees with thick leathery, alternate leaves and fleshy pendant five-petaled flowers. Both species are forest plants, revelling in cool moist loamy soils in shady positions in cultivation. They do particularly well in the milder counties of the west of Britain; fine specimens can be seen in gardens on the west coast of Scotland and in Cornwall and Ireland.

Crinodendron hookerianum = *Tricuspidaria lanceolata* (Pl.20), the Lantern Tree, is a superb plant of temperamental habit forming a stiffly branched bush or small tree up to 7m tall, rarely more. The leaves are rather leathery, oblong or lanceolate, 4–13cm long, dark green above but pale beneath. Rich crimson urn-shaped flowers 2.5–3.2cm long occur singly at the leaf axils, each borne on a long drooping thickened stalk. [May–June, HH, PN, Chile & the island of Chiloe]

A beautiful plant which, when grown well, festoons itself with a myriad of drooping lantern flowers. It should not be planted where it will catch cold or drying winds and the leaves may scorch in strong sunlight. The flower buds appear in the autumn so that any damage caused to plants during the winter will impair flowering the following season.

Crinodendron patagua = *C. dependens*,the Lily Tree, is a bush to 6m with reddish young shoots and oval leaves 2.5–8cm long. The white bell-shaped flowers are smaller than those of the previous species, generally being about 2cm long. [Aug–Sept, HH, PN, Chile]

An attractive plant when flowering freely. It is more tender than its red-flowered cousin but a faster grower and more readily propagated from cuttings.

Plate 18 Evergreen and Deciduous Shrubs 1 *Abutilon megapotamicum* (p.166), 2 *A.* ×*suntense* (p.166), 3 *Abelia triflora* (p.116), 4 *Acacia armata* (p.168), 5 *A. dealbata* (p.167).

CYTISUS (Leguminosae)

These are the popular brooms of our gardens. Although there are many species only two are generally grown as wall shrubs. *Cytissus battandieri* is semi-deciduous, but is included here with *C. monspessulanus*.

***Cytisus battandieri** (Pl.20), the Pineapple Broom, is semi-evergreen especially in mild areas or in a warm winter. It can reach 5m in height, and has the young shoots clothed with whitish silky hairs. The leaves have three leaflets which are 3.5–8cm long and covered on both surfaces with whitish silky hairs. The flowers are bright yellow and smell of pineapple; they are borne in fat racemes up to 12cm long. The pods are 3.5–5cm long, erect, with six or seven seeds and are covered in silvery hairs. [June–July, H, PA–PN, Morocco]

A beautiful shrub which needs plenty of space, ideal on a high wall. If pruned after flowering, the new growth will produce the flowers for the next year. The large leaflets with their silvery sheen are almost as attractive as the delightfully scented flowers.

Cytisus monspessulanus, the Montpelier Broom, is usually semi-evergreen, but can be evergreen in a mild winter. It grows to 2m tall, the leaflets 1.25–2cm long, hairless above but hairy beneath. Yellow flowers about 1.25cm long, are borne in three to nine-flowered racemes. Pods, 1.25–2cm long are covered in long shaggy hairs. [Apr–June, T, PN, Europe, N Africa & Asia Minor]

DAPHNE (Thymelaeaceae)

Small popular shrubs, usually with very fragrant flowers. The commonest is *Daphne mezereum* much liked for its winter flowers. Two species and an hybrid are suitable for wall culture. The leaves are alternate. Flowers with a tubular corolla-like calyx with four spreading lobes are borne in axillary or terminal clusters. They lack petals but there are eight stamens. The fleshy fruit contains one seed.

Propagation of *D. odora* and *D.* ×*hybrida* is best by cuttings; *D. bholua* can be successfully grafted, using *D. mezereum* or *D. laureola* as a stock.

***Daphne odora** is evergreen and grows to about 2m. The narrow leaves are up to 8cm long, dark green and hairless. Fragrant reddish-purple flowers, 12–14mm across are borne in terminal clusters 2.5–5cm across. The fruits are red, but rarely produced in British gardens. [Feb–Mar, H–HH, PN, China]

This is one of the most fragrant Daphnes. In a mild location or in a warm winter, it will flower before February.

'Alba' has white flowers.

'Aureo-Marginata' has leaves with an irregular yellow margin and is a little more hardy than the type. The flowers are often whitish inside.

Daphne bholua is evergreen or sometimes semi-evergreen and will reach 3m in height. The leaves are oval to oblanceolate, 4–10cm long. The flowers are produced mostly in terminal clusters of up to 20 and are white, suffused with purple on the outside. The flower tube is 6–10mm long and the width across the lobes is 5–6mm. [Nov–Feb, HH, PN, Central & E Himalaya]

A variable species in habit and degree of winter leaf retention as well as hardiness and it is safest to give it wall-protection. It is still fairly rare in gardens. The stems of this species, growing wild, are widely used for making paper, especially in Nepal.

Daphne odora.

Daphne × hybrida = *D. dauphinii* is probably an hybrid between *D. odora* and *D. collina*. It is an evergreen growing to about 2m with narrowly oval leaves 2.5–7.5cm long. Flowers very fragrant, reddish-purple and hairy outside measuring 5–6mm across, the lobes borne in small terminal clusters. [All year round, H, PN, Garden origin] ◐

Although it can flower at any time, there are flushes of flower in spring and autumn and a falling-off in flowering at midsummer. Useful for its continuous heavy fragrance, but sadly rarely grown.

DENDROMECON (Papaveraceae)

A beautiful Californian genus containing only two species, related to the poppies, *Papaver*, but most closely allied to *Romneya*. The latter has white flowers and coarsely lobed leaves.

Dendromecon rigida (Pl.13), the Tree Poppy, is a handsome shrub 3m tall, or more in very favoured positions. The stems are slender and semi-woody, bearing alternate, thick, bluish-green ovate or lanceolate leaves, 2.5–8cm long. The glorious 'poppy-flowers' are brilliant yellow, 5–7.5cm across, borne singly on slender stalks; they each have four petals. [June–Sept, T, PN, USA (California)] ☼

This beautiful plant is worth a try in any garden where the climate is reasonably mild and a sheltered sunny wall can be provided. It was introduced to cultivation in the middle of the last century, having first been discovered by that great plant explorer David Douglas. What a pity *D. rigida* is not hardier, for in bad winters it will be killed even in the mildest districts. However, it is worth persevering with and keeping a stock of young cuttings in a frost-free corner to ensure a supply. Cuttings are best taken from firm shoots in the summer, cutting these up into three-node lengths and inserting them in a sandy compost in moderate heat.

Young plants are best placed outside in the spring. A loamy soil which is well-drained by the addition of sand and mortar rubble is best. In the wild it is found growing on dry rocky hill slopes. The flowers have a pleasing fragrance.

DESFONTAINIA (Potaliaceae)

A beautiful genus with five species native to South America, at one time included in the family Loganiaceae which contains the well-known *Buddleia*. Only one species is cultivated.

◐ △ **Desfontainia spinosa** (Pl.20) is an evergreen, rather holly-like, shrub up to 3m tall, generally less. The stems are shiny and hairless and bear opposite pairs of spine-edged, leathery green leaves, each 2.5–6cm long. The solitary crimson-scarlet flowers are drooping trumpets, 3.5cm long, each with five rounded lobes flushed with orange-yellow. There is a small green calyx and five stamens. [Late July–Sept, HH, PN, S America]

This glorious shrub deserves to be more widely known, but unfortunately it is not one of the easiest of species to satisfy. In the wild it is a plant of the cool mountain cloud forests of the Andes from Colombia to the straits of Magellan — the drier parts of the British Isles are certainly not to its liking. It grows particularly well on the west coast of Scotland or northern Ireland. Cool moist places in the west and south-west of Britain and Ireland will also be suitable. Lashings of peat and leaf mould as mulches in the spring and summer are greatly appreciated.

*'**Harold Comber**' is a fine cultivar well worth obtaining if stocks are available.

DRIMYS (Winteraceae)

Handsome evergreen trees and shrubs with alternate untoothed leaves. The flowers are borne in clusters and have two to twenty petals and many stamens. There is a single whorl of carpels.

Two species are suitable for growing against walls. Propagation is by layers, or by cuttings of half-ripe shoots under glass.

☼ ***Drimys winteri**, the Winter's Bark, is a tall shrub or tree which will grow to 13m high. The bark is aromatic and the young shoots reddish. The leaves are oblong to oval, 12–22cm long, deep green above but blue-green underneath. Each fragrant white or cream flower, 2.5–3.5cm across, has five to 20 oblong petals, and each carpel becomes fleshy in fruit. [May–June, HH, PN, Chile & Argentina]

This tree is a lovely sight in full flower, studded with clusters of ivory-white flowers. Both bark and leaves are aromatic. It needs no pruning apart from the removal of old or damaged wood in the spring. The best flowering specimens occur in the mildest districts.

☼ **Drimys lanceolata** = *D. aromatica*, the Mountain Pepper, makes a small tree or dense shrub 3m or more tall. Young stems are deep red, and young leaves reddish-brown. The leaves are oval to oblanceolate, up to 5cm long. Flowers fragrant, borne in clusters, each with three concave deciduous sepals, about 5mm long, and usually six to eight linear whitish petals. Male and female flowers are separate; males have numerous brownish stamens and females a single carpel. The fruit is globose and black when mature. [Apr–May, T, PN, SE Australia]

The leaves are aromatic and have a strong taste of pepper — hence the common name.

ELAEAGNUS (Elaeagnaceae)

A Northern Hemisphere genus of some 45 species of deciduous or evergreen trees and shrubs. Most parts of the plant are covered in tiny scattered brown or silvery scales which give them a mealy appearance. They thrive in most average soils except shallow chalky ones, some species making excellent hedges and windbreaks, particularly in coastal areas.

Elaeagnus glabra is a handsome shrub with a rambling habit which grows to 6m tall normally. Leaves oval to ovate, 3–10cm long, are shiny green above but brownish beneath with a metallic sheen produced by the brown scales. Fragrant flowers, about 1cm long, are white inside and brown-scaly outside. Fruit egg-shaped, 1.2–2cm long, orange with silvery dots. [Oct-Nov, H, PA, China, Japan & Korea]

A vigorous shrub producing long slender growths which will clamber over neighbouring plants. Unless needed, these should be removed after flowering and strong new shoots will grow the following year. *E. glabra* can only be grown on acid or neutral soils.

ERIOBOTRYA (Rosaceae)

A genus best known for the Loquat, *E. japonica,* widely grown fruit in the Mediterranean region and in the subtropics. The genus contains about ten species all native to Eastern Asia.

Eriobotrya japonica = *Mespilus japonicus, Photinia japonica,* the Loquat, is a thickly-branched evergreen tree or bush up to 10m tall, its young branches densely woolly. Leaves large, elliptic, usually 20–30cm long, coarsely toothed and with pronounced parallel ribbing. Yellowish-white flowers, 2cm across, are borne in a stiff, pyramid-shaped panicle at the shoot tips; their fragrance is likened to Hawthorn. Oblong or pear shaped fruits, 3.5–4cm long, are yellow when ripe. [Sept–Oct, HH, PN, China & Japan]

In Britain this handsome plant, primarily grown for its foliage, rarely sets fruit. It produces flowers late in the year, the fruits not ripening until the following spring, so that they easily become prey to winter frosts and chilly winds, even though the plant is reasonably hardy in many districts. A sunny south-facing wall in milder areas suits it best, plants often not flowering until they are well established.

In frost-free areas of southern Europe the Loquat is extensively grown for its delicious fruits which are sometimes called 'nespole'. In this country it is best to obtain a reliable stock, for some are less hardy than others. They are generally propagated from cuttings.

'Variegata' has leaves variegated with white.

ESCALLONIA (Escalloniaceae)

There are about 60 species of *Escallonia,* native to South America, especially the Andes. All the species in cultivation are evergreen, and many are popular flowering shrubs and hedging plants, especially in milder coastal areas. The leaves are alternate and simple, white, pink or red flowers are borne in terminal racemes or panicles. The flowers have five sepals and five petals. The fruit is a dry capsule with many small seeds.

Most of the species described below are tender, except in the south and west, and require wall-protection. They are especially valuable for their prolonged flowering season. They can be propagated by cuttings taken in August and should be pruned immediately after flowering, when the old flowering shoots should be removed to encourage strong new growths.

☼ **Escallonia rubra** var. **macrantha** = *E. macrantha* grows to about 3m high. Leaves oval to obovate, 2.5–7.5cm long and deeply toothed, hairless, dark glossy green above and bearing resinous glands on the lower surface. The flowers are about 1.5cm long and wide, bright pinkish-red and carried in racemes which are sometimes branched, making up a panicle 5–10cm long. [June–Sept, HH, PA, Chile]

This is one of the most commonly grown shrubs in south-western Britain where it is often used for hedges. In other parts of the country it needs the protection of a wall. It was introduced by the plant collector William Lobb in the mid 1840s.

***'C.F. Ball'** is a fine cultivar with large aromatic leaves and crimson flowers.

☼ **Escallonia laevis** = *E. organensis* reaches about 2m with oval to narrowly obovate hairless leaves, up to 7.5cm long, toothed towards the apex. Pinkish-red flowers, 8–13mm across, are borne in short dense panicles. [July–Aug, HH–T, PA, Brazil]

Like the preceding species *E. laevis* was introduced to cultivation by William Lobb.

☼ **Escallonia bifida** = *E. montevidensis* reaches a height of 3m or more. The young shoots are hairless and usually slightly glandular. Leaves narrowly-oval to obovate, 3.5–7.5cm long with tiny marginal teeth, bright green. White flowers, 1.25–2cm across, are produced in rounded panicles up to 22cm long. [Aug–Oct, T, PA, E S America]

☼ **Escallonia 'Iveyi'**, *E. bifida* × *E.* ×*exoniensis,* has young shoots with dark scattered hairs. The oval leaves are 2.5–6cm long, with fine marginal teeth, hairless, deep green above and paler beneath. Scented white flowers, 1.25cm across, are borne in 12–15cm long panicles. The tip of each petal is recurved. [July–Aug, T, PA, Garden origin]

In favoured areas, it will continue to produce flowers until October.

☼ **Escallonia rosea** = *E. pterocladon* is a bushy shrub growing to 5m tall. The narrowly obovate to lanceolate leaves are 8–25mm long, hairless, toothed, shiny green above and paler beneath. Slightly-scented red or white flowers, about 8mm long, are carried in slender racemes 3.5–5cm long. In addition the lower leaf axils often carry solitary flowers. [June–Aug, HH, PA, Chile]

☼ **Escallonia revoluta** reaches 6m and the branches are grey-hairy. The obovate leaves are 2–5cm long, with uneven teeth on the margins and with thick grey down above and beneath. The white or pale pink flowers are 1.5cm long borne in panicles or racemes 3.5–7.5cm long. [Aug–Oct, T, PA, Chile]

☼ **Escallonia pulverulenta** is a downy, sticky-glandular shrub up to 3.8m tall. Leaves oblong, 5–10cm long, finely toothed are glandular are bristly above and below. White flowers are borne in racemes 10–22cm long. [July–Aug, HH, PA, Chile]

Distinguished from the other species by its long slender racemes.

FABIANA (Solanaceae)

A genus of about 25 rather heath-like shrubs native to warm temperate South America.

Fabiana imbricata is a sticky-downy shrub eventually up to 2m tall. The leaves are needle-shaped, densely carried on the branches. Flowers white, 1.25–2cm long, borne profusely on the ends of short branches, are stalkless with the corolla lobes rounded and reflexed. [June, T, PA, Argentina, Bolivia & Chile]

This delightful shrub prefers a light loamy soil and does best at the foot of a sunny wall. It is useful for growing at the base of a leggy wall shrub or climber and can be pruned to keep it tidy once it has finished flowering. Propagation is by cuttings taken at the end of the summer.

*'**Violacea**' has violet flowers and is said to be a little hardier than the type.

× FATSHEDERA (Araliaceae)

This fine bigeneric hybrid was raised on the nursery of Messrs Lizé Frères of Nantes, France in 1910. The parents are not certain but said to be *Fatsia japonica* 'Moseri' and *Hedera helix* 'Hibernica', between which the hybrid lies more or less midway in both habit and the characters of the leaves and stems.

× Fatshedera lizei is an evergreen shrub of rather loose habit with stout erect shoots. Palmate, leathery leaves, 10–25cm across, are shiny dark green above, paler beneath, with five prominent lobes,the long leaf stalks often flushed with purple. Pale green flowers are borne in terminal half-rounded panicles, 20–25cm long at maturity, and composed of many individual umbels. Plants are sterile and do not produce fruits. [Oct–Nov, H, PN, garden origin]

A handsome plant, well-known as a foliage pot plant. Hardy like its parents, it thrives in most average garden soils even in maritime positions or in the polluted atmosphere of cities. The shoots eventually become lanky and should be tied carefully into supports or shortened back to encourage strong new shoots. The flowers are borne late in the season and may not mature properly if there are early sharp frosts.

'**Variegata**' has greyish-green leaves edged by a creamy-white margin. A striking cultivar.

FATSIA (Araliaceae)

A well-known genus containing a single species, *Fatsia japonica*, which is a commonly cultivated ornamental evergreen grown in the garden, but most often seen as a house plant and in conservatories. Very much hardier than is generally supposed, it grows quite happily in a variety of situations and thrives on most average garden soils.

***Fatsia japonica** = *Aralia japonica* is an evergreen shrub or small tree 2–5m tall, producing a rather bushy plant. The thick stems are covered below by the large leaf scars left where leaves have fallen. Large leathery and deep glossy green, the leaves vary in size according to the age and vigour of the plant, measuring some 30–45cm across. They are palmate, generally with nine pronounced lobes and a long slender stalk which is often more than 30cm long. The milky white flowers are borne in broad 'hogweed-like' flowerheads at the branch tips, each flower is small but the massed affects of many aggregated flowers is very striking. The pea-sized fruits are green to begin with but turn black when ripe. [Oct–Nov, H, PN, Japan]

This handsome plant is the largest-leaved of all hardy evergreens. Plants thrive in sheltered places in shaded or semi-shaded positions. Although hardy the leaves may be damaged in fierce winds, but at the same time it is a particularly good species in maritime areas. It is also a fine plant for urban environments. Plants can be propagated from cuttings of firm young wood made in the late summer and placed singly in pots. A little bottom heat will speed rooting and young plants can be placed out-of-doors in the late spring of the following year.

Fatsia japonica has been crossed with *Hedera helix* to produce a fine intergeneric hybrid, ×*Fatshedera lizei*.

'Aurea' is a fine form with deep green leaves with golden-yellow variegations.

'Variegata' is a form with the ends of the leaf lobes blotched with white.

FEIJOA (Myrtaceae)

A handsome genus of two species from central South America allied to the Common Myrtle *Myrtus communis*, but most closely related to the Guavas, *Psidium*. The genus commemorates Don Feijo, a botanist of San Sebastian, Spain.

Feijoa sellowiana (Pl.20) is an evergreen shrub of dense habit to 5m, the young shoots, buds and undersurface of the leaves dotted with whitish down. Leaves opposite, oval, 2.5–7.5cm long, untoothed, dark green and somewhat shiny above. Flowers whitish, flushed with red in the centre, solitary, carried on the lower part of the current year's shoots, 3–4.5cm across, each with four reflexed felted sepals and four broad oval, concave petals and a prominent bunch of crimson stamens. Fruit a plum-shaped berry 3–5cm long with a pleasant flavour, somewhat aromatic. [July, HH, PN, S Brazil & Uruguay]

This attractive shrub is rather neglected in gardens and is probably hardier than generally supposed. Admittedly it is not beautiful at a distance, but individual branches with several flowers viewed close-up are most attractive. It requires a sunny south or south-west sheltered wall and will survive outdoors even in Scotland or cold counties such as Norfolk, although it may need extra protection there during the winter in the form of screens. Plants rarely set seed in cultivation, at least in this country, and are best propagated from cuttings of half-ripe wood with some bottom heat, during July or August. Fruits are more readily set if two plants of different stocks are grown side by side.

FREMONTODENDRON (Sterculiaceae)

There are many exciting shrubs from California and adjacent areas, however, few take kindly to our temperate climate. Those that do so will, in most instances, succeed only on a sunny south-facing wall. The two species of *Fremontodendron* formerly called *Fremontia* are amongst the finest and most widely known of these shrubs. The yellow or orange-yellow flowers lack petals, the colour coming from the large five-lobed calyces, each lobe with a deep nectar-filled pouch at the base. The stamens are also interesting, being united together in a short column around the slender style. The fruit is a bristly capsule containing numerous seeds.

Fremontodendrons should be purchased as young pot-grown plants. They dislike being moved and are best planted in the early spring to avoid any check to growth. Plants do best in a rather poor sandy soil and are particularly good subjects for coastal gardens in mild districts, if a sheltered niche can be provided. Plants are not long-lived at the best of times and need to be replaced from time to time. Propagation from seed is the most reliable method, although some people are very successful with tip cuttings taken in the early summer using a mist propagating bench. Young seedlings should be potted on as soon as possible.

The genus is named in honour of Capt. J.C. Fremont who discovered *F. californicum* in 1846.

Fremontodendron californicum = *Fremontia californica* (Pl.14), the Californian Buttercup is an evergreen or semi-deciduous shrub reaching 10m tall, though generally less. The downy twigs bear alternate leaves, each 5 – 10cm long, with three main lobes, dull green above but brown with fine starry down beneath. The solitary flowers are golden-yellow, widely cup-shaped or flattish, 6 – 8cm across, with rounded lobes that are downy on the back. [May – Aug, HH, PN, SW USA]

F. californicum is native to western slopes of the Sierra Nevada coastal ranges from California to Arizona. It has been cultivated since the 1850s, although as already stressed plants are not long-lived, a specimen of 20 years being considered to have reached old age. Plants may collapse and die quite suddenly and apparently inexplicably. This should not, however, put the gardener off for this species and its ally are well worth growing and, provided that a small stock of young plants is kept aside, sudden gaps can always be filled.

Fremontodendron mexicanum = *Fremontia mexicana, F. californica* var. *mexicana,* is similar to the previous species, although rarely exceeding 6m in height. The young shoots are densely clothed with pale brown down. The leaves vary from 2.5 to 7.5cm long, each with five to seven shallow lobes. The flowers are orange-yellow, 6 – 10cm across, more starry than those of *F. californicum* and often stained with red on the outside towards the flowerstalk. [June – Sept, HH, PN, USA (California) & Mexico]

This species is rarer in cultivation than its cousin and certainly less hardy. However, seedlings may often flower during their first season. The main distribution of the species is in Baja California (Lower California), which is one of the Mexican states, but, it does 'creep' across the border into the San Diego area of California proper.

***'Californian Glory'**, *F. californicum* × *F. mexicanum* (Pl.14), an outstanding hybrid, combining the best features of the two species described above, has leaves similar to the second parent but with five lobes only. The lemon yellow flowers are deeply cupped, 4.5 – 6.5cm across, slightly flushed with red on the outside as they age.

FREYLINIA (Scrophulariaceae)

A South African genus with some five species of evergreen shrubs. The flowers are tubular with five spreading lobes and the leaves are borne in opposite pairs.

Freylinia lanceolata = *Capraria lanceolata* is an evergreen shrub eventually reaching 3 – 4m in height, with slightly hairy and angled young shoots. Leaves dark bright green, linear, 5 – 13cm long. Sweetly-scented flowers, yellow or creamy outside, deep yellow inside, 12mm long, are borne at the shoot tips in slender panicles up to 30cm long. [Aug – Sept, T, PN, S Africa]

An elegant and rather lovely shrub in full flower, but in Britain it seldom blooms profusely. It relishes as much sunshine as it can get, doing particularly well after an all too rare sunny hot summer. A warm sunny sheltered wall and a well-drained loamy soil are the chief requirements. *F. lanceolata* is sometimes seen as a conservatory plant or in gardens in Mediterranean countries where it does very well. The flowers are sometimes tinged with pink.

GARRYA (Garryaceae)

Garrya elliptica is one of the most striking of all wall shrubs, the long silvery-grey catkins contrasting with the deep green leaves through the winter months. The genus contains about 18 species native to the western United States, Mexico and the West Indies. They have simple opposite leaves. All species bear male and female flowers on separate plants and usually carry them in hanging catkin-like racemes. The flowers lack petals but have four sepals, the male flowers with four stamens and the female flowers with two styles. The fruit is a berry containing one or two seeds only.

In all but the mildest counties, *Garrya* species need the protection of a wall or high fence. In the south and west, *G. elliptica* and *G.* ×*thurettii* are hardy in a sheltered position. *Garrya* is good at withstanding both atmospheric pollution and salt-laden air and will grow in any well-drained soil, although light loams are the best. It is useful for north- or east-facing walls. Propagation is by cuttings of half-ripened wood placed in gentle heat, taken in the autumn.

***Garrya elliptica** (Pl.20), the Tassel Bush, will grow 5–6m tall and has downy young shoots. The oval to almost round leaves are 3.5–7.5cm long with wavy margins, deep glossy green above and grey-hairy underneath. The greenish-grey flowers are crowded into pendulous catkins 7.5–15cm long in most districts, although they can reach 30cm in mild areas. [Nov–Feb, HH, PA, USA (California & Oregon)]

The male plant is the usual form sold by nurserymen and is far more desirable than the female as it produces longer catkins. A useful and attractive winter-flowering plant which does not like wet conditions and should be planted where it is to grow as it dislikes being moved. *Garrya elliptica* was introduced by the plant collector, David Douglas in 1828. The genus was named by him in honour of Mr. Garry of the famous Hudson's Bay Company.

'James Roof' is a vigorous male form with extra-large catkins up to 35cm long.

Garrya × thuretii, *G. elliptica* × *G. fadyenii*, is a stout shrub, quick-growing and reaching 5m tall. The leaves are narrowly-oblong, 6–10cm long, glossy above and grey-downy below. The greyish catkins, 3.5–7.5cm long, are more or less erect. [June, HH, PA, Garden origin]

This hybrid is good at withstanding wind. It is named after Gustave Thuret, who raised it in the south of France from *G. elliptica*, crossed with *G. fadyenii* which is a tender species native to the West Indies and not in cultivation in Britain.

GREVILLEA (Proteaceae)

There are nearly 200 species of *Grevillea*, found in tropical south-east Asian islands and Australia. They have alternate leaves and pairs of flowers borne in many-flowered racemes. The calyx and corolla are not differentiated; there is a tubular perianth of four segments, and there are four stamens which are joined to the perianth. The style is long and conspicuous, the fruit pod-like and contains one or two seeds. Propagation is by cuttings of half-ripened shoots in July, in a propagating frame.

Grevillea rosmarinifolia is a loose shrub growing to 2m in height, with downy young shoots. The needle-shaped leaves, 2.5–5cm long are stalkless with under-rolled margins, dark greyish-green above and adpressed-hairy underneath. Dark pinkish-red flowers up to 2.5cm long are arranged in dense stalkless racemes. The perianth, silky inside, hairless outside, has two long and two short segments. The red style protrudes from the perianth. [June–July, T, PN, Australia (New South Wales)]

***Grevillea sulphurea** is a sturdy bush which reaches 1.8m tall and has downy young shoots. Needle-shaped leaves, 1.25–2.5cm long have recurved margins and pale hairs beneath. Pale yellow flowers, occasionally tinged with red, are borne in short 12- or more-flowered racemes. Each flower is 1.25cm long with silky hairs outside and is deeply slit on one side, the long style protruding through the slit. [May–June, T, PN, Australia (New South Wales)] ☼ Δ

A pretty shrub which is a little hardier than *G. rosmarinifolia*, but can still be grown only in the milder areas of Britain. It does well against a sheltered wall in most southern counties. Both species have beautiful and unusual flowers.

HAPLOPAPPUS (Compositae)

There are some 150 species of this American genus but only the one described below is grown as a wall shrub. In catalogues it is sometimes erroneously listed as *Aplopappus*.

Haplopappus ericoides is a small heath-like shrub, growing only 0.5m tall. There are several dark green filiform leaves at each node, each 3–12mm long, with resin glands, and with dense clusters of leaves in their axils. The flowers are borne in heads 8–125mm across which have usually five, occasionally two to six yellow ray florets. The heads are clustered into long-stalked terminal panicles. [Aug–Sept, T, PN, USA (California)] ☼

This pretty little shrub can be readily increased by cuttings taken during July and rooted with gentle heat. It is not commonly grown but does particularly well in southern coastal districts. Plants are not long-lived and need replacing from time to time.

HYPERICUM (Guttiferae)

Of the numerous species of *Hypericum* which we cultivate there is one tender species which appreciates being grown against a wall, even in the mildest areas.

Hypericum leschenaultii is an evergreen shrub of lax habit, growing to 3m, which in the colder parts of the country is semi-evergreen or even deciduous. It has slender reddish-brown branches and opposite ovate-oblong to lanceolate leaves, 3.5–6cm long, dotted with glands, dark green above but paler beneath. The bright yellow flowers are 6–7.5cm in diameter, borne singly or three together at the ends of the shoots. There are five petals which are slightly concave. [July–Oct, T, PN, Malaysia] ☼

A lovely plant with a long flowering season. If the main shoots are attached to the wall, the lateral branches can be allowed to hang downwards. Pruning is only necessary to remove weak growth or to control the size.

Hypericum 'Rowallane', *H. hookerianum* 'Rogersii' × *H. leschenaultii*, is a magnificent graceful semi-evergreen cultivar reaching 2m high. The bowl-shaped flowers, 5–7.5cm across are deep golden-yellow [Aug–Oct] ☼

This cultivar is sometimes found under the incorrect name of *H. rogersii*.

HOHERIA (Malvaceae)

A delightful genus in the Mallow Family, mostly preferring well-drained loamy soils and sheltered sites away from driving winds.

The genus *Hoheria* is native to New Zealand and all five species are cultivated in Britain. They are evergreen or deciduous trees and shrubs, with alternate simple leaves which vary in size and shape as the plant ages. The white flowers are usually borne in clusters at the leaf axils, rarely are they solitary or the clusters terminal. Each flower has five petals and numerous stamens arranged in five bundles. There are five to fifteen often winged carpels, each developing into a dry capsule containing a single seed.

Pruning is generally unnecessary, but if the size needs to be restricted, pruning may be carried out in the spring. Propagation is by cuttings.

The leaves of young plants are usually smaller than those of adult plants, and are often more lobed or toothed.

The deciduous *H. glabrata* and *H. lyallii* are described on p.136.

☼ ***Hoheria sexstylosa** = *H. populnea* var.*lanceolata* (Pl.21) is a densely branched vigorous evergreen, reaching 7.5m high. The young growths are clothed in starry down. The shiny lanceolate leaves are 6–7.5cm long, sharply pointed at the tip and deeply toothed. The white flowers, about 2cm across are produced singly or several together. There are six or seven broadly winged carpels. [July–Aug, HH–T, PN, New Zealand]

The *Hoheria* most commonly grown in gardens. It is fast-growing and makes a beautiful sight when it flowers. In really bad winters, plants will drop some or perhaps all their leaves.

var. ovata has broader ovate leaves which are usually slightly smaller.

'Crataegifolia' is the juvenile form with coarsely toothed smaller leaves.

Hoheria 'Glory of Amlwch', *H. sexstylosa* × *H. glabrata,* is a free-flowering hybrid with ovate and slender-pointed leaves about 8cm long. Flowers, borne in clusters of three to eight, are about 3.5cm across.

This fine cultivar has the largest flowers of the evergreen *Hoheria* species.

☼ **Hoheria populnea** is an evergreen tree, hairless except for some starry hairs on the young leaves and flower-stalks. The adult leaves, 7.5–16cm long, are broadly to narrowly ovate, the margins with double teeth. Juvenile leaves may be similar or smaller and variable in shape. White flowers, 2–2.5cm across, are solitary or in clusters. There are five or six broadly winged carpels. [Aug–Sept, T, PN, New Zealand]

A number of cultivars have been raised in New Zealand and are available in Britain.

'Alba Variegata' = has leaves with a white margin.
'Osbornei' has leaves which are purplish underneath. The flowers have blue stamens.
'Purpurea' = 'Foliis Purpureis' has leaves which are brownish-purple beneath.
'Variegata' has leaves variegated with pale yellow.

☼ **Hoheria angustifolia** = *H. microphylla* is very similar to *H. populnea* but has smaller leaves with large, rather distant, spine-tipped teeth. The flowers are smaller, 1.5–2cm across, and more often borne singly than in clusters. There are five carpels. [Aug–Sept, HH, PN, New Zealand]

ILLICIUM (Illiciaceae)

A genus of some 40 aromatic shrubs related to the Magnolias. The leaves are alternate, entire and rather leathery. The starry flowers are solitary or two to three together, each with up to 30 petals. The fruit is a star-shaped circle of single-seeded carpels. The species thrive on acid soils, although tolerant of a little lime and benefiting from peat mulches. Pruning is unnecessary except to limit growth. Propagation is by cuttings or layers.

Illicium floridanum, the Aniseed Tree, is an evergreen shrub growing ◐ 1.8 – 3m tall and has hairless lanceolate to narrowly oval leaves, 7.5 – 10cm long. The solitary nodding flowers, produced at the ends of the shoots, are 3.5 – 5cm in diameter with strap-shaped maroon petals and 30 – 40 stamens. [May – June, H – HH, PN, S USA]

All parts of this plant are fragrant. It was first introduced to England as early as 1771.

Illicium anisatum, the Star Anise, will grow to 6m tall and has green young ◐ branches which are spotted with brown. The narrowly-oval leaves are 5 – 10cm in length. The flowers are unscented, borne singly or in pairs in the leaf axils and about 2.5cm in diameter. They have narrow greenish-yellow petals and 17 – 25 stamens. [Mar – June, H – HH, PN, China & Japan]

Like *I. floridanum*, this plant is scented, and smells of aniseed. It is slow-growing and a little hardier than *I. floridanum*.

Illicium henryi has 10 – 15cm long, glossy green leaves and solitary bright rose- ◐ pink fragrant flowers which are produced singly at the leaf axils. [May – June, H – HH, PN, W China]

ITEA (Escalloniaceae)

Shrubs with alternate toothed leaves and flowers in axillary or terminal racemes. The flowers have five sepals and petals and the fruit is a five-valved capsule containing flattened seeds.

Propagation is by cuttings of fairly ripe wood, taken in the autumn.

***Itea ilicifolia** is an hairless shrub reaching about 3.8m in height. The young ☼ growth is a bronzy colour. Leaves broadly oval, 5 – 10cm long, with stiff spiny marginal teeth, hairless except for tufts of hair in the vein axils of the lower surface. Scented flowers, with greenish-white narrow petals about 4mm long, are borne in slender pendulous racemes 15 – 30cm long. [July – Aug, T – HH, PN, C & W China]

The flowers are small, but the long racemes make the shrub conspicuous and lovely in flower. No regular pruning is necessary but unwanted shoots may be removed in February. In most parts of Britain wall-protection is essential, west- and south-facing walls being preferred.

Itea yunnanensis is similar to *I. ilicifolia*, differing in its narrower, less spiny ☼ leaves and shorter racemes of flowers. [July, T, PN, China (Yunnan)]

Less spectacular than *I. ilicifolia* and less commonly grown.

JASMINUM (Oleaceae)

The shrubby evergreen Jasmines are treated on p.100 with the other species of *Jasminum*.

JOVELLANA (Scrophulariaceae)

A small genus of six pretty species of herbs or subshrubs native to South America and New Zealand, which are closely related to *Calceolaria* but with more open equal-lobed flowers. Only one species is suitable for outdoor culture.

☼ **Jovellana violacea** = *Calceolaria violacea* is a loosely branched evergreen shrub reaching 1–2m tall with erect branches, spreading by the production of suckers. The opposite leaves are oval, coarsely toothed or lobed, 2–2.5cm long, deep green and slightly hairy above, paler and smooth beneath. Pale violet flowers, spotted with purple and with a yellowish throat, are borne in loose elegant clusters at the stem tips. [June–July, T, PS, Chile]

An attractive plant suitable only for a warm sheltered sunny nook, preferably against a south-facing wall. Plants thrive reasonably well in the mildest parts of the country, but although often surviving outdoors in less mild districts, plants rarely flower well there. In a severe winter plants may lose some or all of their leaves. Pruning mainly consists of removing weak, dead or damaged growths in the spring as growth commences. *J. violacea* is most often seen as a greenhouse or conservatory plant.

LEPTOSPERMUM (Myrtaceae)

This genus which is closely allied to the Myrtles, *Myrtus*, contains about 30 species, native primarily to Australia and New Zealand. They are evergreen shrubs or small trees generally with small alternate, leathery, untoothed leaves, which on close inspection are seen to be gland-dotted. The flowers are solitary or in groups of two or three, borne in the leaf axils towards the shoot tips. There are usually five tiny sepals and five round petals, and a prominent cluster of stamens which form a rosette in the centre of each flower. The fruit is a small woody capsule, clearly different from the berry-like structure in *Myrtus*.

Like the myrtles, Leptospermums are plants for mild sheltered areas, doing particularly well in maritime districts. They thrive on well drained soils which should be neutral or tending towards acidity in reaction. Full sun is essential.

☼ Δ **Leptospermum scoparium**, the Manuka or Tea Tree of New Zealand, is the commonest cultivated species, making a rather dense bush of rounded habit 2–4m high, although it may reach 7m in the wild. The young shoots are somewhat hairy, and the deep green leaves range in shape from narrowly oblong to ovate-lanceolate, pointed, 8–13mm long, pleasantly aromatic when crushed. The single white flowers, 11–13mm across, are borne in large numbers. The woody fruit-capsule is about the size of a small pea. [May–June, HH, PN, Australia & New Zealand]

This lovely shrub has been cultivated since about 1772 and as a result there are a number of fine cultivars with flowers ranging in colour from white to the palest pink, crimson or cherry-red. Most are readily propagated from cuttings taken in midsummer and placed in gentle heat in a propagating frame. For those who are unable to grow it out-of-doors a sunny spot in a conservatory will prove most satisfactory.

'Album Flore Pleno' has a compact rather erect habit and double white flowers.

'Boscawenii' has larger flowers, 22–25mm across, which are pink in bud but open white with a pink centre.

'Chapmanii' has attractively bronzed leaves and deep rose-red flowers.

***'Keatleyi'** has attractive grey-green foliage which is flushed with crimson when young. The flowers are as large as 'Boscawenii' but soft pink when open.

'Leonard Wilson' has pure white double flowers.

***'Nichollsii'**, the Crimson Manuka, has narrow lanceolate leaves which flush a deep bronzy-purple in full sunshine. The flowers are crimson with a deeper centre, larger than the type.

'Roseum' has large pale pink flowers with a crimson centre, 23–25mm across.

'Red Damask' forms a dense bush up to 2m tall with double cherry red flowers, 12–13mm across.

'Roseum Multipetalum' bears a profusion of double rose-pink flowers.

var. **eximium** is a robust variety with broad, more or less rounded leaves. Flowers pure white, 17–18mm across. [Tasmania]

var. **incanum** has narrow lanceolate leaves and white flowers tinged with pink, larger than the type [New Zealand] 'Keatleyi' may belong under this variety.

Leptospermum lanigerum = *L. pubescens* is a rather variable leafy shrub (or small tree in the wild) to 2–4m tall, with a rather erect habit and slender, downy twigs. The oblong or oval pointed leaves, 8–18mm long, are glossy green or greyish above, hairless or rather silky. White flowers, 12–13mm across, have a downy white calyx. [Late June–Aug, HH, PN, Australia & Tasmania]

There are two rather different forms of this attractive plant in cultivation. One has small greyish-leaves which are flushed with pinkish-brown when young. This is sometimes found under the name *L. cunninghamii*. The second has larger narrower leaves which are glossy green tinged with purple when young. This latter form comes into flower rather earlier than the former.

Leptospermum liversidgei, the Lemon-scented Tea Tree, is a rather elegant evergreen shrub 2–4m tall, with drooping branches which are hairless even when young but densely clothed in leaves. The small leaves are narrowly-oblong to obovate, only 4–6mm long and with a delightful though rather faint fragrance of lemon when crushed. The solitary white flowers, 6–8mm across, are borne on short stalks near the shoot tips. [June, HH, PN, Australia (New South Wales)]

This fine shrub will do well on a west- or south-facing wall in a sheltered position. Plants may suffer badly in severe winters, but they have been known to sprout afresh from the old wood so damaged plants should not be removed until it is certain they are quite dead.

LOMATIA (Proteaceae)

This genus hails from South America and Australia where there are perhaps a dozen species. They are allied to the Proteas but come closest to *Embothrium coccineum*, the Fire Bush, which is amongst the most spectacular of all evergreens grown in the British Isles. Lomatias are striking evergreen shrubs or small trees with handsome leaves and attractive, rather bottlebrush-like racemes of flowers, somewhat reminiscent of those of the Honeysuckle.

Lomatia myricoides = *L. longifolia* is a splendid shrub 1–2.5m tall, rather slow-growing, with angled slightly downy young stems. The hairless leaves are lanceolate or almost oblong, coarsely toothed in the upper half or sometimes untoothed, 7–15cm long. Fragrant, creamy-white or pale yellow flowers each only 12mm long, are borne in terminal or subterminal racemes. [June–July, HH, PN, SE Australia]

This shrub deserves to be better known but it does need a warm sunny sheltered niche. Once established, plants are more or less hardy in the extreme south of the country and flowers are generally freely produced. Cut blossom is excellent for flower arrangements.

LOROPETALUM (Hamamelidaceae)

A genus similar to *Hamamelis*, the Witch Hazel, but evergreen and with white flowers. There are three species but only *Loropetalum chinense* is cultivated in Britain.

☼ Δ **Loropetalum chinense** grows to 2m and has wiry crooked twigs thickly covered with brown, starry down. The leaves are alternate, ovate or oval, 2.5–6cm long with a finely toothed margin and sparse hairs on the upper surface. The sweetly scented flowers are borne in small clusters and have four white strap-shaped petals which are about 2cm long. The fruit is a dry woody egg-shaped capsule. [Feb–Mar, T, PN, China & NE India]

A useful shrub which flowers at a time when little else is out. It requires wall-protection in almost all parts of the country. Propagation is by cuttings. This species was introduced to cultivation during 1880 by the plant collector Charles Maries.

LYONOTHAMNUS (Rosaceae)

A genus with a single species found only on a few islands off the coast of California. The type species *Lyonothamnus floribundus* is not in fact in cultivation in Britain but is represented by a ferny-leaved variety, var. *asplenifolius*.

☼ Δ **Lyonothamnus floribundus** var. **asplenifolius** = *L. asplenifolius* is a graceful evergreen shrub or small tree of slender habit reaching 10–16m. The trunk has red-brown and greyish peeling bark and the young shoots are completely hairless. The leaves are oppositely arranged and are pinnate, 10–20cm long, with 3–9 greyish-green leaflets cut into a number of wedge-shaped segments and giving a pleasant ferny appearance. The bunches of creamy-white spiraea-like flowers are borne in terminal panicles 7.5–15cm long, each flower scarcely 6mm across. [May–June, HH, PN, USA (Californian coastal islands, particularly Santa Catalina & Santa Cruz)]

This is an unusual plant, sadly rare in cultivation and unreliably hardy even in the mildest parts of the country. However, it will survive average winters in southern counties given the shelter of a sunny sheltered wall of south, west or even south-east aspect. Plants are fast- growing from seed. The typical form of the species has simple uncut foliage, and it grows in the same locality as var. *asplenifolius*. All possible intermediates between the extremes of leaf type are said to occur in the wild.

MAGNOLIA (Magnoliaceae)

Magnificent and extremely popular plants with species suitable for most gardens. A few require wall culture. They are evergreen or deciduous trees and shrubs with alternate, simple untoothed leaves; their large flowers are borne singly at the end of the twigs and have a perianth of usually six to nine petal-like segments. The numerous stamens and carpels are arranged in a spiral pattern on a fleshy cylindrical or conical structure called the torus; the stamens are at the base and the carpels on the upper part. When the fruits are ripe, the torus enlarges and the carpels split open to release one or two large orange or red seeds.

Beautiful plants which will grace any garden, magnolias are tolerant of atmospheric pollution and can grow well in industrial areas. They thrive on rich deep loamy soils with plenty of humus and moisture. Propagation is by layers, grafts or seed. Seed should be sown as soon as possible and may prove very slow to germinate. The deciduous *Magnolia liliiflora* is described on p.140.

***Magnolia grandiflora** is evergreen and will grow to 9m in Britain. The oval to obovate-oblong leaves, 15–25cm long, are deep glossy green above and have reddish-brown felt underneath, particularly when young. The huge, creamy-white, broadly globular flowers, 20–25cm across, have a powerful fragrance. The 'petals' are 6–12cm long, broadly obovate, concave and thick. [July–Sept, H, PN, SE USA]

Perhaps one of the finest of all wall shrubs, *M. grandiflora* is commonly seen adorning the walls of stately homes and large buildings. Introduced to Britain early in the eighteenth century, it will grow on a wall of any aspect but flowers best on a south-facing wall. It needs a tall wall and can look very effective against a house. It is only necessary to attach the main growths to the wall. Should any pruning be needed, it is best done in July. Propagation is best by layers or cuttings as plants raised from seed take much longer to flower.

The following cultivars are available commercially.

'Angustifolia' has lanceolate to oblanceolate leaves, 15–20cm long with wavy margins.

***'Exmouth'** = 'Lanceolata' has leaves which are oval to oval-obovate. The flowers are very large and are produced on fairly young plants.

'Ferruginea' has reddish-brown leaves very thickly felted beneath but becoming almost hairless with age.

***'Goliath'** has shorter and broader leaves than the type, and they are green underneath. The flowers are exceptionally large, produced at a young age.

'Undulata' has leaves which are green beneath, with strongly wavy margins.

Magnolia nitida is evergreen and like *M.grandiflora*, can grow to 9m. The oval to ovate leathery leaves are 5.5–11cm long, bronzy-red when young, becoming dark green above, paler beneath, hairless. The fragrant creamy-white flowers are 5–7.5cm across, with nine to twelve 'petals', the outer ones sometimes marked with a purple streak. [May–June, T–HH, PN, China (Yunnan) & SE Tibet]

A species which is only occasionally seen in gardens. It will not grow on chalky or limy soils.

Magnolia delavayi is a spreading evergreen tree, reaching 9m or more. The bark of old specimens is brownish-white, rather corky and with characteristic fissures. The leaves, ovate to oblong, with the midrib extending beyond the blade into a short point, are 20–35cm long, greyish-green and rather dull above and downy underneath. The fragrant, cup-shaped white flowers 17–20cm across are usually composed of about ten 'petals' each about 10cm long. [June–Sept, T, PN, China(Yunnan)]

Easily distinguished from the other Magnolias described here by its enormous leaves, it was first discovered by the French missionary Père Delavay in 1886, and introduced by E.H. Wilson in 1899. It grows best on a south- or west-facing wall.

MAYTENUS (Celastraceae)

A large genus of evergreen trees and shrubs centred on Central and South America, but also with species in Africa which were once included in the genus *Celastrus* or *Gymnosporia*. *Maytenus* is closely allied to the spindle trees

Euonymus as well as to *Celastrus*, all three genera including species in which the seeds are enclosed or partly enclosed in a colourful fleshy aril.

Maytenus boaria = *M. chilensis*, the Maiten, is the only species suitable for wall protection. It is an elegant shrub or small tree reaching 20m or more in the wild, but less in cultivation. The slender drooping branches are quite hairless and bear alternate lanceolate leaves 2.5–5cm long. They have a short stalk and a finely toothed margin, the upper surface a shiny mid-grey but the lower surface paler. The greenish-white flowers are small and of little consequence, being borne in small clusters of 2–5 in the leaf axils of the previous year's growth. The flowers are mostly either wholly male or female, although they occur on the same plant; hermaphrodite flowers are occasionally produced. The small pea-sized fruit-capsules contain two red-coated seeds. [Apr–May, HH, PN, Argentina, Bolivia, S Brazil, Chile & Peru]

An interesting plant, but a rare one in cultivation. It will succeed equally well on a well-drained acid or alkaline soil. In the wild it is an attractive feature of many of the lower Andean pastures in light places away from denser forest. Cattle are said to be very fond of foraging amongst the foliage of this species, hence its specific name — *boaria* 'for cattle'. The generic name *Maytenus* comes from the plant's South American Indian name 'maiten'.

MEDICAGO (Leguminosae)

There are about 100 species of Medick, *Medicago*, native to temperate Eurasia, the Mediterranean area and southern Africa. Most species are herbs, but *M. arborea*, described below, is a semi-evergreen shrub.

Medicago arborea, the Moon Trefoil, can grow to 4m high but is usually shorter. Its branches are clothed with silky hairs. The leaves, 2.5–3.5cm long, are composed of three wedge-shaped leaflets, 6–18mm long and untoothed or with tiny teeth towards the apex. Fragrant yellow pea-flowers, 1.25–1.5cm long, with wings longer than the keel, are carried four to eight together in short racemes produced in the leaf axils. The fruit pod is flat and curled into a spiral, rather like a ram's horn. [Apr–Sept, T, PN, S Europe]

A valuable shrub for its long flowering season, thriving on most well-drained soils. It needs pruning only to remove damaged wood after a bad winter. Propagation is by cuttings.

METROSIDEROS (Myrtaceae)

A charming genus containing a number of evergreen trees and shrubs, or climbers from the Antipodes, related to the 'Bottlebrushes', *Callistemon*. The inflorescences are usually brilliantly coloured, like those of the true 'bottlebrushes. None is completely hardy in Britain, even in the very mildest places, and they generally require the protection of a warm sunny wall. A loamy well-drained soil is best, preferably a neutral or slightly acid one, although plants will tolerate small amounts of lime. Plants will need winter protection in all but the very mildest districts and are readily propagated from cuttings in a propagating frame. The most conspicuous parts of the flowers are the prominent showy stamens.

***Metrosideros excelsa** = *M. tomentosa*, known as the Christmas Tree in New Zealand, will eventually form a large vigorous bush or small tree 2–7m or more high. The leaves are elliptic or oval, leathery, 3.5–10cm long, dark shiny green above but white-downy beneath. The large broad 'bottlebrushes' each 25–30mm long are brilliant crimson, often borne in large numbers, especially on well-established plants. [July–Aug, T, PN, New Zealand]

A splendid plant seen at its best in the mildest gardens of south-west Britain.

***Metrosideros kermadecensis** = *M. villosa* is like the preceding species but smaller in all its parts and covered in soft down and with bright scarlet 'bottlebrushes'. [July–Aug, T, PN, New Zealand & Polynesia]

***Metrosideros lucida** forms a dense bush or small tree 2–6m or more tall. The lanceolate leaves, 2.5–7.5cm long are shiny deep green, bronzed when young and the 'bottlebrushes' are bright crimson, each flower 20–25mm long. [Late Aug–Sept, HH, PN, New Zealand]

Probably the best species to grow outdoors in Britain, but unfortunately seldom seen away from the milder districts.

***Metrosideros robusta**, the Rata of New Zealand, forms a bush or small tree 2–6m or more tall. Dark green, oval or elliptic leaves, 2–3.5cm long are leathery and hairless. The coppery-scarlet small, rounded 'bottlebrushes' are singularly beautiful, each flower only 10–12mm long but making up rounded clusters at the branch tips. [Aug–Sept, T, PN, New Zealand]

A very fine species. Some trees may reach 20m tall in favoured localities.

Metrosideros diffusa is a very slow-growing shrub or semi-climber of compact habit, eventually reaching 3–4m tall. Its hairless leaves 1–3.5cm long are lanceolate to elliptic and the 'bottlebrushes', 11–13cm long, pink or crimson with yellow anthers. [Apr-May, T, PN, New Zealand]

Metrosideros hypericifolia is a small shrub or semi-climber with slender branches to 3–4m or more tall, with young shoots angular and reddish. Leaves small, oblong, 0.8–2.5cm long, closely set. Pink or white flowers are borne in small axillary clusters 8–9mm long. [Aug–Sept, T, PN, New Zealand]

MICHELIA (Magnoliaceae)

A genus of some 50 species of trees or shrubs related to *Magnolia*, from which it can be distinguished by the flowers being produced in the leaf-axils instead of at the ends of the branches. The flowers are also generally smaller, many resembling those of the stellate Magnolia, *M. stellata*, in shape.

***Michelia doltsopa** is a semi-evergreen shrub or tree, growing to 12m tall, with somewhat warty young stems. The alternate oval to oblong leaves are 7.5–18cm long, shining green above and paler below. The flowers are beautifully fragrant, 7.5–10cm across, with 12–16 obovate to oblanceolate white or pale yellow 'petals' each 3–7.5cm long, flushed with green at the base. [Apr, T, PN, W China & E Himalaya]

The flower buds are formed in the autumn and open in the following spring. *M. doltsopa* can only be grown in milder counties, but is the finest of those grown in Britain.

Michelia compressa is a slow-growing evergreen tree which reaches 12m high. The alternate oblong or obovate leaves, 5–7.5cm long are leathery, hairless and glossy. The fragrant flowers, 3.5–5cm across, have pale yellow or cream 'petals'. [Apr–May, T–HH, PN, S Japan]

Not commonly grown as the flowers are only occasionally produced in Britain.

Michelia doltsopa (p.211).

☼ △ **Michelia figo** = *M. fuscata* is an evergreen shrub growing to 6m high, its young shoots covered with dense brown hairs. The alternate narrowly oval leaves, 3.5–10cm long, are clothed with brown down when young, later becoming more or less hairless, and shiny green. The scented flowers are borne on brown-downy stalks. The 'petals', 1.8–2.5cm long are yellowish-green suffused with purple. [Apr–June, T, PN, China]

Only suitable for the south and west of Britain. It is not conspicuous but is grown for the fruity scent of its flowers. In the USA it is known as the 'Banana Shrub'. Propagation is by cuttings.

MYRTUS (Myrtaceae)

The genus *Myrtus* is large and diverse, indeed so diverse that some botanists split it up into a number of different genera, based upon characters of the seeds and embryo and other minutiae which need not concern us here.

Myrtles are evergreen shrubs, often aromatic with small leathery leaves which are opposite and untoothed. Their flowers are borne singly or in small groups towards the shoot tips, and the four or five petals and large bunch of prominent stamens are the most important decorative features. The fruit is a small woody vessel usually about the size of a pea.

Myrtles are easily cultivated, but they are plants for warm sheltered localities, revelling particularly in mild areas on or near the coast. They like well-drained loamy soils and are readily propagated from cuttings given gentle bottom heat in a propagating frame.

☼ ***Myrtus communis,** the Common Myrtle, is a densely branched shrub reaching 3–4.5m tall against a wall. The young stems are somewhat downy and the oval or lanceolate leaves, 2.5–5cm long, glossy dark green above but paler beneath with a pleasant fragrance when crushed. The fragrant white flowers, borne singly at the uppermost leaf axils, are each about 18mm across with five rounded petals. The fruit, a purplish-black berry, 11–13m long, is more or less oblong. [July–Aug, HH, PN, S & SE Europe & W Asia]

This well known and popular shrub has been long grown in gardens, particularly in Mediterranean countries. Its use in bouquets goes back to ancient Greece and it is still widely used at weddings today. In Britain the Common Myrtle has been cultivated since the sixteenth century.

'Flore-pleno' has double flowers.

'Microphylla' is an attractive plant smaller in all its parts than the typical plant.

'Variegata' is a cultivar with the leaves attractively variegated with cream.

var. **tarentina** = 'Jenny Reitenbach' the Tarentum Myrtle has smaller narrowly oval leaves, 1.2–2cm long, which may be both alternate and opposite on the same plant. The fruits are whitish.

Myrtus communis.

Myrtus chequen = *Eugenia chequen, Luma chequen,* is a densely branched leafy shrub up to 2m tall with brownish young stems covered with white down. The elliptic or ovate leaves are 1.5–3cm long, smaller on the lateral shoots, deep green above but paler beneath, with a slightly wavy margin and aromatic when crushed. The white flowers, 10–14mm across are borne singly or two to three together, each with four or sometimes five petals. The fruit is a small black berry 6–8mm across. [Sept–Nov, HH, PN, Chile]

A plant for a very sheltered sunny nook.

Myrtus ugni = *Ugni molinae, Eugenia ugni,* the Chilean Guava, is a rather stiff, erect shrub, eventually 1.5–2m tall, with hairy young stems. The ovate or rather oblong leaves, 2–2.5cm long are pointed, deep green above but paler beneath. The fragrant white flowers, each rather globular in shape, 12–14mm across and borne singly towards the shoot tips, are tinged with rose-pink, especially in bud. The rounded dark reddish-brown berries are aromatic when ripe, 8–10mm, and said to be delicious. [May, HH, PN, Chile]

This slow-growing shrub has considerable charm and deserves to be more widely known. However, it is really only at its best in a sheltered nook in mild maritime districts.

'Variegata' has attractive green leaves shaded with grey and outlined with cream.

OLEARIA (Compositae)

A genus of about 100 trees and shrubs from New Zealand, Australia and New Guinea, generally referred to as Daisy Bushes. They have alternate or opposite simple leaves, which are hairy beneath and usually leathery. The typical 'daisy' flowerheads may be solitary or in clusters. Daisy Bushes prefer a light, well-drained soil. Propagation is by cuttings taken in late summer.

☼ **Olearia erubescens** grows to 1.5m, sometimes more, and has slender shoots clothed in brownish down. The alternate leaves are stiff and leathery, oval to oblong, with coarse marginal teeth. They are 1.25–3.5cm long, shiny green above and covered with brownish down beneath. Flowerheads, produced in axillary clusters on the shoots of the previous year, have a yellow central disk and three to five white ray florets. [May–June, T–HH, PA, Tasmania]

*var. **ilicifolia** has larger flowerheads and larger leaves, up to 7.5cm long. A charming plant, more commonly found in gardens than the type and a more vigorous grower. [SE Australia] A fine plant for a low wall or for masking the base of wall climbers, clematis and honeysuckle in particular.

☼ **Olearia virgata** reaches 4.8m tall and has very slender hairless four-angled shoots. The leaves are opposite, narrowly linear-obovate, up to 2cm long and white-felted on the undersurface. The flowerheads are borne in opposite clusters and each head has three to six pale yellow ray florets. [May–June, H, PA, New Zealand]

☼ **Olearia solandri** grows to 4.8m tall and has angled shoots covered with yellow down. The opposite leaves are linear-obovate with the margins rolled under, up to 1.5cm long, deep green and hairless above and covered with pale yellow felt below. The yellowish flowerheads are solitary. [Aug–Oct, T–HH, PA, New Zealand]

O. virgata and *O. solandri* are both rather dull shrubs and scarcely worth growing.

OSMANTHUS (Oleaceae)

A genus of 15 trees and shrubs native to east and south-east Asia. They have opposite leaves and flowers usually in terminal or axillary clusters. The calyx and corolla are both four-lobed and each flower has only two stamens. The fruit is fleshy and single-seeded.

Propagation is by cuttings in mid-summer, placed in a propagating frame with gentle bottom heat.

☼ **Osmanthus delavayi** = *Siphonosmanthus delavayi* grows to about 2m high and has spreading stiff branches which are downy when young. The oval to ovate leaves are 1.25–2.5cm long, hairless, toothed, shiny above and spotted with tiny glands on the lower surface. The deliciously scented flowers are white, borne in small clusters; the corolla has a cylindrical tube 1–1.25cm long, with four reflexed lobes at the mouth. The fruit is egg-shaped, about 1.2cm long and bluish-black when ripe. [Apr, H, PA, W China]

A fairly slow-growing but delightful shrub which does best with wall-protection to reduce the likelihood of frost-damage to the flowers. It is named after Père Delavay, the French missionary who introduced it to cultivation in Europe in 1890.

Osmanthus fragrans is a shrub with oblong-lanceolate to oval leaves, 6–10cm long, untoothed or with fine teeth. The white, very fragrant flowers are solitary or in few-flowered clusters. They are smaller than those of *O. delavayi.* [June–Aug, T, PS, Himalaya, China & Japan]

A very tender plant, only suitable for the mildest areas; in most places it is grown under glass.

'Aurantiacus' = forma *aurantiacus* has orange flowers.

OSTEOMELES (Rosaceae)

A small genus of trees and shrubs from China and south-east Asia of which only two species are in cultivation. Both are evergreen shrubs with unequally pinnate leaves, each leaflet untoothed but ending in a characteristic bristle-tip. The flowers are white and are followed by haw-like fruits which each contain five seeds. Plants can be propagated from cuttings of half-ripened shoots in midsummer. Seed is rarely available being seldom set in this country.

Osteomeles schweriniae = *O. anthyllidifolia*, is an elegant evergreen shrub 2–2.5m tall, sometimes more, with long, somewhat flexuous branches clothed in short grey hairs. The leaves, 5–10cm long, consist of 17–31 oblong leaflets which are grey-downy beneath. The white flowers each 13–17mm across occur in branched clusters at the ends of lateral shoots. The egg-shaped fruits are 7–10mm long, dark red at first but becoming almost black when ripe. [June, HH, PN, SW China]

An attractive shrub, in its native habitat a plant of hot dry river valleys; if it can be acquired it is worth growing on a sunny sheltered wall.

var. **microphylla** is scarcely distinguishable from the type but has denser growth and smaller less downy leaves. It is said to be a rather hardier plant. Plants sold under *O. subrotunda* often prove to be this variety.

Osteomeles subrotunda is a dwarf shrub growing to 0.5m with twisting branches and silky young shoots. The leaves, 2–4cm long, have 9–17 pairs of tiny oblong leaflets, silky beneath but somewhat shiny above. Small white flowers about 12mm across are borne in leafy lateral clusters. [June–July, T, PN, Ryukyus & Bonin Is]

PELARGONIUM (Geraniaceae)

A genus of some 250 species, many of which come from South Africa, including the garden geraniums or zonal pelargoniums, the regal pelargoniums, the scented-leaved geraniums, miniature geraniums and the ivy-leaved geraniums. The ivy-leaved geraniums are normally planted out in the summer in hanging baskets or window boxes, but in mild areas especially near the coast, they can be trained up a wall or trellis. If given winter protection such as a covering of straw or polythene, they can survive the winter. The main shoots need to be tied carefully to wall wires. They are readily raised from cuttings struck during the summer months and overwintered in a frame or frost-free place.

Pelargonium peltatum, the Ivy-leaved Geranium, has a slender hairless, scrambling stem which will reach 2m in height against a wall. The thick, rather fleshy, bright green leaves, 5–7.5cm across, have five lobes and the leaf stalk is attached to the blade at a little distance from the margin. Sometimes there is a reddish zone towards the leaf centre. The flowers are borne in clusters of four to eight, on stalks up to 10cm long produced in the leaf axils. Each flower has five sepals, the upper one with a nectar-bearing spur. The five petals are irregularly arranged into two upper and three lower and are obovate and notched at the apex. They can be mauve, pink or white, the upper petals veined and spotted with deep pink, are 1.8–2.5cm long — longer than the lower petals. The fruit is beaked and separates into one-seeded parts, each of which bears a twisted hairy awn. [June–Aug, T, PN, S Africa]

Although scarcely a shrub in the true sense this plant is more appropriate to this chapter than any other. A large number of cultivars have been selected and bred. This selection shows the range of flower colour and form which is available.

'Abel Carrière' is semi-double, tyrian purple.
'Audrey Clifton' is double, cerise-crimson.
'Can-Can' is semi-double, coral-pink. Produces flowers almost all the year round.
'Duke of Edinburgh' is single, pink. The leaves are silvery.
'Galilee' is double, bright pink.
'La France' is semi-double, mauve. Free-flowering.
'L'élégante' is single, pale mauve. The leaves are dark green with cream and purple variegation.
'Mme. Crousse' is semi-double, pale pink.
'Mrs. W.A.R. Clifton' is double, bright red.
'Mexican Beauty' is semi-double, deep crimson. Free-flowering.
'Rouletta' is single, white striped and edged with red.
'Snowdrift' is double, white.
'Ville de Paris' is single, rose-salmon. Produces lots of flowers.

PENSTEMON (Scrophulariaceae)

A well-known genus with about 250 species in North America noted for their bright, often pink or red, tubular flowers. Most of the species are herbaceous although a number from California are shrubby. Penstemons prefer a well-drained light soil in a sunny position. They are easily increased by cuttings taken of moderately ripened wood struck in midsummer. The two species described here require little pruning except to remove dead wood or shorten back weak growth in the early spring.

☼ ***Penstemon cordifolius** is a rather straggling evergreen shrub 1m high with downy young shoots. The heart-shaped leaves are opposite, 1.5–5cm long, coarsely toothed, and glossy dark green above. The rich scarlet flowers, about 3.7cm long are borne in long terminal leafy panicles. The outside of the corolla is downy-glandular and the anthers yellow. [June–Aug, HH, PS, USA (California)]

An attractive shrub discovered in 1831 by David Douglas. On a sheltered south wall it will reward the grower with a fine display of blooms throughout the summer. It is certainly one of the very best of the shrubby Penstemons.

☼ **Penstemon corymbosus** is similar but a dwarf shrub rarely over 0.5m tall. The leaves are rather variable in shape but generally ovate to oblong, 1.5–3cm long, with a finely toothed or untoothed margin. The scarlet flowers are borne in rather flat-topped clusters. [July–Aug, HH, PS, USA (California)]

PHYLLOCLADUS (Podocarpaceae)

A coniferous genus of six species, native to the Southern Hemisphere, but not really looking like a typical conifer. The male cones are borne in terminal clusters and the female cones tend to be solitary.

Phyllocladus trichomanoides, the 'Tanekaha', is a graceful tree eventually growing to 18m bearing its 'leaves' (phylloclades) in opposite whorls on short shoots 5–10cm long. Each phylloclade (a stem structure which has become leaf-like) is 6–25mm long, obovate or rhombic with shallow lobes towards the apex. When young, the phylloclades are reddish. The true leaves are reduced to mere scales. The male cones are produced in cylindrical terminal branches of five to ten, each bunch being 8–12mm long. The female cones are usually solitary, borne at the margins of small phylloclades. The seed is solitary, and set in a cup-shaped receptacle. [T, PN, New Zealand]

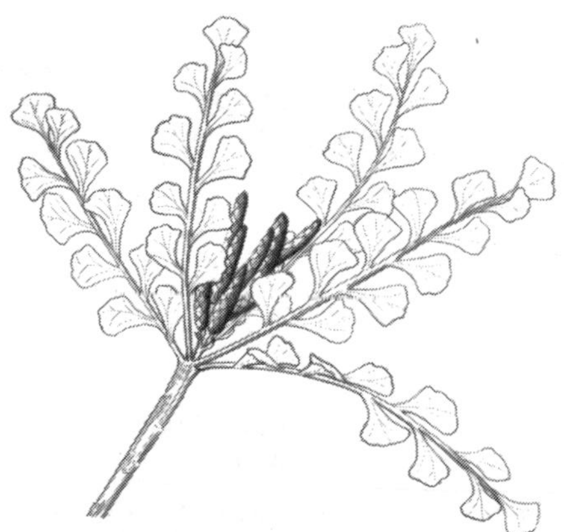

Phyllocladus trichomanoides.

An unusual plant benefiting from wall protection in most areas. It will not tolerate dry conditions and thrives better in areas of higher rainfall. Propagation by raising imported seed is preferable to taking cuttings.

PIPTANTHUS (Leguminosae)

There are eight species of *Piptanthus* native to Central Asia, China and the Himalaya. They have alternate leaves composed of three leaflets. The yellow pea-flowers are borne in erect terminal racemes. The fruit is a flat narrow pod which splits open to release the seeds.

***Piptanthus laburnifolius** = *P. nepalensis* (Pl.15), the Evergreen Laburnum, is normally evergreen although it can lose most of its leaves in a bad winter, or in northern localities. It grows to 3.5m or more. The lanceolate and untoothed leaflets, 7.5–15cm long, are covered with silky hairs when young, glaucous beneath. The hairy, scented flowers, 3–3.5cm long, have a brown-downy calyx and are borne in dense racemes 5–7.5cm long. The pods are downy, 7.5–13cm long. [May–June, HH, PA, Himalaya]

In most areas this fine plant needs wall-protection. It is not very long-lived, but is easily raised from seed and will succeed on most average garden soils if they are well drained and, once established, will flower freely. Young container-grown plants transplant best. Older branches can be pruned out close to the ground to encourage vigorous new growths. Frost-damaged shoots should be removed in the spring.

PITTOSPORUM (Pittosporaceae)

A genus of some 150 evergreen shrubs and small trees, found mainly in tropical and subtropical regions of the Old World. The leaves are alternate, or sometimes in distinct whorls. The flowers have five sepals and petals and five stamens which alternate with the petals. The fruit is a woody or leathery capsule.

Most *Pittosporum* species are tender in British gardens and need wall-protection, except in the mildest areas. They grow especially well in coastal situations. They are generally grown for their foliage, the flowers usually being inconspicuous and fairly dull although some are delightfully fragrant — *P. tobira* for instance.

Propagation is by seed or by cuttings of half-ripe wood helped with gentle heat. Pruning is not usually necessary, but should it become so, it is best undertaken in the spring; as soon as flowering ceases in the case of spring-flowering species.

***Pittosporum tobira**, the Tobira, is a bushy rather stiff shrub which grows to 6m or more. The obovate leaves are borne in whorls and are 3.5–10cm long, leathery, hairless and deep green with a pale midrib, the margins rolled under. Flowers creamy-white and very fragrant, about 2.5cm across, borne at the ends of shoots in clusters 5–7.5cm across, yellow with age. The fruit is a three-valved, pear-shaped downy capsule. [Apr–May, T, PN, Japan, China, Taiwan & Korea]

Worth growing for its fragrance which is reminiscent of orange-blossom. In Mediterranean countries it is often planted as a hedge or a small street tree.

'Variegatum' has the leaves margined with white.

Pittosporum adaphniphylloides = *P. daphniphylloides* is a shrub or small tree reaching 9m with slightly downy young shoots. The leaves are 6–23cm long, narrowly oblong to narrowly obovate, dark green and slightly downy beneath. The flowers are borne in several dense clusters 2–3.5cm wide which form a terminal panicle. Each flower is about 6mm wide, with creamy or greenish-yellow oblong petals. The capsule is 6–9mm long, globular, red and wrinkled. [Apr–July, T, PN, W China]

First introduced from Szechwan province by E.H. Wilson in 1904.

Pittosporum crassifolium, the Karo, is a dense shrub growing to 4.8m. The leathery leaves are obovate to oblong, 3.5–10cm long, with under-rolled margins and whitish or brown felt on the undersurface. The sweetly scented flowers are unisexual, and borne in terminal clusters of up to ten male or up to five female flowers. Both types of flower have deep purplish-crimson, strap-shaped, recurved petals. The roundish capsule is up to 2cm long and covered with grey down. [Apr–May, H–HH, PN, New Zealand]

P. crassifolium flowers freely only in mild localities where it can be used as a shelter-hedge.

Pittosporum ralphii is very similar to *P. crassifolium*, differing in its larger leaves which are more sharply narrowed towards the stalk and have flat, not under-rolled margins. The fruit is smaller. [Apr–May, H, PN, New Zealand]

***Pittosporum tenuifolium**, Kohuhu, is a shrub or small tree reaching about 9m high and with blackish young bark. The pale shiny green leaves can be oblong, oval or obovate, 2.5 – 6.5cm long, and hairless with a wavy margin. The flowers are produced in the leaf axils, usually singly but occasionally two or three together, with dark brownish-purple petals, 6 – 12mm long. The capsule is about 1.25cm across and wrinkled when old. [Apr – May, T, PN, New Zealand]

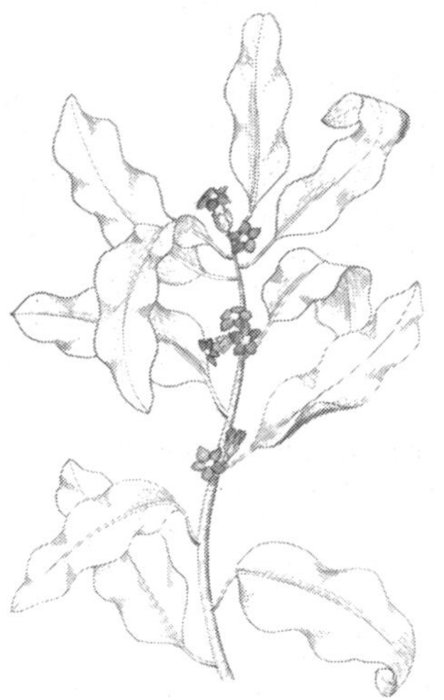

Pittosporum tenuifolium.

P. tenuifolium is the most common species in cultivation and it is sometimes seen as a hedging plant in the west country. The cut foliage is sold by florists. There are a number of fine cultivars.

'Garnettii' has oval or broadly oval leaves up to 5.5cm long and slightly hairy beneath. They have a white margin, flushed with pink in the winter.
'James Stirling' has silvery-green roundish leaves about 1.5cm long.
'Purpureum' has purple leaves and is more tender than the type.
'Silver Queen' has leaves suffused silvery-grey and with a whitish irregular margin.
'Variegatum' has leaves with a creamy-white margin.
'Warnham Gold' has leaves which are golden-yellow when mature.

Pittosporum colensoi is a shrub or small tree reaching 9m in height. The leaves are oblong, oval or somewhat obovate, 3.5 – 10cm long, downy when young, dark glossy green and pale below with netted veins. One to three flowers, 1.5cm across, are borne in the leaf axils. Their dark red petals are oblong and recurved. [Apr – June, T, PN, New Zealand]

Very close to *P. tenuifolium* and sometimes regarded as a subspecies of it.

Pittosporum bicolor reaches 12m high and has a smooth grey bark. The young shoots have a covering of light brown felt. The linear leaves, 2.5 – 6cm long, with the margins rolled under, are hairless and dark green above, felty beneath, at first white, later brown. The fragrant flowers are solitary or in small clusters with oblong petals, 9mm long, which are deep crimson, or yellow marked with red. The globose capsule is 6 – 8mm long. [Nov – Apr, T, PN, SE Australia]

Despite the long flowering season, most of the flowers are borne in the spring.

☼ **Pittosporum patulum** grows to about 4.5m and has downy young shoots which become hairless with age. Young plants have very narrow, lobed leaves, 2.5–5cm long; mature plants have wider shorter leaves which are entire or shallowly toothed. Strongly scented bell-shaped flowers are borne four to eight together in terminal clusters, their deep crimson petals about 12mm long and recurved. The globose capsule is about 8mm long. [May, H, PN, New Zealand]

One of the hardiest of the cultivated Pittosporums which can be tried in colder areas.

☼ **Pittosporum cordifolium** is a shrub 0.6–1.8m tall with slender hairless young shoots. The narrowly-oval or narrowly-obovate leathery leaves are 3.5–8cm long, clustered at the end of the shoots. The flowers, about 8mm wide, are usually unisexual, borne two to five together at the ends of the shoots, musk-scented and with purplish or dull red petals. The capsule is 1.25mm wide, egg-shaped. [Feb–Mar, T, PN, New Zealand]

One of the lowest cultivated species of *Pittosporum* suitable for growing against a low wall.

☼ **Pittosporum undulatum** is a tree, 9–12m tall. The leaves are lanceolate to oblong, 7.5–15cm long, hairless, paler below than above, untoothed and undulate. The fragrant, creamy-white flowers, 1.25–2cm across are borne in a four- to fifteen-flowered terminal cluster, 5–7.5cm across. The almost globose capsule is up to 1.25cm across, orange when mature. [May–July, T, PN, E Australia]

'Variegatum' has the leaves variegated with silver-white.

☼ **Pittosporum dallii** will grow to 6m in the wild; the bark of mature plants is pale grey, the young shoots are reddish. The leaves are clustered towards the ends of the shoots, narrowly oval, 6–11cm long, toothed or untoothed, leathery and hairless when mature. The fragrant flowers are borne in a terminal cluster 2.5–5cm in diameter; each is 6–16mm long with narrowly obovate, white petals. The egg-shaped capsule, about 1.25cm long, has a short apical spine. [June–July, H, PN, New Zealand]

One of the hardiest species, although unfortunately it does not flower well in Britain.

☼ **Pittosporum eugenioides,** the Tarata, is a large shrub or small tree up to 12m with a pale grey trunk and dark hairless twigs. The aromatic leaves are narrowly oval to oblong, 5-12cm long, pale beneath, hairless and with a wavy margin. The flowers are honey-scented, about 4mm wide and carried in terminal clusters. The petals are 3mm long, strap-shaped and pale yellow. The capsule is egg-shaped, 6mm long. [Apr–May, T, PN, New Zealand]

'Variegatum' is hardier than the type and the leaves have an irregular creamy-white margin.

PROSTANTHERA (Labiatae)

An attractive genus of about 50 species native to Australia and Tasmania. The 'Mint Bushes', as they are sometimes called, are shrubby relatives of well-known plants such as Marjoram, Thyme, Sage and Mint itself. All the species of *Prostanthera* cultivated are evergreen shrubs with opposite leaves and small clusters of two-lipped flowers, each with five short lobes and four stamens. The two grown most commonly are not reliably hardy in our climate except in the very mildest districts. They are plants for sheltered warm walls on lime-free soils. Cuttings of young shoots taken in early summer generally root rather readily.

Prostanthera melissifolia var. **parvifolia** is an aromatic shrub reaching as much as 4m in height, the whole plant covered in tiny glands. The ovate to elliptic leaves are small, generally 1–1.5cm long, dark green above but bright green beneath, the margin with or without one or two small teeth. The attractive lilac-mauve flowers have whitish calyces and are borne in small clusters of about eight at the shoot tips. Each flower is a small tubular bell about 12mm long. [Apr–May, T, PN, Origin unknown]

A charming plant which is well worth a try if it can be found for sale. It is generally known in gardens under the name *P. sieberi*, however, this is quite a distinct species, not in cultivation. The type *P. melissifolia* from south-eastern Australia is not in cultivation either. The origin of var.*parvifolia* is unknown but it was originally obtained from a New Zealand nursery about 40 years ago.

***Prostanthera rotundifolia** is a most beautiful shrub 1–4m tall with slender grey-white, downy young shoots. The dark green leaves are oval or roundish, 4–8mm long, usually with several coarse teeth, somewhat shiny above, but dull beneath. Rich bluish-purple or deep lilac flowers about 9mm long, are rather bell-shaped with five rounded lobes; calyx purplish. They form loose terminal clusters of five or more. [Apr–May, T, PN, SE Australia & Tasmania]

This truly delightful plant is seen outdoors most frequently in the south-west of Britain, however, it deserves a try in other districts, if not outdoors then against a sunny conservatory wall. It is quite one of the very best of all of the Tasmanian shrubs and was introduced from there in 1824. Even in the mildest districts it can be killed during a severe winter or in cold spring winds and it is always the wise gardener who keeps a few young rooted cuttings tucked away. In any case plants are not long-lived and need regularly propagating.

PRUNUS (Rosaceae)

For general remarks and the deciduous *P. argentea* and *P. triloba* see p.141.

Prunus ilicifolia = *Cerasus ilicifolius, Laurocerasus ilicifolia*, the Holly-leaved Cherry, is a striking evergreen shrub of dense, compact habit, reaching 2–3m tall. The young branches are hairless and the ovate leaves are leathery and glossy green above, 2.5–5cm long, with a spiny margin. White flowers about 8mm across are borne in drooping racemes 4–8cm long. The small 'cherries' are green at first, then red, but finally purplish-black when ripe. [June–July, T, PN, USA (California)]

This unusual cherry is rare in cultivation: a collector's plant, perhaps more fascinating than beautiful. Young plants are vulnerable to frosts, but once established they prove more resistant. To be seen at its best, *P. ilicifolia* requires a warm sunny wall. *Prunus lyonii* = *P. ilicifolia* var. *occidentalis*, known from Santa Catalina and several other islands off the coast of California is a taller shrub with scarcely spiny leaves and longer racemes of flowers. It is even rarer in cultivation than *P. ilicifolia*.

PYRACANTHA (Rosaceae)

The Firethorn or Pyracantha needs little introduction for it is one of the most common wall shrubs, easily grown and trained and needing very little support. *Pyracantha coccinea* is the common Pyracantha of gardens often represented by its cultivar 'Lalandei'; however, there are seven species in cultivation as well as numerous cultivars.

Pyracanthas are evergreen shrubs with alternate leaves and white flowers. The flowers are attractive at close quarters but they cannot be described as showy. It is the bright berries, produced in the late summer and autumn, that make the firethorns such popular garden plants. The berries vary in colour from yellow to orange or brilliant red and are often borne in great profusion.

Most of the species are hardy, but nevertheless ideal for training against walls and fences, being relatively slow growing. They thrive on most garden soils but dislike cold heavy clays. Their dense growth is perfect for blanketing walls where they can be trained with the minimum of support. However, strong young growths should be carefully trained and tied in to direct the shape of the plant. The current season's growths can be shortened back to a quarter of their length during the summer. Walls or fences of most aspects are suitable except those facing due south. Most of the species and cultivars are good at withstanding severe frosts and biting winds, although *P. angustifolia*, *P. crenulata* and *P. koidzumii* are less hardy than the others.

Young plants should be planted out in March, care being taken to ensure that they are not allowed to dry out, especially during the first season. Plants can be propagated easily from cuttings of the current year's growths, taken in midsummer and inserted in a sandy compost. Seeds are also an easy means of propagation though the resulting plants may not necessarily prove to be as good forms as their parents.

Like apples and pears, the firethorns may suffer attacks of scab, generally seen as a sooty coating on the foliage and fruit, causing die-back and often the loss of many of the leaves. This unsightly disease can be controlled by spraying with Captan two or three times in March and April and twice later in June. Plants may sometimes be infected by fireblight which can suddenly kill an entire plant.

Pyracantha is closely allied to the Hawthorns, *Crataegus*, but differs in having evergreen untoothed or toothed leaves borne on leafy thorns; the leaves are never lobed.

***Pyracantha coccinea** = *Mespilus, Crataegus* or *Cotoneaster pyrancantha* (Pl.21), the Common Pyracanth, is a dense, leafy, evergreen shrub reaching 5m tall, sometimes more. The young shoots are grey with down and bear slender spines. The narrowly oval leaves are finely toothed, 4–6.5cm long, smaller on the flowering shoots, dark shiny green above but paler beneath. The white flowers are borne in dense rounded clusters on shoots springing from the previous season's wood, each flower about 8mm across. Brilliant coral-red berries, 7mm in diameter, are borne in great profusion on established plants. [June, H, PA, S Europe & W Asia]

This is one of the finest of evergreen wall shrubs despite the fact that the berries are much loved by blackbirds and other birds which can soon strip an entire bush in some gardens. The species has been cultivated in Britain since the early part of the seventeenth century. Plants will bear quite hard pruning and are easy to keep in shape, however, mature specimens should never be moved.

'Kasan' is a very hardy form which can be grown in some of the coldest districts of Europe. Unfortunately not often seen in Britain.

***'Lalandei'** is the best cultivar of all with larger leaves than the type and a more upright habit. The large berries are yellowish-red or orange. This firethorn was raised in France by M. Lalande of Angers round about 1874.

Pyracantha crenulata = *Crataegus* or *Mespilus crenulata*, the Nepalese White Thorn, is similar in many respects to the preceding species but the leaves are blunt-tipped, not pointed, and the whole shrub has a more slender and elegant appearance. The flowers are smaller and the berries orange-yellow when ripe. [June–July, HH, PA, Himalaya]

A species far less often seen in cultivation than perhaps it should be. However, it is not hardy in all districts, although some may prefer its more elegant form to that of *P. coccinea*. At one time it was regarded as a variety of *P. coccinea*, and an inferior one at that, but most botanists now agree that the two are quite distinct botanically.

***Pyracantha rogersiana** = *P. crenulata* var.*rogersiana* is a rather erect spiny evergreen shrub to 3.5m tall, with dense growth and greyish-downy young stems which become hairless and pale brown in their second season. The hairless oblanceolate leaves, 1.5–4cm long are tapered at both ends with shallowly toothed margins, each tooth tipped by a characteristic blackish gland. White flowers, 6–7mm across are borne in small rounded clusters. Berries 6mm in diameter are golden-yellow to reddish-orange. [June, H, PA, S China]

A fine shrub of dainty appearance with its small leaves and slender habit. Fortunately it is hardy in most districts and bears a heavy crop of fruit. It is also probably the most attractive species of *Pyracantha* in flower. *Pyracantha rogersiana* was discovered in Yunnan in 1889 by Père Delavay, but it was not introduced to cultivation until 1911 when that intrepid plant hunter George Forrest collected it in fruit.

'Aurantiaca' is an orange-berried form.

***'Flava'** is an excellent form with yellow berries.

'Golden Charmer' and **'Orange Charmer'** are both hybrids raised in Germany between *P. coccinea* and *P. rogersiana* and are well worth growing if they can be obtained. The former has orange-yellow berries and the latter orange-red berries, both about 9mm in diameter. Both these hybrid cultivars are apparently resistant to scab.

Pyracantha koidzumii = *Cotoneaster koidzumii* is allied to *P. rogersiana* but the leaves are always untoothed except on vigorous young growths. The flower stalks are downy as are the calyces. The berries are deep orange. [June–July, HH, PA, Taiwan]

This species, commonly grown in the south-eastern USA, is rather rare in Britain. It appears hardy in the south on a sheltered wall where it will fruit freely.

'Mohave' is a fine hybrid between *P. coccinea* and *P. koidzumii* raised in the USA. It has large orange-red berries from mid-August onwards and is apparently scab-resistant.

Pyracantha atalantioides = *P. gibbsii* is a rather erect evergreen shrub up to 7m tall, though often less. The branches are spineless, the young ones downy at first but becoming bright olive-brown in the autumn. The oblong or oval leaves are finely toothed or untoothed, 2.5–7.5cm long, dark shiny green above but paler and duller beneath. The white flowers are borne in rounded clusters 4–5cm across on short leafy twigs from the previous year's wood, each flower 8–12mm across. The scarlet berries are small, 5–6mm in diameter, and borne from autumn well into the new year. [May–June, H, PA, Central China]

This species is a vigorous grower introduced early in the twentieth century. It is closely related to *P. crenulata* but is much hardier than that species, with the added advantage of being quite without spines. The berries are smaller than most of the species but have the advantage over species like *P. coccinea* in persisting until March, and apparently are not such a delicacy to birds.

'Flava' has yellow berries.

◐ ***Pyracantha 'Watereri'** is a fine cross produced between *P.atalantioides* and *P.rogersiana*. It is a vigorous shrub to 3m tall with densely downy young stems and elliptic leaves 2–3.5cm long, which are minutely toothed in the upper third and downy beneath. The large berries are deep orange-red.

This is a fine cultivar which does not reach the height of most of the species and is therefore more suitable for the average wall, especially on bungalows, by doorways or between windows.

◐ ***Pyracantha angustifolia** = *Cotoneaster angustifolia* is an evergreen, somewhat spiny shrub 3–4m in height with dense growth and more or less horizontal lateral branches. The young stems are greyish-downy at first. The narrowly oblong leaves are dark green above but grey-felted beneath, 1.5–6cm long, only the largest with a few tiny teeth near the apex. White flowers are borne in dense clusters about 5cm across, each 6–7mm in diameter. The brilliant orange-yellow berries, 7–10mm in diameter, are retained on the bush well into the new year.[June, HH, PA, W China]

A beautiful species when seen heavily laden with fruit, especially after a good hot summer, although perhaps the least attractive in flower. *Pyracantha angustifolia* is not reliably hardy in the less mild districts and will require the shelter of a tall wall or fence. The berries are present until about March which gives them a great advantage over *P. coccinea* whose fruits have generally been eaten by birds before Christmas.

◐ **Pyracantha crenato-serrata** =*P. yunnanensis, P. gibbsii* var.*yunnanensis*, is an evergreen shrub up to 9m tall, closely related to *P. atalantioides* and *P. rogersiana* but differing from both in its rather coarsely toothed leaves which are broadest above the middle, 2.5–8cm long. The flower stalks are distinctly downy. [June, H, PA, China]

This species has never been widely cultivated and is certainly not so fine a plant as the two cultivars below which probably have *P. crenato-serrata* as one of their parents. The berries will survive until the early spring, birds permitting.

'Taliensis' = *P. crenulata* var.*taliensis* is intermediate between *P. crenato-serrata* and *P. rogersiana*. A handsome plant with its shiny yellow berries which are mature in October, but alas generally gone long before those of *P. crenato-serrata*. This plant probably originally came from the Tali Range in Yunnan.

***'Orange Glow'** is a vigorous, free-fruiting hybrid from Holland which probably has its parentage in *P. coccinea* and *P. crenato-serrata*. The berries are bright orange-red, and more or less tangerine-shaped. This cultivar is apparently scab-resistant or at least less prone to it than most of the species.

RHAPHIOLEPIS (Rosaceae)

A small genus of about 15 species closely allied to the apples, pears and quinces, grown chiefly for their attractive racemes or panicles of five-petaled flowers that terminate the leafy shoots in the early summer. The alternate leaves are leathery and short-stalked. They are seen at their best when planted against a warm, sunny, sheltered wall and prefer well drained soils. Plants resent disturbance and should be bought as young pot-grown specimens. Only two species are cultivated, both are evergreen and can be propagated from seed or cuttings of half-ripened wood.

☼ **Rhaphiolepis indica** = *Crataegus indica* is a graceful shrub growing to 2.5m with narrowly lanceolate, toothed leaves, 5–7.5cm long. Pretty white flowers tinged with pink, about 1.5cm across, are borne in short racemes at the shoot tips.

Plate 19 Evergreen Shrubs 1 *Bigelowia graveolens* (p.172), 2 *Callistemon salignus* (p.174), 3 *Ceanothus dentatus* (p.185), 4 *Clianthus puniceus* (p.189), 5 *Camellia japonica* 'Lady Ardilaun' (p.176), 6 *C. japonica* 'Kimberley' (p.178).

1
2
3
5
4
6

1
2
3
4
5

They are further enhanced by a large number of pink stamens which point upwards from the centre. [June, HH, PS, China]

Rhaphiolepis umbellata = *Laurus umbellata, Rhaphiolepis japonica,* is a sturdy shrub of rounded habit growing to 3.5m with downy young stems and leathery oval leaves that are tapered at the base and toothed towards the top, 4–9cm long. The fragrant white flowers are borne in stiff terminal panicles or racemes, each flower about 2cm across. These are followed by small pear-shaped fruits, 1.25cm long that turn bluish-black when ripe. [June, HH, PS, Japan & Korea]

An attractive shrub for a sheltered position, although it is probably hardier than is generally supposed.

Rhaphiolepis × delacourii a hybrid between the two species mentioned above is a bushy shrub to 3m with leaves like *R. umbellata*. The attractive rose pink flowers are 1.25–2cm across, being borne in terminal panicles up to 10cm long. [May–June, H]

First raised by Delacour, a gardener at Villa Allerton, Cannes, in the last century, although this handsome plant flowers in the late spring often some flowers are produced out of season. 'Coates Crimson' is a particularly good cultivar.

RHAPHITHAMNUS (Verbenaceae)

There are only two species in this genus which comes from Chile and Argentina. They have opposite simple leaves. The calyx is five-toothed and the corolla has four or five unequal lobes. There are four stamens. Only one species is cultivated.

Rhaphithamnus spinosus = *R. cyanocarpus* is a shrub or small tree of dense growth, reaching 7.5m tall. The young shoots are covered with rather bristly down and armed with spines; on year-old branches these spines are about 2.5cm long. The opposite leaves are often borne in threes, broadly ovate, 0.6–1.8cm long, sharply toothed and paler on the underside. Pale blue or lilac flowers are produced singly or in pairs in the leaf axils, each with a very short bristly stalk, and a tubular corolla 1–1.25cm long. The globose fruit, 0.8–1.25cm long, is bright blue when ripe. [Apr–June, T–HH, PA, Chile & Argentina]

This shrub is more attractive in fruit than in flower. It does best in the south and west of Britain. It was first introduced in the early 1840's by William Lobb. Propagation is usually by cuttings. In catalogues it is sometimes listed incorrectly as *Rhaphithamus*.

RIBES (Grossulariaceae)

Ribes is the Currant genus, containing both the Blackcurrant, *R. nigrum* and the Redcurrant, *R. rubrum*. It is a deciduous or evergreen genus of some 150 species spread across nothern temperate regions and down the Andes. The alternate leaves are usually three or five-lobed. The flowers are carried in racemes or few-flowered clusters. The most showy part of the flower is the receptacle which bears four or five sepals and a similar number of petals, the latter usually small and inconspicuous. There are four or five stamens. The fruit is a berry, usually edible.

The Redcurrant can be grown as a cordon against walls and fences, see p.281. The often deciduous *R. speciosum* is described below for convenience.

Ribes viburnifolium is an unarmed shrub growing to about 2.8m in height. The very young shoots are slightly downy, covered in many glands. The coarsely

---

Plate 20 Evergreen Shrubs 1 *Crinodendron hookerianum* (p.193), 2 *Cytisus battandieri* (p.194), 3 *Feijoa sellowiana* (p.200), 4 *Desfontainia spinosa* (p.196), 5 *Garrya elliptica* (p.202).

toothed, oval or ovate leaves, 1.8–4cm long, are shiny and hairless above, dotted with glands below. Dull pink flowers, about 8mm across with spreading sepals, are borne in terminal erect racemes about 2.5cm long. The oval red berries are 8mm long. [Apr, T, PA, Mexico (Baja California).]

Not one of the most attractive *Ribes* and very tender, suitable only for the very mildest localities. The aromatic leaves smell of turpentine when crushed.

***Ribes speciosum** (Pl.15) is a semi-evergreen, spiny shrub which can lose all its leaves in a bad winter, and grows to 3·7m tall. The reddish young shoots are clothed with gland-tipped bristles. Leaves, three- or five-lobed, 1.5–3cm long and wide, and usually hairless, with some marginal teeth. The bright red flowers which resemble little fuchsias are borne several together in pendulous clusters. The receptable is glandular and about 1.25cm long, bearing four erect sepals and four petals; long red stamens protrude about 1.8cm beyond the receptacle. The red berry, 1.25cm long, is glandular-bristly. [Apr–June, H, PA, USA (California).]

A lovely *Ribes* which deserves to be more widely grown. It can be grown in the open in mild areas but needs wall-protection in cooler places. It is best increased by layering. The small flowers reward close inspection as they are most beautifully formed.

ROMNEYA (Papaveraceae)

A genus of two species only, commonly referred to as 'Tree Poppies'. They are delightful plants with their somewhat crumpled, showy white flowers which have a large central 'eye' of golden stamens. Both species are subshrubby with rather fleshy cut leaves. The flowers have three sepals, six petals and numerous stamens. The fruit is a capsule, similar to that of the Poppy.

Romneyas are plants for sunny sheltered spots — they come from the warm valleys of California and Mexico. They will succeed in the open garden in mild districts but look magnificent against a wall where they generally grow taller. They are not the easiest plants to establish and young container-grown plants should be purchased, planting them out in the spring. Once established, however, they will increase by the production of suckers, often spreading over quite a wide area. Plants should not be moved once established and suckers cut away from the parent plant may prove difficult to establish, mainly because they often have a very small fibrous root system. Success is generally increased by cutting such 'offsets' hard back the moment they are dug up, removing them from the ground with a good ball of soil. Seed is sometimes available and this a more reliable way of increasing stock, but young plants will take a number of years to flower.

***Romneya coulteri** (Pl.15), the Californian Tree Poppy, or Matiliya Poppy, is a subshrub reaching 1.3m in height depending on the situation. The erect stems are rather flexuous, branched only in the upper half. The bluish-green leaves are cut into a number of lanceolate or oval, pointed lobes. The flower-buds are beaked, smooth with purple-tipped sepals. The large white flowers are solitary, 10–15cm across. The fruit capsules are covered in spreading bristles [July–Oct, HH, PN, USA (California) & Mexico]

A delightful and beautiful plant, which, once established, will reward the grower with flowers over a long season.

Romneya trichocalyx is very similar to *R. coulteri* but with more slender stems and bristly, not beaked flowerbuds. [July–Sept, HH, PN, USA (SW California)]

Romneya trichocalyx is rarely seen in cultivation and as a garden plant has no advantages over its cousin.

Romneya × hybrida is a fine hybrid between the two species which was raised in the United States. The cultivar 'White Cloud' is a vigorous large-flowered clone from this cross.

RUBUS (Rosaceae)

The 250 or so species in this large genus include the Blackberry, the Raspberry and a host of lesser known Brambles. The genus has an almost world-wide distribution and the complexities of *Rubus* classification are such that many a botanist has struggled over their study. Most of the problems seem to arise from the wide range of variation seen in many 'species', and interpretation is hindered by the fact that many produce fruit apomictically — that is without true fertilisation. The gardener need not trouble himself with the complexities of classification.

Apart from the few grown for their delicious fruits there are quite a number grown for their handsome stems and leaves or their showy flowers. Most cultivated species are best suited to the wild garden where their vigorous and often rampant characters can be seen to advantage. However, some of the less hardy ones need the protection of a wall or fence.

The cultivated species of *Rubus*, often collectively called Rubi, present little problem to the grower, succeeding on most average garden soils. The scandent or weak-stemmed ones require the support of a wall, fence or trellis, or alternatively a stout post stuck into the soil, to which the main stems are tied. They are rambling shrubs, not climbers in the true sense. Pruning consists mostly of cutting out old or unwanted wood and shortening back extra-long stems. This can be carried out during the winter or in the case of the half-hardy or tender species, in the early spring. Young shoots need to be tied in carefully to maintain some order. Propagation from cuttings or layerings is generally fairly easy, at least of the species mentioned here. Deciduous species are treated here with the evergreen species.

Rubus cissoides = *R. australis* var. *cissoides* is a rambling shrub forming a dense tangle of zig-zag stems, which in its native habitat reach the tops of quite lofty trees, however, in cultivation it can often be kept to 2–4m. The main stems are smooth but the side shoots are covered in small reddish prickles. The leaves consist of three to five leaflets radiating out from a central point. The rather leathery leaflets, glossy green above, are generally ovate or subrounded, 6–15cm long, with a finely but sparsely toothed margin. Small white flowers, about 12mm across, are borne in large handsome branched panicles anything up to 60cm in length. The flowers are unusual in being unisexual, a character shared with the next species. Small bramble fruits, about 7mm across are reddish-orange when ripe. [June–Aug, HH, PS, New Zealand.]

A handsome species for a large old wall in a sheltered spot but quite unsuitable for the small garden where it would quickly swamp its neighbours — or indeed your neighbours. Fruits are only produced when both a male and a female plant are grown side by side.

This species is sometimes seen under the name *R. australis*, a quite distinct and little-grown species.

Rubus squarrosus = *R. cissoides* var. *pauperatus*, closely related to the previous species, is a peculiar plant which forms a mass of tangled stems beset with tiny white prickles. The curious, thread-like leaves are reduced mainly to their midribs giving them a spidery appearance. Small yellowish flowers are carried in panicles. Female plants bear orange-red fruits, but they are seldom produced in cultivation in this country. [June–Aug, HH, PS, New Zealand]

An interesting *Rubus*, although it could scarcely be described as handsome or beautiful. Those who study curious growth forms will be intrigued by it!

◐ **Rubus flagelliflorus** is a rather graceful evergreen to 3–4m tall with slender stems that are covered in white felt when young as well as a number of tiny recurved prickles. The dark green leaves are often marbled above, this contrasting strangely with the yellowish-felted undersurface. They are generally ovate and pointed, or heart-shaped, 7–18cm long with a finely toothed margin. White flowers are borne in small lateral clusters and succeeded by shiny edible blackberries about 12mm across. [June–Aug, HH, PS, C & W China]

A handsome species which was first introduced to cultivation by E.H. Wilson, in 1901. It receives its name from the numerous whippy shoots produced from the base of the plant annually, these generally flowering in their second season. Plants are best trained to a post or pillar or trellis work against which the shoots, which may often grow 1.5–2m in a single season, can be trained. In the milder districts of the country *R. flagelliflorus* is almost completely hardy.

☼ **Rubus henryi** is another quick-growing and vigorous evergreen scrambling species producing long whip-like stems which have a sparse covering of small prickles. Plants may attain 6m tall in a suitable position. The leaves are three-lobed, or have three distinct leaflets, 6–15cm long, dark green above but with a thick coat of white felt beneath. Pink flowers, 18–20mm across, but of little beauty, are borne in small clusters, either laterally or at the shoot tips. The small shiny 'blackberries' are about 12mm across [June–Aug, HH, PS, C & W China]

Another species introduced at the turn of the century by E.H. Wilson, *R. henryi* is an elegant and rapid grower, grown as much for its handsome foliage and growth as for its attractive fruits. It is particularly striking trained against a post with the lesser growths allowed to arch outwards. The form in cultivation has leaves with three distinct leaflets and is generally referred to as var. *bambusarum*.

◐ ***Rubus hupehensis** is a scrambling evergreen with slender dark stems which have a sparse covering of whitish down when young, together with a few curved prickles. The oblong or lanceolate leaves are long-pointed, 7.5–11cm long, with a finely toothed margin, smooth above except for tiny bristles spaced along the main veins but covered with grey felt beneath. The white flowers are borne in small clusters and are followed by red fruits which turn black when ripe. [June–Aug, HH, PS, C China]

An interesting *Rubus* grown mainly for its handsome and quite distinctive foliage. The flowers are of no real beauty but are easy to recognise because of the glandular hairs which cover the flower stalks.

☼ ***Rubus lineatus** is a semi-evergreen or even deciduous bramble 1–3m tall or forming a broad mass over a low wall. The stems are slender and downy with a few tiny prickles. The handsome leaves are dark green above but shiny-white and silky beneath with numerous parallel veins. Each leaf is divided into 3–5 oblong or elliptic leaflets which radiate out from a central point, each leaflet 6.5–23cm long with a fine saw-edged margin. White flowers of little beauty are produced in small clusters at the leaf bases and succeeded by small red or yellowish fruits [June–Aug, HH, PS, SE Asia, SW China & E Himalaya]

This is the finest species for grace and foliage: mature plants can look very beautiful despite their rather poor flowers. Plants require a sunny sheltered spot and are very fine trained on a fence or trellis if the correct aspect can be found. *R. lineatus* was introduced to cultivation in 1905 from seed collected in Yunnan by George Forrest.

Rubus playfairianus is a rambling evergreen or semi-evergreen shrub of graceful habit with slender stringy stems beset with tiny hooked prickles and covered in whitish-down when young. The leaves have three or five leaflets radiating from a central point. The leaflets themselves are lanceolate, 2–15cm long, dark green above but covered in grey felt beneath. Small white flowers, scarcely 12mm across, are borne in small close-branched clusters at the shoot tips. Fruits are small 'blackberries' the size of a raspberry. [June–Aug, HH, PS, C & W China]

A particularly good species for a stout post or trellis where its handsome and rather distinctive foliage can be best appreciated.

***Rubus laciniatus** = *R. fruticosus* var. *laciniatus* is a deciduous species which deserves consideration amongst those species suitable for culture on walls or other sheltered sites such as fences or pergolas. It is indeed amongst the most striking of all Rubi. The Cut-leaved Bramble is a vigorous deciduous rambling shrub, 2–3m high or more, with hairy angled stems bearing stout curved prickles. The handsome leaves of ferny appearance, consist of three or five deeply lobed and toothed leaflets which are downy, particularly beneath. The leaflets vary greatly in size but are mostly between 5–9cm long. The small flowers are rather dingy pinkish-white of little beauty, but are borne in large terminal panicles. They are succeeded by numerous large juicy 'blackberries' of excellent flavour. [June–Aug, H, PS, Origin unknown]

This handsome bramble is worth growing for its attractive foliage as well as for its mouth-watering fruits. Its origin is not known but it was in cultivation in the seventeenth century. It may be indigenous to Britain or, more likely, a sport of another species. *R. laciniatus* is a fine plant, particularly good on boundary walls and fences or on pergolas if carefully trained. Seedlings often appear close to the parent plant and generally grow true to type. Some forms have been especially selected for their fine fruits and there is even a thornless one. *R. laciniatus* is naturalised in parts of North America.

'Oregon Thornless Blackberry' is the best cultivar producing large crops of juicy berries. Also known as 'Thornless Evergreen'.

SALVIA (Labiatae)

A genus best known for the culinary sage, *Salvia officinalis*, commonly grown in gardens and the scarlet bedding Salvia, *S. coccinea*, beloved of formal bedding in parks and gardens. However, the genus is represented by over 500 species distributed in temperate and subtropical regions of both the northern and southern hemispheres. Most are aromatic or pungent herbs or shrubs with opposite leaves and two-lipped flowers in whorls, clusters or spikes.

Four species only are suitable for culture against a warm sunny wall or fence in a sheltered position. They prefer a light, well-drained soil. Propagation is from cuttings in midsummer, overwintering young plants in a frost-free place before they are planted out the following spring.

Salvia microphylla = *S. grahamii*, is a small shrub, 0.5–1.2m tall, with hairless or slightly downy stems. Oval blunt leaves, 1.5–3.5cm long, are short-stalked and more or less hairless. Deep crimson flowers, 20–25mm long, which turn to purplish-red, have two whitish spots on the lower lip and are borne in 'spikes' up to 15cm long. [June–Sept, HH, PS, Mexico]

A variable plant generally found in catalogues under the name *S. grahamii*. When crushed the leaves smell strongly of blackcurrant. Plants are half-hardy in most districts but more or less hardy in the mildest places.

Salvia neurepia = *S. grahamii* var. *neurepia* is very similar, although often taller, with larger, paler, or yellowish-green leaves, 3–5cm long, clearly downy beneath. Larger, clear rosy-carmine flowers have a rather flat lower lip. [Aug–Oct, HH, PS, Mexico]

With its larger flowers an all together finer plant than *S. microphylla*.

***Salvia greggii** is a small shrub up to 1.2m tall with more or less hairless slender branches. The leaves are rather leathery, narrowly oblong, untoothed, 2–4cm long. Flowers six to eight together, carmine or purplish-red, each flower about 25mm long with a narrow slightly glandular calyx, are borne in a short spike 5–7.5cm long. [Aug–Oct, HH, PS, Mexico & USA (Texas)]

A splendid showy species well worth growing if plants can be obtained and especially valuable for its late-flowering habit. Less hardy than *S. microphylla*.

'Alba' is a white flowered form.

Salvia rutilans the Pineapple-scented Sage, is another small shrub or subshrub up to 1m tall. The heart-shaped, softly downy leaves are scented of pineapple when crushed. Bright scarlet flowers are borne in leafy spike-like panicles, each flower with a slender tube and a deflexed lower lip [July–Oct, HH, PS]

Another attractive red-flowered species. Its origin is unknown but it appears to have been in cultivation since at least 1873. It comes close to the Mexican *S. elegans*. *S. rutilans* is a good subject for a cool greenhouse where it will flower through the winter.

SOPHORA (Leguminosae)

A tropical and warm temperate genus of about 50 evergreen and deciduous trees and shrubs. They have alternate odd-pinnate leaves with opposite leaflets. The typical pea-flowers are borne in racemes or panicles and have a calyx with five short teeth and an orbicular to oblong-obovate standard.

Beautiful shrubs with attractive flowers. They should be tried more often and do best in the warmer areas where the wood is more readily ripened and better able to stand winter cold. Young container-grown plants should be planted out in the spring. Older plants do not transplant readily. Most are easily raised from seed. The deciduous *S. davidii* is included here.

Sophora tetraptera (including var. *grandiflora*), the Kowhai, is an evergreen or semi-deciduous shrub or small tree 5–12m tall. The branches are spreading or drooping. The young shoots, leaf-stalks, flower-stalks and calyces are all brown-hairy. The leaves, 4–15cm long, have ten to twenty pairs of leaflets, each 1.25–3.5cm in length and silky above and below. Golden-yellow flowers, 2.5–5cm long, are borne in drooping racemes of up to ten. The pod is 5–20cm long, strongly constricted between each seed, and four-winged. [May-June, T, PN, New Zealand]

A lovely plant for a south- or west-facing wall. In a good summer it will produce abundant seed.

***Sophora microphylla** = *S.tetraptera* var. *microphylla* (Pl.21), is very similar to *S. tetraptera* but has smaller, more numerous, deeper-green leaflets and shorter fruit-pods. [May, HH, PN, New Zealand]

This species is hardier than *S. tetraptera* and is equally beautiful and certainly a very distinctive wall shrub, guaranteed to attract attention.

Sophora macrocarpa is an evergreen tree growing 6–12m tall. The young growth is clothed in brownish-red down. The leaves, 7.5–12.5cm long, have 6–24 pairs of leaflets which are 2–4cm long and downy, especially on the underside. Yellow flowers, 2.5–3cm long, with a downy calyx, are carried in short racemes of up to twelve. The pod is 10cm or more long, constricted between the seeds, but not winged. [May, T–HH,PN, Chile]

Similar to *S. tetraptera* but with wingless pods. It has the advantage of flowering when still quite young.

* **Sophora secundiflora** is an evergreen tree 7.5–10.5m tall. The leaves, 10–15cm long, have three to four pairs of leaflets which are 2.5–5cm long and notched at the apex. Violet-blue flowers, about 2.5cm long and smelling of violets, are produced in terminal racemes 5–7.5cm long. The pod, up to 20cm long, contains scarlet seeds. [Apr, T, PN, SW USA to Mexico]

This pretty shrub can be grown only in the mildest countries but it has not yet been tried very much in Britain and should be grown more in the future.

***Sophora davidii** = *S. viciifolia* is smaller than the species described above, growing only to 3m in height. It also differs in being deciduous. The young branches are covered with greyish down and the year-old branches are spiny. The leaves are 3.5–6.5cm long with six to ten pairs of oval or obovate leaflets, 6–9mm long and silky-hairy below. The terminal racemes measure 5–7cm in length. The flowers are white to bluish-violet, about 1.8cm long and with a violet-blue downy calyx. The pod is 5–6.5cm long, downy and with constrictions between the seeds; it is not winged. [June, H, PN, China]

A beautiful plant which appreciates full sun and a good loamy soil.

TELOPEA (Proteaceae)

A small genus of evergreen Australian shrubs with alternate leathery leaves and flowers borne in dense terminal racemes. The fruit is a leathery capsule containing winged seeds.

***Telopea truncata**, Tasmanian Waratah, is a shrub reaching 7.5m tall, with thick, brown-hairy shoots. Leaves thick, oblanceolate, 5–12cm long, sometimes with two or three large teeth, glaucous on the underside. Young leaves often have a deeply notched apex. Bright crimson flowers, about 2.5cm long, have a slender perianth which is split to expose the style which protrudes, and terminates in a large globose stigma; they produce abundant nectar. [June, H, PN, Tasmania]

A very beautiful shrub which is usually hardy provided it has wall-protection. It does not like limy or dry conditions and grows best with its roots in the shade and its head in the sun. It can be grown on an east-facing wall but in northern areas it may need extra winter protection such as sacking or straw. It well deserves to be grown more frequently.

TEUCRIUM (Labiatae)

A large genus of attractive small herbs or subshrubs belonging to the deadnettle family which contains such well-known plants as the salvias, mints, thymes and rosemary, many of which are aromatic herbs or shrubs, whose leaves are used to add flavour to cooking. Only one species of *Teucrium* is included here.

☼ **Teucrium fruticans** = *T. latifolium*, the Shrubby Germander, is a pretty, rather loosely branched and untidy evergreen subshrub, reaching 1m high against a wall. The square stems are covered in white woolly felt and bear opposite pairs of blunt oval leaves, 1.5–4cm long. The dark green upper surface of the leaf blade contrasts strongly with the white-felted lower surface. The flowers are borne in loose racemes at the stem tips, one flower to each leaf or branch. The colour ranges from pale purple to lavender, each flower about 25mm across, with two small upper petal lobes and three larger lower lobes, the anthers arching out of the centre of the flower on long filaments. [July–Oct, HH, PN, S & SW Europe & N Africa]

This attractive species deserves a place in any garden where a warm sheltered niche can be provided. It prefers a light loamy soil and no pruning, save to remove dead growth in the spring and to trim the bush after the main flush of flowers — in late August. In the milder parts of the country it is often grown away from the confines of the wall environment but even there may succumb during a harsh winter. Plants are easily propagated from cuttings of half ripened wood struck during August.

The Shrubby Germander has been cultivated in this country since the early part of the eighteenth century.

***'Azureum'** is a delightful plant, more tender than the type, with deeper blue flowers. The original plants came from the Atlas Mountains in Morocco.

VESTIA (Solanaceae)

This genus contains only a single species which is closely related to the more widely known *Cestrum*.

☼ ***Vestia foetida** = *Cantua ligustifolia, Periphragmos foetidus, Vestia lycioides* (Pl.21), the Huevil, is a semi-erect rather densely branched evergreen shrub 1.5–2m tall, the young stems slightly downy at first. The alternate leaves are bright shiny green and like the stems have a rather unpleasant scent when bruised. They are generally oblong or elliptic, untoothed, 2.5–5cm long and hairless. The graceful semi-nodding flowers are pale yellow, tubular, 25–32mm long, the stamens and style protruding prominently beyond the mouth of the corolla which has five short spreading lobes. The fruit is a small many-seeded capsule [May–July, HH, PN, Central Chile]

This charming plant is probably rather hardier than is generally supposed and will succeed by a sunny, sheltered south-facing wall in milder districts. It is sometimes seen as a greenhouse or conservatory plant. It has been cultivated in Britain since about 1815 and is readily raised from seed or from short cuttings struck during midsummer. In catalogues it is sometimes still found under the name *V. lycioides*.

VIBURNUM (Caprifoliaceae)

A very popular genus of plants in our gardens, grown for their pleasing shape and fragrant flowers and some for their showy display of bright berries in the autumn. Some species are well known, the Guelder Rose, *V. opulus*, the Wayfaring Tree, *V. lantana*, and the deliciously scented winter-flowering *V. farreri*, better known to most gardens under the more familiar name of *V. fragrans*.

The genus is native mainly to the temperate regions of the Northern Hemisphere where there are over one hundred distinct species, however, a few others reach south-east Asia and South America. Most are quite hardy though a few require the protection of a warm sunny wall. The winter flowering *V. farreri*, and the hybrids *V.* ×*burkwoodii* and *V.* ×*bodnantense* are often seen at their best against a sheltered wall or fence where their blooms are less affected by frosts and chill winds, although they are all quite hardy. Viburnums mostly relish a deep moist loamy soil and rich supplies of leaf mould dug into the surface soil or added as a summer mulch. They are, in the main, easy to propagate from late summer cuttings struck in a propagating frame, or by layerings. Seed is erratic in germinating and may not come true to type in some instances.

Viburnums are shrubs or small trees with opposite, generally simple, toothed leaves. The inflorescence is either a small cluster of flowers or a broad umbel-like cluster or panicle, borne either at the stem tips or on short lateral branches. Individual flowers are white or pink and have a small five-lobed calyx with the ovary beneath (inferior) and a cup, funnel or trumpet-shaped corolla with five rounded petal lobes. There are five stamens which join the tube of the corolla below the mouth. In some species the outer flowers are much larger and flattish and quite sterile without any sexual parts. These act as 'flags' to passing insects, attracting them to the flower clusters and hence to the fertile flowers. The same situation is found in Hydrangeas. In some cultivated forms the whole flower cluster is replaced by sterile florets of this type, which are highly ornamental in gardens but of little use for the proliferation of the species. The fruits are small berries, red, blue or black. Species grown for their fruits should be planted in pairs to ensure a good set.

Viburnum×burkwoodii, *V. carlesii*× *V. utile*, is a charming hybrid, a semi-evergreen shrub reaching 2.5m tall, sometimes more, with brown-downy young shoots. The ovate leaves are dark green and slightly bronzed above, but brown-downy beneath, 4–10cm long with a finely toothed margin. The fragrant flowers are pink in bud but soon open to pure white, borne in five-rayed clusters, 6–9cm across. Individual flowers are about 12mm across with five spreading petal lobes. [Mar–May, H, PA, Garden origin]

One of the most popular and most widely planted of all Viburnums, quite hardy but relishing the shelter of a high wall or fence. There are a number of fine clones besides the original cross. These include 'Anne Russell', 'Chenaultii' and 'Park Farm Hybrid' which vary slightly in habit and flower size.

Viburnum japonicum = *Cornus japonicus, Viburnum macrophyllum*, is a sturdy evergreen shrub of slow growth, ultimately reaching 2m or more high, the young shoots thick and hairless. Leathery, ovate or rounded leaves, 7.5–15cm long, are toothed in the upper half only, hairless, rough and dark glossy green above but pale beneath. Very fragrant, white flowers about 10mm across, are borne in rounded, short-stalked clusters 7–llcm across. The ovoid red berries are 7–8mm long. [June, H, PN, Japan]

A handsome slow-growing shrub said to attain the proportion of a small tree in its native haunts. *Viburnum japonicum* is quite hardy in most districts but it is slow-growing and is probably seen at its best in a warm niche under a sunny wall. It well deserves to be more widely known. It is sometimes confused with the next species.

Viburnum odoratissimum = *V. awabuki* is a much larger shrub than the preceding species, attaining 4–7m in height or more. The young wood is noticeably warty and the leathery evergreen leaves are oval, 8–20cm long. Fragrant, pure white flowers are borne in panicles 8–16cm long. The berries are red at first but finally ripen to black. [Aug–Sept, HH, PS, NE India & SE Asia, including the Philippines & Celebes, Japan & Taiwan]

An attractive plant only reliably hardy in the mildest districts of the south-west of Britain. Elsewhere a wall or fence of south or west aspect is necessary if plants are to succeed. The species has been cultivated in Europe since 1818. The leathery leaves often assume an attractive reddish or bronze tint during the autumn and winter.

Viburnum suspensum = *V. sandankwa* is another evergreen species, reaching 2–4m in height. The young branches are warty and downy. The leathery leaves are ovate or oval, pointed, toothed in the upper half or scarcely toothed, glossy green and hairless, 5–13cm long. Fragrant white flowers, borne in flattish clusters 6–10cm across, are often flushed with pink in bud. The rounded red berries are only rarely produced in cultivation. [Mar–Apr, HH, PN, Taiwan & Ryukyus Is.]

A rare species in cultivation, only reliably hardy in the mildest districts of south-western Britain. Unfortunately *V. suspensum* is a shy flowerer, requiring long hot summers to prove otherwise. This species has been cultivated in Japan for several centuries.

***Viburnum macrocephalum** is a deciduous or semi-evergreen shrub, up to 7m tall, forming a broad rounded bush with scurfy-downy young shoots. Ovate or oblong leaves with a rounded base, 5–10cm long, are dull green above but paler and downy beneath. Pure white flowers, all sterile, are borne in dense globular heads 8–16cm across, with individual florets 25–32mm across. [May–June, HH, PA, China]

A very beautiful shrub, perhaps the finest of all Viburnums, introduced from China in 1844 by the plant collector Robert Fortune, but long before cultivated in Chinese gardens. The plants are quite sterile and are not known from a wild habitat. The wild counterpart which has small fertile flower heads ringed by sterile florets is known as forma *keteleeri* but is probably not in cultivation in Europe. *V. macrocephalum* is half-hardy in most districts and requires wall-protection. Plants can be kept in bounds by careful pruning immediately flowering ceases.

Viburnum rigidum = *V. rugosum, V. tinus* var. *strictum, V.tinus* var. *rigidum*, is a bushy evergreen shrub 2–3m tall, with hairy young shoots. Plants are not unlike a large-leaved *V. tinus* which is a widely grown species. Leaves oval, untoothed, 5–15cm long, and dark dull green above, paler and greyish-downy beneath, with a hairy edge. White flowers with pink stigmas, are borne in dense flattish clusters 7.5–11.5cm across. Egg-shaped blue berries, 6–8mm long, become black when fully ripe. [Feb–Apr, HH, PA, Canary Is.]

V. rigidum is more or less hardy in the coastal south and south-west of Britain, however it is scarcely a better plant than the hardier and more easily obtainable *V. tinus* and probably not worth wall space in a small garden.

Viburnum rhytidophyllum is a rather upright evergreen shrub 3–7m tall with stout main branches, the young shoots covered in a felt of greyish down. Large, oblong or oval leaves, 7–19cm long, are rough and shiny deep green above, grey-felted beneath. Dull yellowish-white flowers, 6mm across are borne in large umbel-like heads 10–20cm across. Oval berries 8mm long, are red at first but shining black when ripe. [May–June, H, PA, C & W China] ◐

A handsome shrub introduced from China in 1900 by E.H. Wilson for Messrs. Veitch. Although hardy, plants need a sheltered niche to be seen at their best, for the leaves can become unsightly and torn in cold buffeting winds. A semi-shaded wall is ideal where space permits. Plants like a richer soil than most other *Viburnums*. Unfortunately *V. rhytidophyllum* is often disliked by gardeners because of its rather loose ragged appearance and rather dingy flowers, however, well grown specimens can be very handsome.

forma **roseum** has pink buds which open white with a faint flush of pink. Finer than the more typical form.

The popular deciduous species *V. farreri* = *V. fragrans* and the hybrid *V.* × *bodnantense* can be found on p.145.

WEINMANNIA (Cunoniaceae)

There are some 170 species of *Weinmannia*, found mainly in the tropics. They are evergreen shrubs or trees with opposite, simple or pinnate, leaves. The small flowers are borne in clusters or erect racemes. The flowers have four or five sepals and petals and eight to ten stamens. The fruit is a rather leathery capsule, containing many seeds which are usually hairy.

Weinmannia trichosperma is a tree reaching about 12m tall. The young shoots are covered with brown down. Pinnate leaves, 3.5–7.5cm long, have up to 19 oval or obovate leaflets which are toothed. The stalk between each pair of leaflets has a triangular wing on each side. Scented white flowers are carried in a slender raceme 3.5–5cm long. Each flower has stamens with conspicuous pink anthers. The capsule is 3mm long and red when young. [Apr–June, T, PN, Chile] ☼

An unusual plant with distinctive ferny leaves. In most parts of Britain it will only grow with wall protection.

Weinmannia racemosa, Kamahi, has juvenile leaves which are three-lobed or have three leaflets. The leaves of adult plants consist of a single toothed leaflet which is oblong-lanceolate or ovate, up to 10cm long. The flowers are white or sometimes pink, in racemes up to 10cm long. [June–July, T, PN, New Zealand] ☼

Rarely grown, and lacking the attractive foliage of *W. trichosperma.*

Herbaceous and Annual Climbers

This group of climbers differs from all the others in this book, except a few of the herbaceous Clematis, in that they are not permanent: they die down at the end of the season. These plants are either annuals, which have to be regrown from seed each season, or herbaceous perennials dying down to a resistant rootstock from which fresh shoots grow each year, the shoots in effect behaving as annuals.

Annual and herbaceous climbers are particularly good for clothing temporary screens or trellises, or for walls and fences where a permanent cover would be undesirable. The latter include walls which need to be painted regularly and wooden fences that may need treating with creosote or other preservatives. Having said this, it is wise to point out that many wood preservatives are harmful to plants, especially if they seep into the soil.

Most of the climbers mentioned in this section require only a lightweight support. Strong peasticks, canes or strings may be quite sufficient and these can be removed at the end of the season. Annual species are particularly useful for masking the lower half of other wall plants or for temporarily filling in gaps, such as where a wall shrub has been removed. Away from the wall or fence, clusters of sticks or a tripod of canes of a suitable height prove useful temporary supports.

Many of these climbers are readily grown from seed and most are best planted out in the spring, the less hardy species being protected from frosts or cold winds at first. Diligent collection of seeds each year will ensure further generations of plants. They are a rewarding group of plants, especially as, in most instances, they flower so quickly from seed.

ABOBRA (Cucurbitaceae)

There is only one species in this genus, which, although perennial, is not frost-hardy and is best treated as an half-hardy annual. Plants raised under glass from seed should be planted outside in June. In the autumn the tuberous roots may be lifted and stored in a frost-free place until the following season.

☼ **Abobra tenuifolia** will grow 3–4m tall and climbs by tendrils which are usually forked. The alternate, glossy green leaves are broadly ovate with three or five deep lobes cut into narrow segments. There are male and female flowers, borne on separate plants, solitary or in racemes. They are scented, pale green and with a five-lobed corolla which is hairy inside; male flowers have three stamens and females have a three-celled ovary. Egg-shaped, berry-like fruits, up to 1.25cm long, are bright red when ripe. [July–Aug, HH, temperate S America]

ACONITUM (Ranunculaceae)

A genus of about 60 species which contain the well known Monkshoods and Wolfsbanes. The genus is native to the temperate Northern Hemisphere including the Himalaya. Most species are tuberous-rooted herbaceous perennials with digitately-lobed leaves. The flowers are borne in few- or many-flowered racemes, the flowers irregular, with coloured sepals, the upper of which forms a prominent 'hood' or 'helmet'. There are numerous stamens and the fruit consists of three or five follicles, rather similar to those of *Delphinium* and *Aquilegia*.

Plants are easily grown in most average garden soils and can be increased either by division or by seed sown the moment it is ripe. All the species are poisonous, containing an alkaloid aconitine or pseudaconitine. Only one species is suitable for culture on walls, fences or trellises.

***Aconitum volubile** (Pl.22) is a slender twining herbaceous perennial, which may reach 5m tall, although often less. The leaves have five to seven divisions, each wedge-shaped or lanceolate and further lobed and toothed, deep shiny-green above, paler beneath. Violet-blue flowers, 3–3.8cm long are borne in loose, rather drooping racemes. The 'helmet' is strongly arched with a prominent beak. [Aug–Oct, HH, USSR (Altai)] ◐

An attractive and rather unusual plant that deserves to be more widely known.

BOWIEA (Liliaceae)

An unusual genus containing a single species suitable for a sunny border beneath a wall. Plants require a light well-drained soil and some protection during the winter. Plants can be propagated easily from offsets or seed.

Bowiea volubilis is a perennial with a stout fleshy bulb which can get very large when mature. Its green twining stems reach 3–4m tall, the lower shoots much branched and flowerless, the upper little branched and bearing flowers. The leaves are short and linear and soon fall leaving the stems bare. Small green flowers 10–14mm across, have six similar persistent green tepals. The green, globose fruit contains many seeds.[Sept–Oct, HH, S Africa] ☼

A rather fascinating plant like a bunch of twisted asparagus, more of botanical interest than garden merit. It was introduced from South Africa in 1866. The bulbs should be half or fully buried and kept dry until growth is seen to commence. In the autumn, as the growth begins to die back, water should be withheld gradually. Bulbs may survive best if lifted and stored overwinter in a dry frost-proof place.

CLITORIA (Leguminosae)

A tropical and subtropical genus of perennials, many of which are climbers. The alternate leaves are pinnate and the curious upside-down pea-flowers are often borne in racemes at the leaf axils. The standard is large and notched at the apex. The fruit is a flat narrow pod which splits open to release the seeds.

Clitoria mariana climbs to about 1m tall by means of its somewhat twining stem. The leaves have three ovate to obovate leaflets, 2–8cm long. The lilac flowers are about 5cm long, borne one to three together. The pod is up to 5cm long. [June-Aug, T, USA & Mexico] ☼

This beautiful climber is usually grown under glass, but can be cultivated outside if treated as an annual and raised from seed each year.

COBAEA (Cobaeaceae)

Shrubby climbers from tropical America with alternate pinnate leaves which end in a branched tendril. The flowers are usually solitary and borne in the leaf axils.

They have a five-lobed calyx, the lobes rather leaf-like, and a bell-shaped five-lobed corolla. The five stamens protrude from the mouth of the corolla. The fruit is a capsule containing winged seeds.

☼ ***Cobaea scandens** (Pl.9) is an hairless climber with angled stems, growing to 7.5m, although generally only 2–3m if treated as an annual. The pinnate leaves have four or six oblong or oval leaflets which are up to 10cm long. The solitary flowers are carried on long stalks up to 25cm long, the calyx is about 2.5cm long and the corolla is about 5cm long, with roundish lobes shorter than the tube. At first the flowers are white or greenish and as they age they turn a striking violet. [July-Oct, T–HH, Mexico]

C. scandens is a most attractive plant, but will not survive winter frosts so is normally grown as an annual in this country or as a longer lived conservatory plant. To encourage a branched plant with plenty of flowers, the tips of the growing shoots should be pinched out regularly. The flowers are very handsome and it is a delight to see them change from pale green to deep violet as they age.

'Alba' has completely white flowers.

'Variegata' has leaves variegated with cream.

CODONOPSIS (Campanulaceae)

A genus of 30–40 species native to Central and Eastern Asia, the Himalaya and Malaysia, which usually have tuberous roots. They generally have a twining habit, and die back each winter. The leaves can be alternate or opposite, and are simple. The bell-shaped flowers are usually solitary and have a five-lobed calyx and a five-lobed corolla. There are five stamens and three stigma-lobes. The fruit is a dry, or occasionally fleshy, capsule which opens at the apex.

Codonopsis species are easily raised from seed and will thrive in a light good soil. They can be trained on a wall but are at their best when allowed to scramble over a suitable wall shrub. The flowers have a quiet beauty and many are more attractive viewed inside than they are outside. Unfortunately these delightful plants are not seen as often as they might be and several are now difficult to acquire.

◐ ***Codonopsis convolvulacea** = *C. vinciflora* is perennial and has slender twining hairless stems which grow to 2m tall. The ovate to narrowly lanceolate leaves, 1.25–5cm long, have toothed or untoothed margins. Shallowly bell-shaped, violet-blue flowers 3–5cm across, are borne on twining stalks which arise singly in the leaf axils. [June–July, H, Himalaya & W China]

var. **forrestii**, has larger leaves and flowers, and climbs higher.

☼◐ **Codonopsis clematidea** is a smaller plant than *C. convolvulacea*. Leaves 2–3cm long, untoothed and shortly hairy or almost hairless. Flowers white, tinged with blue, with darker veining and two purple rings inside, are about 2.5cm long; usually solitary and nodding. [July, H, Central & W Asia]

A pretty plant, but one which has rather an unpleasant smell, especially when the foliage is touched. It can be grown in light shade.

◐ **Codonopsis lanceolata** is perennial and has hairless, often purplish stems up to 1m tall. The leaves, crowded at the ends of the lateral branches, are narrowly ovate, 2.5–6cm long, untoothed or with rounded teeth. The bell-shaped flowers, up to 4cm long, are pale bluish or lilac with violet spots or lines inside. [Aug–Oct, HH, China & Japan]

Codonopsis tangshen is a perennial with almost hairless stems which grow to 3m tall. The ovate leaves are 3–6cm long. The calyx is divided into lobes almost to the base. Bell-shaped, flowers, 3–4cm long, are greenish, flushed with purple, with purple spots and stripes inside. [Jul–Aug, HH, W China] ◐

Codonopsis affinis has oblong-ovate leaves, deeply heart-shaped at the base and hairy beneath, 5–10cm long. The flowers are solitary, or sometimes produced a few together, and borne on the lateral branches. The calyx-lobes are very narrow and the bell-shaped corolla is greenish with purple markings. [July–Aug, HH, E Himalaya] ◐

Codonopsis viridiflora twines to about 1m. Ovate to lanceolate leaves, about 2.5cm long, have wavy or revolute margins. The flowers are borne at the ends of the shoots. The ovate calyx-lobes have toothed margins and the bell-shaped corolla is 1–1.5cm long, yellowish-green, and with purple spots inside at the base. [July–Aug, HH, C to E Asia] ◐

Codonopsis handeliana has downy stems which twine or clamber to about 1m. The ovate leaves have rounded marginal teeth. The corolla is about 2cm long, broadly bell-shaped, and greenish-yellow flushed with purple. [July–Aug, HH, China]

COLUMELLA (Vitaceae)

A genus of 16 or so species of climbing, rather shrubby, vines closely related to *Vitis* but differing mainly in having flowers with their parts in fours rather than fives. Cultivation is the same as for *Cissus* (see p.93).

Columella japonica = *Cissus* or *Vitis japonica*, is a herbaceous vine with slender ridged stems and tendrils in the leaf axils. Digitate leaves have five oval toothed leaflets, the central one larger and more pointed than the others. Greenish flowers in forked lateral clusters are followed by small pea-sized berries. [July-Aug, HH, Australia, Japan & Java] ◐

An herbaceous species which is hardy in some districts providing the roots are protected during the winter.

var. **marmorata** has leaves blotched with yellow.

CUCURBITA (Cucurbitaceae)

This genus contains the marrows and some of the gourds. They are trailing or climbing annuals or perennials native to America, with alternate lobed-leaves and yellow flowers. Male and female flowers are borne on the same plant; the males have a five-lobed bell-shaped calyx, a five-lobed bell-shaped corolla and three stamens, whilst the female have a calyx which narrows towards the top or is bell-shaped and a five-lobed bell-shaped corolla. The fruit is often large and contains many seeds which germinate readily in a warm greenhouse or frame. Young plants need to be hardened off with care. Plants thrive on moist, humus-rich, soils with plenty of moisture during the summer.

Cucurbita pepo, the Vegetable Marrow, is an annual with an harshly-hairy running or climbing stem reaching 3–4m long. The broadly ovate leaves have a heart-shaped base and five blunt-toothed lobes; like the stem they are clothed in stiff hairs. The calyx is constricted below the narrowly lanceolate lobes. The ☼

deep-yellow corolla is 7–10cm in diameter, with pointed lobes. The fruit can be smooth or warty and is extremely variable in size, shape and colouring. [June–July, HH, N Central America]

The Ornamental Gourds which are grown for their fruit which can be dried and preserved for decoration, are forms of *C. pepo*.

☼ **Cucurbita ficifolia**, French Melon, Malabar Gourd or Fig-leaved Gourd, is a perennial which can reach 9m during a British summer! The ovate or roundish leaves have a heart-shaped base and five rounded lobes, resembling the leaves of the Common Fig. They are pale green, occasionally marbled with paler green or white. The calyx is short and bell-shaped and the corolla is yellow or pale orange. The fruit can be up to 30cm long, roundish or egg-shaped, green-speckled or striped with white and containing black or brown seeds. [July-Aug, HH, C & S America]

The main stems like those of most ornamental gourds need to be trained to some extent, tying them in loosely to supports to train the direction of growth. They can be pinched out if they become too invasive.

CYNANCHUM (Asclepiadaceae)

Climbers with opposite leaves and clusters of small flowers. The flowers have a five-lobed corolla and a membranous double, ten-lobed corona which forms a cup around the five anthers. The fruit is a pair of fleshy pod-like follicles.

☼ **Cynanchum acutum** has twining hairless stems reaching up to 3.5m tall. Lanceolate leaves, up to 15cm in length, are heart-shaped at the base. Scented white or pink flowers are borne in few- to many-flowered clusters, the corolla hairless and 8–12mm across; the corona segments triangular. The follicles are about 8cm long when mature. [July, H, S Europe]

DICENTRA (Fumariaceae)

Every gardener knows the Bleeding Heart, *Dicentra spectabilis*, but few realise that the genus also contains some attractive herbaceous climbers which climb by means of fine-branched tendrils at the leaf tips. *Dicentra* is a close cousin of the fumitories, *Fumaria* and *Corydalis*, the genus being native to North America and Asia including the Himalaya. The flowers are fascinating and well worth a close examination. They are basically heart-shaped with four petals, the outer two rather flat with a broad, rounded pouch forming the outline of the 'heart'. The inner two petals are small and sandwiched between the outer. Dicentras like moist loamy, though well drained, soils and are readily raised from seed or careful division of old clumps.

◐ **Dicentra torulosa** is a slender climber with a tuberous rootstock. The bipinnate leaves terminate in branched tendrils and have narrow elliptic leaflets 0.5–2cm long. Yellow flowers 1.3–1.5cm long are borne in drooping clusters. The plant gets its name from the slender fruit pods, 4.5–6cm long, which are constricted between each seed. [Aug, HH, SW China & Assam]

☼ **Dicenta chrysantha** = *Dielytra chrysantha* is the better known of these two, however, it is an herbaceous plant rarely reaching more than 1m tall and without climbing tendrils. The plant has a semi-woody base from which arise the erect annual stems. The pale bluish-green leaves are bi- or tri-pinnately divided, the leaflets linear or wedge-shaped, 1.5–4cm long. The bright yellow flowers are borne in erect clusters at the stem tips, each 1.25–2.5cm long. [late June–Sept, HH, USA (California)]

This species was discovered by David Douglas and was introduced to cultivation as long ago as 1852. However, plants are not long-lived in cultivation and have to be propagated regularly to maintain the species. In the wild it is a plant of dry sunny hill slopes, so in cultivation a light loamy soil at the base of a sunny south-facing wall is ideal. Definitely a plant for the drier southern counties.

DIOSCOREA (Dioscoreaceae)

A genus of some 200 species of mostly tropical twining climbers with handsome, usually heart-shaped, or digitate leaves. Most have large tuberous roots which are generally referred to as 'yams'. The Common Yam is *Dioscorea batatas* which is grown and eaten in many tropical countries. Only three species are suitable for outdoor culture in our temperate climate. The tubers are best stored in sand in a cool, frost-proof place overwinter and placed out-of-doors in late spring or early summer. A sunny, sheltered position and a light, well-drained soil with added well-rotted farmyard manure are the chief requirements. During the growing season they need plenty of water, but this should be withdrawn gradually as the herbaceous shoots begin to die down in the autumn. The flowers are small, male and female usually borne separately but on the same plant, the female in small clusters, the male in long slender racemes or spikes.

Dioscorea batatas, the Common or Chinese Yam, has large elongated tubers, 60–90cm long when fully grown, which reach down deep into the soil. The herbaceous stems are smooth, 2–3.5m long, green or purplish. Large glossy, deep green opposite leaves are heart-shaped or lyre-shaped, with seven to nine prominent veins; the lower leaves generally bear small axillary tubers in their axils. The small white flowers have a pleasant cinnamon fragrance and are borne in axillary racemes. [July–Aug, HH, Philippines]

Dioscorea fargesii has small globular root tubers which are edible as in the previous species. The stems are slender, reaching 2–3m in height. The leaves are digitate or lobed, with three to five divisions, the leaflets oval or almost lanceolate, pointed. [July–Aug, H, W China] Very rare in cultivation.

Dioscorea caucasica has a thick horizontal rhizome-like rootstock producing smooth stems reaching 1–3m in height. The heart-shaped leaves have wavy, sometimes lobed, margins. The lower leaves are in whorls of three to five whilst the others are opposite or subopposite. Small greenish flowers are borne at the upper leaf axils in slender sparse spikes. Fruits with three broad, rounded, papery wings, are 1.5–2.5cm across. [July–Aug, HH, USSR (Caucasus)]

ECCREMOCARPUS (Bignoniaceae)

An attractive small group of South American subshrubby climbers. One species, *Eccremocarpus scaber*, is widely cultivated, being treated as an annual generally, although it will overwinter in mild areas. The tubular flowers are very attractive, each containing four stamens and a solitary style.

***Eccremocarpus scaber** (Pl.9), the Glory Vine, is a semi-woody climber with slender ribbed stems. The leaves are borne in opposite pairs, each twice pinnate and terminating in a fine branched tendril; the leaflets are 5–30mm long, ovate, but with irregular lobes. The nodding flowers are orange-red, occurring in racemes, each flower 2–2.5cm long with a narrow mouth surrounded by five small rounded lobes. The fruit pods are spongy and inflated, about 3.5cm long, and containing numerous small papery winged seeds that float readily away on the wind. [June–early Oct, HH, Chile]

The Glory Vine is among the most handsome of climbers and worthy of a place in any garden where a sheltered semi-shaded or sunny nook can be found. In mild winters, or as a conservatory plant, the shoots may survive from one year to another, otherwise the shoots will die back to the thicker semi-woody basal growth, however, plants are never very long-lived. This does not matter as plants are readily raised from seed and will flower profusely in the same year. Seeds can be sown in gentle heat in February or March, pricking the the young plants off singly into small pots as soon as they are a manageable size. Young plants can be placed out of doors in May once frosts have ceased. A south- or west-facing wall is ideal, the plants being allowed to scramble up shrubs, fine mesh or twiggy branches stuck into the soil. Few climbers flower for such a long season. The yellow-flowered form is often found under the cultivar name 'Aurea'. There is also a carmine-flowered form, 'Carmineus'.

ECHINOCYSTIS (Cucurbitaceae)

An American genus of 15 annual species which carry separate male and female flowers on the same plant. They climb by branched tendrils and the flowers have five or six corolla-lobes. The fruit is dry and prickly.

☼ **Echinocystis lobata** grows rapidly and can reach 8m in height. The stems are more or less hairless. The alternate leaves, about 5cm long, have three, five or seven deep, triangular, toothed lobes. The flowers are greenish-white, the females solitary in the leaf axils, the males borne in panicles. The egg-shaped fruit, 3–5cm long, is covered with long slender prickles. It eventually bursts irregularly at the top. [July–Sept, HH, E N America]

An unusual plant to grow on wall wires or on a trellis. It needs a rich soil and plenty of water. It is naturalized in parts of central and south-eastern Europe.

HUMULUS (Cannabaceae)

Most people know this genus by the 'Beer Plant', the Common Hop, however there are a number of species. They are twining perennial herbs which produce male and female flowers on separate plants. The leaves are opposite and broadly toothed. The male flowers are borne in loose clusters and have five sepals and five stamens. The female flowers are borne in short, bracted spikes which when mature look rather like a greenish fir-cone; within the spike, each bract encloses two flowers.

◐ **Humulus lupulus**, the Common Hop, will climb to 6m tall and has deflexed hairs on the stem, making it feel rough to the touch. The leaves are usually three- or five-lobed, the lobes being coarsely toothed. Male flowers are about 5mm in diameter and female flower-spikes 15–20mm long. The mature drooping 'cones' measure 20–30mm long. [July–Sept, H, Europe & W Asia]

The fruiting 'cones' are the hops used in brewing beer and this species is grown as a crop in many of the temperate regions of the world. In the garden it is a rather coarse plant, but can look attractive at the fruiting stage and is ideal for covering a fence or growing over large tree stumps.

***'Aureus'** has attractive yellowish leaves.

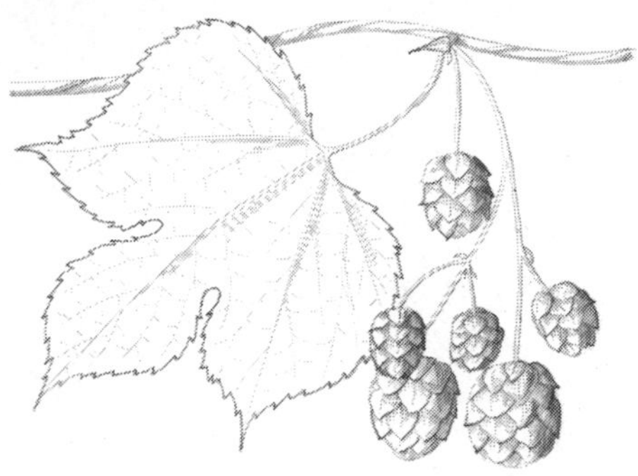

Humulus lupulus, the Common Hop.

Humulus japonicus = *H. scandens* can grow as much as 10m in a season and has deeply toothed leaves with five or seven main lobes. The 'cones' of female flowers do not enlarge in fruit. [July–Sept,HH, temperate E Asia]

In Britain it is best to grow *H. japonicus* as an annual — it rarely survives our winters.

'Variegatus' has leaves mottled with white streaks and splashes.

IPOMOEA (Convolvulaceae)

An exciting genus of plants related to the bindweeds, *Convolvulus,* native to the subtropics of both hemispheres. There are in excess of 500 species of Morning Glory, although only a relatively small number are cultivated and only a handful will succeed out-of-doors in our temperate climate, and then only in warm sheltered niches. Undoubtedly the most well-known is the lovely 'Heavenly Blue' Morning Glory which is a cultivar of *Ipomoea tricolor.* The species are predominantly evergreen or deciduous twining climbers, although some are shrubby or form small trees. They all possess alternate heart-shaped or variously lobed leaves. The showy rather fragile flowers are funnel-shaped, bell-shaped or tubular and open in sunshine, being short-lived but generally produced in abundance.

In cultivation most require plenty of room and love to romp up trellis work against walls or pillars. They need warm conditions, sheltered in the open garden, with a rich moist loam and plenty of water during the growing season. Well-rotted farmyard manure is particularly good, either dug into the soil before planting or used as a mulch. Plants are easily propagated from seed but they greatly resent disturbance once they have germinated and should be potted on with great care. It will greatly assist germination to soak seeds for 12 hours before sowing. Two or three seeds sown to a pot are ideal, placing the pots in a warm position. Young plants should be given branched twigs to start them climbing and they must be hardened off carefully before being committed to the open garden. Most make fine plants for conservatory walls.

***Ipomoea tricolor** = *I. rubrocaerulea, Pharbitis rubrocaerulea, P. tricolor,* is a short-lived twining perennial, but generally best treated as an annual, reaching 7m tall, although generally less. The heart-shaped leaves are pointed, pale to mid- 

Ipomoea tricolor 'Heavenly Blue'.

green. The funnel-shaped flowers are whitish in bud, but the corolla unfurls reddish-purple, azure or china blue, 7.5–10cm long, three or four flowers being borne on each stalk. [July–Oct, T, Mexico]

A very beautiful plant most commonly seen as a conservatory plant but it will succeed well enough on a sunny sheltered wall. The delicate flowers open in the early morning sunshine and generally have faded by mid-afternoon. This species gained notoriety a few years ago because it was discovered (in particular by teenagers) that the seeds contain small amounts of the hallucinogen, LSD. However, the amount contained in each seed is very tiny indeed. *I. tricolor* is easily distinguished from the other species by its tiny linear sepals.

'Heavenly Blue' is the finest and most popular cultivar, bearing large china blue flowers.

☼ **Ipomoea nil** = *I. imperialis, Pharbitis nil,* is an annual or herbaceous perennial twiner reaching 4m tall, sometimes more, with hairy stems. The heart-shaped leaves are entire or tri-lobed. One or several flowers are borne on a common stalk, each funnel-shaped, pale to bright blue at first but usually ageing to red or reddish-purple, with a white tube, 5–6.5cm long. The sepals are long-drawn out and bristly at the base. [July–Sept, HH, N America]

This species includes the group of plants generally referred to as the Imperial Japanese Morning Glories. It is grown in many tropical and subtropical countries and has become a weed in some. *I. nil* is sometimes found under the name *I.*

acuminata, but quite erroneously so, for this name is a synonym of the next species *I. indica*.

'Limbata' has violet-purple flowers edged with white.

***'Scarlet O'Hara'** has deep red flowers.

Ipomoea indica = *I. acuminata, I. congesta*, is a fast-growing twiner reaching 12m tall. Leaves are heart-shaped, entire or 3-lobed. Funnel-shaped, blue or bluish-purple flowers, 5–9cm long, are borne in clusters, only one or two opening at a time. [Aug–Oct, T, S America]

This vigorous grower, indeed sometimes too vigorous, is grown commonly throughout the tropics and subtropics. Frequently confused with *I. purpurea*, it can be easily distinguished by its finely hairy, not bristly, sepals.

'Leari' = *Ipomoea leari, Pharbitis leari*, has silvery hairy leaves, especially noticeable on the undersurface.

***Ipomoea purpurea** = *Convolvulus purpurea, Pharbitis purpurea* (Pl.22), the Common Morning Glory, is an annual or herbaceous perennial twiner up to 3–5m tall, with hairy stems. The heart-shaped leaves may be entire or three-lobed. The flowers are borne one or several to a common stalk, each funnel-shaped, 5–6.5cm long, ranging in colour from dark purple to purple-blue or reddish, with a white tube. [July–Sept, HH, Tropical America]

This widely grown species has been cultivated since 1629. Its flowers are not as large or as spectacular as in the preceding two species but it is hardier. Often confused with *I. indica* and *I. nil*, it can be distinguished by the sepals which are covered in bristly hairs. There are a number of cultivars including those listed below.

'Alba' has white flowers.

'Dickensonii' has blue flowers.

'Flore-pleno' has bluish-white flowers streaked with purple, double, later-flowering.

'Kermesiana' has scarlet flowers.

'Rosea' has blush-rose flowers.

'Tricolor' has blue flowers striped with red and white. Not to be confused with *Ipomoea tricolor*

Ipomoea hederacea = *Pharbitis hederacea*, an annual twiner to 3–5m tall, very variable. The heart-shaped leaves are entire or 3-lobed, pointed. The flowers are solitary or borne in pairs on a common stalk, funnel-shaped, pale blue, 2.5–5cm long. [July–Sept, HH, Tropical America]

Often confused with *I. nil* but with smaller flowers and narrow spreading or recurved sepals. Commonly cultivated.

Ipomoea jalapa = *Batatas jalapa* is a slender hairless twiner up to 5–8m tall with a stout woody tuberous rootstock. The leaves are rather membranous, triangular-heart-shaped, entire or three-lobed, pointed. The narrow funnel-shaped flowers are borne in pairs on a common stem, varying in colour from red, to pinkish-purple or white, 5–6.5cm long. [July–Aug, T, S USA & Mexico]

The tubers can grow very large, some weighing as much as 33kg having been recorded. The tubers have purgative properties like those of *I. purga*.

Ipomoea pandurata = *Convolvulus panduratus* is known variously as Man of the Earth, Wild Potato Vine or Wild Sweet Potato. A perennial twiner, it grows up to 4m tall, with long tuberous roots. The heart-shaped leaves are entire, fiddle-shaped or three-lobed, finely downy beneath. Broad, funnel-shaped flowers, borne in small lateral clusters, white with a dark purple throat. [June–Aug, H, USA]

An attractive species widely cultivated in many parts of the world. It is probably the hardiest species. *I. pandurata* has become a troublesome weed in a number of warm countries, being difficult to eradicate because of its long tuberous roots.

☼ **Ipomoea coccinea** = *Quamoclit coccinea*, the Star Ipomoea, is a twining perennial up to 3m tall. The variable leaves are generally heart- or arrowhead-shaped, with a slender pointed apex, angled, toothed or untoothed. Flowers fragrant, brilliant scarlet, 18–36mm long, with yellow throats, several borne on a common stalk. [Aug–Oct, T, Mexico & USA (Arizona)]

A beautiful climber which produces an abundance of flowers. Unfortunately it is rather tender and for this reason it is more often grown on a conservatory wall or pillar.

'Luteola' is a fine form with yellow or orange flowers.

var. **hederifolia** = *Ipomaea hederifolia, Mina sanguinea,* is like the type but with three to five-lobed leaves.

☼ **Ipomoea quamoclit** = *Quamoclit pinnata*, the Cypress Vine or Indian Pink, is a handsome twining climber with smooth slender stems reaching 5–7m tall. The leaves are short-stalked or stalkless, finely pinnately cut into numerous linear lobes giving them a ferny appearance. The scarlet flowers are often borne in pairs, each 25–36mm long with a narrow tube that broadens into a flattened five-lobed limb. [July–Oct, T, Tropical America]

A beautiful and rather unusual-looking species with finely cut foliage and brilliant flowers. It is a tender species and needs winter protection. Plants should be started off in a warm greenhouse and hardened off carefully before being planted out in the early summer. A sunny sheltered nook is essential.

'Alba' is a white-flowered cultivar.

LAGENARIA *(Cucurbitaceae)*

A small genus of tropical annual climbers with male and female flowers borne separately but on the same plant. They are easily raised from seed.

☼ **Lagenaria siceraria** = *L. vulgaris*, the Bottle Gourd or Calabash Gourd, climbs to 9m and has sticky-hairy stems and usually forked tendrils. Leaves alternate, ovate with a heart-shaped base, are usually unlobed. They are 10–30cm wide, hairy and the leaf-stalk bears two glands at the top. White flowers are borne singly in the leaf axils. The pale yellow fruit is smooth and has a hard skin when ripe. It varies enormously in size, from 7–90cm in length, and in shape, from globose to oblong, club-shaped, bulbous with a crooked neck, or dumb-bell-shaped. [Aug, T, Old World tropics]

This plant is grown mainly for its interesting fruit which are used for domestic utensils in tropical countries and are valued as decorative ornaments in many countries. Like most cucurbits the Bottle Gourd is a vigorous grower requiring a moist humus rich soil. Plants should not be put out-of-doors until all danger of frost has passed, early June is quite soon enough.

LATHYRUS (Leguminosae)

This delightful genus contains the very popular Sweet Pea and the Everlasting Pea. The genus has some 130 species in all, native to northern temperate regions as well as the mountains of South America and tropical Africa. They are annual or perennial herbs many of which climb by tendrils which terminate the leaves. The flowers are produced in axillary racemes and are of the typical pea-type characteristic of the family. The fruit is an oblong compressed pea pod which splits into two to release the seeds.

These flowering peas are normally and easily propagated from seed. Some gardeners advocate chitting the hard-coated seeds or soaking them for twenty-four hours before sowing. Sweet peas can be sown in pots in frames during the early winter or sown directly out-of-doors in the spring. Tips of seedlings can be pinched out to encourage lateral shoots. Perennial species can be sown in a similar way, but they are best raised in pots to begin with. Once established, self-sown seedlings often occur; these should be transplanted while still fairly young.

The climbing species, especially the Everlasting Pea *L. latifolius*, are good plants for scrambling through shrubs or over old walls, or fences or up a trellis. Fine pea sticks are ideal for sweet peas, especially hazel or beech, or alternatively 2–3m long canes. Most species like a moist loamy soil with plenty of well-rotted manure or compost.

Lathyrus odoratus, the Sweet Pea, is an annual climber with a winged, slightly downy stem up to 2m tall. Leaves have one pair of oval to ovate-oblong leaflets, 2–6cm long. Flowers, 2–3.5cm long, are purple and fragrant. The downy pods, 5–7cm long contain about eight seeds. [June–Aug, H, Italy & Sicily]

Lathyrus odoratus is the ancestor of the modern sweet peas which can have white, pink, purple, crimson-red, or even bicoloured flowers. It is a pity that the original species is not more frequently grown. There are many named cultivars on the market and we leave the reader to select his or her own favourites.

***Lathyrus grandiflorus** is perennial with downy, angled, unwinged stems up to 1.5m tall. The leaves terminate in a three-branched tendril and usually have one pair, occasionally three pairs, of ovate leaflets. The racemes bear one to four flowers which are 2.5–3cm long, with a violet standard which pales towards the margin, purple wings and a pink keel. The pods are hairless, 6–9cm long and contain 15–20 seeds. [June–Aug, H, S Europe]

The flowers normally last a day only, but are produced in large numbers during the summer.

***Lathyrus latifolius** (Pl.22), the Everlasting Pea, is an perennial with downy or hairless, strongly winged stems reaching up to 2m, rarely much more. Leaves with one pair of bluish-green lanceolate to almost round leaflets, 4–10cm long, bear a three-branched tendril. Purplish-pink flowers 2–3cm across, are borne in a raceme of 5–15 blossoms. The hairless pod is 5–11cm long and 10–15-seeded. [July–Sept, H, C & S Europe.]

A beautiful plant, with a long flowering season, which dislikes being moved and may take a year or two to settle down. It is superb for masking the lower parts of climbing roses or clematis.

'Albus' has white flowers.
'Pink Beauty' has flowers which are dark purple and red.
'Splendens' has deep pink flowers.
'White Pearl' has white flowers.

Lathyrus rotundifolius, the Persian Everlasting Pea, is a hairless perennial with winged stems growing to 1m in height. The leaves end in a three-branched tendril, and have one pair of ovate-roundish leaflets, 2.5–6cm long. The bright pink to purplish-pink flowers are borne three to eight per raceme, and are

1.5–2cm long. The hairless pods, 4–7cm long contain eight to ten seeds. [June–Aug, H, E Europe & W Asia]

Lathyrus roseus is an hairless perennial with an unwinged stem reaching 1.5m tall. The leaves, with one pair of ovate-roundish leaflets 2.5–5cm long, usually lack tendrils. Rose-pink flowers, 1.2–2cm long, form racemes of one to five blossoms. The hairless pods, 3–5.5cm long contain up to ten seeds. [June–Aug, H, Turkey & USSR (Caucasia)]

***Lathyrus tuberosus** is a perennial which sends up hairless, four-angled stems to 1.2m from a creeping rootstock which produces small tubers. The leaves bear one pair of oblong-oval leaflets up to 4.5cm long, and terminate in a three-branched tendril. The rose-pink flowers are 1.2–2cm long, usually two to seven in a raceme. The hairless pods are 2–4cm long and contain three to six seeds. [June–July, H, Europe & W Asia]

This plant spreads by its creeping roots and new stems will often emerge at some distance from the parent. It can be propagated by division of the tuberous roots as well as by seed. It will tolerate more shade than the other species.

***Lathyrus pubescens** is a vigorous climber with hairy winged stems which climb to 3m or more. The leaves bear one, or occasionally two, pairs of leaflets 2.5–7.5cm long, and end in a three-branched tendril. Lilac or violet-blue flowers, about 2.5cm wide are borne in clusters on the ends of stiff stalks. [June–Aug, T, Chile & Argentina]

This *Lathyrus* can only be grown in the warmer areas of Britain and is best on a south-facing wall where it will produce abundant seed in a hot summer. It may take three years from seed to flower. It is a fine plant to mix with wall roses, 'Maréchal Niel', for instance. There is a fine white form, rare but well worth obtaining.

Lathyrus violaceus is a perennial with an unwinged stem growing up to 2.7m tall. The leaves are composed of four to six pairs of linear to ovate leaflets, up to 5cm long. Violet blue flowers about 1.5cm long, with darker veins on the standard, are borne 10–14 in a raceme. [June–July, HH, W USA (California)]

Lathyrus laetiflorus differs from *L. violaceus* in having larger flowers (up to 2.5cm long) borne in longer racemes, the petals white or flushed with pink, with pink or purplish veins on the standard. [June–July, HH, W USA (California)]

***Lathyrus nervosus** = *L. magellanicus*, Lord Anson's Blue Pea, is a vigorous perennial which climbs by means of three-branched tendrils. Its leaves have one pair of ovate to ovate-oblong leaflets, 3–3.8cm long. Flowers purplish-blue, 1.8–2.2cm long, with a paler keel are borne in many-flowered, long-stalked racemes. [June–Sept, HH, S Chile]

A beautiful pea introduced to Britain in 1744 by Admiral Lord Anson. It is presently rare in cultivation, and deserves to be grown more widely.

MARAH (Cucurbitaceae)

A genus of about six tuberous-rooted perennials, native to the western USA, which are best raised from seed.

Marah fabaceus = *Echinocystis fabacea, Megarrhiza californica*, climbs by the means of tendrils to 6m or more. Alternate, palmately-lobed leaves are silvery-green. Small male flowers are borne in racemes and female flowers are produced singly at the base of the male raceme. The round or oblong fruit, about 5cm long, is densely covered in spines. [July–Sept, H, USA (California)]

Marah macrocarpus = *Echinocystis macrocarpa* is a tendril-climber 3–6m tall with alternate, deeply-lobed leaves, 7.5–20cm wide. The fruit is broadly oblong, 7–10cm long, densely spiny with the spines of different lengths. [July–Sept, H, USA (S California)]

MAURANDIA (Scrophulariaceae)

A small Central American genus of perennial herbs and climbers of considerable charm. The climbing species are excellent for walls and fences, in warm sheltered positions. They prefer a well-drained fairly light soil. Except in the very mildest districts they are best dug up in the autumn and overwintered in a cool, frost-proof place. Alternatively, cuttings can be struck in August in gentle heat using these for the following season. Seed is easily germinated and young plants flower in the first season. However, they may prove rather variable, so that cuttings may be the only safe way of maintaining a particularly good form.

The climbing species have opposite or alternate, more or less heart-shaped leaves and tubular, foxglove-like flowers borne on long stalks. The flowers broaden at the apex into two lips, the upper two-lobed and the lower three-lobed. The plants climb by means of twisting leaf-stalks and flower stalks which wrap themselves around supports, although some shoots often need tying in to keep the plants tidy. Most species are tender or only half-hardy and make excellent plants for cool conservatories and greenhouses.

***Maurandia barclaiana** (often spelt *barclayana*) is a perennial climber somewhat woody at the base, with slender greenish stems reaching 2m tall. The heart-shaped leaves are rather angular, pointed and with long twining stalks. The flowers are pale to deep purple with a whitish throat, downy outside, 65–70mm long. [July–Oct, HH, Mexico]

A charming plant worth growing in the milder districts for its dainty flowers borne over a long season. Flowers are variable in colour and a number of cultivars have been recognised most of which have previously been given species status.

'Alba' = *M. alba* has white flowers.

'Rosea' = *M. rosea* has rose-pink flowers.

'Purpurea Grandiflora' = *M. purpurea-grandiflora* has purple flowers, larger than the type.

Maurandia erubescens = *Lophospermum erubescens* is a slightly woody twining climber reaching up to 3m tall sometimes more, the stems and leaves covered in glandular hairs. The leaves are triangular-heart-shaped, sharply toothed, with a twining stalk, the lower ones opposite, the upper alternate. Rose-pink flowers are 70–75mm long. [July–Oct, HH, Mexico]

Maurandia lophospermum = *Lophospermum scandens* is very close to the previous species and often treated as a variety of it. The slender stems bear heart-shaped, somewhat lobed leaves and rosy-purple flowers which have a whitish tube, the throat faintly dotted inside. [July–Sept, HH, Mexico]

A handsome plant, certainly better in our gardens than *M. erubescens* and, like *M. barclaiana*, quick to flower from seed. In gardens it is often found under the name *M. scandens*, but this latter is a quite distinct species, rarely seen in our gardens, with smaller flowers, only about 36mm long, ranging in colour from pale violet to lavender or reddish-purple.

MINA (Convolvulaceae)

An interesting genus closely related to, and once included in, *Ipomoea*. It is easily distinguished by its one-sided racemes of tubular, rather pouched flowers that are not expanded into a broad limb.

☼ **Mina lobata** = *Ipomoea versicolor, Quamoclit lobata*, is a vigorous, twining perennial climber with green stems reaching up to 7m in height although generally less. Leaves are three-lobed with a heart-shaped base, the central lobe longer than the adjacent ones. Pouched and slightly curved flowers, 13–25mm long terminating in five small rounded lobes, are borne in paired one-sided racemes; they are crimson fading to orange, then pale yellow. [July–Sept, T, S Mexico]

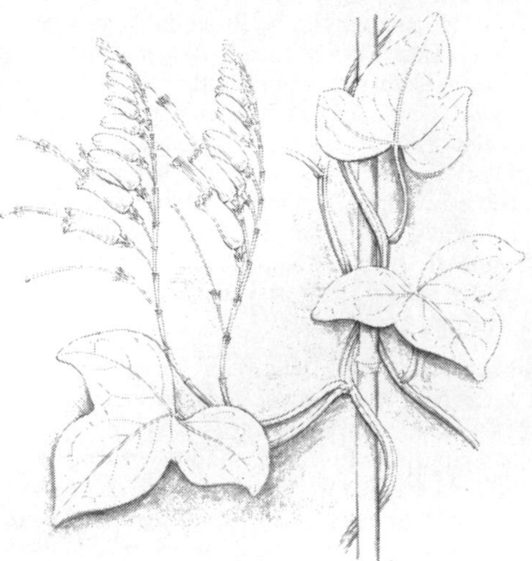

Mina lobata.

A rapidly growing twiner of great beauty which is unfortunately suitable only for a sunny sheltered niche in milder districts. Plants can be overwintered in a frost-proof place and planted out in early summer, once the danger of frost has passed. They are readily raised from seed and flower in the first season if started off in warmth early in the year. *M. lobata* makes a good subject for a conservatory wall. The flowers are borne in profusion over a long season.

MOMORDICA *(Cucurbitaceae)*

There are about 45 species of *Momordica* found throughout the tropics. They are annuals or perennials and climb by means of simple or forked tendrils. The leaves are alternate. Male and female flowers are usually produced on the same plant, solitary in the leaf axils, with a five-lobed calyx and five corolla-lobes.

Most species need to be grown under glass, but the following two species can be planted out in the summer. They are both annual and must be raised each year from seed. They grow best in good soil with plenty of water.

Momordica balsamina, the Balsam Apple, has hairless, shiny leaves, 2.5–10cm wide, with five, toothed, sharp lobes. The flowers are yellow with brown spots, the stalk of the male bearing a toothed bract above the mid-point. The orange fruit, up to 7.5cm long, is roundish to egg-shaped and angled, almost smooth or quite warty, and bursts when ripe. [June–July, HH, Tropics of Africa, Asia & Australia]

Momordica charantia, the Balsam Pear, has five-lobed leaves which are less sharply pointed than those of *M. balsamina*, toothed and hairy. Both leaves and flowers are larger than in *M. balsamina*. The flowers are yellow and the bract on the male flower stalk is untoothed and borne below the mid-point. The angled oblong or ovoid slender-pointed fruit, 2.5–20cm long, is orange-yellow or orange-red with a warty surface. It bursts at maturity to expose seeds with red arils. [June–July, HH, Tropics of Africa & SE Asia]

OXYPETALUM (Asclepiadaceae)

There are about 150 species of *Oxypetalum* native mainly to Mexico, the West Indies and Brazil. They have opposite leaves and bear their flowers in loose axillary clusters. The corolla has five lanceolate to strap-shaped lobes and is united to a corona of five scales.

Oxypetalum coeruleum = *Tweedia caerulea* is a weakly twining perennial with densely white-downy stems which reach 1m or more in height. The leaves are narrowly oblong with a heart-shaped base, up to 10cm long and hairy on both surfaces. Fleshy, pale blue flowers, up to 2.5cm across, becoming darker and somewhat purplish with age, are borne in a few-flowered cluster. The deep blue corona scales are erect. The spindle-shaped fruit is up to 15cm long. [July, T, Brazil, Uruguay]

In Britain this plant is usually treated as an annual and raised each year from seed.

PHYGELIUS (Scrophulariaceae)

There are very few shrubs or subshrubs hailing from South Africa that can be grown out-of-doors in our northern climate. The genus *Phygelius* which contains two species in cultivation is reasonably hardy. They are subshrubs which can be trained up a wall, but which in the open garden are generally killed back to ground level every winter. The genus is a distant relation of the foxglove, *Digitalis*, and *Penstemon*, similarities being seen in the tubular, five-lobed, flowers containing four stamens, and in the two-parted fruit capsules.

Phygelius capensis (Pl.22) is the most commonly seen, making a subshrub 2–3m tall, sometimes more in a particularly favoured position. The stems are four-angled and completely hairless, bearing opposite pairs of ovate, toothed leaves, each 3–13cm long. The nodding flowers are borne at the shoot tips in elegant loose panicles, the slightly curved corollas scarlet with a yellowish throat, 2.5–3.2cm long. [Aug–Sept, HH, S Africa]

This attractive plant has been in cultivation since the middle of the last century. It can be cut back during a hard winter but will generally sprout anew from ground level when spring arrives. For this reason it is often treated as an herbaceous perennial. In very mild districts some specimens have been known to reach 6m in height if the main shoots are tied into horizontal wires, a glorious sight in full flower. Like its cousin described next, this species prefers a well-drained soil and a sunny wall. In the spring all dead, weak or untidy growths should be trimmed out. Both species are easily propagated by cuttings in mid-summer.

*'**Coccineus**' is the finest cultivar with brillant scarlet flowers.

☼ **Phygelius aequalis**, rarely seen in cultivation, is a subshrub woody in the lower part, but seldom much more than 1m tall. The leaves are ovate or lanceolate, 2.5–10cm long. The nodding flowers are borne in terminal panicles, the slender, almost straight corollas, 2.5–4cm long, buff pink outside with a yellow throat edged with red. [Aug–Oct, HH, S Africa]

A smaller plant than *P. capensis* requiring a sunny, sheltered wall if it is to do its best, but even there it will be killed to ground level during most winters.

PUERARIA (Leguminosae)

A genus of some 35 Old World twiners or subshrubs. The leaves are alternate, with three leaflets and the pea-flowers are borne in axillary racemes. The fruit is a narrow pod.

☼ **Pueraria lobata** = *P. hirsuta, P. thunbergiana*, the Kudzu Vine, is an hairy twiner reaching 5m. The leaflets are broadly ovate, sometimes with shallow lobes on the margin, up to 15cm long and hairy on the lower surface. The racemes can measure up to 30cm long with fragrant reddish-purple flowers 2–2.5cm long. The hairy pod is up to 8cm in length. [July–Aug, HH, China & Japan]

In warmer areas the roots will overwinter, sending up new stems in the spring, but in colder parts of the county the plant will not survive and it is then best treated as an annual. It only flowers well in a good summer and even then the large leaves tend to hide the flowers. In the south-eastern United States it is grown both as a fodder plant and to control erosion, and in some parts it has escaped and become a weed.

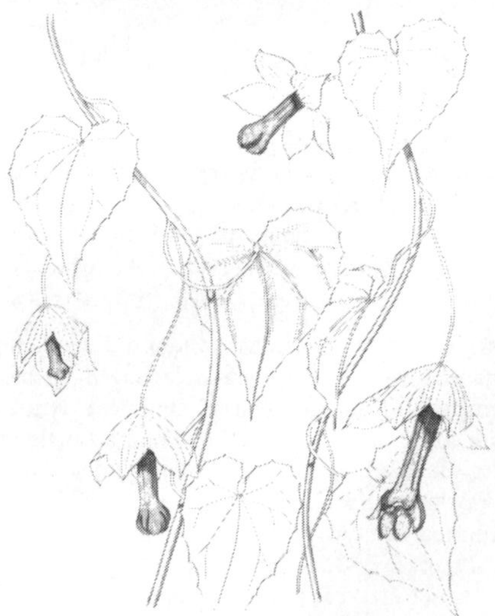

Rhodochiton volubile.

RHODOCHITON (Scrophulariaceae)

This genus contains only one species which is normally grown under glass as a perennial, but which may be planted outside in the summer and treated as an annual. The unusual flowers always attract attention and this plant should be tried more often.

***Rhodochiton volubile** = *R. atrosanguineum* has slender stems up to 3m tall, clothed with downy glandular hairs and climbing by means of twining leaf-stalks and flower-stalks. The alternate, heart-shaped leaves are 7 – 8cm long, with sparse glandular hairs and a few marginal teeth. The flowers are pendulous and produced singly at the leaf axils. The five-lobed calyx is broadly bell-shaped, about 2.5cm long, reddish-purple and glandular-downy. The corolla is long-tubular, about 5cm long, blackish-purple, glandular-downy and with five rounded lobes at the apex. [Aug – Oct, T, Mexico] ☼

A splendid plant, although often a rather short-lived one even when grown under glass. It is guaranteed to attract attention.

SICYOS (Cucurbitaceae)

A genus of 15 tendril-bearing annual climbers mainly from tropical America and the Pacific Islands. *Sicyos angulatus* is the only species cultivated in Britain, and it has become naturalised in southern Europe.

Sicyos angulatus, the Bur Cucumber, has glandular-downy stems up to 6m tall with branched tendrils. The alternate, broadly ovate leaves, about 7cm long and wide, have an heart-shaped base and five shallow lobes. Whitish male and female flowers are produced in clusters on the same plant. The males have five stamens which are united. The spiny, egg-shaped fruits are 1.2 – 1.5cm long. [July – Sept, HH, E N America] ☼

This species is raised annually from seed sown in the open once the danger of frost is past.

THLADIANTHA (Cucurbitaceae)

A genus of 15 perennial climbers with tuberous roots, native from eastern Asia to Malaysia. Usually they are grown under glass, but *Thladiantha dubia* is hardy enough to grow outside.

Thladiantha dubia has softly hairy stems climbing to 1.5m tall by means of simple tendrils. The alternate leaves are ovate, heart-shaped at the base, 5 – 10cm long, minutely toothed and usually hairy on the lower surface. The male and female flowers are produced on separate plants and have a bell-shaped calyx with five narrowly lanceolate lobes and a golden yellow corolla with five recurved lobes which are hairy beneath and warty-glandular above. Male flowers have five stamens and are borne in crowded racemes 5 – 7.5cm long. Female flowers are solitary in the leaf axils, on a stalk 5 – 7cm long. The red, hairless fruit is oblong or egg-shaped, 3.5 – 5cm long, with ten longitudinal grooves. [July-Oct, H, N China] ☼

T. dubia has become naturalized in C and SE Europe.

TRICHOSANTHES (Cucurbitaceae)

A genus of 15 herbaceous climbers native to Australia and Indomalaysia. The plant described below is an half-hardy annual which must be raised from seed each year.

☼ **Trichosanthes cucumerina** var. **anguina**, the Common Snake Gourd or Serpent Cucumber, is an annual with a five-angled, downy, somewhat twining stem with branched tendrils. The alternate leaves, up to 22cm long, are broadly ovate, sometimes with three, five or seven shallow lobes. Male and female flowers are borne on the same plant, the male flowers containing three stamens and carried in long-stalked racemes, the female flowers solitary. The corolla is white, divided almost to the base into five lobes, each lobe being deeply fringed. The slender, often curved or coiled fruit varies in length from 30–180cm. When young it is green- and white-striped, but turns bright orange when it is ripe. [July–Sept, HH, India]

TROPAEOLUM (Tropaeolaceae)

There are about 90 species of *Tropaeolum* native to Mexico and the Andes of South America. They are beautiful climbers with attractive and often unusual flowers, characterised by the common Nasturtium and the Canary Creeper. They can be grown on a trellis or up a shrub or another stronger climber; for example, *T. peregrinum* can be grown on *Clematis montana*, to bloom when the clematis has finished flowering. They are annual or perennial herbs which climb by twisting their leaf-stalks round a support. The leaves are alternate, usually with long stalks attached to the centre of the blade which is untoothed or lobed. The showy flowers are solitary and borne on long stalks at the leaf axils. There are five sepals and the uppermost is lengthened into a spur which is full of nectar. There are five petals, with the upper two differing from the lower three giving the flower a characteristic irregular appearance. The eight stamens are borne in two whorls. The fruit is three-lobed and separates into three one-seeded parts.

Propagation is by seed, or by tubers in the case of the tuber-bearing species. The caterpillars of cabbage white butterflies can be a nuisance. The butterflies lay their eggs on the underside of the leaves and the caterpillars can do considerable damage if not controlled.

☼ **Tropaeolum majus**, the Garden Nasturtium or Indian Cress, is a somewhat succulent rather vigorous annual generally reaching 2–3m high, with hairless stems and leaves. The leaves are almost round, usually untoothed and 5-17cm across. The fragrant flowers are up to 6cm across and have rounded yellow, orange or red petals. The spur is about 2.5cm long. [June-Sept, HH, Peruvian Andes]

Semi-double and double-flowered forms are offered by the trade, as well as dwarf non-climbing forms. The Garden Nasturtium is best grown in a soil that is not too rich, otherwise a lot of large leaves and few flowers will be produced. A shady position will have the same effect. A popular plant for training up strings or wires or left to scramble over a trellis or old fence. Plants are subject to attack from blackfly and this needs to be controlled the moment it is spotted. The young fruits can be used in salads or pickled and have a pleasing peppery taste.

◐ ***Tropaeolum speciosum** (Pl.22), the Scottish Flame Flower or Flame Nasturtium, is a perennial with 3m hairless stems growing from a creeping rhizome.

The leaves have five or six obovate lobes which are hairy below. Flowers bright scarlet, up to 3.5cm long with notched petals and a spur 2.5–3cm long. The fruits are bright blue, set in the persistant calyx which turns deep red. [June–Sept, H, Chile]

A splendid species which is a wonderful sight in full flower. It will grow on a north- or east-facing wall and in any position is happiest if its roots are in the shade. It is unpredictable in its needs, but as a general rule, grows more successfully in the northern parts of Britain and seems to appreciate a cool leafy soil. It can be grown on trellis or netting on a wall and looks especially good if it can be persuaded to grow up an evergreen such as yew or box.

***Tropaeolum tuberosum** is a perennial with hairless stems reaching up to 2.5m, produced from large underground tubers which are yellow, attractively streaked with crimson. The leaves have three to six lobes which have minute points at the tips. The flowers are up to 2cm long, with red sepals and untoothed orange-yellow to orange-red petals. The spur is reddish. [June–July, Sept–Oct, HH, Andes of Peru & Bolivia]

The tubers which tend to be produced at the soil surface will survive the winter only in the mildest areas and should normally be dug up and stored in a frost-free place during the winter. They can be planted out again in May or when the danger of frosts is over. There appear to be two forms of *T. tuberosum* in cultivation, one flowering earlier than the other, and there also seems to be a form which only produces sparse flowers.

In its native country, *T. tuberosum* is grown as a crop for its edible tubers.

Tropaeolum tricolorum is a perennial, 1m tall producing small underground tubers. The leaves have five to seven obovate or narrowly obovate lobes. The calyx is the most conspicuous part of the flower; it varies in colour from bluish to red or yellow but is usually orange-red, the lobes tipped with black. The spur is 1.8–2.5cm long and similar in colour to the calyx. The petals are rounded, shorter than or slightly longer than the sepals and orange or yellow. [May–July, T, Chile & Bolivia]

An elegant plant, rarely over 1m in height, with unusually-coloured flowers.

Tropaeolum pentaphyllum is a perennial up to 1.5m tall, producing long underground tubers and hairless purplish stems. The leaves are five-lobed, with oval lobes and purplish stalks. The flowers, 2.5–3cm long, have a green and red spur about 2.5cm long and the upper sepals spotted with red. The scarlet petals are rounded and the stamens protrude. [June–July, T, S America]

Tropaeolum brachyceras is an hairless slender perennial, up to 1m tall, with small tubers. The leaves have five to seven lobes which are obovate to narrowly linear. The flowers are about 1.25cm long with yellow, somewhat notched petals, the upper petals marked with purplish lines. The spur is about 6mm long with a blunt end. [June, HH, Chile]

***Tropaeolum peregrinum** = *T. canariense* (Pl.22), Canary Creeper, is an hairless perennial reaching about 2m. The leaves have five lobes and are greyish green. Bright yellow flowers, about 2.5cm in diameter, have a greenish curved spur 1.25cm long. The upper two petals, erect and deeply fringed, often with red spots at the base, are much larger than the three lower petals. [June–July, HH, Peru, Ecuador]

This pretty species is usually treated as a half-hardy annual. It used to be far more popular in our gardens than at present. Like *T. majus* it is readily raised from seed and is offered by several seed companies.

Tropaeolum peltophorum = *T. lobbianum* is an annual hairy climber up to 2m tall. Its roundish leaves are hairy beneath with a wavy margin. The red or orange-red flowers, about 2.5cm long, have a curved spur about 3cm long. The three lower petals are fringed. [June–July, T, Ecuador & Colombia]

Tropaeolum leptophyllum is a perennial, up to 1.5m tall, with underground tubers. The leaves have six or seven lobes. The flowers are about 3.5cm long and have a straight spur about 1.8cm long. The petals are notched and vary from pinkish-white to yellow or orange. [June–July, HH, Chile & Bolivia]

Tropaeolum azureum is an hairless perennial, climbing to 1.3m with small underground tubers. The leaves, up to 5cm across have five obovate to narrowly lanceolate lobes. The flowers, about 3.5cm across, have a conical spur about 4mm long. The petals are notched and purplish-blue. [Aug–Oct, T, Chile]

A lovely species with flowers of a colour rarely seen in *Tropaeolum*. Seed is now more readily available than in past years.

VINCETOXICUM (Asclepiadaceae)

Very similar to *Cynanchum*, differing in the flowers having a single corona with five lobes.

Vincetoxicum ascyrifolium = *Cynanthum acuminatifolium*, the Cruel Plant, or Mosquito Plant, is a more or less erect herbaceous perennial about 1m tall with greyish angled stems which twine at the tips. The opposite leaves are broadly ovate, untoothed and grey-hairy on the under surface. The white flowers are produced in clusters. [June–Aug, H, Japan]

Like *Araujia* the common name refers to the fact that the flowers trap visiting insects.

Wall Fruits

Growing various fruits against walls and fences can prove a most interesting aspect of gardening on walls as well as a rewarding one. Wall fruits can look very attractive, but as a group they require more regular care and attention than any of the other groups of plants referred to in this book, at least they do if you want to get a good crop of fruit. Well-grown wall fruits often produce very fine quality fruit, and the wall environment allows the less hardy varieties to ripen their wood satisfactorily and lay down plenty of those all-important fruit buds. Apples and pears are the first choice of most people, but we shall also consider apricots, blackberries and hybrid berries, cherries, figs, grapes, peaches, plums, currants and gooseberries. Other plants which produce edible fruits, but which are grown primarily in this country for their ornamental value, are to be found in their appropriate section — evergreen climbers, deciduous shrubs etc.

From the start it is essential to purchase fruit trees and bushes of good healthy stock. Suitable plants should be bought from a nursery or centre which sells Government certified stock.

Fruit, particularly apples and pears, can be grown in many parts of Britain and Ireland and will succeed on a wide range of soil types. Before planting dig the site deeply and thoroughly, breaking up the subsoil if it is near the surface. The general treatment of soils is outlined in the introduction.

The sunniest possible aspect suits most fruits, but not all. Sites should be protected from strong winds, which may damage growth, inhibit the formation of fruit, cause young fruitlets to drop off and even keep important pollinating insects away. Frost can prove a problem to early-flowering fruits, especially peaches and apricots, and if you are unfortunate enough to be in a frost pocket it is certainly wiser to avoid planting these, or indeed any early-flowering varieties of apples and pears, unless they are known to be frost-tolerant. Some varieties are more frost-tolerant than others and it is always a good idea to hunt around your neighbourhood to discover which varieties do particuarly well in your area.

Nowadays, plants can be purchased as container-grown stock or as recently lifted stock. If ordering by post most will arrive with the roots bound in hessian or a synthetic wrapping. Planting can take place any time between November and March during suitable mild spells. However, planting should be deferred if the ground is frozen or sticky, storing the plants in a cool frost-free place until conditions improve. On the other hand, if the weather is mild and the ground is not ready, plants can be heeled in firmly in a temporary site. Root coverings such as hessian should first be removed.

Before planting fruit trees, damaged roots should be trimmed back to healthy tissue, at the same time cutting back any thick downward directing roots in order to encourage a good system of lateral roots. Dig out a large hole so that the roots can be spread out widely before the soil is filled in around them. Firm planting is essential and make quite sure that the young tree is planted at about the same depth as it was previously. The union of grafted stock, that is the point at which the variety or scion was grafted on to the rootstock should be above the soil surface, by about 7–10cm. Cordons, which are generally planted at an angle of

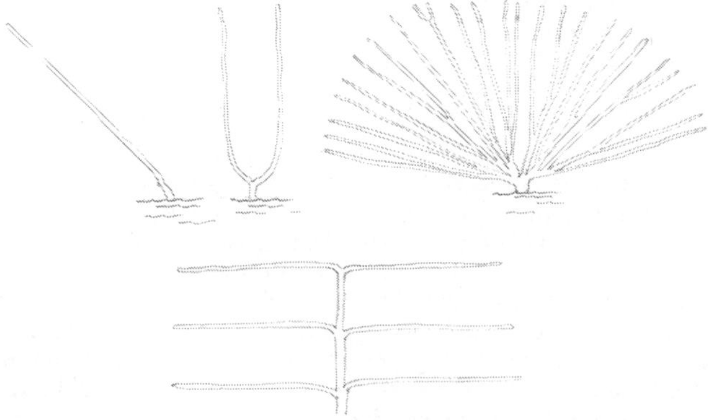

Fruit tree forms suitable for walls and fences. Top, left to right: cordon, double cordon and fan; bottom: an espalier with three tiers of branches.

about 45°, should have the scion uppermost. This will avoid the weight of the tree breaking the graft in future years and also prevent the scion from rooting.

The form of tree or bush is important. There are three main types for wall culture, but many variations on these can be seen.

Cordons consist of a single stem along which a series of short fruiting branches or spurs are developed so that the fruit is borne close to the main trunk. Cordons are very suitable for apples and pears and are normally planted about 1m apart at an angle of about 45°, if possible with the ends of the plants directed northwards. Cordons have a considerable advantage in small gardens in that quite a number of varieties can be grown close together. For instance, in a 10m stretch of wall or fence you could grow about eight varieties allowing for the inclination of the trees. Cordons need not be planted at an angle if there is a wall sufficiently tall. Vertical cordons can be trained with one, two or more vertical stems.

Espalier. These consist of a series of parallel branches or tiers one above the other. Branches are trained in pairs in opposite directions from the main trunk. A new tier can be added each year until the required height is reached. Espaliers can be trained with three to five or more tiers, depending on the type of rootstock. As in cordons the fruit is borne fairly close to the main stems. The espalier form is the ideal way of growing most apples and pears against walls or fences.

Fan. Fan-trained fruit trees can be most attractive. Trees are trained on a short leg about 30cm high, with the main branches radiating out fanwise against the wall. This is an ideal form for the more vigorous fruits such as peaches, nectarines, plums, cherries and figs. Apples and pears can be grown in a fan shape but this is not generally to be recommended.

Trees can be purchased as one-year-old plants, commonly called 'maidens', which generally have a single stem. Those with short lateral branches are referred to as feathered maidens. Maidens have to be trained right from the start and this may put some people off, however, the procedure is relatively simple and it can be very rewarding to form your own fans or espaliers. The faint-hearted can purchase partially trained trees from most large garden centres and nurseries. These are very much more expensive, but they do save two, sometimes three, years before the trees begin to bear fruit in any quantity. Whatever the type of tree, correct pruning is essential if good results are to be obtained.

The training and pruning of the different fruits is described separately under each in turn.

A regular system of spraying against various pests and diseases must be established if you want good quality fruit. Winter washes and spring and summer sprays are usually necessary. This subject is too complex to be covered in this book and we would refer readers to any book dealing solely with fruit growing but most especially to those listed in 'Books for Further Reading'. Early flowering varieties and the less hardy ones such as figs, peaches and apricots must be protected from frost. A curtain of hessian or a close 'coat' of straw or bracken through the winter months should help a lot. Frost damage to early flowering fruit trees and bushes, especially those grown against walls and fences can be alleviated by spraying the plants all over with water in the early morning, an effective trick used by many gardeners. Siting so that the trees avoid early morning sunshine can also help to reduce frost damage.

The height and position of walls or fences governs the type of fruits that can be grown. Walls and fences 2–2.5m high are ideal for apples and pears grafted on to dwarfing or semi-dwarfing rootstocks and trained as cordons, espaliers or fans. The more vigorous stone fruits such as the plums, cherries and peaches require a wall or fence at least 2.5m tall, preferably 3m. Extra height can be given to walls or solid fences by adding trellis-work.

SOUTH-, SOUTH-WEST- OR SOUTH-EAST-FACING aspects which are sunny and warm are ideal for apples, apricots, cherries, gages, figs, grapes, nectarines, pears and plums. The soil on such sunny sites tends to dry out quickly and they need careful watering and mulching, especially throughout the summer if the fruits are to succeed.

WEST-FACING walls and fences receive the afternoon sunshine but are more exposed to the predominating westerly winds. They are suitable for all the fruits mentioned above as well as hybrid and blackberries and various currants and gooseberries.

EAST-FACING aspects are more tricky, since they receive not only the early morning sunshine but also those nasty biting easterly winds, particularly during the winter and early spring. Cherries and plums will succeed as well as early fruiting varieties of apples and currants, gooseberries, hybrid berries and blackberries.

NORTH-FACING aspects are the most difficult and fruits that succeed here are those that grow and fruit in cold sunless situations. Acid cherries and damsons, currants, gooseberries and blackberries will all surprisingly thrive in such a situation, though the fruit will ripen later than those in sunnier positions. Some early culinary varieties of apples can also be grown on north-facing walls.

APPLES AND PEARS

Apples and pears are dealt with under the same heading because their cultural requirements are very similar. They are the most popular fruit trees grown in Britain. Although quite hardy in the open garden they are ideal grown against walls or fences in a sunny or partially shaded position. Trees are easily controlled by a variety of dwarfing or semi-dwarfing rootstocks which make them far better subjects for the average gardener to handle than, say, wall-grown cherries, plums or peaches. Pears are rather more difficult to grow and control than apples. They tend to flower rather earlier and the danger of frost damage to the blossoms is an obvious hazard.

As with all fruits trained against walls, tending them demands time and patience. A regular annual system of pruning should be adopted from the start to obtain the best results.

There are many varieties of both apples and pears which have different flavours, different dates of ripening and, furthermore, different keeping qualities. By carefully selecting varieties it is possible to have fruit available over a long season, from, say, late August until March the following year. On the whole, the earlier a particular variety ripens the poorer are its keeping qualities. Another important factor is pollination. Some varieties are self-fertile, but many are not, and the choice of variety must be carefully governed by selecting the right combination of pollinators. Frost hardiness and time of flowering are other important considerations. In colder districts or if one is unfortunate enough to have a garden, or part of it, in a frost pocket, then it is wiser to plant the later flowering cultivars. Some apple cultivars exhibit a certain degree of resistance to frost damage as far as the flowers are concerned — these include 'Ellison's Orange', 'Epicure', 'James Grieve', 'Lane's Prince Albert', and 'Worcester Permain'.

Both apples and pears will succeed on a wide variety of soils provided that they are well-drained. Very acid soils can be improved by the careful addition of lime. Mildly acid loams are perhaps the very best soil of all for most top fruit. Over-heavy soils can be helped by generous amounts of well-rotted composts and manures. Highly calcareous soils are equally unsatisfactory and generally give rise to various mineral deficiencies in the trees. Manures and composts should, however, be added with some degree of caution as it is important to try to keep a good balance of minerals in the soil. Dressings of well-rotted manure or compost given as mulches during the late winter or early summer are probably the best way of adding humus to the soil. In addition an annual dressing of Sulphate of Ammonia at 22gm per sq m (¾oz per sq yd), twice as much for pears, 44gm (1½ozs), and 22gm per sq m (¾oz per sq yd), of Sulphate of Potash should be applied annually in the late winter, before growth commences. Superphosphate can be given as a bonus every three or four years at a rate of about 44gm per sq m (1½oz per sq yd). These together should help to keep the nutrient balance correct in the average soil. Care must be taken not to overdo the nitrogen, which will result in a healthy looking tree with lots of shoots and large green leaves, but little blossom and even less fruit. Both apples and pears produce two types of shoot: long, leafy, vegetative shoots and short shoots with leaf clusters and flowers known as 'spurs'. The spurs are built up over succeeding year's and form a permanent framework which bears the fruit. In time the spurs may become over-congested and eventually need thinning. Pruning must take the spurs into account, for they bear the following year's flowers and, of course, fruit.

Two main forms of tree are suitable, cordons or espaliers: they can generally be purchased partly-formed, or the gardener can train a maiden tree into the correct framework. This is not as difficult as it looks although patience and a little knowledge are needed.

Summer and winter pruning of established apples and pears. Left: to prune in summer shorten extension growths by a third to a half their length. Right: to prune the same branch in winter shorten back the same shoots to three buds.

Cordons are generally planted at an angle of about 45° with the tip of the tree directed northwards if possible. Planting distance is 75–90cm for both apples and pears. Cordons can be grown vertically on tall walls, say 3m high or more. More complex cordons with double or treble stems are also possible on such walls. The planting distance of espaliers is directly related to the vigour of the rootstock.

Apples and pears can also be purchased as partly trained fan trees, though this form is really more suitable for cherries, plums and peaches.

Before describing how to form your own cordon or espalier from a young tree we will take a brief look at rootstocks. There are a number of rootstocks suitable for cordon or espalier apples. 'Malling 9', known simply as 'M9' is a dwarfing rootstock very suitable for cordons or for low espaliers which are not required to grow more than 1.5m high. 'M26' is equally satifactory, equally dwarfing, but less used. 'M7' and 'MM106' are semi-dwarfing rootstocks ideal on average soils for cordons and espaliers. 'M2' and 'MM111' are more vigorous and really only suitable for cordon or espalier trees on poor soils, although excellent on a good soil for extra large espaliers.

The planting distances for espaliers on different rootstocks are as follows: 'M9', 3.5m apart; 'M26, 3.5–4m apart; 'M7' & 'MM106', 4–5m apart; 'M2' & 'MM111' 5–6m apart.

Pear rootstocks are far less complicated. Most cultivars are grafted onto a quince rootstock, either Quince A or Quince C. The former is the best for a standard espalier or cordon on most soil types. Quince C is more dwarfing and is suitable where a low espalier, perhaps of only two or three tiers, is required. Planting distances for espalier pears are 4–5m apart for those grafted onto Quince C and 5–7m apart for those on Quince A.

Cordons are secured along canes 3–3.5m long driven into the soil at an angle of 45°, or vertically for vertical cordons. These canes are tied to horizontal wires fixed to straining eyes on the wall or fence about 0.75m, 1.35m and 1.95m from the ground. The wires should be as taut as possible, using galvanised wire strainers (adjustable straining bolts) if necessary. If the fence is not suitable for fixing wires to, then wires can be strained between stout posts securely fixed in the ground immediately in front of the fence. Cordons are trained along the canes and tied to them. Ties need to be checked and replaced every two years.

Espaliers are trained to horizontal wires which should be 30cm apart and fixed the same way as for cordons. The number of wires depends on how many tiers are required. The 'arms' or tiers of the espalier are tied directly to the wires.

Trees can be planted at any time between October and March provided that the weather is mild, the soil has been prepared and it is in a suitable condition for planting.

The training of a cordon from a young maiden apple or pear tree is relatively straight-forward. After planting, the leading shoot, the leader, should be left unpruned and should remain unpruned until the cordon has reached its desired length, perhaps in two or three years time. The only exception is in varieties which bear fruit on the branch tips; in such cases the leader is best cut back by a quarter of its length during the winter.

Maiden laterals, or 'feathers' as they are usually called, can be left unpruned, although if they are quite strong they are best pruned back to three buds — also during the winter.

During the first season a system of summer pruning is immediately established. This consists of cutting back all the strong lateral shoots to three leaves beyond

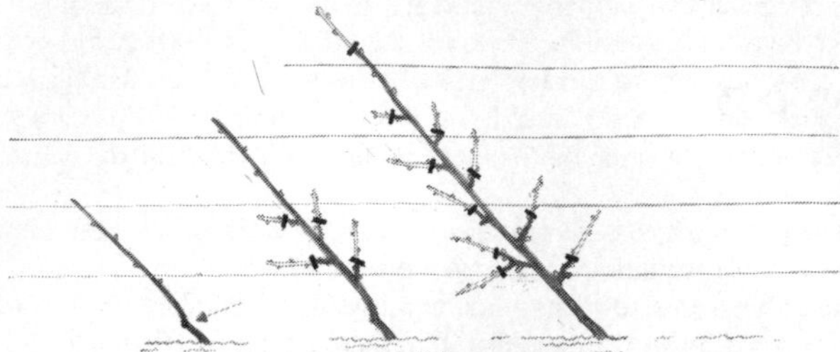

Training cordon apples and pears as described in the text. Left to right: first, second and third years. The fruiting spurs are built up evenly along the main trunk by a careful system of summer and winter pruning. The union between rootstock and scion is indicated by an arrow.

the basal cluster. Shoots arising from a 'spur' should be pruned back to one leaf only. Summer pruning should commence in early July in southern Britain for pears, the wood of which ripens first, and mid-July for apples. In colder districts and in the north this should be about a fortnight later than in the south.

The pruned lateral shoots will produce secondary shoots during the late summer and these should be pruned to one bud in the late autumn after leaf fall, although it should be carried out before winter sets in, bringing the risk of frost damage to the young growths.

This system can be carried on until the cordon leader reaches the topmost wire. It can then be stopped at the desired length, May being the best month for this operation. It sometimes happens that a young cordon does not produce enough laterals, which will form the system of spur branches to bear the fruit. Further laterals can be induced by carefully nicking out of a small notch of bark from above a latent bud. This is best carried out in May when the lateral buds remaining latent can easily be distinguished. The alternative is to cut back the leader by up to one third of its length to a suitable wood bud, however, this can delay the establishment of the full-length cordon. In most instances such treatment is not necessary.

Once the cordon has been formed summer pruning is carried out annually as described. In time it may be necessary to thin overcrowded fruit spurs and this is best undertaken in winter when it is easy to see the whole framework of the cordon.

The training of espaliers is more complex. The young maiden is tied into a vertical cane fixed to horizontal wires. During the winter it is cut back to about 5cm above the lowermost wire. The cut should be made close to where there are three good buds the lower two of which should oppose each other on the main stem, one to the right and on to the left. When growth commences the uppermost bud will grow out to form the new leader and the opposing two will grow out to form the branches or 'arms' of the first tier. All other buds between these can then be rubbed off.

When the growths have reached 30cm long or more they can be tied in to train the direction of growth. The leader is tied loosely to the vertical cane and the 'arms' to two temporary canes at about a 45° angle, though if one 'arm' is weaker it is best left untied or in a more vertical position until it has caught up with the more vigorous 'arm'. The temptation to tie the arms into the lowermost horizontal wire during the summer should be avoided as it will impede the growth of the shoots. Instead it is best to wait until the winter and then untie them from the canes and bring them down to tie onto the wire. During the summer any other laterals arising from the main stem of the espalier should be pruned back to four or five leaves.

During the second year the second tier is formed following the same system of cutting back the leader and training the laterals as outlined for the formation of the first tier. This is repeated each year until the desired number of tiers is reached — four to six are common.

It should be remembered that the leader of each 'arm' should be left unpruned until it has reached the desired length. The lateral shoots of 'arms' are treated as for the cordon, shortening them back during the summer to three leaves beyond the basal cluster, or to one if they arise from an existing spur. Secondary shoots are pruned back to one bud during October or early November.

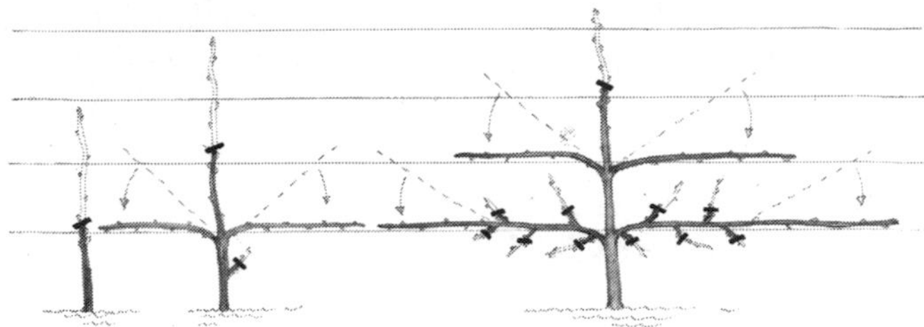

Training espalier apples and pears, as described in the text. Left to right: first, second and third years. The tier branches (broken lines) are secured to horizontal wires or canes at the end of the growing season.

When the espalier has produced the desired number of tiers the central leader is cut out immediately above the uppermost tier, being careful not to leave a snag behind.

It is best to sacrifice potential fruit and remove all flowers produced during the first and second year to allow the tree to build up sufficiently. Only the flower buds themselves should be removed, leaving the young leaves and shoots undamaged. Fruits will require some thinning in most years, except for those varieties which are known to bear rather light crops. Some apples bear heavy crops only every two or three years. Thinning is necessary if a crop of good-sized, even fruits are wanted, besides which, heavy cropping may damage a tree or reduce its capacity in the succeeding years. Thinning can be done in two stages. During early June any mishapen, small or damaged fruitlets should be removed using a pair of sharp pointed scissors. In late June a phenomenon known as 'June drop' affects many varieties and fruitlets are shed. This is quite natural and often results in sufficient thinning, however in bumper years further fruitlets will have to be removed. Clusters are usually thinned to two fruits, and the central fruitlet in each cluster, generally the largest, is best removed. Large-fruited apples are best thinned to a single fruitlet in order to obtain good-sized fruits. Pears require less thinning because the clusters set are usually smaller. However, thinning to one or perhaps two fruitlets per cluster is to be recommended.

The pests and diseases of apples and pears are too numerous to deal with in detail here. They are all very adequately dealt with in the books mentioned in our reading list. Suffice it to say that a regular system of winter spraying with tar oil washes will control overwintering pests and their eggs, but this needs to be followed up by applications of Malathion and/or HCH after flowering. This should control pests such as aphids, sawflies, codling moth, capsid bugs and fruit tree red spider mite.

Birds will attack some varieties of apples, but more especially pears, just as they ripen, and netting may be needed to protect the trees. Fruit buds are frequently attacked by bullfinches or greenfinches and unless suitable measures are taken a tree may be completely ruined. Wasps generally only attack fruits which have already been pecked by birds, although they can be a nuisance, particularly during harvesting.

There are far too many varieties of apples and pears to deal with adequately in this volume, so we have applied author's discretion and recommend the following, although we know full well that everyone has their own particular favourites.

In this and the following lists the dates indicate when the fruit is ripe (cropping time). Numbers in brackets refer to the numbers preceding other cultivars and indicate varieties which are good pollinators for each. Hence 1 'Beauty of Bath' can be pollinated by varieties 4,10,14,17 etc.

APPLE CULTIVARS: DESSERT.

†1 **'Beauty of Bath'** Aug (4,10,14,17,21,23,28,41)
2 **'Blenheim Orange'** Nov–Jan (3,6,7,8,12,13,18,19,24,25,26,29,30,32)
3 **'Charles Ross'** Nov–Dec (2,6,7,8,12,13,19,24,25,26,30,32,35)
4 **'Christmas Permain'** Nov–Jan (1,10,14,17,21,23,28,41)
5 **'Claygate Permain'** Dec–Feb (9,11,15,20,29,31,38,39)
6 **'Cox's Orange Pippin'** Nov–Jan (2,3,7,8,13,18,24,25,30,32,35)
7 **'Crispin'** Dec–Feb (3,6,8,12,13,18,19,24,25,30,32,35)
8 **'Discovery'** mid-Aug–early-Sept (2,3,6,7,12,13,18,19,24,25,30,32,35)
9 **'Duke of Devonshire'** Jan–Mar (5,11,20,29,31,38,39)
10 **'Egremont Russet'** Oct–Dec (1,4,14,17,21,23,28,41)
11 **'Ellison's Orange'** Sept–Oct (5,9,15,20,29,31,38,39)
12 **'Epicure'** mid-Aug–mid-Sept (2,3,6,7,8,13,18,19,24,25,30,32,35)
13 **'Fortune'** Sept–Oct (2,3,6,7,8,12,18,19,24,25,30,32,35)
14 **'George Cave'** mid-Aug (1,4,10,17,21,23,28,41)
15 **'Golden Delicious'** Sept–Oct (5,9,11,20,29,31,38,39)
16 **'Gravenstein'** Oct–Dec (1,4,10,14,17.23.28.41)
17 **'Idared'** Dec–Apr (1,4,10,14,21,23,28,41)
18 **'James Grieve'** early Sept–Oct (2,3,6,7,8,12,13,19,24,25,26,31,33,36)
19 **'Kidd'**s Orange Red' Nov–Jan (2,3,7,8,12,13,18,24,25,26,30,32,35)
20 **'Laxton's Superb'** Nov–Feb (5,9,11,29,31,38,39)
21 **'Lord Lambourne'** Oct–mid-Nov (1,4,10,14,17,23,28,41)
22 **'Merton Beauty'** Sept–Oct (5,9,11,20,27,29,31,38,39,40)
23 **'Ribston Pippin'**Oct–Jan (1,4,8,10,14,17,21,41)
24 **'Spartan'** Nov–Jan (2,3,6,7,8,13,18,19,25,26,30,32,35)
25 **'Sturmer Pippin'** Jan–Apr (2,3,6,7,8,13,18,19,24,26,30,32,35)
26 **'Sunset'** Nov–Dec (2,3,6,7,8,13,18,19,24,25,30,32,35)
27 **'Suntan'** Dec–Mar (5,9,11,20,22,29,31,38,39,40)
28 **'St. Edmund's Pippin'** late Sept–Oct (5,9,11,20,31,38,39)
29 **'Tydeman's Late Orange'** Dec–Apr (5,9,11,20,27,29,32,39,40,41)
30 **'Worcester Permain'** early Sept–Oct (2,3,6,7,8,13,18,24,25,26,32,35)

†Also a good culinary variety.

Plate 21 Evergreen Shrubs 1 *Hoheria sexstylosa* (p.204), 2 *Punica granatum* (p.142), 3 *Jasminum humile* 'Revolutum' (p.101), 4 *Pyracantha coccinea* (p.222), 5 *Sophora microphylla* (p.231), 6 *Vestia foetida* (p.232).

1
2
3
4
5
6

1
2
3
4
5
6

APPLE CULTIVARS: CULINARY

31 **'Annie Elizabeth'** Dec–June (5, 9, 11, 20, 29, 38, 39)
32 **'Bramley Seedling'** Nov–Feb (2, 3, 6, 7, 8, 13, 19, 24, 25, 26, 30, 35)
33 **'Crawley Beauty'** Dec–Mar (22, 27, 34, 39)
34 **'Edward VII'** Dec–Apr (22, 27, 33, 40)
35 **'Emneth Early'** = 'Early Victoria' July–Aug (2, 3, 6, 7, 8, 13, 19, 24, 25, 26, 30, 32)
36 **'George Neal'** late Aug–early Oct (1, 4, 10, 14, 17, 21, 23, 28, 41)
37 **'Grenadier'** Aug–Sept (2, 3, 6, 7, 8, 13, 19, 24, 25, 26, 30, 32, 35)
38 **'Howgate Wonder'** Oct–Jan (5, 9, 11, 20, 29, 31, 39)
39 **'Lane's Prince Albert'** Nov–Mar (5, 9, 11, 20, 29, 31, 38)
40 **'Newton Wonder'** Nov–Mar (22, 27, 33, 34)
41 **'Rev. W. Wilks'** late Aug–Nov (1, 4, 10, 14, 17, 21, 23, 28, 36)

PEAR CULTIVARS

1 **'Beurré Dumont'** Nov–Dec (2, 3, 5, 8, 9, 12, 13, 17, 21)
2 **'Beurré Hardy'** Oct (1, 3, 5, 8, 9, 12, 13, 17, 21)
3 **'Beurré Superfin'** Oct (1, 2, 5, 8, 9, 12, 13, 17, 21)
4 **'Bristol Cross'** Sept–Oct (6, 10, 11, 14, 16, 18, 22)
5 **'Conference'** Oct–Nov (1, 2, 3, 8, 9, 12, 13, 17, 21)
6 **'Doyenne du Comice'** Nov (10, 11, 14, 16, 18, 22)
7 **'Easter Beurré'** Mar–Apr (15, 19, 20)
8 **'Fertility'** Oct (1, 2, 3, 9, 12, 13, 17, 21)
9 **'Fondante d'Automne'** Sept–Oct (1, 2, 3, 5, 8, 12, 13, 17)
10 **'Gorham'** Sept (6, 11, 14, 16, 18, 22)
11 **'Improved Fertility'** Sept–Oct (6, 10, 14, 16, 18, 22)
12 **'Joséphine de Malines'** Dec–Jan (1, 2, 3, 5, 8, 9, 13, 17, 21)
13 **'Jargonelle'** Aug (1, 2, 3, 5, 8, 9, 12, 17, 21)
14 **'Laxton's Foremost'** Sept–Oct (6, 10, 11, 16, 18, 22)
15 **'Louise Bonne of Jersey'** Oct (7, 19)
16 **'Marie Louise'** Oct–Nov (6, 10, 11, 14, 18, 22)
17 **'Merton Pride'** Sept–Oct (1, 2, 3, 5, 8, 9, 12, 13, 21)
18 **'Onward'** Sept–Oct (6, 10, 11, 14, 16, 22)
19 **'Packham's Triumph'** Nov–Dec (7, 15, 20)
20 **'Seckle'** Oct–Nov (8, 20)
21 **'William's Bon Chrétien'** Sept (1, 2, 3, 5, 8, 12, 13, 17)
22 **'Winter Nelis'** Nov–Jan (6, 10, 11, 14, 16, 18)

CHERRIES

Cherries can be divided into two main groups, sweet and acid (sour) cherries. They are vigorous plants and not easy on walls. Sweet cherries are the greater problem for they are very vigorous and fast-growing and require a good deal of space. Furthermore they are not self-fertile, requiring a different variety as a pollinator, so at least two varieties must be grown to produce a worthwhile crop. These must be selected with the utmost care. Until recently no dwarfing rootstocks for cherries were known, however, a semi-dwarfing rootstock, the Colt rootstock, has now appeared and this seems to promise a far more satisfactory plant for growing against a wall.

Acid cherries are far more rewarding as wall fruits. They are easier to control and have the advantage of being self-fertile and set a full crop of fruit with their own pollen.

Plate 22 Herbaceous and Annual Climbers 1 *Aconitum volubile* (p.237), 2 *Phygelius capensis* (p.251), 3 *Ipomoea purpurea* (p.245), 4 *Lathyrus latifolius* (p.247), 5 *Tropaeolum peregrinum* (p.255), 6 *T. speciosum* (p.254).

Cherries like a deep moist soil to which has been added a generous supply of compost or well-rotted manure. They dislike dry soils and will not succeed on soils that dry out during the summer — nor on water-logged soils either. Careful watering and liberal mulches throughout the summer are essential, especially for trees growing against a sunny wall. A semi-shaded aspect suits most varieties and Morello cherries will do particularly well even on a north-facing wall.

Trees should be planted as maidens or partly fan-trained specimens. Planting can be carried out at any time between October and March, weather permitting. Planting distance varies from 3.5–6m according to vigour.

Fan training is the only satisfactory method of growing cherries against a wall and the fan-shape can be built up in much the same way as for peaches and nectarines, outlined on p.270.

The pruning of cherries is very critical, the vigour and health of the tree being the prime controlling factors. Any form of winter pruning must be avoided because of the risk of silver leaf infection, which will enter the gummy cut surfaces during the winter months. Pruning should therefore be carried out either in April or in August and September. The framework should be built up spacing branches about 30cm apart to avoid overcrowding. Once the main shoots reach the top of the wall the temptation to cut them off at wall height should be avoided as this will not help to control the vigour of the plant. Instead the leading shoots should be bent over and tied down for a year. The new growth will then be weakened and in the early autumn (September) it is usually possible to shorten the leading shoots back to a weak lateral. Shoots growing directly away from, or towards, the wall should be removed carefully during the early part of the growing season. Excess pruning should be avoided and wounds should be sealed with a proprietary bitumen tree compound. With older trees it is often necessary to cut back an old branch or two annually to encourage new young branches to form.

Once the fan has been shaped pruning should be confined to pinching back all lateral shoots to five or six leaves, unless a particular lateral is required to fill a gap in the framework. Usually this is carried out during June. These pinched laterals will grow out again but each should be pruned back to three, or perhaps four, buds in the early autumn — September. Any dead wood can be removed at the same time. Side shoots should be 5–8cm apart along the branches in a well-balanced tree and excess laterals can be carefully thinned during the summer pinching period.

Cherries should be left on the tree until they are fully ripe. Once picked they should be consumed or used as quickly as possible. Trees will need protecting from birds which can destroy a fine crop with alarming rapidity.

Cherry Black Fly can prove troublesome, less so on trees in shady conditions. They can disfigure and damage the growing shoots. Regular spraying with a tar oil winter wash should greatly alleviate the problem.

ACID CHERRIES

These are normally grafted onto Malling F12/1 rootstock. Trees should be spaced at a distance of 4.5–6m apart. Trees grafted onto Colt rootstock can be planted 3.5–5m apart. Acid cherries only fruit on the previous year's wood so after the framework has been built up (which normally takes four or five years) a few shoots should be cut back annually into two- or three-year-old wood to encourage strong even new growths to bear the fruit the following year. This is best carried out in spring as the buds burst so that wood buds, which produce vegetative shoots, can be distinguished, the cut being made just above a suitable one. There is also less danger from silver leaf infection at this time of the year.

VARIETIES

'Kentish Red', cropping late June – early July, is self-fertile and generally sets a heavy crop.
'Morello' cropping mid – late July, is completely self-fertile and the finest and most reliable acid cherry.
'Wye Morello' cropping mid – late July, is self-fertile.

SWEET CHERRIES

Traditionally these are grafted onto Malling F12/1 rootstock and such stocks were all that was available for fan-trained trees. The advent of a less vigorous rootstock, the Colt, should however, greatly help, making it easier to grow sweet cherries against a wall. Planting distances are the same as for acid cherries, although the widest spacing is most satisfactory.

Pollination is a complex business as most sweet cherries are self-sterile. Only 'Stella' is self-fertile and this is an ideal cultivar for the smaller gardens where there may only be space for a single tree. In the following list, the cultivars are numbered and the numbers of suitable pollinators are given in brackets for each cultivar. Several possible pollinators are recommended for each cultivar. Asterisks indicate highly recommended pollinators. Dates are cropping times.

VARIETIES

1 **'Bigarreau de Schrecken'** (4*, 5, 12, 14) late June
2 **'Bigarreau Gaucher'** (7, 10, 13) July
3 **'Bradbourne Black'** (2, 8) late July
4 **'Early Rivers'** (1*, 11, 12, 16) mid to late June
5 **'Elton'** (1, 9, 11, 12, 14, 15, 16) early July
6 **'Governor Wood'** (1, 9, 11, 12, 13*, 14, 15, 16) late June
7 **'Kent Bigarreau'** (2, 5, 6, 9, 10, 13, 14, 15) early July
8 **'Late Black Bigarreau'** (2, 3, 7, 10, 13) late July
9 **'Merton Bigarreau'** (5, 7, 12, 13, 14) July
10 **'Merton Crane'** (5, 6, 7, 13, 14) July
11 **'Merton Favourite'** (4, 5, 12, 14) late July
12 **'Merton Glory'** (1, 4, 5, 9, 11, 14, 15, 16) mid July
13 **'Napoleon'** (2, 5, 6*, 7, 9, 10, 14, 15) late July
14 **'Roundel'** (1, 5, 9, 11, 12, 15, 16) early July
15 **'Van'** (5, 7, 12, 13, 14) July
16 **'Waterloo'** (4, 5, 12, 14) late June – July
17 **'Stella'** (self-compatible) late July

PLUMS, GAGES & DAMSONS

Plums, gages and damsons do particularly well against walls or fences, especially in more northerly gardens where the fruits of a number of varieties ripen very late in the season. Wall-trained trees produce fine dessert fruits, depending upon the variety.

Plums and their cousins will thrive on a wide variety of soils, but they must be well-drained. Trees will not do well on very acid soils unless lime is added to improve them.

Plums flower early so if you live in a frost pocket it is best to concentrate on the later-flowering cultivars. Most like a light, sunny position, although damsons can be grown on a shady wall, even one of northerly aspect. Most are rather vigorous growers and need regular feeding, however, some caution is needed for over-feeding will result in over-vigorous growth which is especially difficult to control in wall grown trees. Light mulches of well-rotted manure in the spring plus a dressing of 15gm per sq m (½oz per sq yd) each of sulphate of ammonia and sulphate of potash should suffice.

Plums are rather unpredictable as crop bearers and vary greatly in the amount of fruit set from one year to another. They are grafted on to various rootstocks but by far the best for wall-trained trees is the semi-dwarfing St Julien A which is also frequently used for peaches and nectarines. Trees should be spaced at a distance apart of 4.5–6m and about 22cm from the base of the wall or fence.

The most suitable type of tree is a fan-trained one. Young trees can be bought as maidens or already partly fan-trained. The initial training of the fan from a one-year-old maiden is exactly as that described for peaches and nectarines. Once the framework has been established a different treatment is required. Plums, gages, and damsons all flower on old wood as well as one-year-old shoots, so that any undue cutting out will reduce the potential crop. Shoots can be trained to extend the framework as with the peach, at the same time training young shoots to fill in any gaps present in the framework. Any young shoots growing towards or away from the wall or fence should be removed in the spring. All lateral young shoots, except those required for extension purposes, should be pinched out after the sixth or seventh leaf. In plums these laterals can be closer together than in the peach, 5–8cm apart is quite adequate. After cropping, all dead or diseased growth should be removed and all the pinched laterals shortened back to half their length, to three or four buds.

Vigorous erect shoots must be carefully controlled. They can either be cut out or, better still, bent and tied down to reduce their vigour.

The most important thing to remember is that pruning must not be carried out during the autumn and winter due to the risk of Silver Leaf infection, one of the worst, and perhaps best known of all fruit diseases. Pruning is therefore carried out in the spring or the late summer as described. Large cuts should be protected by a covering of bitumen paint.

The root systems should not be disturbed by forking the soil unnecessarily, for they are prone to suckering. Suckers produced should be removed by pulling, rather than cutting, and are best removed as soon as is possible.

Some plums and gages are self-fertile, setting fruit satisfactorily with their own pollen, but many are self-incompatible or partly so. This means that varieties should be chosen with great care.

Fruit must be thinned during years of heavy fruit set. This is done for two main reasons. Firstly, in order to produce a good crop of large well- and even-ripened fruits. Secondly, to lessen the weight of fruits on the rather brittle branches which can easily break under too heavy a crop. Thinning can be done in two phases: the initial thinning in late May or early June and a second one during mid or late June. The aim is to end up with a fruit spaced every 5–8cm on the branches. This procedure may seem rather drastic but the results will prove it well worth while. The temptation to thin in one go should be avoided because there is often a drop of young fruits in June — nature's way of getting rid of excess, damaged or diseased fruits. The second thinning should come after the June drop.

Most plums and gages are best left on the tree until ripe. This applies particularly to dessert varieties. However, slightly under-ripe fruit are often preferred for bottling or jam making. All the fruits will not ripen at once and trees normally need to be picked over three or four times. Varieties, especially of gages, which are prone to split during wet weather may be picked before they are fully ripe, and ripened in shallow trays, placing the fruits on soft packaging to protect them from bruising. Varieties prone to split are more suited to the sunnier, drier parts of Britain.

Aphids can damage young shoots, but are generally controlled by regular sprays of tar oil wash applied during December or January, preferably followed by a spray of Malathion shortly before flowering.

Birds, especially bullfinches and greenfinches, can cause considerable damage to the buds of plum trees, particularly to young flower buds. Trees prone to attack should be protected with suitable netting.

Wasps can also damage ripening fruit and are less easily dissuaded.

There is a large number of varieties of plums and gages. A selection of dessert and culinary varieties is listed below in a numerical sequence. Self-fertile varieties are indicated. The others will require a pollinator and suitable pollinators are indicated in brackets after the self-incompatible varieties, the numbers referring to those of the list; dates are cropping times.

DESSERT VARIETIES

1 **'Ariel'** mid–late Sept (3, 5, 11, 18, 19, 21, 25)
2 **'Cambridge Gage'** Aug–Sept (7, 9, 16, 17, 18, 20, 21, 22, 23)
3 **'Coe's Golden Drop'** late Sept (1, 5, 9, 18, 19, 20, 21, 23, 25)
4 **'Count Althann's Gage'** Aug (2, 6, 7, 9, 15, 16, 17, 18, 20, 21, 22, 23, 24)
5 **'Denniston's Superb'** late Aug (Self-fertile)
6 **'Early Laxton'** late July–Aug (8, 9, 10, 17, 18, 20, 21, 23)
7 **'Early Transparent Gage'** Aug (Self-fertile)
8 **'Edwards'** Sept (Self-fertile)
9 **'Golden Transparent'** Sept (Self-fertile)
10 **'Goldfinch'** Aug (6, 8, 9, 14, 17, 18, 20, 21, 23, 24)
11 **'Jefferson'** late Aug–Sept (1, 5, 19, 25)
12 **'Kirke's'** late Aug–early Sept (4, 7, 15, 16, 22)
13 **'Laxton's Delight'** Sept (Self-fertile)
14 **'Merton Gem'** Sept (6, 8, 9, 10, 17, 18, 20, 21, 23, 24)
15 **'Old Greengage'** late Aug–early Sept (4, 12, 16, 17, 22)
16 **'Oullin's Gage'** mid Aug (Self-fertile)
17 **'Severn Cross'** Sept (Self-fertile)
18 **'Victoria'** late Aug–early Sept (Self-fertile)

CULINARY VARIETIES

19 **'Black Prince'** Aug (1, 3, 5, 11, 25)
20 **'Czar'** early–mid Aug (Self-fertile)
21 **'Early Rivers'** late July–early Aug (6, 8, 9, 10, 14, 17, 18, 20, 23, 24)
22 **'Marjorie's Seedling'** late Sept–Oct (Self-fertile)
23 **'Pershore'** = 'Yellow Egg' Aug (Self-fertile)
24 **'Purple Pershore'** Aug (6, 8, 9, 10, 14, 17, 18, 20, 21, 23)
25 **'Warwickshire Drooper'** Sept (Self-fertile)

PEACHES & NECTARINES

These are dealt with under the same heading. Nectarines are a smooth-skinned form of peach and one with a rather less robust constitution. Their cultural requirements are the same.

Peaches and nectarines are generally grown as fan-trained trees against walls or fences, although in some of the milder parts of the country they can be grown as bushes in the open garden. Usually they are vigorous plants and require a lot of space — a wall 3–5m high is ideal. They like good drainage and plenty of sunshine. Walls or fences facing south or west are the best; north should be avoided and east is not generally suitable because of the danger of frost damage in the early morning to the young shoots and flower buds which swell very early in the year.

As with all fruit the soil should be deeply dug and well prepared. Acid soils should be lightly limed and heavy soils can be lightened and better drained by the addition of well-broken mortar rubble added in moderation. Plants will not succeed on highly alkaline soils.

Planting is best carried out in the autumn, during October and November. Peaches and nectarines are usually grafted on to a rootstock, either St Julien A which is semi-dwarfing suitable for smaller gardens, or on to Brompton, which is more vigorous. There is no truly dwarfing rootstock. Trees can be grown quite satisfactorily on their own roots and will fruit freely when seven or eight years old, although it is often more difficult to control their vigour. Many gardeners have grown peaches successfully from a 'stone'.

Young trees can be purchased as maidens with a single stem and often a few short laterals or as partly trained trees, which, although more expensive, save one or perhaps two years of initial training and produce fruit more quickly. Those grafted on to St Julien A can be planted at a distance of 5–6m from one another, whilst those on Brompton rootstock require more space, usually 6–8m. Plants should be placed 15–22cm away from the base of the wall or fence. Young trees will soon require some support if they are to be trained correctly from the start. Horizontal galvanised wires 15–20cm apart are the most satisfactory method.

The choice of variety is up to you but it is wise to choose the earlier maturing ones if you live in more northerly climes.

Trees should never be allowed to dry out at the roots. If they do premature leaf fall and, worse still, fruit drop, may result. Regular watering during dry periods and the application of mulches starting in the spring should help to alleviate the problem. Once cropping starts it is wise to add some well-rotted manure or compost, either lightly forked into the soil surface or applied as a mulch. May is the best month for such action. The addition of too much nitrogen will result in over-vigorous growth and a sparsity of fruit.

The training of peaches and nectarines and the pruning of established trees is a rather complex business and is best dealt with stage by stage. It should be noted that the initial training of apricots, cherries and plums, to build up a fan-shaped framework, follows the same basic system.

Consider the way peaches and nectarines grow. Fruits are borne only on the previous year's shoots. If you examine such a shoot you will see two types of buds. One type is long, thin and pointed: these are called wood buds and grow into long vegetative shoots. The other type is plump and rounded: the young flower or fruit buds which will never produce vegetative shoots. Quite often buds occur in threes, a central wood bud, with a fruit bud on either side. In pruning, if a vegetative shoot is required always cut back to a single wood bud or to a triple bud.

The treatment of a newly planted maiden tree is relatively simple. In the early spring the maiden should be cut back to about 60cm above the ground, if possible to a lateral. At the same time any laterals should be removed close to the main stem. As growth commences two opposing young shoots should be selected, preferably about 22cm above the ground or slightly higher. Having made a selection remove all other buds or young shoots. The two young shoots will grow out quickly; when 40–50cm long tie them to canes stuck in the soil at an angle of about 45°. At the same time the main stem above the two laterals can be cut out, protecting the wound with bitumen tree paint. The February following, cut back the two laterals to 30–45cm from the main stem. During the following summer (the second) let the terminal bud of each lateral grow on unhindered. At the same time allow three further shoots to grow on each 'arm': select two on the upper and one on the lower side and carefully remove all other laterals. Tie the selected laterals to the wires or, better still, train them along canes to form the framework of the fan. By the end of the summer there should be eight long 'arms' to the fan.

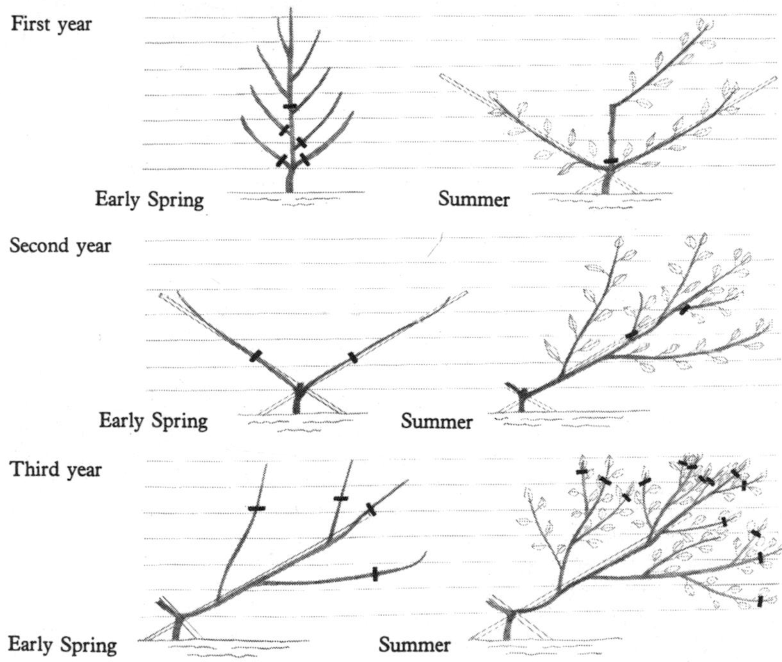

Training a fan peach or nectarine, as described in the text. In the first year the basic framework is built up from a feathered maiden by careful early spring and summer pruning. In the second year further framework branches of the fan are built up and this is continued into the third and succeeding years.

During the following February cut back each of the eight 'arms' to a triple bud or a wood bud, preferably an upward pointing one. These cuts should leave the arms 60–75cm long. During the summer of the third year allow the terminal bud on each of the eight arms to extend unhindered, tying them in at intervals to the canes or wires. At the same time rub out all buds facing into or away from the wall. Leave the rest to grow out so that they are about 10cm apart. If closer the odd ones should be removed. Allow these young laterals to grow until they are about 45cm long and then pinch out the growing point. At the same time carefully tie them into the wires. These pinched laterals will produce the first crop of fruit in the following season. Any laterals required to build up the framework of the fan should not be pinched out.

By the end of the third year the permanent framework of the peach fan will have been established. The pruning system thereafter consists of replacing fruiting shoots, pinching out and cutting out.

For a start, at the beginning of each season, as growth begins, all shoots growing towards or away from the wall should be removed. At the base of each flowering lateral allow one or two wood buds to grow out into leafy shoots. These will replace the existing laterals at the end of the season and provide flowers the following year. All other leafy laterals are best pinched out after two leaves only, whilst the terminal shoot is pinched after having produced six leaves. This selecting and pinching can be spread out over several weeks, starting with the uppermost branches and working downwards. During the summer, any further leafy laterals produced from those already pinched out should in their turn be pinched out, having produced a single leaf.

Two important things need to be remembered. Firstly, the idea is to produce new laterals each season to replace those currently flowering and fruiting. Once fruiting has finished all shoots that have borne fruit are cut out to just above the replacement laterals which are then tied in to replace them. Secondly, some shoots will be required to form part of the framework, especially on older trees where old damaged or diseased branches have had to be removed. The fan framework should be maintained always.

This initial training and subsequent culture seems immensely complicated to the beginner, but it is quite easy once the principles have been understood. Although peaches and nectarines require a good deal of attention it is a joy to see a well-trained tree and the rewards are obvious.

Flowers open very early in the year, often in March, before the leaves appear and are very beautiful in their own right. During frosty weather they may be damaged if not given a little protection. Most gardeners advocate hand pollinating to ensure a good fruit set. This can be carried out with a small soft brush or a rabbit's tail tied to a cane, passing carefully from one flower to another. Peaches and nectarines are self-fertile.

Some thinning is necessary if you want a crop of good-sized fruits. Two thinnings are generally recommended. The first in late May or early June, when the young fruits are about 1cm long, should leave single fruits about 10cm apart. The second thinning can take place at the end of June when the fruits are about 2–2.5cm long, leaving them finally about 22cm apart on the branches.

Fruit should be handled with care when ripe. When properly ripe they should pull away from the branches with ease. Place them on soft material in boxes kept in a cool place until you want to eat them.

Peach Leaf Curl is the worst disease of peaches and nectarines. It causes characteristic red blisters and curling or distortion of the leaves. It can be controlled by two sprayings a fortnight apart of Bordeaux Mixture or liquid copper during January or February, followed by a further single spray just before leaf fall in the autumn.

Aphids can be controlled as with most fruit by a tar oil winter wash applied during December.

On warm walls Red Spider Mite may be a problem. Infested leaves become mottled with brown and soon fall. Regular spraying with Malathion is an effective control but should not be applied close to fruit harvesting.

Split stone is a physiological disorder in peaches and nectarines which results in the fruit and stone splitting open and the embryo rotting. The degree of splitting varies according to the season and the variety but it can spoil fruit. Furthermore earwigs often find their way into the cracks. The cause is not understood and there is no ready cure. However, the disorder can often be prevented by careful mulching and watering, not allowing the trees to dry out, by hand pollinating the flowers, or, in some instances, by careful liming of acid soils.

In the following lists dates are cropping times.

NECTARINE VARIETIES

'Early Rivers' mid July
'Elruge' late Aug
'Humblodt' mid Aug
'Lord Napier' mid Aug
'John Rivers' mid July
'Pine Apple' early Sept

PEACH VARIETIES

'Bellegarde' early – mid Sept
'Duke of York' mid July
'Dymond' mid – late Sept
'Hale's Early' mid – late July
'Noblesse' Aug – early Sept
'Peregrine' early Aug
'Rochester' early Aug
'Royal George' late Aug

APRICOTS

Apricots are hardy in the milder parts of Britain and half-hardy elsewhere. They are ideal as fan-shaped trees trained on high walls or fences.

Apricots require a warm sunny wall if they are to succeed, preferably one of south or west aspect. A slightly alkaline loam is the ideal soil. Sandy or poorly drained soils are not suitable.

Plants can be purchased as maidens or partly fan-trained and are normally grafted on to St Julien A plum rootstock. The mid or late autumn is a good time to plant. Make sure that the young trees are well firmed in 15 – 20cm from the base of the wall. Trees should be planted about 5m apart. Mulches of well-rotted manure are valuable, especially during the dry summer months.

Apricots are self-fertile, compatible and, under ordinary circumstances, fruit is set freely. However, they flower very early in the year when few pollinating insects are about so that hand pollinating is advisable as with peaches and nectarines.

Fruits need thinning when they are the size of a small marble, removing any that are damaged or malformed. A second thinning a fortnight later should leave the fruitlets 7 – 10cm apart.

The initial training of the fan framework from a maiden tree is the same as that described for peaches and nectarines. Horizontal wires for securing the fan need to be about 22cm apart.

Apricots, like plums and gages, can become infected with Silver Leaf: they must never be winter pruned.

By the third year the young fan should have made eight arms or leaders. These should be cut back in late February by about 75cm. During the summer, late July or August, select three strong shoots from each pruned leader and carefully tie them in. At the same time remove all other lateral shoots, pinching them out carefully from the main stems. The following February (the fourth year) cut back all the leaders by a quarter of their length. Treat the resultant growth as before. The fan framework will now be established.

Summer pruning of established fans consists of pinching out lateral shoots after they have made six good leaves. After cropping these same pinched laterals are pruned back by half, in the same way as for plums and gages. These will bear the flower buds the following season. The best fruits are borne on short spurs on two- and three-year-old wood.

The main pests of apricots are aphids and red spider mite.

APRICOT VARITIES

'Alfred' July – early Aug
'Breda' mid Aug – Sept
'Early Moorpark' late July – early Aug
'Farmingdale' late July
'Hemskerk' early – mid Aug
'Moorpark' late Aug

FIGS

In no part of Britain are figs completely hardy; even in the very mildest districts they may be cut back in a severe winter, but in these milder places they can be grown in the open. They make a very handsome ornamental bush or tree, but will fruit well only in an exceptionally sunny hot summer. To fruit regularly they require the close protection of a sunny sheltered wall, preferably facing due south or south-west. They can be grown with success in this way in much of southern and south-western Britain. Elsewhere they are more reliable when confined to the protection of a sunny conservatory wall.

Figs need as much warmth and sun as they can get. The aim in growing figs is to produce strong sturdy shoots with short internodes. Figs are vigorous plants and planted in a rich soil with an unlimited root-run they will run riot, producing a mass of strong leafy soft growth, but no fruit. They should be given a restricted root-run. This can sometimes be arranged by planting the fig in the narrow space between a path and a wall, or in the angle between two high walls. However, more often than not, a specially prepared confined space has to be created. This can be done close to a suitable wall by digging out a space about 1.25m long, 0.75m wide and 1m deep. Line the hole with closely-packed bricks, concrete or rubble to a depth of 20 – 30cm. Fill the remaining hole with loam, preferably mixed with finely broken mortar rubble and a little bone meal.

Because plants are not hardy, especially when young, they should be planted in early spring (March). Figs are grown on their own roots and need to be firmed in well. Young pot-grown plants are the best to purchase. If more than one is planted, 6 – 7m should be left between plants. Figs are completely self-compatible; a single plant is sufficient in an average garden.

During the first year no pruning or manuring need be given. However, if the summer is a dry one, plants must be watered regularly. Mulches can be very beneficial. In succeeding years, especially when the trees begin to fruit well, both feeding and watering through the summer will prevent the fruits dropping off before they are ripe. Mulches of well-rotted manure are very useful.

Figs are generally trained on walls as fans. At the end of the first season the growths should be trained roughly into a fan shape. Subsequently any pruning must be carried out before the end of June. This is because fruit is produced on well ripened shoots of the previous season. Pruning after June will result in a lot of semi-ripe, non-productive wood. The young figs are initiated towards the tips of the current season's growths, but do not develop into mature figs until the following summer. Early summer pruning consists of shortening back shoots to the fifth leaf. During July excessive growths can be cut out of the plant allowing the remaining shoots plenty of space. Figs have large leaves and too many shoots will result in some shoots being completely shadowed and fruits not ripening properly. The shoots selected to remain should be tied in closely and securely to the wall supports, training them carefully into a broad even fan as far as is possible. The fans can be built up over the first few years in much the same way as for peaches.

Some winter pruning may be necessary. This should not be carried out until March due to the danger of late frost damage to the shoot tips. Any weak, diseased or frost damaged shoots should be cut out at this season, retraining shoots to fill gaps which occur in the fan. Large cuts should be treated with a protective paint. The shoots remaining should be well-spaced with undamaged tips where the embryo figs will be clearly visible.

Where figs are grown out-of-doors in colder districts winter protection will be needed. This can be provided by straw, hazel screens, sacking, or indeed any insulator placed carefully and closely around the plant. Polythene should be avoided.

Outdoor figs usually ripen in August or September in Britain, rather earlier during a hot sunny summer. The lower figs on the shoots are the first to ripen and the upper ones often fail to do so before the first frosts of autumn.

Plants with an unrestricted root run will grow very vigorously and will need to be kept in check by judicious root pruning. This is best carried out during the late winter. Remove the soil as a trench around the plant, but about 60cm from the base. Cut and remove only the strongest roots, leaving the finer roots intact. Replace the soil as quickly as possible making sure that it is firmed in well.

Figs can be affected by Fig Mosaic Virus which often produces discoloured leaves and makes the leaf lobes narrow and irregular. Destroy affected plants, for there is no cure. Fig Canker is a fungal disease seen as oval cankers on the bark. Remove and burn infected and dead branches and coat the resultant wounds with a fungicidal wound paint. Older branches can be affected by brown scale and the fruit can succumb to grey mould.

FIG VARIETIES

'Bourjassotte' **'Brown Turkey'** **'White Marseilles'**

The last two named are the best in most districts. 'Bourjassotte' is late- fruiting and most suitable for the mildest districts.

GRAPES

Grapes, like figs, love the sun. That is why they do so well in Mediterranean areas or in the warmer parts of Europe where hot, relatively dry summers are more usual. They are fairly widely grown in this country but cannot always be relied upon to produce sweet edible grapes, although various varieties have been selected over the years which will do better under our more temperate climate. Even so, the best crops are always produced during those hotter, drier, summers which are followed by a mild autumn.

Grapes make admirable greenhouse or conservatory vines in many parts of Britain, given a sunny well-ventilated aspect. Except in the mildest districts they cannot be grown in the open garden without the protection of a wall. Against a wall they make a fine sight, decorative as well as fruitful, once they are established.

Walls, fences or the side of a shed are all suitable. The aspect should be as sunny as possible, south- or south-west-facing being ideal, but it should at the same time be as sheltered as possible. Grapes dislike strong cold winds and the young growths may be damaged at the start of the season if the position is too exposed. Grape vines have the advantage that they can be trained low or high, so low or high walls or fences are equally suitable: 1–7m, or higher. In more northerly districts it is wise to protect even wall-grown plants with hessian or straw during the winter. On the whole grapes should be grown against a wall or fence north of a line from Bristol to Cambridge. Further south they can be grown in the open on sunny slopes at low altitudes, but wall-grown specimens can still be expected to produce the best grapes, especially of dessert varieties.

Grapes will succeed on a wide variety of soils, but they need to be well-drained. The vines are deep-rooted so that heavy clay soils which are often poorly-drained below the surface layer are the least desirable. Calcareous soils, especially thin soils above chalk, require the addition of humus in the form of compost or well-rotted manure. Some varieties are better on calcareous soil than others. Acid soils can be improved by the addition of lime. Soils are best double dug and organic matter should be applied only to poor soils, and then sparingly.

Today most plants will be purchased as pot or container-grown specimens. These can be planted at almost any time of the year, although between October and March is best. If you live in a colder area or if the plants are rather weak it is better to delay planting until the late winter, storing the plants in the meantime in a cool frost-free place. Most plants are grown on their own rootstock, however, grafted plants can be obtained. These have some advantages in that the various rootstocks behave differently on different soil types. These stocks are given numbers and letters to distinguish them: 125AA will cope well with most soil types, 5BB is good on poor or heavy or chalky soils, whereas 5C will be better on the richer deeper loams under acid or alkaline conditions. The rootstock influences the vigour of the plant as well as coping with a particular soil condition. They are also resistant to Vine Phylloxera, an aphid-like pest which is a menace on the continent but which is thankfully absent from Britain.

Vines should be planted about 22cm from the base of the wall or fence, firmed in well and given a mulch of well-rotted compost which can be allowed to cover the lower buds or the graft union on grafted plants. This will help to protect the graft during frosty spells, however, the scion must not be allowed to root or the purpose of the graft will be lost.

In late winter young plants can be cut hard back to about one-third their length, usually 10–15cm. Vines planted in full growth should be left unpruned until the following winter.

Young and established plants must be looked after with care. The soil, especially that below a sunny wall, must never be allowed to dry out completely. Regular watering and mulches will help to overcome this. Regular feeds of weak liquid manure or National Growmore at a rate of 70gm per sqm (2oz per sqyd), plus susphate of potash at 15gm per sqm (½oz per sqyd) are most beneficial, especially during the summer months.

The training and pruning of grape vines is rather complex. Vines can be grown in various ways but on walls and fences it is best to establish a permanent framework. This framework can be in the form of a simple vertical cordon or rod, or it can be turned at right angles above or below a window. Alternatively a series of rods can be formed from a single plant, producing a multiple cordon. The vertical rods need to be about 1.2m apart to allow room for the lateral shoots which will bear the fruit in the years to come. Horizontal tiers or arms need to be about 40–50cm apart. The type and shape of the framework depends primarily on the size and space of wall to be occupied, and the variations possible are numerous.

Whatever the shape of the framework it will require a system of support in the form of horizontal galvanised wires spaced about 18cm apart for vertical cordons. For a single cordon choose the strongest shoot from the young vine and lead it in the required direction until it reaches the limit proposed. This may take several seasons, although a growth of 2m or more in a single year is common. After leaf

First year Second year

Training a single cordon grape vine during first and second years, as described in the text.

fall shorten back this shoot to firm, not soft, wood, at the same time trimming back any side shoots produced to two buds. The lead shoot is extended each summer until it reaches the desired length. Pinch out the lateral shoots after five or six leaves have been produced, during the summer. Pinch out any subsequent laterals after one leaf only. If you want a multiple cordon select the two strongest shoots of the young vine and train them horizontally in opposite directions. In the following season, a series of vertical shoots is established from them which should be treated in the same way as the single cordon first mentioned. The main idea during these formative years is to encourage the maximum shoot extension.

Having established a permanent framework, a regular routine of pruning is essential to produce good quality grapes. Winter pruning should be attempted during November or December shortly after leaf fall. If carried out later vine cuts tend to 'bleed' profusely — this is difficult to stop and may impair the vigour of the plant. Pruning during the early winter consists of shortening back all lateral shoots to two buds only. At the same time vines can be given a tar oil winter wash to kill off insects or insect eggs lurking on the plant. This also should not be carried out too late in the winter for fear of damaging the young swelling buds — it should certainly have been completed by the end of January.

The spring and summer pruning or pinching is rather more complex. Each leader pruned in the winter will probably produce two shoots. The most vigorous of these is selected to carry the fruit, the other being pinched out after it has made two or three leaves. Young shoots are brittle and easily broken off at the base causing 'bleeding' as well as a loss of potential fruit. They must be handled with care until they begin to harden. They should be tied in carefully, using long, loose ties. The unpinched laterals will continue elongating and after they have made several leaves, some 40–60cm of growth, the flower trusses (one or perhaps two per shoot) will be seen. These shoots should be pinched out two leaves beyond the first flower truss. Any shoot not producing a truss should be pinched out after having made seven or eight leaves.

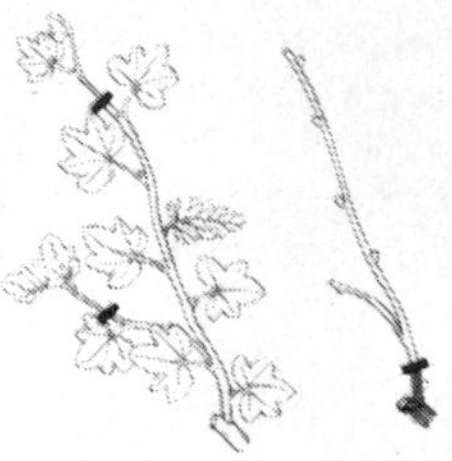

Pruning of a simple cordon grape vine. In summer (left) shoots are pinched out two leaves beyond a flower cluster. In winter (right) the same shoot is pruned back to a single bud above the main stem.

Some varieties of grapes set fruit easily, others, especially those grown against a wall rather than in the full open garden, need a little help. When they are in full flower the branches can be shaken or tapped gently to scatter the pollen. Alternatively run your hands over one truss after another to aid pollination. Grapes grown for dessert require careful thinning as the berries swell. It is often necessary to remove up to half the potential grapes in order to produce bunches with good-sized berries. Sharp pointed scissors are required for this operation, (if you have a number of vines you may wish to purchase special grape scissors). Malformed or damaged grapes should be removed first, followed by further thinning if necessary. Grapes grown for wine-making need not be thinned as only the juice is required. One word of warning here — avoid damaging the natural bloom produced by the young fruits for this both removes the water-repellant coating of the berries and spoils their appearance.

Ripening bunches of grapes often need protecting from birds and wasps which can quickly ruin the crop just as it begins to ripen. Some varieties are more prone to attack than others. Use fine netting or protect individual bunches within a piece of old nylon stocking.

Grapes are prone to various diseases, of which Grey Mould and Downy and Powdery Mildews are the most troublesome. Grey Mould attacks the grapes, causing them to rot and covering them in a mass of furry grey mould. Plants are particularly prone during wet weather and the mould spreads very rapidly. A spray of Dichlorofluanid at blossom time, followed by regular spraying at two-week intervals is sufficient control. Plants should not be sprayed within three weeks of harvesting.

Powdery Mildew is common on some varieties of grapes grown on walls. It appears early in the season as a white powdery covering on the shoots and young leaves and it can be very disfiguring. Bad attacks will also spread on to the flowers and young fruits. Overcrowded shoots and leaves will exacerbate the problem. Sprays of Benomyl or Thiophanate-methyl should help to control the fungus.

Downy Mildew causes pale green or yellowish patches on the leaves which show as downy mildew patches on the lower surface. These eventually dry out causing the leaves to curl and fall prematurely. Berries and stems may also be affected. All affected parts should be removed and burnt. A protective spray of Bordeaux Mixture, Zineb or liquid copper, applied at 10–14-day intervals should alleviate the problem. Spraying should not take place during flowering time or as the berries mature.

WHITE VARIETIES

'Chasselas Late' late Oct. A good grape for growing on a wall and useful for dessert or wine making. There are several clones available: 'Chasselas d'Or', 'Chasselas 1921', 'Chasselas Rose Royale' and 'Royal Muscadine'.
'Madeleine Angevine 7972' late Sept – early Oct. A vigorous grape, especially good in colder areas, but best for wine making.
'Muller Thurgau' = 'Riesling Sylvaner' mid Oct. The most widely grown grape, especially good for dessert.
'Precose de Malingre' late Sept. A good early grape, although not prolific, for dessert or wine making.
'Seyval' = 'Seyve Villard 5276' mid – late Oct. A heavy cropper which is resistant to mildew. Particularly good for wine making.
'Siegerrebe' late Aug – early Sept. The earliest grape to mature, although prone to wasp damage. Can be used for dessert or wine making.

BLACK VARIETIES

'Brant' mid Oct. A fine small sweet grape good for dessert or wine. A very useful wall vine which has striking autumn colouring as well as the bonus of fruit. Can be used for dessert or wine making.
'Cascade' = 'Siebel 13.053' early Oct. A good wall grape, especially for wine making. Resistant to mildew.
'Noir Hatif de Marseilles' late Sept. A small grape for dessert or wine making, best on a sunny wall.
'Pinot Noir' late Oct. A heavy but late cropper suitable for the milder districts of the country, for dessert or wine.
'Strawberry Grape' late Oct. A well-known grape producing small bunches of grapes most suitable for wine making, but with a flavour faintly suggestive of strawberries. There are a number of clones available, some have pink or greenish berries.

BLACKBERRIES AND HYBRID BERRIES

Blackberries and various hybrid berries which are crosses between different blackberry species and varieties, or between blackberries and raspberries, are fine cane fruits for training on fences, on walls or even over arches. They are particularly good on boundary fences where they can grow relatively unrestricted. Some are too vigorous for the small garden, but the Loganberry and Boysenberry, which are less vigorous and fairly easily trained, are ideal for the average small garden.

Blackberries and hybrid berries will succeed on a wide variety of soil types, light or heavy, acid or alkaline. A fairly heavy loam is ideal, but not essential. The judicious use of composts or well-rotted farmyard manure is the best way to improve light soils. Dig all soils deeply before planting. Position is not critical: sun or partial shade is preferred: plants will succeed in a fully shaded position but fruits will ripen later.

Canes will be purchased as young pot or container-grown plants or as recently-lifted stock grown on open ground. They can be planted at any time from late October until the end of March, weather permitting. Plants should be spaced at a distance of 2 – 3.5m from one another according to the vigour of the particular cultivar. Immediately after planting, cut back the stems to about 15cm if this has not already been done.

Plants benefit from liberal applications of mulches and manures, especially when young. If these are not available an annual spring dressing of sulphate of ammonia, applied at 60gm per sqm, (2 oz per sq yd) will suffice.

The training of these fruits is important. Most have prickly stems and are rather difficult to handle. If new and old canes are allowed to grow together, pruning out of all the old canes each year can prove tricky and the young canes can easily be damaged. Ideally you should train the new growth away from the older canes; to do so you need to understand their growth. A newly planted cane will put out new shoots from the ground during its first summer. These will bear the first crop of berries the following year. At the same time, in the second year, the plant will be producing more vigorous young shoots. By the time the one-year-old canes are in flower and fruit the new growths will already be 1 – 2m long or more. If these are carefully trained away from the fruiting canes then a tangle will be avoided and pruning made simple.

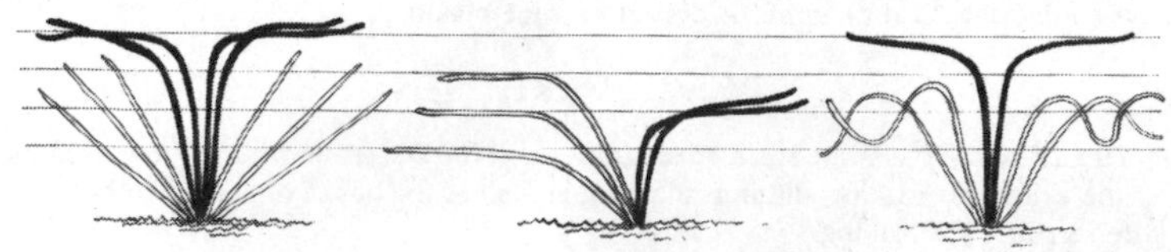

Many systems can be employed to train blackberries and hybrid berries, however they all aim at training the strong new growth (dark canes) away from the fruiting canes. Three different methods are shown. At the end of the season the canes which have fruited are cut out and replaced by new canes.

Canes can be trained in a number of ways, the system adopted depending on your individual whim and the space available. A system of galvanised wires 30cm apart, to a height of 1.75 – 2m should be aimed for, although a top wire at 1.5m will be sufficient for the less vigorous varieties. Young canes should be tied into the wires as they elongate. At the same time excessive shoots or weak or damaged ones can be removed. Old canes can be cut out the moment they finish fruiting, which is generally in the late autumn or early winter. The new canes can then either be left as they are or retied to fill the space left by those that have been removed, according to the system adopted.

Clean healthy stock is essential. Cane fruits are subject to virus diseases and these can greatly decrease the vigour of plants and reduce cropping. Greenfly can prove disfiguring and may spread virus from a neighbouring garden. They can be controlled by tar oil winter washes in the same way as for other fruits — apples and pears for instance.

Raspberry beetle can also be a menace. Derris is the best means of controlling this beetle. On blackberries this should be applied as the first flowers open followed by a second application a fortnight later. On Loganberries the first application is best undertaken towards the end of the flowering period, again followed by a second application a fortnight later.

Blackberries and hybrid berries are generally easy to propagate. The simplest method is to peg down to the ground the tip of a vigorous young shoot during July. These root readily and can be severed from the parent plant for replanting early in the following spring.

Plate 23 Crevice Plants 1 *Aethionema pulchella* (p.285), 2 *Antirrhinum majus* (p.286), 3 *Asplenium trichomanes* (p.287), 4 *Campanula portenschlagiana* (p.288), 5 *Erysimum linifolia* (p.294), 6 *Cymbalaria muralis* (p.292), 7 *Corydalis lutea* (p.291).

1
2
3
4
5
6
7

1
2
3
4
5
6
7

BLACKBERRY VARIETIES

'Bedford Giant' early, July – Aug. A vigorous variety particularly suitable for poorer soils.
'Himalayan Giant' mid-season, Aug – Oct. Another vigorous variety which grows well on poor soils.
'Japanese Wineberry' mid-season, Aug – Sept. A cultivar of *Rubus phoenicolasius*. Most of the fruits mature at once.
'John Innes' mid-season, Sept – Oct. A semi-vigorous, heavy-cropping variety.
'Merton Early' early, Aug. A semi-vigorous variety with fine-flavoured berries.
'Oregon Thornless' = 'Thornless Evergreen' late, Sept – Oct. Semi-vigorous. A fine cultivar of *Rubus laciniatus* and a very decorative plant.
'Parsley-leaved Blackberry' mid-season, Aug – Sept. A selected form of *Rubus laciniatus*.
'Smoothstem' late, late Aug – Oct. A vigorous, but thornless variety.

HYBRID BERRY VARIETIES

'Boysenberry' early, July – Aug. A loganberry/blackberry/raspberry hybrid which is particularly good on lighter drier soils. There is a thornless sport introduced fairly recently — 'Thornless Boysenberry'.
'Loganberry' early, July – Aug. A blackberry/raspberry hybrid which is very popular in gardens being particularly well-suited to the smaller garden.
'Thornless Loganberry' a thornless sport of the preceding.
'Phenomenal Berry' mid-season, Aug – Sept. A fine, vigorous hybrid berry.
'Tayberry' early, July – Aug. A fine new blackberry/raspberry hybrid. A similar plant to the Loganberry but higher yielding.

When choosing which berries to plant bear in mind the vigour of the plant and the season of fruiting — early, mid or late to fruit. Thornless varieties are less vigorous on the whole and are ideal for planting near the house, on a shed or by a gateway, or wherever people are likely to walk close by.

There are a number of interesting related berries in the genus *Rubus* to be found on p.227. These, although grown primarily for their ornamental value, can also be grown for their fruits.

CURRANTS AND GOOSEBERRIES

Both red and white currants and gooseberries can be grown to advantage against wall and fences. The usual form is a vertical cordon, although double or treble cordons are often formed. All three fruits flower on one-year-old wood but they form a system of short fruiting spurs from older wood, and these bear the majority of the fruit. It is thus possible to build up a permanent framework such as the cordon.

Currants and gooseberries like a well-drained loamy soil, preferably one that is slightly acid or neutral. However, they are not overfussy and will succeed on a wide variety of soils, but light sandy soils or highly calcareous ones are not suitable. The position can be sunny or shaded so that walls or fences of almost any aspect will do, although the quality of fruit produced by completely shaded plants cannot be expected to be as good as those ripened in the sun.

These fruits are not long-lived and begin to decline after about ten years. However, they are very easily propagated by simply heeling in 30cm lengths or strong, young, well-ripened wood in the autumn in the open garden. The lower buds are removed so that the first bud is about 5cm above the soil surface, allowing half the cutting to be buried. These will be well rooted within a year and can be planted out the following autumn.

Plate 24 Crevice Plants 1 *Erinus alpinus* (p.294), 2 *Saxifraga paniculata* (p.300), 3 *Haberlea rhodopensis* (p.295), 4 *Sempervivum arachnoideum* (p.303), 5 *Sedum acre* (p.301), 6 *S. reflexum* (p.301), 7 *Centranthus ruber* (p.290).

The best time to plant is October – November, but any time until February will do. Mulches of well-rotted manure are very beneficial, especially for those plants in sunny exposed positions.

The training of single cordons is fairly straight-forward. Young plants should be spaced about 45cm apart and 15 – 25cm in front of the wall or fence. During the winter the young plants should be cut back by about a half their length to an outward-facing bud. At the same time prune back any lateral shoots to about 2.5cm from the leading shoot. At the end of June or in July of the first year pinch out all lateral shoots after four or five leaves. Do not attempt this earlier or a lot of unwanted secondary growth will be produced. At this stage leave the leader unpruned, but tie it in to protect it from damage.

During the second winter prune back all the pinched laterals to about 2.5cm and cut back the leader again to an outward facing bud, leaving 15cm of new growth. This annual routine is repeated until the cordon has reached the desired height, usually between one and two metres. The leader is then treated as a lateral to prevent it from gaining more height.

Multiple cordons are trained by cutting back the original shoot to two strong opposing buds and training the resultant shoots sideways at first. The upright arms of the cordon should be about 15cm apart and future pruning to form the verticals should take this into account. Each vertical arm of a multiple cordon is treated as an ordinary single cordon.

Currants and gooseberries are self-fertile and readily pollinated by garden insects so there are no worries about fruit setting. Picking differs between the two types: red and white currants are picked as trusses when ripe; use a pair of sharp, pointed scissors to avoid damaging the cordons. Gooseberries can be removed as individual fruits; pick some early fruits from dessert gooseberries for cooking, allowing the later fruits to ripen well and grow to a good size.

Birds can greatly damage the crop and bushes will need suitable protection. Birds may also attack the fruit buds during the winter and can quickly devastate a plant.

Aphids and sawflies are the worst pests of both currants and gooseberries and appropriate measures should be taken to protect plants using a systemic insecticide.

Gooseberry mildew can be lessened by spraying with Dinocap or Benomyl, though severely infected shoots should be removed and burnt.

RED CURRANT VARIETIES

'Jonkheer van Tets' July
'Laxton's No 1' July
'Red Lake' July – Aug
'Rondom' Aug
'Wilson's Long Bunch' Aug

WHITE CURRANT VARIETIES

'White Dutch' July
'White Grape' mid July
'White Versailles' July

GOOSEBERRY VARIETIES

'Careless' June. Green-fruited
'Golden Drop' June. Yellow-fruited
'Green Gem' June. Green-fruited
'Howard's Lancer' June – July. Green-fruited
'Lancashire Lad' July. Red-fruited
'Leveller' June – July. Yellow-fruited
'Whinham's Industry' June – July. Red-fruited
'Whitesmith' June – July. White-fruited
'White Lion' July. White-fruited

Plants to Grow in Wall Crevices

Every gardener knows that old walls accumulate plants. They often appear quite spontaneously, growing directly on the bricks or in various holes and crevices that appear with age due to the processes of weathering, especially in the mortar. Wallflowers, Snapdragons, Valerian, Yellow Corydalis, Stonecrops and Ivy-leaved Toadflax often appear casually on walls.

Mortar crumbles with age, allowing roots to penetrate deeply. Soil and seeds can be blown into crevices together, and plants can soon become established.

Some plants are less desirable on walls, especially young shrubs and trees. Buddleia is a common example, though Sycamore, Yew, Berberis, Laburnum and many others have been recorded. As these grow the roots swell and sections of wall can be brought down. Such plants should of course be discouraged.

There are a large number of plants that will grow on walls, but it is difficult, often impossible, to establish plants on new mortared walls and gardeners can waste countless frustrating hours trying to do so. Older walls in which the mortar has begun to crumble are easier and suitable cracks can be extended and deepened to allow some soil to be rammed in. Dry walls can serve better, although holes must be packed with suitable soil allowing no air pockets to remain. Best of all are dry walls which are inclined back against an earth bank. Such retaining walls can often support many plants. Mortared retaining walls can support plants providing spaces are left at intervals in their construction.

Walls do not, after all, provide the best environment for plants to grow. They dry out rapidly, especially on the sunny side and there is little room for roaming roots. Retaining walls allow roots to penetrate through wall spaces into the soil behind, where conditions are more equable. Plants which survive on free-standing walls are able to withstand drought or can survive in the minimum amount of soil, or are those whose roots can penetrate the tiniest cracks and crevices. Shaded walls, which are often more moist, will harbour rather different plants from dry sunny walls. Yet it is surprising how, once established, wall plants will flourish year after year with scarcely any attention. Some will even spread by seeding into other crevices.

The ideal wall pocket is one which slopes backwards and downwards thus allowing the roots to extend down. They also prevent the soil from falling out, or being washed away. The best soil is a compost made up of equal parts of loam, peat, sand and finely chopped well-rotted manure or leaf-mould. The compost should be rammed into crevices with a suitable stick.

It is best to use young plants or seedlings, making sure the roots go well down into the soil. Larger plants are seldom easy to introduce without damaging the root system, even if there is room for it in the first place. Many gardeners advocate planting the wall, especially a dry retaining wall, as it is being constructed, and indeed this is by far the best way of establishing plants in such situations. However, most people will have walls already and it is a case of making the most of existing structures. Plants can be wedged in with small chips of rock and this will also help to stop the soil from tumbling out.

Seeds can be sown directly into wall crevices or soil pockets. The best way of

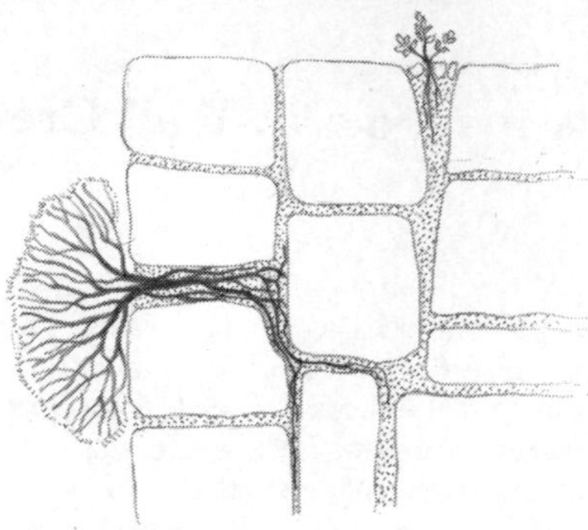

Plant roots penetrate between blocks of stone or bricks on suitable walls, seen here in section. Dry retaining walls with soil rammed into the crevices are the most suitable.

doing this is to make small pellets of soil with seeds included, and to press them into suitable spots on walls. The success rate will not be high although, as in establishing mistletoe on an apple tree, the more seeds that are tried the greater the chance of success.

Newly-planted walls must be kept watered during dry weather, although care should be taken not to wash out either seeds or small seedlings. Retaining walls can be watered from behind.

This can all seem a lot of effort together with a good deal of chance, but an established wall sprouting various colourful plants can be a most attractive and charming feature. Those who have explored the limestone or granitic walls of Devon and Cornwall or the stone walls of the Cotswolds will already know how delighful such walls can be, both for their wild flowers and tiny ferns, and for their range of common garden plants.

It is not our intention here to instruct on the construction of dry walls and retaining walls, for there are numerous detailed accounts for those who wish to start from scratch. Below we have listed some of the plants which are easy to establish and loveliest for cultivating on walls, although the list is far from complete. We have also included some rare, though fine wall plants.

ACANTHOLIMON (Plumbaginaceae)

There are some 90 of these cousins of the Thrift, *Armeria,* and Sea Lavender, *Limonium*. They form tight hedgehog-like cushions of narrow spiny leaves and come mostly from the Middle East and Western Himalaya, but also from Greece. They are excellent plants for dry sunny walls. Seeds germinate very slowly so propagation is probably more satisfactory by division or cuttings.

☼ **Acantholimon glumaceum** = *Statice ararati* forms small dark green cushions with dense leaves. Six to eight bright rose flowers, 11–12mm across, are borne in slender spikes. [June–July, HH, USSR (Armenia) & E Turkey]

☼ **Acantholimon venustum** forms silvery-grey, rather loose cushions with broader leaves than the previous species. Flowers are vivid rose, 10–12mm across, twelve or more to a spike. [June–July, HH, Turkey (Cilicia)]

ACHILLEA (Compositae)

A large and well known genus which includes the Yarrows, Milfoils and Sneezeworts. A number are grown in the herbaceous border and some of the smaller ones are especially fine in the alpine garden.

Achillea umbellata is a low tufted perennial with silvery, rather ferny-looking leaves. Six to eight white flowerheads share a common stem. [June–Sept, H, Greece]

var. **argentea** is an even more silvery plant.

AETHIONEMA (Cruciferae)

An attractive little genus allied to the Candytufts, *Iberis*, with some 60 species present mainly in Europe and Asia. They may be annual, perennial or subshrubby with fleshy leaves and small four-petalled flowers. The cultivated species revel in light sandy soils in warm sunny spots. They are readily raised from seed or cuttings. The less hardy ones may not survive bad winters unprotected and cuttings overwintered in a frame will insure against loss. The small, flat, heart-shaped fruits are very characteristic of the genus.

***Aethionema cordifolium** = *Iberis jucunda* is an erect perennial up to 20cm high, branching from a woody base, the stems with crowded linear bluish-green leaves. Rosy-lilac flowers form dense rounded racemes. [June, H-HH, Turkey]

'Warley Rose' is a beautiful cultivar with deep pink flowers. The leaves are also edged with pink.

Aethionema pulchellum (Pl.23) is similar to the previous species and sometimes confused with it. However, plants are smaller and the stems produce numerous side shoots. The rosy-lilac flowers are smaller and borne in longer, narrower racemes. [May–June, H-HH, Iran]

Aethionema grandiflorum is a loosely branched perennial up to 45cm tall, generally less. Leaves are oblong, blunt, blue-green. Flowers larger than the above species, are warm rose, in crowded racemes. [May–Aug, HH, Lebanon]

ALYSSUM (Cruciferae)

A popular garden genus, although only a handful of the 80 or so species are cultivated. They are readily and quickly raised from seed, although especially good forms can be increased by cuttings.

***Alyssum saxatile**, the Rock Alyssum, is a deservedly popular plant frequently seen on walls, in rock gardens or lining pathways in our gardens. The plant forms a tufted subshrub, up to 30cm across or more, with hoary greyish-green lanceolate leaves. The small, bright golden-yellow flowers are borne in branched clusters on slender stems. [Apr–June, H, E & SE Europe]

A vigorous and colourful plant which soon increases by seeding into cracks and crevices. Seedlings, if need be, should be moved whilst still young. Plants often produce a few late flowers after the main season has finished.

'Citrinum' = 'Sulphureum' is a form with pale lemon-yellow flowers.
'Plenum' is more intensely golden than the type.
'Variegatum' has leaves variegated with yellow and grey-green.

ANTIRRHINUM (Scrophulariaceae)

The Common Snapdragon, *A. majus*, is one of the very best wall plants, often arriving there by chance from other parts of the garden. On walls it often makes a splendid more compact plant and although often treated as a half-hardy annual it will survive for a number of years in the right place. The genus *Antirrhinum* is relatively small, its species confined primarily to southern Europe.

***Antirrhinum majus** (Pl.23), the Common Snapdragon, is a branched rather erect perennial up to 100cm tall, but often only 20–40cm on a sunny wall. The deep green leaves are lanceolate, crowded mostly in the lower half of the plant. The fragrant typically pouched snapdragon-flowers are 2.5–5cm long, varying in colour from white through yellow, orange, pink, crimson to scarlet or bicoloured. [May–Oct, H-HH, S Europe]

Plants are easily raised from seed, although particularly good forms can be increased by cuttings. There are many named varieties available in the trade.

ARABIS (Cruciferae)

Another popular genus in our gardens, although of the 100 or so species only a handful are worth cultivating. They are readily raised from seed.

Arabis blepharophylla is a perennial forming a loose cushion of leafy rosettes, the rough, deep green leaves being spoon-shaped or oblong. The flowers are rosy-purple, produced in rather open racemes. [Mar–May, HH, USA (California)]

Plants may be killed in a severe winter but produce seed readily and a young stock can always be kept in hand.

Arabis albida is the common Arabis of gardens forming broad loose mats of hoary green, rather rough foliage. The lower leaves occur in rosettes and are oblong or obovate and toothed, whereas the upper leaves are heart-shaped, clasping the stem with their base. The flowers are borne in loose racemes up to 20cm tall, white and pleasantly fragrant. [Feb–May, H, SE Europe & W Asia]

A popular and easily grown plant, useful for the top of a retaining wall or for the side of a wall if a suitable crevice can be found. Plants are rather sprawling and soon become untidy and need to be trimmed every year or so to keep them in check. Good forms are best propagated from cuttings rather than from seed.

'Flore-Pleno' has double white flowers.
***'Rosa-bella'** is a form with large soft pink flowers of great charm.
'Variegata' has leaves variegated with green and yellow.

ARENARIA (Caryophyllaceae)

Generally referred to as the Sandworts, this large genus contains perhaps 150 species. Most are rather insignificant herbs with opposite leaves and white flowers. A few make good, though dainty garden plants, easily increasing from seed. They are sometimes included in the genus *Minuartia* in catalogues, however, *Arenaria* species have rounded rather than notched petals.

***Arenaria balearica,** Creeping Sandwort is a small creeping perennial forming a close mat of tiny shiny green leaves. The small solitary white flowers are borne on slender stalks 5–7.5mm long. [Mar–Aug, H-HH, Balearic Is, Corsica]

A quick-growing, excellent and fascinating little plant for a moist, partially shaded spot, especially a wall ledge, or the top of a wall.

Arenaria ledebouriana is a tufted hairless perennial 10–18cm tall, with densely congested leaves, each slender and rather stiff. Small, white flowers are borne in loose clusters. [Apr–May, H, E Turkey] ◐

Arenaria montana is an hairy creeping perennial with lanceolate, oblong or linear leaves. Large, white flowers are borne on slender stalks. [May–June, H-HH, France & Spain] ◐

ARMERIA (Plumbaginaceae)

The Sea Pink or Thrift, *A. maritima*, is a well known plant, however, several different species are cultivated. They all have basal tufts of leaves and globular flowerheads borne on long slender stems.

***Armeria maritima**, Sea Pink or Thrift, is a low perennial forming dense tufts of slender grassy leaves. Bright pink or reddish flowers form heads 10–15mm across. [June–Aug, H, Europe] ☼

A good plant for the top of a retaining wall or a cavity wall. There are a number of colour variants including a white one.

ASARINA (Scrophulariaceae)

Closely related to the Snapdragons *Antirrhinum*, but with solitary flowers borne along long trailing stems.

Asarina procumbens, the Creeping Snapdragon, is a stickily hairy perennial with sprawling stems and opposite pairs of heart-shaped or oval leaves. The flowers are pale whitish-yellow with a yellow patch in the throat, each 30–35mm long. [June–Sept, H-HH, S France & Spain] ●

ASPLENIUM (Aspleniaceae)

A large and diverse genus of ferns with some 700 species distributed in temperate and tropical regions of the world. Many of the hardy ones relish a deep crevice in limestone or mortar but *A. septentrionale* requires acid rocks.

***Asplenium trichomanes** (Pl.23), the Maidenhair Spleenwort or Wall Spleenwort, is a common British fern. Plants make spidery rosettes of fronds, each 5–35cm long, slender and tapered with a series of hard green, oval or rounded leaflets set upon a shiny slender black stalk. [H, Europe & Asia]

A charming little fern which is easily grown and surprisingly drought-resistant. On old walls in many parts of Britain it is frequently seen in large numbers.

Asplenium viride, the Green Spleenwort, is similar to the previous species but more delicate and with green stalks. [H, Europe & Asia]

Asplenium ruta-muraria, the Wall Rue Spleenwort, is common in many parts of Britain on walls, bridges and limestone rocks. Plants often form thick masses of grey-green fronds, each 2–15cm long, irregular in shape and with numerous rounded, or wedge-shaped leaflets. [H, Europe & Asia]

A tough little fern, although slow to establish. It was at one time used as an herbal remedy for rickets.

Asplenium adiantum-nigrum, the Black Spleenwort, is another common British fern forming tufts of hard, shiny-green fronds, 10–45cm long, which are narrowly triangular in outline and deeply lobed. The stalks are purplish-brown. [H, Europe & Asia]

◐ **Asplenium septentrionale** is a rare fern in Britain, a rather dainty species of acid rocks and walls in Wales and northern England. The narrow, forked fronds are deep green, 5–15cm long and borne on shiny dark stalks. [H, Europe & Asia]

AUBRIETA (Cruciferae)

Aubrieta deltoidea and its numerous cultivars are some of the most widely planted garden plants, forming bright mats of colour in the spring. They are valuable plants, easily grown and spreading by self-sown seedlings. Keep plants from becoming too straggly by clipping them back as soon as flowering is finished.

◐ **Aubrieta deltoidea** is a compact or trailing perennial forming rather flat cushions of grey-green obovate or wedge-shaped, toothed leaves. The four-petalled flowers are lilac or purplish red, borne in loose racemes. [Apr–June, H, Sicily, Greece & Turkey]

Many cultivars are available ranging in colour from white and pink to deep red and purple. There are also double-flowered forms.

BUGLOSSOIDES (Boraginaceae)

A genus of 30 or more perennial herbs or subshrubs. Mostly Mediterranean in distribution but with species in northern Asia as well as North America. The species were at one time all included in the genus *Lithospermum* along with *Lithodora* and *Moltkia*.

☼ **Buglossoides gastonii** = *Lithospermum gastonii* is a leafy perennial up to 45cm tall, occasionally more, with rough ovate or lanceolate leaves. The flowers, 12–14mm across are violet or purple to begin with but soon change to deep blue, with a white throat; they are borne in small terminal clusters. [June–Aug, H, W Pyrenees]

◐ **Buglossoides purpureo-caeruleum** = *Lithospermum purpureo-caeruleum*, the Blue Gromwell, is a tufted perennial with arching non-flowering stems and erect flowering stems. The rough leaves are lanceolate with under-rolled margins. The salver-shaped flowers start off red but change to deep blue, 14–19mm across, borne in paired terminal clusters. [Apr–June, H, Europe & W Asia]

Both species are suitable for the top of a wall given a good deep pocket of soil.

CAMPANULA (Campanulaceae)

This is the Bellflower or Harebell genus, one of the most popular groups of delightful species for growing on walls. There are some 250 species, mostly in Europe and Asia. They can be annuals, biennials or long-lived perennials with milky juice and typical bell-shaped flowers, which may be in long spikes or clusters or solitary. They are readily raised from seed, but the perennials are more rapidly increased by divisions or cuttings. Most like to get their roots deep into crevices, some managing to penetrate the tightest cracks. Plants generally like a sunny position.

☼ ***Campanula portenschlagiana** = *C. muralis* (Pl.23) is a smooth tufted perennial with stems up to 22cm long bearing shiny-green kidney-shaped, toothed leaves. Light bright purple widely bell-shaped flowers, are borne in loose racemes. [June–July, H, S Europe]

Perhaps the best of all 'wall campanulas', despite its tongue-twisting name, although it can become rather invasive. It is free-flowering and long-lived. Flower stems can be clipped off once flowering has finished, this sometimes stimulating a few more flowers later in the year.

var. **alba** has white flowers.

Campanula poscharskyana is a vigorous tufted perennial with a rather sprawling habit, the stems 30cm long, sometimes more. The leaves are pale green, the lower heart-shaped and toothed, the upper narrower. The lavender-blue flowers, almost white in the centre, are open rather starry bells borne in loose, branched clusters. [June–Nov, H, Yugoslavia] ◐

Another tongue-twister, but a delightful plant, especially for its long flowering season. Like the previous species this one seeds itself freely and may have to be restricted from time to time.

***Campanula cochlearifolia** = *C. pusilla*, Fairy's Thimble, is a tiny creeping harebell usually scarcely 10cms tall which forms a close carpet of pale green leaves. The flowers, usually solitary, are nodding, blue bells, 12–16mm long, on very slender stems. [June–Aug, H, C & S European mountains] ◐

A charming little Campanula especially good for the top of a wall where there are wide cracks for it to run along.

'Alba' has white flowers.

'Pallida' has flowers of very pale blue.

var. **tyrolensis** = *C. bellardii* is more robust than the type and with deeper blue bells.

Campanula caespitosa is a densely tufted perennial up to 5cm tall with a deep tap root but no runners. Shiny-green leaves are ovate and toothed. The several clear blue, narrow-mouthed bells are borne on a wiry stem. [June–July, H, Italy (Dolomites)] ◐

***Campanula carpatica** is a spreading tufted perennial with stems 20–45cm long. The lower leaves are heart-shaped and toothed and the large solitary, broad, blue bells are erect, borne on long naked stalks. [June–Aug, H, E Europe (Carpathian Mountains)] ☼

A fine and striking plant for a sunny wall where its roots have a deep run. It is a variable plant and the best forms are well worth securing.

'Alba' has white flowers.

'China Cup' has flowers of palest blue.

'Isabel' has flowers of purple-blue.

'Riverslea' has rather flat deep blue flowers.

'White Star' also has rather flat flowers, but they are white.

Campanula isophylla = *C. floribunda* is a prostrate or trailing perennial with ovate, toothed leaves and numerous lilac-blue, rather starry flowers, each 20–25mm across. [July–Aug, HH, S Italy] ◐

This fine plant is often sold as a pot plant in the summer. However, it is hardy in milder districts in all but the most extreme winters.

'Alba' has white flowers.

Campanula garganica is a tufted perennial. The basal leaves are kidney-shaped whilst those higher up are heart-shaped. All have blunt teeth. The large broad rather flat, bell-flowers are blue with a whitish centre, borne in axillary clusters of great charm. [May–Sept, H, S Italy] ☼

A lovely, though variable, species but often not long-lived so requiring frequent propagation.

'Alba' has white flowers set above the downy-grey leaves.

Campanula latifolia, the Giant Bellflower, frequently grown in gardens, sometimes finds its way on to an old wall. Plants grow up to 100cm tall, sometimes more, with simple leafy stems, the leaves large and heart-shaped. The flowers are large blue deep bells, 4–5.5cm long borne in a long, loose raceme. [July–Sept, H, Europe & Asia]

'Alba' has white flowers.

A number of other Campanulas are suitable for wall culture, although less frequently seen. These include *C. elatines* and *C. elatinoides*, *C. fragilis* = *C. barrelieri*, *C. macrorhiza* and *C. mirabilis*.

CENTRANTHUS (Valerianaceae)

This attractive genus contains the Common or Wall Valerian which is such a feature of walls and cliffs in certain parts of the country, especially in Devon and Cornwall. The species at one time were all to be found in the genus *Valeriana*, although the characters of separation are rather slight.

***Centranthus ruber** = *Valeriana ruber* (Pl.24), Common Valerian, is a stout, rather fleshy perennial forming a bushy plant 60–90cm tall. The bluish-green leaves are lanceolate and untoothed. Small flowers, borne in large pyramidal clusters, are a vivid carmine-red, although pink, cream and white forms can be found. [June–Sept, H, Europe]

This superb plant is a British native and is one of the most decorative of all wall plants. Established plants are long-lived and they seed freely. Plants do particularly well in maritime districts.

CERASTIUM (Caryophyllaceae)

This large genus occurs in many parts of the world. They are mostly small plants with opposite leaves and white flowers with notched petals. The Chickweeds, or Mouse-ears belong here. Most are simply not worth growing.

Cerastium tomentosum, Snow-in-Summer, is a widely grown and well-known species which forms a low mat of woolly-white growths from which rise slender, branched flower stems. The flowers are pure white, 15–25mm across, with deeply notched petals. [July–Aug, H, S Europe]

Snow-in-summer is an invasive plant but always attracts attention when in flower. It looks fine draped over the top of a wall, but beware lest it swamps its neighbours. Plants are easily increased by division. In some parts of Britain *C. tomentosum* has become naturalised.

CETERACH (Aspleniaceae)

A small genus of ferns once included in *Asplenium*.

Ceterach officinarum = *Asplenium ceterach*, the Rusty-back Fern, is a small tufted species with tough deep green fronds, 5–25cm long, which are narrow with alternating oblong or oval leaflets set close together along the midrib. The underneath surface of the fronds is silvery with scales at first but soon changes to rusty-brown giving the fern its common name. [H, Europe & Asia].

An attractive and common fern typical of mortared walls in many parts of Britain. Plants are very drought resistant but variable in size according to where they are growing.

CHEIRANTHUS (Cruciferae)

A genus best known for the Wallflower, *Cheiranthus cheiri*, which is, as its common name implies, a most splendid wall plant, indeed often looking more at home on a wall than in the garden border. Plants are easily raised from seed and, once established on an old wall, usually increase readily.

***Cheiranthus cheiri**, the Wallflower, is a short-lived perennial reaching 60cm tall, often less on a dry wall. The slender lanceolate leaves are 2–10cm long. The flowers are borne in long racemes and vary in colour from yellow and bronze to orange, red and mauve; individual flowers 1.5–2.5cm across and richly fragrant.[Apr–June, H, SE Europe & W Asia, but widely naturalised]

CHELIDONIUM (Papaveraceae)

This genus contains a single species which is native to Britain. Plants are easily raised from seed and quickly spread by this means. It makes a fine and easily grown wall plant if given a semi-shaded moist site and a deep crevice.

***Chelidonium majus**, Greater Celandine or Swallow-wort, is a loosely growing perennial herb, 30–60cm tall, with erect rather brittle stems with yellow juice. The soft green leaves are variously lobed and the small yellow poppy-like flowers are 18–25mm across, borne in small umbels. The seed pod is a long, thin, pointed capsule. [May–Oct, H, Europe & Asia Minor]

'Flore-Pleno' has double yellow flowers.

'Laciniatum' = *C. laciniatum* is a form with the leaves cut into slender lobes.

CHIASTOPHYLLUM (Crassulaceae)

A genus containing only a single species — a lovely rather succulent plant distantly related to both the stonecrops and the houseleeks.

***Chiastophyllum oppositifolium** = *Cotyledon oppositifolia* is a tufted perennial 15–30cm tall with opposite pairs of fleshy, roundish leaves which are coarsely toothed. The small, golden-yellow flowers are borne in delicate, drooping, branched racemes. [June–July, H, USSR (Caucasus)]

CORYDALIS (Fumariaceae)

A delightful genus of tuberous- or fibrous-rooted plants allied to the Fumitories, *Fumaria*, and included by some authorities in the Poppy Family, Papaveraceae. Only the fibrous-rooted species are suitable for growing in wall crevices.

***Corydalis lutea** (Pl.23), the Yellow Corydalis, forms loose, rounded tufts of thin, succulent stems and ferny grey-green leaves. The golden-yellow flowers, each 12–20mm long, are borne in loose, often branched racemes. [May–Oct, H, Europe]

A delightful plant which spreads readily by seed once plants have become established. Plants can be clipped back in the autumn or when they become untidy. Young plants can be easily introduced to suitable wall crevices and flower when still quite young.

***Corydalis ochroleuca** is similar to the previous species but the flowers are cream with a yellow centre. [June–Sept, H, Italy]

◐ ***Corydalis cheilanthifolia** is another accomodating species. The fern-like, bright green leaves are 10–20cm long and the yellow flowers, each 12–13mm in length, are borne in crowded many-flowered racemes. [May, H, China]

CYMBALARIA (Scrophulariaceae)

Cymbalaria is a small genus closely related to the toadflaxes, *Linaria*, but with solitary flowers rather than racemes.

◐ **Cymbalaria muralis** (P1.23), Ivy-leaved Toadflax, is a charming trailing plant with small lobed leaves and tiny snapdragon-flowers which are lilac or violet with a yellow patch on the lower lip; each flower is 9–15mm long, borne on a delicate thread-like stem. [Apr–Oct, H, Europe]

This little plant often appears on old walls, both in gardens and in the countryside. It is not a spectacular plant but it is very dainty and well worth looking at closely.

CYSTOPTERIS (Athyriaceae)

● **Cystopteri's fragilis** = *C. alpina, C. regina*, the Brittle Bladder Fern, is a delicate little fern with deeply cut feathery fronds which unfurl early in the year. The fronds vary from 6–35cm in length depending on aspect, with dark brittle stalks. [H, Europe & Asia]

A charming fern for moist shaded pockets, doing especially well on old mortared walls.

● **Cystopteri's bulbifer**, the Bladder Fern, is closely related with narrow, less lobed fronds, but with characteristic pea-like green buds at intervals along the midrib. [H, N, America]

The pea-like buds can be removed and propagated to produce new plants.

DIANTHUS (Caryophyllaceae)

This popular genus contains the ancestors of the Garden Pink, the Sweet William and the Carnation, together with a host of exciting little species for the rock garden and flower border. The genus is large and complex, many of the species being difficult to tell apart. They like sunny, dry places on the whole and are easily propagated from cuttings or seed. A number are useful for the top of a broad wall or retaining wall; those listed below are only a selection.

☼◐ ***Dianthus deltoides**, the Maiden Pink, is a mat-forming species with numerous leafy stems, which are grass-green, sometimes flushed with red. Flower stems 15–22cm tall, rise from the mat with purple or crimson-red flowers, with brighter spots, each 12–17mm across with fringed petals. [June–Sept, H, Europe]

A delightful little plant which grows wild in Britain.

'Albus' has white flowers.
'Brilliant' has flowers of bright rose-pink.
'Glaucus' has attractive grey-green leaves.
'Superbus' has flowers of dark purplish-red.
'Wisely Var' has crimson flowers with a purplish eye.

☼ **Dianthus gratianopolitanus** = *D. caesius*, the Cheddar Pink, forms a low, rather flat cushion of bluish-green leaves from which the flowering stems arise.

The flowers are deep pink or purple, 20–30mm across, and delightfully fragrant, with toothed petals. [May–July, H, C & W Europe.]

This is the famous pink of the Cheddar Gorge, a plant worthy of a home in any garden.

'Baker's Var' has flowers of even deeper colour than the more usual form.

Dianthus plumarius is the Pink before it was modified into the myriad of forms that we see in our gardens today. It is rather like the previous species but the cushions are less tight and the flowers white to bright pink, 24–36mm across, usually solitary and with deeply fringed petals. [June–July, H, C & SE Europe]

A charming plant, grown as much for its flowers as for its powerful fragrance, but largely succeeded by modern garden forms and hybrids.

Dianthus superbus forms tufts of linear green leaves from which the shiny green flower stems arise, to 30–60cm. The branching stems each terminate in a solitary flower which is lilac or rosy-lilac, spotted finely with green near the centre and generally also with a reddish beard; each flower is 34–38mm across with deeply fringed petals. [June–Sept, H, Europe & N Asia]

A variable but lovely species. The flowers are very fragrant in some forms, less so in others.

Dianthus superbus.

ERIGERON (Compositae)

This large genus known commonly as the Fleabanes, occurs in most temperate parts of the world. They are daisies closely related to the Aster and on the whole easily grown.

Erigeron karvinskianus is a small much branched perennial herb reaching 45cm tall at the very most. The thin stems bear small elliptic or obovate leaves, untoothed or with few teeth. The solitary flowerheads, about 18mm across, terminating wiry stems are white turning pink or reddish-purple and with a yellowish disk. [May–Oct, H–HH, C & S America]

This rather charming little daisy has become naturalised on walls in some parts of the country, particularly in Devon and Cornwall. It requires very little attention once established. Seedlings generally appear quite readily.

ERINUS (Scrophulariaceae)

A small genus containing eight species of which only one is commonly cultivated.

***Erinus alpinus** (Pl.24), the Fairy Foxglove, is a small tufted perennial only 7–15cm tall, with small deeply toothed leaves and racemes of small purple or rose-pink flowers, each only 6–9mm across. [Mar–June, H, Mountains of W Europe]

A dainty and lovely little plant which has become naturalised on walls and bridges in parts of northern Britain. An easy plant to establish, particularly from seed, it generally spreads on a suitable wall.

'Albus' is a form with pure white flowers.
'Carmineus' has carmine flowers.
'Hirsutus' is a form with hairier stems and leaves.

ERODIUM (Geraniaceae)

A genus containing about 50 species which are closely related to *Geranium*, and natives of Europe, Asia, parts of Africa and Australia. They are on the whole readily raised from seed, but plants can also be increased from cuttings.

***Erodium petraeum** forms small tufts up to 15cm tall with soft-hairy greyish or silvery pinnate leaves which smell strongly when crushed. The pink flowers, 15–25mm across are borne in small clusters on a common stalk. [Apr–May, H, C Pyrenees]

There are various forms and subspecies of this species cultivated in our gardens. Some have white flowers veined with pink or purple or with dark blotches on the upper two petals. They prefer limy rocks and walls.

Erodium corsicum forms mats or low cushions of silvery-grey or grey-green ovate or oblong, rather crumpled leaves. The small pink flowers 8–12mm across, have deeper veining and are borne singly or several together on a common stalk. [June–Aug, H–HH, Corsica & Sardinia]

A lovely little species requiring a sunny spot and a deep crevice.

ERYSIMUM (Cruciferae)

Attractive tufted perennials related to the wallflowers, *Cheiranthus*. The species are readily increased by cuttings or seed. The genus contains many species.

***Erysimum linifolium** = *Cheiranthus linifolius* (Pl.23), is a loose plant of rounded habit reaching 40cm tall with oblong leaves and slender, dense racemes of purple-violet flowers with greyish-green anthers. [May–July, H–HH, Canary Is]

'Bowles Purple' is a particularly splendid cultivar.

***Erysimum purpureum** is an handsome, ash-grey plant, subshrubby in habit, with narrowly oblong or linear leaves and racemes of purple flowers, each 12–13mm across. [May–July, H–HH, Turkey]

Both species are well worth growing and look particularly fine on a wall where they will spread by natural seeding.

GLOBULARIA (Globulariaceae)

A delightful little genus of sun-loving plants which usually make dense mats of leathery green leaves and small globose heads of blue flowers borne on slender leafless stems. The two species below are particularly suitable on old limestone walls and can be propagated from seed or by division.

Globularia cordifolia has shiny, dark green, obovate or wedge-shaped leaves, mostly borne in loose rosettes. The lilac-blue flowerheads rise on stalks 3–5cm high, each 10–20mm across. [June–Aug, H, C & S Europe & W Asia]

Globularia bellidifolia = *G. cordifolia* var. *nana* is a more compact and densely tufted cousin with smaller leaves and flowerheads 8–12mm across. [June–July, H, S Europe]

GYPSOPHILA (Caryophyllaceae)

This genus is best known for *G. paniculata* with its white or pale pink sprays of flowers which are often cut and mixed with sweet peas and other summer flowers. There are over 100 species, mostly from Europe and Asia, which are closely related to the Catchflies, *Silene*. Most are easily raised from seed.

Gypsophila repens, the Alpine Gypsophila, is a sprawling often mat-forming perennial with narrow bluish-green leaves. The flower stems spring upwards from the prostrate mat with branched loose clusters of white, pale pink or lilac five-petalled flowers, each 8–10mm across. [May–Sept, H, C & S Europe]

A delightful plant which grows best on the top of a broad retaining wall where its roots can delve down deep into soil-filled pockets. Plants can be trimmed back when they become too untidy.

HABERLEA (Gesneriaceae)

Close cousins of the Ramondas which are also distantly related to the African Violets, *Saintpaulia*. Like the Ramondas they revel in moist peaty soil pockets on shaded or partially shaded walls. Plants need to be carefully wedged into the crevices but, once established will continue happily for many years. Unlike the Ramondas, Haberleas build up a series of close rosettes of leaves and do not continue as a solitary rosette from year to year. They can be increased by division or from seed.

***Haberlea rhodopensis** (Pl.24) is a softly-hairy perennial with basal rosettes of obovate to ovate, toothed leaves. From these rise funnel-shaped flowers, two to five to a stem, pale lilac and white with a yellowish throat and each about 25mm long. [Apr–May, H, Bulgaria]

Haberlea ferdinandi-coburgii is a larger cousin less often seen in cultivation. [Apr–May, H, Balkans]

IONOPSIDIUM (Cruciferae)

Ionopsidium acaule, Violet Cress, is a small tufted annual only 5–7.5cm tall with green, spoon-shaped leaves, mostly in a basal cluster. Flowers are 4–6mm across, lilac, or white tinged with lilac. [July–Nov, H–HH, Portugal]

A charming little annual which will seed along suitable wall cavities once established.

JANKAEA (Gesneriaceae)

There is only one species of *Jankaea*, which is one of the choicest of all mountain plants, although not the easiest to cultivate. Most gardeners who are lucky enough to possess it, grow it in an alpine house, but with the right site and some luck it will succeed on a suitable wall. The genus is closely related to *Ramonda* and *Haberlea*. Like the Ramondas it needs a shaded wall and a moist peaty pocket, preferably where the rain will not strike the plant directly.

Jankaea heldreichii.

Jankaea heldreichii is a perennial with silvery-grey, furry rosettes of oval leaves which are reddish-downy beneath. The violet, bell-shaped flowers are four-lobed, several borne together on delicate arching stems. [May–June, HH, N Greece]

This lovely plant is only found on Mt Olympus at the southern edge of Greek Macedonia. It is generally propagated by division, or seed if obtainable.

LEWISIA (Portulacaceae)

A showy genus of semi-succulent rosette-leaved plants from western North America. The starry flowers usually have five or more petals and numerous stamens. Most are not easy plants to cultivate and require the more equable conditions of a frame or alpine house. A few can be tried in a sunny wall crevice. Like most rosetted species the plants must be wedged firmly into the crevice and checked carefully from time to time. Now available are some hybrid Lewisias, produced from crosses between various species but particularly *Lewisia columbiana*, *L. cotyledon* and *L. rediviva*; they make excellent wall plants, many being more accommodating and longer-lived than their parents.

Lewisia columbiana forms rosettes of narrow, spathulate, deep-green leaves. The flowers, 14–18mm across, have four to seven white or pink petals with dark red veins. They are borne in clusters on long stalks rising from the centre of the rosette. [May–July, HH, SW USA]

***Lewisia cotyledon** has obovate-spathulate leaves and white flowers veined with pink, each flower with seven to ten petals. [Apr–July, HH, USA (California)]

Lewisia tweedyi is a very beautiful species, although by no means easily grown, having broad ovate or obovate leaves and delightful flesh pink flowers, 5–7cm across. [May–June, HH, USA (Washington)]

A superb plant but not easy and prone to root rot.

LINARIA (Scrophulariaceae)

The Toadflaxes represent a moderate-sized genus, mainly of European and western Asian origin. The two included below are easily cultivated perennials readily raised from seed, or increased by division. Seldom deliberately planted on walls but, like the Wallflower and the Snapdragon, often occuring there by chance, and looking very attractive in such situations.

***Linaria vulgaris**, the Common Toadflax, forms erect tufts up to 90cms tall, the stems clothed in slender leaves, particularly in the lower half. The narrow racemes of pale or mid-yellow flowers are very distinctive, each 25–33mm long. [May–Sept, H, Europe & W Asia]

Linaria purpurea is often taller with smaller, purplish-blue flowers in elegant spike-like racemes. [July–Sept, H, S Europe]

This species is naturalised in Britain, especially on roadside banks and in waste places.

LITHODORA (Boraginaceae)

Lithodora rosmarinifolium = *Lithospermum rosmarinifolium* is a dwarf evergreen shrub 30–60cm tall with narrow elliptic or lanceolate leaves. The bright blue flowers are lined with white, 16–17mm across, salver-shaped and borne in small terminal clusters. [Jan–Apr, HH, S Italy & Sicily]

A charming plant for a sheltered wall, not easy to grow but well worth giving a try.

MECONOPSIS (Papaveraceae)

This beautiful genus contains both the Welsh Poppy and the stunning Blue Poppies of the Himalaya and China. The Welsh Poppy often finds its way on to old walls, particularly in the more westerly parts of Britain. Plants are vigorous and seed profusely.

***Meconopsis cambrica**, the Welsh Poppy, forms tufts of rather yellowish-green dissected leaves. The long slender stems, up to 60cm tall, bear a solitary yellow, sometimes orange flower with four delicate petals. These are followed by slender oblong pods. [June–Aug, H, Britain, France & Spain]

MOLTKIA (Boraginaceae)

A delightful little genus containing eight species of subshrubs native to southern Europe and western Asia. They are closely related to *Buglossoides*.

Moltkia suffruticosa = *Lithospermum* or *Moltkia graminifolia* is a widely spreading subshrub forming a loose cushion with rough grassy, deep green, linear leaves. Pale blue flowers, each 13–16mm long, are borne in arching sprays on stems up to 24cm tall. [June–Aug, H–HH, N Italy]

A delightful little shrub to grace the top of a limestone wall.

ONOSMA (Boraginaceae)

The Onosmas are amongst the finest of all the members of the Borage family. The genus contains 40 or so species distributed in southern Europe and Western Asia. Most form dense tufts of narrow, bristly, untoothed leaves and coiled clusters of pretty, drooping, tubular flowers which open in succession towards the shoot tips. They revel in sunny, well-drained positions away from excessive winter wet.

Beware of the bristly stems and leaves which can cause a good deal of irritation to the skin.

***Onosma albo-roseum** is a dense subshrub, up to 30cm tall, with bristly narrowly-oblong leaves. The flowers, about 25mm long are white at first but becomes deep rose with age. [June–Aug, H–HH, Turkey Syria & Iraq]

Onosma echioides is a rather smaller plant with narrow spatula-shaped silvery-grey leaves and pretty, pale yellow flowers. [June–Aug, H, S Europe]

PHLOX (Plumbaginaceae)

A well-known genus in gardens especially for the many cultivars grown in the herbaceous border, adding colour and scent from midsummer onwards. Several of the smaller species make good wall plants provided that they are allowed a long root run.

Phlox subulata, the Moss Phlox, grown in many gardens, is a mat-forming plant with rigid awl-shaped leaves. The flowers are purple, rose, lavender or lilac, with a darker centre, 15–20mm across, borne in small clusters; the petals are notched. [Apr–May, H, E USA]

A very popular rock garden plant, although equally at home on a wall. Plants need to be trimmed from time to time to keep them from becoming straggly. This is best undertaken shortly after flowering ceases.

'Alba' is a fine white-flowered form.

Phlox nivalis is very similar to *P. subulata* but with generally paler flowers of lilac, pale purple, pink or white, and the petals not notched. [Apr–May, H, E USA]

Phlox nivalis and *P. subulata* have been crossed to produce a fine range of hybrids. These go under the names *P.×frondosa*, *P.×henryae*, *P.×lilacina* and *P.×procumbens* in books and catalogues and listings will include a number of cultivar names. Most are well worth growing.

PHYLLITIS (Aspleniaceae)

A small genus of tropical and temperate ferns.

Phyllitis scolopendrium = *Scolopendrium vulgare*, the common and well-known Hart's Tongue Fern, forms circular tufts of rather leathery fronds which are pale green at first but soon turn deep green. The fronds are narrow, 10–60cm long, undivided and tapering from a heart-shaped base. [H, S, W, & C Europe]

A common fern on rocks, walls and banks in shaded places throughout Britain and also one that is widely cultivated. The fronds persist through the winter until the new ones begin to unfurl in the late spring. Plants can be increased by division once established. Many different forms are cultivated, some with curled or cleft fronds.

POLYPODIUM (Polypodiaceae)

A cosmopolitan genus of some 70 species of ferns which are very diverse in their vegetative characters.

Polypodium vulgare, the Common Polypody, has rather flat, deeply lobed fronds, 10–40cm long, which are produced in early summer amongst those of the previous year. [H, Europe & Asia] ◐

This fern is not often cultivated, although it is a native species found widely on trees, rocks or wall crevices, particularly in western and northern Britain and Ireland. It prefers acid or neutral conditions primarily and has the habit of creeping about rather than forming close tufts.

RAMONDA (Gesneriaceae)

A delightful little genus of only three species native to Europe, all of which are in cultivation. They form flat rosettes of rather rough leaves and small clusters of flattish 'African violet'-like flowers borne on a common stalk. They are plants for moist, shaded rock crevices and do well on north-facing walls. They can be propagated from seed or division, or from leaf-cuttings.

*__Ramonda myconi__ = *R. pyrenaica* forms deep green rosettes of oval, coarsely toothed leaves that are rusty with hairs beneath. The flowers, 20–30mm across, range from violet-blue to purple, each with five corolla lobes and yellow anthers. [June–Aug, H, Pyrenees] ●

The finest species which, once established, will flower for many years. Although plants prefer a moist crevice they are surprisingly drought resistant, soon recovering after a dry period.

'Alba' has white flowers.

'Rosea' is a fine form with rose-pink flowers.

Ramonda nathaliae is similar but the leaves are ovate, bright glossy green and corrugated. The lavender-blue flowers have an orange 'eye' and only four corolla lobes. [June–July, H, Bulgaria & S Yugoslavia] ●

Ramonda serbica is like *R. nathaliae* but with smaller, more cupped flowers which are lilac-blue with five corolla lobes. [June–July, H, Balkans] ●

The rarest of the three in cultivation and generally only seen in the collections of specialist growers.

RESEDA (Resedaceae)

The mignonettes are an interesting group of annual or perennial plants with small flowers usually making up long slender spikes. Some have a powerful fragrance which has endeared them to gardeners, particularly *R. odorata*.

Reseda lutea, the Wild Mignonette, is a biennial or perennial species which occasionally seeds on to old walls. The erect stems bear pinnate leaves and terminate in long spikes of yellowish-green flowers, each flower only 6mm across. [June – Sept, H, Europe & W Asia]

SAPONARIA (Caryophyllaceae)

Attractive cousins of the Catchflies, *Silene*, commonly called the Soapworts. The genus is a small one with some 20 species scattered in Europe and temperate Asia. On the whole those grown in our gardens are fairly readily raised from seed.

***Saponaria ocymoides**, the Rock Soapwort, is a mat-forming perennial with opposite pairs of obovate or oblong leaves which are grass green, though often flushed with red or purple. The rose-red flowers, each 12 – 13mm across, are borne in small umbel-like clusters, with purplish calyces. [May – Sept, H, Mountains of C & SW Europe]

A pleasing plant with a rather trailing habit, often producing flowers in great abundance.

'Albiflora' has white flowers.

'Carnea' has flowers of flesh-pink.

'Splendens' has flowers of deep rose, deeper than the typical form.

'Versicolor' has flowers which are white to begin with but which gradually become pale rose-pink.

Saponaria calabrica is far less often seen. A small erect annual up to 30cm tall with branched, rather sticky stems and oblanceolate or lanceolate leaves, its flowers are pale rose, 12 – 14mm across. [July – Aug, H – HH, S & SE Europe]

A plant for the wall top.

'Alba' has white flowers.

'Scarlet Queen' is a splendid cultivar with flowers redder than the more typical plant.

SAXIFRAGA (Saxifragaceae)

This large and popular genus contains many exciting garden plants, especially ones for the rock garden, but relatively few are suitable for wall culture. There are some 370 species distributed in many parts of the world. Most form rosettes of leaves which build up large cushions of foliage. The leaves vary enormously from species to species, being variously lobed and toothed, as well as long, slender and spear-like. Some are plain green, others are encrusted with lime exuded from pores along the leaf margin. The flowers may be solitary, in clusters or borne in large branched heads or panicles. Most are five-petalled with ten stamens and a two-part ovary in the centre. Many dislike both brilliant baking sun and deep shade. On walls an easterly or westerly aspect is probably the best.

***Saxifraga paniculata** = *S. aizoon* (Pl.24) forms small encrusted rosettes, rounded in outline which in time form quite large cushions. White or cream flowers, 8 – 11mm across, are borne in loose panicles on long arching stems up to 30cm long. [May – July, H, C & S European mountains & SW Asia]

Saxifraga hostii is similar but larger in all its parts, with larger, dark green rosettes with leaves up to 10cm long in some vigorous plants. [May – July, H, Europe (E & SE Alps)]

This species is best on limy walls.

Saxifraga callosa = *S. lingulata* forms large, rather untidy, encrusted greyish rosettes with long, narrow, spoon-shaped leaves. The white flowers, 11–16mm across, are borne in long arching panicles up to 40–50cm long; the petals are usually spotted with red. [June–Aug, H, SE France & N Italy]

***Saxifraga longifolia** is the king of the encrusted saxifrages. It forms large solitary rosettes up to 30cm across, generally less, composed of numerous strap-shaped symmetrically arranged leaves. White flowers, 9–11mm across, are borne in large, arching, narrow sprays up to 60cm in length. [June–Aug, H, Pyrenees]

A truly wonderful plant to see in full flower. Rosettes build up in size over a number of years and die once they have flowered. Occasionally plants produce lateral rosettes, which generally prove to be hybrid plants between this and one of the preceding species. The finest of these is Saxifraga 'Tumbling Waters' which is one of the most splendid Saxifrages in cultivation, although it is not easy to get the best forms of this particular cultivar.

Saxifraga cotyledon, the Pyramidal Saxifrage, forms large, rather flat rosettes of oblong, deep green leaves, each up to 6cm long. The flowers are white, occasionally spotted with purple, 11–18mm across. [July–Aug, H, Pyrenees & S Alps, S Sweden (Gotland)]

A plant for acid rocks.

SEDUM (Crassulaceae)

The Sedums or Stonecrops are a large genus of succulent plants with clusters of starry flowers. Many are ideal plants for wall crevices being long-lived, easily propagated and, perhaps most important of all, drought resistant. Small pieces broken off or even single leaves will root readily and most of those commonly grown easily seed about. A selection of species is presented below.

***Sedum acre** (Pl.24), the Wall-pepper or Biting Stonecrop, is perhaps the best known species forming small evergreen mats or tufts, generally only 3–6cm tall. Bright yellow flowers, only 10–12mm across are borne in small clusters. [June–July, H, Europe & W Asia]

This plant is a characteristic plant of dry walls, tiled roofs and pathways in many parts of Britain, particularly in the south.

Sedum sexangulare, is similar to *S. acre* but its leaves are narrower and borne in five or six regular rows. Its flowers form larger, branched clusters. [June–July, H, C & S Europe]

***Sedum reflexum** (Pl.24), the Rock Stonecrop, is another common plant which forms large mats with trailing stems covered in slender fleshy cylindrical leaves. The flower stems reach 20–30cm tall and the tips droop characteristically in bud. The flowers are yellow, 12–14mm across, borne in rounded branched clusters. [June–July, H, Europe]

A vigorous species which will grow equally well in sun or half-shade, although it flowers best in a sunny, exposed position.

***Sedum ochroleucum** = *S. anopetalum* is similar to *S. reflexum* but with greyer leaves and cream or greenish-white flowers which are erect in bud. [June–July, H, C & S Europe]

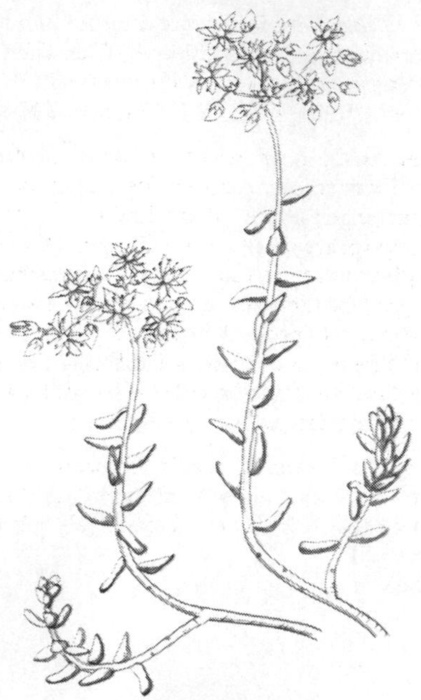

Sedum album.

Sedum album, the White Stonecrop, forms bright green, loose mats, its short, cylindrical leaves often tinged with red. Small white flowers, 4–8mm across are borne in loosely branched clusters. [June–Aug, H, Europe & W Asia]

A widely grown and naturalised species, although perhaps less desirable than the preceding species.

Δ **Sedum anglicum**, the English Stonecrop, forms small greyish or reddish mats with thin stems and rather globose leaves. The white or pink flowers are borne in few-flowered clusters. [June–Sept, H, W Europe]

A dainty species which grows best on acid rocks.

Sedum telephium, the Orpine, is a stouter though variable species 20–60cm tall. The leaves are large, up to 7cm long, fleshy but flattened, rounded to oblong and toothed. The purplish-red, yellowish-green or whitish flowers are small, 8–10mm across, but borne in dense flattened clusters at the ends of erect shoots. [July–Sept, H, Europe & W Asia]

Sedum kamtschaticum is a creeping and branching species with dark green narrow spathulate leaves borne on short over-wintering shoots which elongate in the spring to produce flowers. The flowers are orange-yellow, 17–18mm across, borne in a rather loose head. [June–Sept, H, N China & E USSR]

'Variegatum' has leaves edged in white.

SEMPERVIVUM (Crassulaceae)

The Houseleeks are amongst the best of all wall plants. They are easy to grow, need little attention, and furthermore are very drought-resistant. They are plants for a sunny position growing as well on the side as the top of the wall. On the whole propagation is best effected by pulling off spare rosettes, and rooting these first in pots if they do not have roots already.

Houseleeks have rosettes of succulent leaves, the rosettes often borne in tight clusters. Each year a few of the largest rosettes push forward a stem which carries a cluster of starry flowers at the top. In the wild most are plants of rocky mountain pastures, screes and cliffs.

***Sempervivum tectorum**, the Common Houseleek, is a variable plant forming stout, blue-green, rather flat rosettes, up to 8cm across, each leaf tinged with red or brown and edged by rough white bristles. The flowers are dull pink or purple, 18–20mm across, borne in large clusters. [July–Oct, H, C & S Europe]

The Common Houseleek is frequently seen on old walls in this country, although perhaps more often on the tiled roofs of cottages where it will build up large mounds of rosettes over the years.

Sempervivum tectorum growing on a wall.

Sempervivum calcareum is rather like the previous species but the leaf-rosettes are more globular, and the leaves broader and blue-green tipped with purplish-brown. The flowers are pale pink, 14–16mm across. [July–Sept, H, SE France]

Sempervivum montanum is the Mountain Houseleek, forming low mats or tufts of small dull green hairy rosettes each up to 2cm across. The reddish-purple flowers are 24–30mm across. [June–Aug, H, C & S Europe]

This species thrives best on walls of acid rather than calcareous rocks.

***Sempervivum arachnoideum** (Pl.24), the well-known Cobweb Houseleek, forms low mats of small rosettes up to 1.5cm across, each covered in a cobweb of whitish hairs, which links the leaf tips. The flowers are reddish-pink, 14–18mm across, borne in small rather dense clusters. [July–Sept, H, C & S Europe]

A popular plant which is primarily grown for its fascinating cobwebbed leaf-rosettes. It is best on acid rocks but will tolerate calcareous ones. There is a var. *tomentosum* from the Pyrenees and Western Alps with larger rosettes, 1.5–2.5cm across.

Other species of Houseleeks are cultivated, although less commonly so. Amongst these must be included *S. wulfenii* and *S. grandiflorum* both of which have yellow flowers. The former has handsome bluish-green leaf-rosettes, up to 5cm across whilst those of the latter are dark green and hairy, each leaf tipped with reddish-brown.

SYMPHYANDRA (Campanulaceae)

This genus contains only seven species which are attractive cousins of the Bellflowers, *Campanula*, from Western Asia. They have broad, often heart-shaped, leaves and drooping bell-shaped flowers. The cultivated species can be grown from seed, by root divisions or alternatively by rooting young shoots in the spring.

◐ **Symphyandra hofmannii** is a softly hairy perennial 30–60cm tall with lanceolate, pointed leaves. The nodding, creamy-white flowers are 25–30mm long. [June–Sept, H, Yugoslavia]

◐ **Symphyandra pendula** is a less robust species up to 60cm tall with ovate, pointed leaves of velvety green. Cream flowers are borne in a broad panicle. [June–July, H–HH, USSR (Caucasus)]

TANACETUM (Compositae)

◐ ***Tanacetum parthenium**, Feverfew, is a strongly aromatic erect perennial reaching 60cm tall with downy stems and yellowish-green cut leaves with numerous rounded lobes. The small, white, daisy flowers, with a yellow 'eye' or disk are 10–25mm across, and borne in flat-topped clusters. [June–Sept, H, SE Europe]

The Feverfew is an handsome plant, long cultivated for ornamental and medicinal purposes. It has become widely naturalised in Britain and many parts of Europe. Double forms exist which are partly or wholly white without the yellow disc, but they are scarcely as attractive as the ordinary type.

GLOSSARY

Aerial root a root originating above ground level.
Alternate describing leaves placed alternately along the stem, not opposite or whorled.
Annual a plant which completes its whole life cycle, from seed to flowering, fruiting and death, within the same year.
Anther the terminal part of the male organ (stamen) of the flower, usually borne at the top of the filament, and containing pollen.
Aril a fleshy or sometimes hairy appendage borne on the seed.
Awn a long stiff bristle.
Axillary in the axil, i.e. the angle between the stem and the leaf stalk.
Berry a fleshy fruit, usually rounded and containing several hard seeds embedded in the flesh.
Bipinnate a pinnate leaf in which the segments are themselves pinnately divided.
Biternate a ternate leaf in which the segments are themselves ternately divided.
Bract a small leaf-like or scale-like organ which bears a flower or an inflorescence in its axil — not always present.
Calyx refers to the sepals as a whole — these may be separate, or joined to one another in whole or in part to form a tube (the calyx tube).
Capsule a dry fruit which splits open to release its seeds.
Carpel the structure containing the ovules.
Chitting removal of a tiny chip from the seed coat to aid germination.
Composite a collective name used to describe members of the Daisy Family, Compositae.
Corolla refers to the petals as a whole — these may be separate, or joined to one another in whole or in part to form a tube (the corolla tube).
Corona an outgrowth from the corolla or the stamens, which is usually petal-like.
Cucurbit a collective name used to describe members of the Melon Family, Cucurbitaceae.
Cultivar a variant or race that has originated and persisted under cultivation. Cultivar names are enclosed in single quotation marks e.g. *Clematis montana* 'Tetrarose'.
Deciduous describes trees and shrubs that shed all their leaves in the autumn.
Digitate with finger-like lobes arising from one point, e.g. a lupin leaf.
Dioecious with male and female flowers on separate plants.
Disk florets in Composites, refers to the tubular flowers which make up the central 'eye' or disk of the daisy flowerhead. The flowerhead may sometimes consist solely of disk florets — see also ray florets.
Even-pinnate a pinnate leaf which lacks a terminal leaflet. The total number of leaflets is an even number.
Evergreen describes trees and shrubs that retain their leaves throughout the winter.
Family a group of genera, with certain important characters of flower and/or fruit in common. Family names usually, but not invariably, end in — aceae e.g. Ranunculaceae, Rosaceae.

Female flower a flower with styles but lacking stamens.
Filament the stalk of a stamen, bearing the anther.
Flowerhead refers to closely, often tightly grouped clusters of usually stalkless flowers, generally terminating the stem(s), e.g. as in the Daisy Family, Compositae.
Follicle a dry 'pod-like' fruit derived from a single carpel, splitting open along one side to release the several to many seeds. Follicles may be solitary or in pairs or clusters.
Forma a category below the variety, which usually represents variation in a single character such as flower colour e.g. *Wisteria venusta* forma *violacea*. The forma has no distinct geographical distribution.
Genus a group of allied species with important characters in common, e.g. *Clematis, Rosa,* (plural — genera).
Glaucous with a greyish-blue bloom.
Herb a plant which dies back more or less to ground level in the winter and does not develop a persistent woody stem; the term includes annuals.
Inflorescence any arrangement of more than one flower.
Keel the two front petals of a pea-flower which are united along their lower margins.
Lanceolate spear-shaped, pointed at the apex and broadest below the middle.
Leaf axil the angle between the stem and the leaf or leaf stalk.
Leaflet one of the separate parts into which compound leaves are divided. A leaflet is distinguished from a leaf by the absence of a bud in its axil.
Lenticel a corky or wart-like breathing pore in the bark.
Linear long and narrow, with the sides parallel or almost so.
Male flower a flower with stamens but lacking styles.
Mucronate terminated abruptly by a short sharp, often spiny tip.
Mutation a change in the genetic composition of an organism, creating a new inheritable character.
Node the point on a stem where one or more leaves or side branches arise.
Oblanceolate the reverse of lanceolate i.e. broader above the middle.
Obovate the reverse of ovate, i.e. broader above the middle.
Odd-pinnate a pinnate leaf with a terminal leaflet. The total number of leaflets is an odd number.
Opposite describing leaves arising opposite one another on the stem, thus appearing in pairs.
Ovary the hollow basal part of a carpel, containing one or more ovules, and surmounted by the style(s) and stigma(s).
Ovate with the outline of an egg, broader below the middle.
Ovule the structure inside the ovary, which develops into the seed after fertilisation.
Palmate hand-like with three or more lobes, e.g. a Sycamore leaf.
Panicle a much-branched inflorescence.
Pea-flower the typical flower of the Pea Family, Leguminosae, composed of a standard petal, two wing-petals, and a keel petal.
Perennial a plant which lives for more than two years and produces flowers each year.
Perianth the outer sterile whorls of a flower, often differentiated into calyx and corolla.
Petal one of the segments of the corolla, often conspicuously coloured.

Petiole the leaf stalk.
Phylloclade a stem or branch which is usually flattened, and functions as a leaf.
Phyllode a leaf stalk which is flattened and functions as a leaf blade.
Pinnate with several opposite pairs of leaflets borne along each side of a common stalk, and with or without a terminal leaflet.
Pod a long, cylindrical or flattened fruit which is not fleshy and usually splits into two equal halves when ripe. It is characteristic of the Pea Family, Leguminosae.
Quartered referring to a flattened double rose flower in which the central petals are arranged in four rows.
Raceme a flower spike in which the individual flowers are stalked.
Ray florets the conspicuous outer individual flowers (florets) of a daisy head, with a flat strap-like corolla which is tubular at the base and often sterile.
Receptacle the enlarged top of a flower stalk from which all parts of a flower arise.
Revolute with the margin or apex rolled backward.
Scabrid with minute rough projections, rough to the touch.
Scion the upper unrooted part of a graft from which the stem or branches will grow.
Semi-evergreen describes trees or shrubs which retain some of their leaves in the winter, depending on the severity of the wether and the location of the plant.
Sepal one of the segments of the calyx, often green.
Simple describes leaves which are not divided into leaflets.
Spathulate spoon-shaped or paddle-shaped.
Species the basic unit of classifiction, consisting of a group of individuals which are distinct, but interbreed freely with one another. Groups of species with certain features in common make up genera, e.g. *Clematis montana, Clematis orientalis, Clematis texensis.*
Spike a dense elongated group of flowers in which each flower is unstalked.
Sport a plant which has undergone a spontaneous genetic change in one or several characters.
Spur a hollow, usually cylindrical or conical projection from the base of a sepal, petal or corolla tube, often containing nectar.
Stamen the male organ of a flower consisting of a stalk (filament) and an anther which contains the pollen.
Standard the broad upper petal of a pea-flower.
Starry hairs hairs which are divided into several branches, thus shaped like a star.
Stigma the tip(s) of a style which receives the pollen.
Stipule a leaf-like, often small structure, situated at the base of a leaf stalk. Stipules occur in pairs and are not always present.
Style the usually elongated stalk-like organ which links the ovary to the stigma.
Subspecies (abbreviated subsp.), the unit of classification immediately below that of species. Subspecies usually differ from one another in one or two characters, such as flower number or leaf size, but interbreed freely. They normally occur in the wild in different geographical areas.
Tendril a thread-like structure by which a plant grasps and coils round an object and clings to it for support. Structurally it may be part of a leaf or stem.
Tepal one of the segments of a perianth which is undifferentiated into sepals and petals.
Ternate a leaf or leaflet which is divided into three parts.

Trifoliolate divided into three leaflets.
Triternate a biternate leaf in which the segments are themselves ternately divided.
Tuber an underground stem or root, swollen with food reserves and persisting from one year to the next.
Unisexual of one sex.
Valve one of the segments of a capsule after it has split open.
Variety (abbreviated var.), a lower rank than species or subspecies consisting of individuals which differ from the type in one or two characters such as hairiness or leaf width. Although capable of interbreeding and often occuring in the same geographical locality, varieties manage to maintain their identity. E.g. *Clematis montana* var.*rubens, Clematis montana* var.*wilsonii.*
Wing one of the two lateral petals of a pea-flower, usually lying on either side of the lower or keel petal.

FURTHER READING

Baker, H. Fruit (Royal Horticultural Society's Encyclopaedia of Practical Gardening), Mitchell Beazley, 1980.
Bean, W.J. *Trees and Shrubs Hardy in the British Isles*, John Murray, 1970-80.
Brickell, Christopher D. *Pruning* (Royal Horticultural Society's Encyclopaedia of Practical Gardening), Mitchell Beazley, 1979.
Brooks, A. & Halstead, A. *Garden Pests and Diseases* (Royal Horticultural Society's Encyclopaedia of Practical Gardening), Mitchell Beazley, 1980.
Buczacki, Stefan & Harris, Keith. *The Pests, Disorders and Diseases of Garden Plants,* Collins, 1981.
Dahl, M.H. & Thygesen, T.B. *Garden Pests and Diseases of Flowers and Shrubs,* Blandford, 1974.
Hillier's *Manual of Trees and Shrubs,* David & Charles, 1977.
Lloyd, Christopher. *Clematis,* Collins, 1977.
McMillan Browse, P. Plant Propagation (Royal Horticultural Society's Encyclopaedia of Practical Gardening), Mitchell Beazley, 1979.
Royal Horticultural Society & Bles. G. *The Fruit Garden Displayed,* Royal Horticultural Society, 1968.
Thomas, G.S. *Climbing Roses Old and New, Phoenix House,* 1965.

Index of Plant Names

English and Latin accepted names are in roman type; synonyms are in italic. = indicates a synonymous cultivar.

Wall fruits and their cultivars are not included in the index.